MAKE LOVE, NOT WAR

MAKE LOVE, NOT WAR
THE SEXUAL REVOLUTION: AN UNFETTERED HISTORY

DAVID ALLYN

ROUTLEDGE
New York

Published in 2001 by
Routledge
29 West 35th Street
New York, NY 10001

First published in hardcover in 2000 by Little, Brown and Company.
Reprinted by arrangement with Little, Brown and Company.
First Routledge paperback edition, 2001
Copyright © 2000, 2001 by David Allyn

Routledge is an imprint of the Taylor & Francis group.

Printed in the United States of America on acid-free paper.

Library of Congress Cataloging-in-Publication Data

Allyn, David (David Smith)
    Make love, not war: the sexual revolution, an unfettered history / by David Allyn.
        p. cm.
    Includes bibliographical references and index.
    ISBN 0-415-92942-3 (pb. : alk. paper)
    1. Sex customs--United States--History--20th century. 2. Sexual ethics--United
States--History--20th century. 3. Sex in popular culture--United States-History--20th
century. 4. United States--Social life and customs--20th century. 5. United States--Moral
conditions--History--20th century. 6. Nineteen sixties. I. Title.

HQ18.U5 A38 2001
306.7'0973'0904--dc21

                                                                    2001018063

FOR JENNIFER

CONTENTS

PREFACE TO THE
PAPERBACK EDITION

Since the publication of *Make Love, Not War*, many people have asked me: In the final analysis, was the sexual revolution a positive social development or a negative one? Did it result in progress or decay? Should we welcome another era of sexual liberation or should we do everything we can to avoid one?

Needless to say, such questions cannot be answered scientifically. "Progress" and "decay" are statements of opinion, not fact. No amount of archival research will turn up proof of what is "good" and what is "bad." Despite the fact that scholars sometimes enter political and cultural debates, the scholar's first obligation to society is to sift fact from opinion, to distinguish between what is and what we want, feel, or believe about what is.

But, as a citizen, am I glad that birth control is legal, that censorship is no longer commonplace, that college students can have sex without worrying about getting expelled, that homosexuality is no longer considered shameful and abhorrent? Certainly. In my mind there can be no doubt that, on the whole, the sexual revolution of the 60's and 70's improved the quality of life for most Americans.

Obviously, the sexual revolution had its share of ill effects. Most notably, the acceptance of casual sex helped facilitate the spread of sexually transmitted infections, including HIV, the virus that causes AIDS. Some argue that the sexual revolution (especially the pill) also deprived women of the ability to say "no" to sex. Personally, however, I think the ability to say "no"—like the ability to say "yes"—is a function of one's own self-awareness and ability to communicate openly with others, not a function of available birth control or social pressure.

Whether one agrees or disagrees with my own personal evaluation of the sexual revolution, there can be no denying that it dramatically transformed American society and culture. But how? How did it have such a sweeping and powerful effect on our nation in so short a time?

The answer is surprisingly simple: during the sexual revolution of the 60's and 70's people told the truth. They told the truth about their sexual histories. About their secret desires. About the ways they had been pretending to conform to societal norms. Not everyone told the truth all at once, of course. But when a few key people became authentic about their sexuality, others were inspired to follow suit. Eventually, more and more people told the truth about themselves, until there was a critical mass or "tipping point." It turned out that "nice girls" were having sex before marriage, that teenagers were yearning to have homosexual relationships, that some married couples were interested in more than just monogamy. When enough people told the truth, the life of the nation was transformed.

Many cultural critics have denounced the rise of confessionalism in our society. They say that the confessional spirit encouraged by television talk shows and pop psychological movements is really self-aggrandizement in disguise. Of course, most of the confessions on daytime television are actually staged. And even when they are not staged, they are usually done in a spirit of self-justification and bravado.

The real practice of telling the truth is not easy. It is often embarrassing, even humiliating. It forces one to be vulnerable. And it can have enormous consequences for one's family, relationships, and career. That is why the sexual revolutionaries of the 60's and 70's — for all their faults and foibles — remain profoundly inspiring. That is what continues to make reading and writing about the sexual revolution such a rewarding — and sometimes emotionally confronting — experience.

I believe that studying history ought to make one uncomfortable. It should force a person to question his or her assumptions and beliefs. Ultimately, it should lead to the unsettling realization that present-day attitudes and ideas may someday be considered strange and illogical.

My hope is that this book makes readers as uncomfortable and unsettled as any book of history they are likely to find.

ACKNOWLEDGMENTS

I AM DEEPLY GRATEFUL TO ALL THE INDIVIDUALS WHO TOOK the time to assist or encourage me on this project. First, I would like to thank those who granted me personal interviews, including: Ti-Grace Atkinson, Susan Baerwald, Bill Baird, Lee Baxandall, Howard Bellin, Michael Bronski, Helen Gurley Brown, Rita Mae Brown, Susan Brownmiller, Betty Dodson, Hal Call, Sydney Dickstein, Andrea Dworkin, Edward Eichel, Albert Ellis, Sarah Evans, Candace Falk, Roger Fisher, Stanley Fleishman, Larry Flynt, Marsha Gillespie, Barbara Gittings, Bob Guccione, Hugh Hefner, Sarah Holland, Jim Kepner, Anne Koedt, Larry Kramer, Tuli Kupferberg, Jacques Levy, John Lobel, Mimi Lobel, Bob McGinley, Ted McIlvenna, George Mansour, Peter Marcuse, Howard Moody, Osha Neuman, Camille Paglia, Nell Painter, Kenneth Pitchford, John Rechy, Charles Renslow, Margo Rila, Robert Rimmer, Barney Rosset, Maggie Rubenstein, Steven Saylor, Vicki Scharfman, Barbara Seaman, Myron Sharaf, Charlie Shively, Earle Silber, Ronald Smith, Gloria Steinem, Gay Talese, Lynn Tylman, Randy Wicker, Sylvia Weil, Sean Wilentz, Ellen Willis, the Reverend Robert Wood, the staff of Elysium Fields, and all those who shall remain anonymous. They answered my questions—which were often intensely personal—with good humor and grace. Many of these individuals not only agreed to be interviewed, they also welcomed me into their homes or took the time to share a meal with a young writer.

A very special thanks to my advisor, Donald Fleming, and the members of my dissertation committee at Harvard University, Stephan Thernstrom and Allan Brandt. In Washington, D.C., my fellow members of the informal Gender and History Study Group — Anne Little, Kathleen Trainor, and Michael Coventry — and the members of the History Department at American University provided a much needed sense of community. For start to finish, Lauren Asher gave me intellectual and emotional guidance.

Many historians, as well as scholars from other fields, offered their thoughts on the project and the period. Their insights and encouragement were invaluable. I would especially like to thank Henry Abelove, Beth Bailey, Allan Berubé, Paul Boyer, Winnie Brienes, Elizabeth Chabert, Nicole Dombrowski, John D'Emilio, Alice Echols, Paula Fass, Estelle Freedman, David Garrow, James Gilbert, Todd Gitlin, Ellen Herman, John Howard, Drew Isenberg, Michael Kazin, Peter Kuznick, Liz Lunbeck, D. A. Miller, Jeffrey Moran, Susan Moeller, Paul Robinson, Marc Stein, Randy Trumbach, Carole Vance, Elizabeth Watkins, Brad Verter, and Ron Yanovsky.

I would like to thank Toby Simon and Lynn Gorchov for inviting me to speak at Brown University and Johns Hopkins University, respectively. These talks gave me a welcome opportunity to clarify my thoughts on the sexual revolution. Thanks also go to the members of Cheiron, SUNY Binghamton's Department of Romance Languages and Literatures, AHA — Committee on Gay and Lesbian Studies, and the American Studies Association.

Special thanks go to the Rockefeller Archives, Harvard Law School, the Charles Warren Center, Radcliffe College, and the Princeton University Committee on the Faculty for providing funds to support my research. This project would not have been possible without the patience and assistance of many research librarians, including Jennifer Lee, the John Hay Library; Dan Linke, Mudd Library, Princeton University; Deborah Kelley-Milburn, Widener Library; Charles Niles, Boston University Special Collections; Brenda Marston, Curator of the Human Sexuality Collection, Cornell University; and Kathleen Manwaring, Syracuse University Special Collections. Patricia Gossel and Faith Davis Ruffins at the Smithsonian Institution were generous with their knowledge and materials. The staff at the Institute for the Advanced Study of Human Sexuality in San Francisco gave me free reign of the institute's vast library. Mary McCarthy at the *New York Times* Archives and Cleo Wilson and Carilyn Engel at the Playboy Foundation provided me with useful documents. The staff of the Bancroft Library, the Lesbian Herstory Archives, the Rockefeller Archives, the University of Illinois at Chicago Center Special Collections, Countway Medical Library, Catholic University Special Collections, Barnard College Archives, New York Public Library, Harvard Law School Special Collections, and University College, London University made my research productive. The staff at the Kinsey Institute for Research in Sex, Gender and Reproduction were helpful and welcoming. The institute's collections are in disarray, but Kath Pennavaria and Margaret Harter did their best to find the materials I needed. Ian Moritch and Todd Smith made my visits to Bloomington truly worthwhile. Wendy Thomas and the staff at the Schlesinger Library deserve a special word of thanks for helping me to find materials day after day for almost a year.

I am indebted to all who provided me with somewhere to stay in cities across the country: Nick Breyfogle and Jillian Gustin, Adrian Davis, Jacqueline Edelberg and Andrew Slobodian, John Howard, Roberta and Lloyd Hill, Colby Devitt, Zach Karabel, Adam Leffert, Melanie Thernstrom, Mark Molesky, Brian Domitrovic, Meredith Radmondo, Paul Brennan and Paolo Pacheco, Toby and Peter Simon.

Sonja Herbert, Bill Farley of *Playboy*, Michael Bronski, and Jackie Markham, helped me to arrange interviews. John Mitzel, Sol Gordon, Jens Rydstrom, Jefferson Poland, and Suzanne Nichols all sent me materials I would not have been able to obtain otherwise. Betty Dodson and Albert Ellis allowed me to consult their personal collections of manuscripts. Thanks to all those who helped me obtain photographs for the book and especially those who sent me their own personal photos.

From start to finish, I received constant support from John and Pat Wilcha, Christopher Wilcha, my brother, Michael Wallach, and my parents, John and Janet Wallach. A tremendous thanks to David Wrisley for his coaching and insights, and to the seminar leaders and center staff at Landmark Education Corporation.

Thanks to Sarah Saffian for being a true friend; Michael Kaye, Anne Montague, Bob Castillo, and Lauren Acampora at Little, Brown; Svetlana Katz at Janklow and Nesbit; my research assistants, Julia Ott and Katie Farrell; Matthew Snyder at CAA; Kary Antholis and Susan Baerwald at HBO.

To my extraordinary agent and friend, Tina Bennett, who made my dream a reality, and, of course, to Michael Pietsch, my editor, whose patience, insight, and faith made this book possible.

And finally, thanks to my wife, Jennifer, who listened to me talk about this project every day for seven years, shared my sense of excitement, soothed my frustration, and read countless, countless drafts. For these reasons and so many more, this book is dedicated to her.

MAKE LOVE, NOT WAR

INTRODUCTION

WHAT WAS THE SEXUAL REVOLUTION? That's the question this book tries to answer. It is a question that I've wondered about since an early age. Born in 1969, I missed the sixties and, for the most part, the seventies. But I have always been fascinated by stories of the days of sexual liberation. I don't remember when I first learned about the sexual revolution or even when I first heard the term, but I do remember growing up with the vague sense of having missed something magical and mysterious. I remember the adolescent's agony of realizing that my parents and teachers had witnessed extraordinary social transformations, the likes of which we might never see again.

This book, in other words, grew out of my own personal desire to understand how the world as we know it today came to be. Who were the people who rebelled against sexual mores in the sixties and seventies? What sort of personal risks did they take? Why did they challenge the authorities? What forms of resistance did they meet? How did they succeed? How did they fail? What was life like before the sexual revolution and to what extent was it really changed?

This book has two important features. First, it endeavors to combine a traditional narrative with original analysis; my hope is that it will have something to offer to both the reader who knows little about the period and the one who knows a great deal. Second, it is based on written documents from the era as well as interviews with people who lived through it. The documents ensure historical accuracy, while the interviews provide perspective and context. The result, I hope, is a book that allows the reader to understand why and how the sexual revolution took place, why it ended when it did, the many ways it contributed to the overall improvement of American life, and, at the same time, the many ways it left us all less at peace with ourselves.

Where did we get the idea of a "sexual revolution"? The phrase was coined in Germany in the 1920s by Wilhelm Reich, an eccentric Austrian psychoanalyst who hoped to liberate Europeans from centuries of social, political, and psychological enslavement. His book, *The Sexual Struggle of Youth*, helped to disseminate his ideas in the German-speaking world. As one of the leading figures of the sex reform movement that swept Germany in the 1920s, Reich founded several clinics throughout Central Europe for the distribution of information about birth control and abortion, but his campaign was cut short by the political turmoil of the 1930s. In 1945, *The Sexual Struggle of Youth* was reprinted in the United States under the title *The Sexual Revolution.*[1]

Though Reich's dream of a sexually liberated society did not come to fruition, the first half of the twentieth century did see rapid changes in mores in both Europe and the United States. Advertising became more suggestive, avant-garde writers eschewed Victorian proprieties in describing their sexual experiences, magazine publishers began printing sexually titillating images to appeal to their male readers, and young women started to flaunt their "sex appeal." To many, these changes were deeply disturbing. In 1954 Harvard sociologist Pitirim Sorokin decried the "sex revolution" he saw taking place in American society and bemoaned the rising divorce rate, the shrinking family size, the growing popularity of jazz, the spread of ever more "expressive gyrations and contortions called dancing," and the new phenomenon he labeled "sex addiction." These developments, he declared, were evidence that American culture was on the verge of collapse. "We are," he wrote, "completely surrounded by the rising tide of sex, which is flooding every compartment of our culture, every section of our social life." This was a serious matter: "Unless we develop an inner immunity against these libidinal forces, we are bound to be conquered by the continuous presence of a gigantic array of omni-present sex stimuli."[2]

In the early sixties, the "sexual revolution" was used to describe the suspected impact of the newly invented birth control pill on the behavior of white, middle-class, female college students. A few years later, the term was employed to describe the sweeping repudiation of literary censorship by the U.S. Supreme Court. It was borrowed to characterize developments in the scientific study of sexual behavior, most notably by

Masters and Johnson. In the late sixties, the "sexual revolution" was invoked to refer to the new candor in American culture, especially the sudden acceptance of nudity in film and on the stage.

By the early seventies, the "sexual revolution" was taking on new meanings with each passing year. It was adopted to describe the showing of hard-core sex films in first-run theaters, not to mention the opening of private clubs for group sex. It was used to capture the new spirit of the swinging singles life, as well as the popularization of open marriage. For those in the counterculture, the "sexual revolution" meant the freedom to have sex where and when one wished.

In the highly politicized climate of the late sixties and early seventies, the "sexual revolution" was given a range of meanings. Some student radicals used the term specifically to refer to the end of the "tyranny of the genital" and the arrival of an eagerly awaited age of polymorphous pansexuality. Young feminists equated the "sexual revolution" with the oppression and "objectification" of women and saw it, therefore, as something to stop at all costs. Gay men considered the "sexual revolution" to mean a whole new era of freedom to identify oneself publicly as gay, to go to gay bars and discotheques, to have sex in clubs and bathhouses.

Events and developments shaped popular perception of the "sexual revolution." Sex-education courses in schools and colleges were radically redesigned to replace euphemism and scare tactics with explicit visual aids and practical information. New books suggested that women were as eager for one-night stands and other sexual thrills as were men. Many states repealed their sodomy laws and introduced "no-fault" divorce. And in 1973 *Roe v. Wade* ended a century of criminalized abortion. Once again the "sexual revolution" was reinterpreted and redefined.

To this day, the "sexual revolution" remains a resonant and provocative expression, but it evokes different events and eras to different people: It may bring to mind college coeds in tight sweaters learning about the pill, or naked hippie couples frolicking in a park, or men and women waiting in line to see a hard-core porn film as a first date. Each of these images is accurate, but no one alone can tell the whole story.

This book is not about the "sexual revolution" described by Reich or Sorokin but about the social and cultural transformations of the 1960s and '70s. The narrative begins in the early sixties because this was when white middle-class Americans first really began to accept the idea of young women having premarital sex. It ends in the late seventies, when opponents on both ends of the political spectrum waged a largely successful campaign against sexual permissiveness. In the intervening years, the nation went through a period of rapid change that affected nearly everyone in some way or another. Dozens of developments reshaped the American social and cultural landscape. Depending on one's perspective, these developments could be seen as either steps toward social progress or symptoms of social decline. But every one of them has had an impact on how we as a nation have come to think of life, liberty, and the pursuit of happiness.

One cannot write a serious book today on sex without addressing the theories of the French philosopher Michel Foucault. The first volume of his *History of Sexuality* sent shock waves through the academy when it was published in English in 1978 because it challenged the validity of one of the most talked-about ideas of the 1960s and '70s: the idea of sexual "repression."

Ever since American cultural critics discovered Foucault, "repression" has been a dirty word in intellectual circles. It is not my aim to challenge Foucault or to critique his philosophical system, but I do believe it is necessary to appreciate that real sexual repression was always a threat in the 1940s and '50s. That is to say, the state reserved the right to repress sexual deviance and dissent. One could go to jail for publishing the "wrong" book or distributing contraceptive devices to the "wrong" person, or saying the "wrong" word aloud in a public place. Although few people actually served time for such activities, the threat of punishment was always there. In a more subtle yet even more powerful way, the threat of "social death" loomed on the horizon for anyone who broke with convention. There were likely to be severe consequences if one admitted to having had premarital sex, or confessed to a physical attraction for a person of another race, or acknowledged publicly one's homosexual inclinations. No one looked kindly on a "slut" or a "pervert."

Far more people worried about the threat of legal trouble and social ostracism than ever actually experienced either of the two, so it is hard to document the extent of sexual repression in the forties and fifties. If one were to conduct a study that focused on actual police prosecutions for distributing obscenity in the 1950s, for instance, the results would probably be inconclusive. Moreover, people most likely did many things in private that would have cost them dearly if discovered. Professed sexual morality and actual sexual behavior do not always correlate.

But statistics alone do not encompass the vastness of culture, and it was America's culture of repression that had a chilling effect on the arts, publishing, science, and everyday interactions. People were afraid that what they said about sex might come back to haunt them, so they often chose silence and self-restraint. But as I hope this book makes clear, many Americans in the second half of the twentieth century desperately craved freedom from the fear of retribution for sexual misconduct. To that end they wrote books, staged rallies, formed organizations, broke the law, and flouted convention. For them, sexual repression was something very real and very disturbing. They made it their goal to liberate humanity from what they felt were intolerably repressive laws and beliefs.

It takes an unusual person to devote his or her life to challenging society's views about sex. The people who did so in the sixties and seventies certainly formed an eclectic group. They believed passionately in what they were doing, and sometimes they let their passions get the better of their reason. They were not, with a few exceptions, great thinkers; nor were they great artists or activists or writers. Most did not have children; those that did would probably have been judged by their families as mediocre parents. Though they condemned others for hypocrisy, they were often blatantly hypocritical themselves. Often they were motivated less by high-minded ideals than by lust and greed.

But for all their faults, the sexual revolutionaries of the sixties and seventies were individualists in the truest sense of the term. They refused to bow to convention, to dress "appropriately," to act "normally," to "go with the crowd." They were rarely embarrassed by their own peculiarities, and they almost never let the smirks and sneers of others stop them from expressing themselves.

And unlike the great majority of history's revolutionaries, they eschewed violence. Or, rather, to be more accurate, the thought of violence never even occurred to them. Violence was the very opposite of all they stood for. They believed in making love, not war.

If leadership is defined as the ability to enroll others in new possibilities and new futures, then no matter how strange or anti-intellectual or, at times, deeply selfish they may have been, the sexual revolutionaries of the sixties and seventies were the truest of leaders. They made people realize that the future does not have to look like the past.

Part of the reason that there is still so much confusion surrounding the sexual revolution of the sixties and seventies is that the term "revolution" has two meanings: It can denote a calculated contest against the status quo (as in the "French Revolution"); or a sudden, unexpected period of social transformation (as in the "Industrial Revolution"). The sexual revolution of the sixties and seventies involved both elements. There were direct attempts to topple the legal and political pillars of the existing moral regime. There was also an unplanned reconfiguration of American culture, a result of demographic, economic, and technological changes that took many Americans by surprise. Sometimes these two aspects of the sexual revolution operated in tandem, forcefully pushing the nation along one path; sometimes they operated in opposition to each other, pulling the nation in two different directions at once.

Many of the social and cultural changes of the era were not revolutionary at all but evolutionary. Gender roles began to change dramatically in the 1910s and '20s and continued to evolve over time. The birth control movement also got its start in the first decades of the century, and by the 1960s "family planning" was already an acceptable practice for married middle-class couples. Erotic pinup pictures date from the 1940s and only slowly developed into the magazine centerfolds in *Playboy*, *Penthouse*, and *Hustler*. Gay bars and bathhouses existed long before they became visible to the straight world in the late sixties and seventies.

As the following pages reveal, the so-called "permissiveness" of the sixties and seventies was a far more complicated cultural phenomenon than popular memory allows. It was a response to the sense of fatalism created by the military draft and the moral questions raised by the war in Vietnam. It was encouraged by many religious leaders, who came to the conclusion that "traditional" morality was based on a misreading of scripture. The trend was endorsed by judges who could not bring themselves to support censorship or laws regulating private behavior. It was fueled by the hunger for truth.

In some respects, the permissiveness of the era was just the logical extension of the commercial free market to include sexual goods and commodities. In other respects, it marked a literal *revolution:* a return to the secular values and bawdier spirit of the eighteenth century, when the Founding Fathers wrote the Declaration of Independence and the Constitution. It was during the Age of Enlightenment, after all, that the pornographic classic *Fanny Hill* was published in England, that Benjamin Franklin and other champions of liberty penned countless erotic poems, and that most educated people believed science and reason were about to eradicate religious superstition once and for all.

I am suggesting, in other words, that the sexual revolution of the sixties and seventies was a deeply American revolution, filled with the contradictions of American life. It was spiritual yet secular, idealistic yet commercial, driven by science yet colored by a romantic view of nature.

This book was far harder to write than I ever expected it would be. Naively — and arrogantly — I thought I could simply interview a few people and read some out-of-print books and thereby master a topic as sweeping and complicated as the sexual revolution. But more than that, I assumed at the start that my own views on the subject were crisp and consistent. Over time I realized the opposite was true. In fact, there were many moments while writing this book that I wished I had a clear political agenda to organize my thoughts: a marxist framework, a feminist perspective, or even a coherent, moralistic stance. Other times I wished at least that I could write history objectively and impartially without any of the hindrances of hindsight.

Unfortunately, I must beg the reader's forgiveness in advance: I have not found any escape from my own highly idiosyncratic, personal concerns, which shape my perception of both the present and the past. When I read a story in the morning paper about a case of contemporary censorship, I fear for the First Amendment and fire off letters to the editor. But when I see a report on television about pre-teens practicing unsafe sex, I fret about the messages being sent in the mass media. When I hear about government discrimination against gays and lesbians, or attacks on abortion providers, or opposition to sex education in schools, I am overcome with anger. And when I hear about sexual violence against women, sexual cruelty among teenagers, or the sexual exploitation of children, I wonder if my own civil libertarian leanings aren't misguided. I cannot claim, in other words, to possess a consistent socio-sexual ideology. When I began working on this project I was young and single and brashly confident about my own commitment to the cause of sexual freedom. Now that the book is done I am married and a father and just a little bit mortified that one day my daughter will no doubt find this book on a shelf and flip through its pictures and pages.

I suspect that my ambivalence about sexual expression is shared by most Americans. Perhaps, ultimately, this book examines how difficult it is to sustain a consistent political point of view regarding sex. In the 1960s and '70s many tried, but most failed. Sex is far too messy and complex to conform to tidy political postulates.

As recent scandals and controversies suggest, however, the problem of sexuality remains critical for the nation. The meaning of marriage, the psychological significance of gender differences, the relationship between private life and public life, the dynamics of sexual power, the nature of consent, the stigma of sexually transmitted disease, the concept of age appropriateness, the virtue of honesty, the obligation of parent to child, the role of sex education, the causes of unwanted pregnancy, the definition of infidelity (non to mention the definition of sex itself) are all, no matter how hard we may pretend otherwise, unresolved issues in American society. To really understand our relationship to these issues, one must go back to the 1960s and '70s, back to a time when utopianism and hedonism, idealism and opportunism were dramatically transforming the landscape of sexual morality.

CHAPTER 1

SINGLE GIRLS,
DOUBLE STANDARD

W HEN HELEN GURLEY BROWN's *Sex and the Single Girl* hit
bookstores in 1962, the sexual revolution was launched and
there was no turning back. Brown did something few other
American women had dared to do: She gleefully admitted, in print, that
she had lost her virginity before getting married. It was a wild confession, the kind of revelation that could destroy a woman's reputation,
cost her her closest friends, wreck her marriage. But Brown did more
than admit to a single indiscretion, she hinted at a long history of casual
contacts, and she extolled unmarried sex as a positive virtue. "Not having slept with the man you're going to marry I consider lunacy," she
wrote. Unrepentant and unashamed, Brown gently urged other women
to follow her example. As she told those who might feel guilty about
their erotic impulses, "[S]ex was here a long time before marriage. You
inherited your proclivity for it. It isn't some random piece of mischief
you dreamed up because you're a bad, wicked girl."[1]

As Brown and her publisher hoped, *Sex and the Single Girl* proved
just controversial enough to become a sensation. One reviewer called it
"as tasteless a book as I have read" and warned that it showed "a thorough contempt for men," who become "the marionettes" in an artful
and immoral "manipulation."[2] From a literary standpoint, the book was
simply atrocious. Tossing exclamation points right and left, Brown
could barely write a single sentence that didn't include a shriek of
delight over rich men or expensive eyeliner. Most of the book's advice
to women — from makeup tips to cooking lessons — was numbingly

conventional. But the public adored its breezy style, forthright manner, and pragmatic attitude about premarital romance. The book was an instant best-seller: 150,000 hardcover copies were sold the first year alone. Brown got $200,000 for the movie rights to the book — the second-highest figure that had ever been paid for a nonfiction book.

Helen Gurley Brown was an unlikely revolutionary. Born in Green Forest, Arkansas, in 1922, she was bred to be a proper Southern lady. Raised by her mother (her father died when Helen was only four), Helen Gurley prided herself on being a good daughter, always obeying the rules — or at least telling the truth when she didn't. She was more bony than beautiful, suffered from severe acne as a teenager, and spent most of her youth caring for her older sister, who had polio. Helen performed well in school, but like most women in the forties and fifties, the only job she could find after graduation from college was secretarial. A firm believer in the American Dream, the young Gurley felt confident that if she were persistent enough, her literary talents would eventually be recognized. In the meantime, she took advantage of everything that working for wealthy, attractive men had to offer. Even though a company might frown on "intramural dating," Gurley would later write in her book, she believed in workplace romance if there were "good material at hand." If her boss was less than handsome, Gurley simply found a new one: "As long as we're in more or less of a boom economy, it's possible to change jobs easily."[3] After she'd held eighteen different secretarial jobs, Gurley's talent for perky prose landed her a position as a copywriter for an advertising firm.

Gurley had discovered sex at an early age. When she was only eleven, she and a relative, four years older, tried to have intercourse and failed only because her vagina was too tight.

> That was some hot and heavy summer, as you can imagine. I was eleven and he was 15. There's nothing like a country boy who is 15 and horny. Yet I too felt — what would you call it — feelings, cravings, longings. And we once even tried it. But I, of course, was hermetically sealed, a tiny little person, I'd never been touched before, and his heart wasn't in it.

At sixteen, she kissed a boy in the back of a car and had her first orgasm. Four years later she lost her virginity. "Everything was sealed over. I think I bled a little. But I did have an orgasm. I knew then that sex is a wonderful, delicious, exquisite thing . . . after that nothing ever got in the way of my thinking sex was fabulous." The following day "the darling man went to a store and bought me earrings. He wanted me to marry him, but I said no. My mother was devastated."[4]

At thirty-three, Gurley obtained a diaphragm and discovered the joys of sexual independence. After a string of affairs, she finally did marry in

1959. She was already thirty-seven, an old maid by the standards of the day. David Brown, her movie-producer husband, was the one who suggested she write an advice book for young women. He knew a financial opportunity when he saw one, and she knew that there was a large gap between what women did in private and what was said in public. She was appalled by a 1961 article in the *Ladies' Home Journal* warning single women that they had two choices: to marry or remain absolutely chaste. Brown knew from her own experience that many single women were flouting public morals in their private lives. "Theoretically a 'nice' single woman has no sex life. What nonsense! She has a better sex life than most of her married friends. She need never be bored with one man per lifetime. Her choice of partners is endless and they seek *her*."[5] All a woman needed to fully enjoy single life was a little of Brown's advice on fashion, decorating, and sex.

Bubbling with optimism, *Sex and the Single Girl* reflected the spirit of middle-class America during the heyday of Camelot. The economy booming, the misery of the Depression and World War II all but forgotten, America in the early sixties was a vibrant, energetic nation. Brown's combination of coy femininity and pull-yourself-up-by-your-bootstraps ambition was practically a guaranteed success. In the early sixties, anything seemed possible — even the abolition of the age-old double standard.

The sexual double standard is as old as civilization itself. Among the Hebrews of the Middle East, monogamy was strictly enforced for women, while men often took concubines or multiple wives. When Sarah could not bear children for Abraham, he — with God's blessing — simply took a maidservant as his mistress. According to Jewish lore, King Solomon had seven hundred wives and three hundred concubines. Jewish women were required to shave their heads so that they would not prove tempting to other men. According to the Old Testament, women who committed adultery were to be summarily stoned to death. In ancient Athens, men were free to have multiple partners (male or female), while women who were not professional prostitutes lived in virtual slavery. A married woman was not only the property of her husband, she was confined to the upper floors of her home and forbidden to appear in public without a veil. In Greek mythology, the most powerful and revered goddesses remained lifelong virgins. In Imperial Rome, the law was less harsh: A woman who committed adultery was banished from her home and never allowed to marry again. Although early Christians tried to introduce a single standard of sexual restraint for both men and women, they ended up — by glorifying Mary's virginity and demonizing Eve's eroticism — merely reinforcing the double standard and providing a new justification for the punishment of sexually active women.

Despite the fact that gender roles fluctuated throughout the Middle Ages, promiscuous women were consistently attacked and denounced by Church authorities. In the sixteenth and seventeenth centuries, many were burned at the stake as witches. Chastity belts and other devices served where the fear of punishment did not. Despite the Enlightenment and the scientific revolution, the double standard persisted into the modern era. While aristocratic women could afford to play by their own rules, Rousseau and other "modern" thinkers tended to be vocal opponents of female sexual freedom. After the bloodbath of the French Revolution, many observers in England and America blamed the loose morals of French women for the political mess in Paris.

In the nineteenth century, bourgeois notions of propriety and cleanliness lent new import to the notion of female purity. Victorian sensibilities required women to profess a total lack of sexual feeling. A middle-class woman was expected to tolerate her husband's advances only for the sake of having children. Women were simply not supposed to enjoy sex. Since men were known to need sexual release, moralists urged them to visit brothels rather than defile their own wives. As a result, red-light districts flourished in nineteenth-century cities.[6] As in ancient Athens, a woman who appeared on the street alone in the Victorian era was assumed to be a prostitute.

The double standard had several cruel implications for women. Not only did it mean an unmarried woman was supposed to be absolutely chaste, it meant a woman who had been raped was deemed unsuitable for marriage. Not infrequently, a girl who was raped would be pressured by her parents to marry the rapist. Women were often blamed for the assaults.[7] The double standard also led to laws against birth control and abortion, on the grounds that they would encourage female promiscuity. In 1873, the U.S. government made it a crime to send birth control devices — or even information about such devices — through the mail.

In the nineteenth century and early twentieth, a few scattered social reformers tried to dismantle the double standard. But they were almost always dismissed as strange bohemians or dangerous radicals and their writings were often banned. Slowly, however, the double standard began to wane. Anthropologists showed that premarital promiscuity was happily encouraged in some primitive societies without any adverse effects. The vulcanization of rubber led to the invention of modern contraceptives. Marriage manuals encouraged husbands to attend to their wife's sexual pleasure. In the 1910s and '20s, working-class women discovered that money brought freedom. The economic vitality of the era encouraged a relaxed view of sex outside of marriage.[8] But the double standard did not disappear. At the insistence of Catholic authorities, Hollywood drove home the moral that wanton women would ultimately be punished for their sins. In films like *East Lynne* (1931), *Waterloo Bridge* (1931), *Grand Hotel* (1932), *Anna Karenina* (1935), *Jezebel* (1938), and countless others, women were put in their place for expressing their sexual desires. When Mae West insisted on flaunting her sexuality onscreen and refused to abide by the dictates of censors, Paramount Pictures failed to renew her studio contract. As Sylvia Weil, who was born in 1910, remembers, "if it got around that a girl slept with a man before she was married, she was ruined. She would never find a good husband." Women continued to face retribution for "unladylike" behavior, while society generally winked at the sexual antics of young men.[9]

Each new generation of young girls was indoctrinated with the same message: A woman's virginity is her most precious commodity. As actress Dyan Cannon, born in 1937, recalls, "My dad used to tell me that if I let anyone touch me, anyone, they wouldn't respect me and I would be considered a tramp."[10] In the 1950s, as Americans reveled in the "return to normalcy" after years of depression and war, the double standard was reaffirmed in books, movies, television shows, and popular magazines. American males were told that if they were healthy they should hunger for sex, while young women were advised to resist forcefully and demand a ring.[11]

"You have no idea how bad it was," recalls Gloria Steinem, who grew up near Toledo, Ohio, in the thirties and forties. "There was always the fear that you might be punished for being sexual." One author catalogued the rules that the mass media conveyed to young women:

> The young miss, for example, must never take any real initiative in courtship . . . must not show any interest in one male when she is out with another . . . must never try to date a fellow who is going steady with another girl . . . must never go home with a man whom she has just met at a dance, lest he consider her "just a pickup" . . . must not act too intelligent when she's with a boy because "boys don't like you to be smart" . . . must never phone a fellow unless she is going steady with him or has some other legitimate excuse . . . must never be so forward with boys as to "cheapen her in a man's eyes."[12]

Failure to abide by these rules could lead to gossip, insult, and public humiliation.

With the emergence of professional psychoanalysis in the postwar period, the double standard acquired "scientific" legitimacy. Psychologists and psychiatrists claimed that women were not only less sexual than men, they were naturally masochistic. Helene Deutsch claimed that women were inevitably masochistic because they could experience full sexual arousal only by being dominated. Marie Bonaparte argued that women were masochistic because during conception the ovum must be "wounded" by the sperm.[13] Meanwhile, other psychoanalysts insisted that women who experienced only clitoral orgasm were immature and unwell; mature women supposedly transferred their orgasmic sensations from the clitoris to the vagina. The vaginal orgasm, psychoanalysts maintained, was the only true orgasm. Such ideas caused many women to feel inadequate and inferior.

Most teenage girls in the fifties did not even know orgasms existed. "I didn't know anything about orgasms," one woman recalls.

> The first time [we had sex] we were in his dorm room. It was fast — he came in and came out. It was a sharp, poignant pleasure that had no resolution . . . He would come in and then pull out and come into a handkerchief. I was always left hanging. I used to come back to my dorm and lie down on the floor and howl and pound the floor. But I didn't really know why I was so frustrated. It felt so lonely.[14]

So long as the double standard was dominant, men and women were caught in a war of the sexes. Boys lusted after girls and tried to seduce them without getting trapped into marriage, while girls distrusted boys — often with good reason. "When I was a kid," *Penthouse* publisher Bob Guccione remembers,

> finding a girl who screwed was like finding gold. It was a great piece of news if you heard about a girl who screwed, because it was extraordinarily unusual for a girl to screw without a lot of problems — having to take her out, court her, spend money on her. When you did hear about one, she was inevitably the object of many a gang bang. I remember going to see a girl in Teaneck, New Jersey, and there were four or five carloads of guys, and we picked this dame up, drove her to the schoolyard, and one by one, twenty guys screwed her on the grass.

Ronald Jones, who was a student at Ohio State during the fifties, remembers one weekend at his fraternity house when "over a hundred guys had sex with the same woman."[15] Under the double standard, a woman who publicly expressed the slightest interest in sex effectively forfeited her right to say no. As these examples show, the reward could be gang rape.

As Helen Gurley Brown revealed, women in the 1940s and '50s publicly claimed to observe official morality but often followed their own rules privately. There is no reliable data on sexual behavior from the period, but in 1957 alone, 200,000 babies were born out of wedlock in the United States. In 1953, Alfred Kinsey, a zoologist turned sex researcher at Indiana University, reported in his book *Sexual Behavior in the Human Female* ("the Kinsey Report") that roughly 50 percent of the 5,940 white American women he surveyed admitted to having had sex before marriage. He also noted that approximately 25 percent admitted to having had an extramarital encounter. Since Kinsey's sample was not random, his findings cannot be treated as nationally representative, but they do suggest a discrepancy between official morality and private behavior.[16]

As a result of the double standard, girls who acquired a reputation for being "fast" or "easy" were both scorned and envied by other girls. Worse, sexually active girls tended to feel terrible guilt about their own behavior. Eunice Lake (a pseudonym), who was born in 1930 and grew up in a working-class family in rural Indiana, was, in her words, "very promiscuous" between the ages of seventeen and twenty-two. During that period, she had intercourse with twenty-three boys, six of whom she felt "in love with." Later, she wrote in a diary, it was a time of "mental grief." "*Promiscuous, whore, prostitute, slut,* and *nymphomaniac* were some of the words I chose to call myself, I suppose, as some sort of mental punishment for not being a 'nice girl.'"[17]

No matter what was really going on behind closed doors, those who publicly criticized the double standard could suffer severe consequences. As long as one championed sexual restraint for both sexes, there was no need to fear. But as soon as one advocated sexual freedom for women as well as men, the public responded with outrage. When, for instance, Ben Lindsay, a judge in charge of the juvenile court in Denver, began advocating "trial marriage" for young men and women in the 1920s, he was summarily removed from office.[18] In 1940, New York City authorities prevented faculty members at City College from hiring the famed mathematician and philosopher Bertrand Russell because he had defended sex outside of marriage in his book *Marriage and Morals* (1929). As soon as Russell's proposed appointment was announced, he was branded a "professor of paganism" and a "desiccated, divorced, and decadent advocate of sexual promiscuity." The Registrar of New York County said that Russell should be "tarred and feathered and driven from the country." The New York state legislature ruled that "an advocate of barnyard morality is an unfit person to hold an important post in the educational system of our state at the expense of taxpayers." Eventually the matter went to court, and a judge ruled that if City College granted Bertrand Russell a position on the faculty, it would be tantamount to creating "a chair of indecency." In observance of the court order, the New York City Board of Higher Education rescinded Russell's appointment.[19]

Alfred Kinsey suffered a similar fate. Because his study of female sexual behavior implied that many women were likely to have sex before marriage and that traditional morality should therefore be scrapped, his book was viciously attacked. Though Kinsey was highly respected by fellow scholars and maintained a scrupulous public persona (his taste for crew cuts, bow ties, and classical music was well known), *Sexual Behavior in the Human Female* earned him a reputation as a public menace. Republican Congressman B. Carroll Reece branded Kinsey a Communist and demanded a federal investigation of the Rockefeller Foundation, Kinsey's major source of financial support. The foundation eventually cut off Kinsey's funding. Even Margaret Mead, who had made her name in the twenties as one of the first anthropologists to study the sexual behavior of other cultures, criticized Kinsey's "amoral" approach. At a 1954 conference, the American Medical Association charged Kinsey with creating a "wave of sex hysteria."[20] In 1956 Kinsey died a defeated man.

Wisconsin Senator Joseph McCarthy died the year after Kinsey, and as the anti-Communist hysteria of the '50s waned, Kinsey's posthumous prestige grew. His statistics slowly gained the weight of scientific orthodoxy. Though Kinsey did not live to see the long-term impact of his work, by the late 1950s his numbers were beginning to make the double standard suspect. Other developments played a role in its decline. The backlash against McCarthyism, and the realization that ultraconservatives were apt to be as authoritarian and intolerant as their Communist enemies, led to a general disgust with moral hypocrisy. The discovery of penicillin as a cure for syphilis took much of the danger out of sex. Meanwhile, middle-class white women were increasingly entering the paid workforce, and as a result they had less patience with restrictions on their personal behavior. The huge number of teenagers (there were some 13 million in 1956) led to general friction as they rejected the moral assumptions of their parents. Because the economy was so strong, these teens had money to spend and could spend it as they pleased. Corporate America quickly learned to cater to their tastes and values — including their contempt for "preachy" sexual moralism.

These teenagers tore through copies of *Peyton Place*, the 1956 novel by Grace Metalious about sexual secrets in a small New England town. *Peyton Place* offered the same indictment of American hypocrisy as Kinsey's report on female sexual behavior. In one typical episode, Metalious describes the plight of a young woman raped by her stepfather. When she realizes she is pregnant, the girl must plead with a local doctor to perform an abortion. He agrees but, afraid of public censure, pretends that it is an appendectomy. Not just victims, Metalious's female characters were sexually assertive, independent, and determined to satisfy their desires, regardless of morality. In one scene, Betty Anderson, "an over-developed seventh grade girl," demands rough sex from her boyfriend, Rodney:

> "Come on, honey," she whimpered. "Come on, honey," and his mouth and hands covered her. "Hard," she whispered. "Do it hard, honey. Bite me a little. Hurt me a little."
>
> "Please," murmured Rodney against her skin. "Please. Please."
>
> His hand found the V of her crotch and pressed against it.
>
> "Please," he said, "please."
>
> It was at this point that Betty usually stopped him. She would put both her hands in his hair and yank him away from her, but she did not stop him now. Her tight shorts slipped off as easily as if they had been several sizes too large, and her body did not stop its wild twisting while Rodney took off his trousers.
>
> "Hurry," she moaned. "Hurry. Hurry."

Metalious walked a fine line between the bold and the conventional. On the very same page that Betty has her torrid affair, she learns that she is pregnant, suggesting that she must be punished for her actions.

Born into a lower-middle-class French Canadian family, Metalious always felt alienated from the puritanical morality of her New Hampshire neighbors. Pregnant at eighteen, she had a shotgun wedding and began the life of a fifties housewife. After writing several novels without success, she was inspired by a string of tragic events in her hometown. A young woman, the victim of her father's sexual advances, killed him in a combination of revenge and self-defense. Metalious realized that incest was the perfect centerpiece for a novel exposing the sadness and hypocrisy of small-town life. A New York publisher fell in love with Metalious's novel, and *Peyton Place* soon became a best-seller.[21]

The eager consumption of Grace Metalious's fictional exposé and the eventual public acceptance of Kinsey's report on female sexual behavior paved the way for Albert Ellis's sustained assault on the double standard. An irreverent, iconoclastic psychologist with a doctorate from Columbia University, Ellis first made a name for himself as a marriage counselor and therapist. Like Metalious, Ellis came from a working-class background and found himself at odds with middle-class definitions of morality. He began to rail against bourgeois niceties and made a habit of using four-letter words in his public lectures. Although he was reviled by many of his colleagues, Ellis attracted many New York clients, who liked his iconoclasm and rationalist — though sometimes flippant — approach to sexual attitudes. In a series of books in the 1950s and '60s, including *The Folklore of Sex, The American Sexual Tragedy, Sex Without*

Guilt, and *The Art and Science of Love,* Ellis attacked the double standard as a barbaric remnant of primitive societies in which men owned women as property. Some critics blasted Ellis as they had Russell and Kinsey, but Ellis couched his critique of the double standard in terms midcentury Americans could not afford to ignore.[22] According to Ellis (and contrary to Kinsey and Brown), women were reluctant to have premarital sex with men, and this was driving men to seek satisfaction through homosexual relationships. If women didn't abandon the double standard soon, the nation would be swarming with homosexual men. Marriage and the family might disappear and the nation would suffer the consequences. Lawmakers, sociologists, and psychologists concerned about "rising" rates of homosexuality took note of Ellis's predictions and began to slowly accept the necessity of sexual freedom for women.

As the fifties came to a close, various forces were conspiring against the double standard. But moralists made a last-ditch effort to prevent the spread of sexual liberalism. In 1960, administrators at the University of Illinois fired professor Leo Koch simply because he criticized the double standard and defended premarital sex in a letter to the student newspaper, while FBI Director J. Edgar Hoover launched a nationwide crusade against "pornography," a term he used to describe everything from titillating comic books to avant-garde literature. A 1961 issue of *Reader's Digest* offered "The Case for Chastity." That same year, in *Better Homes and Gardens,* another writer offered advice on "How to Tell Your Daughter Why She Must Keep Her Self-Respect." The president of Vassar College told female undergraduates in 1962 that premarital sexual activity was cause for expulsion. But women were beginning to repudiate the double standard. As one Vassar student told a reporter, albeit under the cover of anonymity, "If Vassar is to become the Poughkeepsie Seminary for Young Virgins, then the change of policy had better be made explicit in admissions catalogs."[23] This was just the kind of sentiment Helen Gurley Brown knew would guarantee sales of her book.

If *Sex and the Single Girl* hadn't come along, those American women who disregarded public morality in their private lives would have continued to do so, and a few might even have risked social ostracism by openly challenging the double standard on philosophical grounds. But Helen Gurley Brown, who had read Albert Ellis with relish, packaged sexual liberalism for early-sixties America as only an advertising copywriter could. Brown combined just the right amount of iconoclasm, individualism, consumerism, and conservatism to appeal to a mass market. *Sex and the Single Girl* was designed to reach sexually active single women and Madison Avenue executives alike.

True to America's Enlightenment tradition, Brown believed human beings were born without shame or sin. In the book's most provocative passages, Brown criticized American child-rearing practices for making girls ashamed of their bodies.

> Well, the truth is everybody starts out sexy . . . or with terrific potential. A sixteen-month-old baby is the prototype of sexiness. . . . She will be sexy all her life if nobody interferes. Unfortunately in our society somebody nearly always interferes! When she touches herself with pleasure and curiosity, her mother will take her hand away and say, "Naughty!" When she expels squashy brown cones not unlike the modeling clay she likes to play with, her mother will put over the idea they are icky, dirty . . . to be flushed away quickly. If the child isn't dim-witted, she figures out that where these cones came from is dirty too.

Brown presented a radical redefinition of sex appeal. "Being sexy means that you accept all the parts of you body as worthy and lovable . . . your reproductive organs, your breasts, your alimentary tract. You even welcome menstruation as the abiding proof of your fertility."

But Brown's enthusiasm for expensive cosmetics and plastic surgery undercut her social critique. "You probably wear lipstick, powder base and a little eye make-up every day. But have you considered drawing in completely new eyebrows, wearing false eyelashes, putting hollows in your cheeks with darker foundation, a cleft in your chin with brown eyebrow pencil or enlarging your mouth by a third?" Brown herself confessed to having had a "nose job" and being "delighted" with the results. She even called herself a "cheerleader" for plastic surgery. "Plastic surgery is admittedly expensive, not covered by Blue Cross, horribly uncomfortable for a few days — but oh my foes and oh my friends — the results! The lovely cataclysmic results are the kind you can't get any other way." She warned overweight women that they were doomed if they didn't diet. "You must *Do Something* or you can't hope to be blissfully single." (As for men who claimed to find fat women attractive, Brown insisted that they were unsure of their masculinity.) A far cry from a serious intellectual, Brown was quick to ignore the wisdom of her own insights into child-rearing practices.

The suggestions about makeup and fashion were relentless, interrupted by only occasional pop psychological insights. She warned that nymphomaniacs were really "frigid" women desperately trying to overcome their sexual anxieties. (This theme was also the centerpiece of Irving Wallace's 1960 novel *The Chapman Report,* inspired by the Kinsey

Report.) She cautioned her readers to be wary of homosexuals. Homosexuals, she wrote, "are little boys, or girls, in an arrested state of sexual development" with "tremendous emotional problems."[24] These asides lent a conservative, contradictory element to Brown's sexual liberalism.

But Brown never claimed to be a radical. In interviews, she disavowed any attempt to encourage premarital sex. "I didn't suggest anybody do anything," she declared, rather disingenously. "I'm always careful to say that I'm not for promiscuity." After the book was published, Brown told reporters that it was meant only for women over twenty. But if her publisher hadn't feared censorship, *Sex and the Single Girl* would have been even more revolutionary than it was. The original manuscript contained a large section on birth control and abortion that the publisher deleted. "I fought for it, but it came out anyway," Brown said.[25]

Though one might think that men would have been delighted by Brown's message — she was, after all, telling women to say yes to premarital sex — men raised to expect modest, demure, diffident female companions were in fact taken aback by Brown's vision of sexual equality. In a roundtable discussion published in *Playboy* in 1962 as "The Womanization of America," Alexander King, an editor at *Life* magazine, said he feared Brown's type of feminism enormously. "The assumption that a woman is supposed to get something out of her sexual contact, something joyful and satisfactory, is a very recent idea. But this idea has been carried too far, too. It's become so that women are sitting like district attorneys, to see what the man can or cannot perform and this has put men tremendously on the defensive." King was unabashedly sexist: "I haven't the slightest doubt that this absolute, unquestioned equality is a great mistake and in violation of all natural laws. It is a mistake because democracy is all right politically, but it's no good in the home." King also believed that women longed to be like men — that they suffered from Freudian "penis envy."

> Penis envy does exist, it's true — I think that perhaps it's not conscious, but it exists. I have no doubt about it. I have known a great deal of women in my life and they've all been enormously competitive on all levels, you see, particularly in the last few years. I think they do deeply and instinctively resent these outward manifestations of masculinity, of which they have none.

According to King, the fact that women were becoming so "dominant" was an important factor in the rise of "pansies."

In the same *Playboy* article, Mort Sahl, a comedian and political satirist, appeared equally angry that women were becoming "cold" and "predatory"; the psychoanalyst Theodor Reik expressed suspicion of all sexually assertive women. "What is astonishing to me is that women, more and more, are taking over the active roles in sex, which was not so before. The men finally will resent it. They should." Reik believed that sexually assertive women would emasculate their male partners. "I would say there is a law — a law as binding as the laws of chemistry or of physics — namely, that a masculinization of women goes with the womanization of man, hand in hand."[26]

Philip Wylie, a popular social critic of the day, warned in a 1963 *Playboy* article that sexually aggressive "career women" were modern versions of Delilah and Salome, "girl-guillotiners" who "used their sex appeal . . . at considerable cost to those males who would impede them." Desperately worried about the fate of the male sex, Wylie warned that

> a man must instantly be on the alert, for most dedicated career women will unhesitatingly use their sexuality in the manner of the Sirens, whose allure had a single professional intent: luring sailors off course and causing ships to be wrecked. The latter-day career woman has much the same obscene compulsion: She must compete with and, if necessary, cripple manhood and masculinity on earth.[27]

Sex and the Single Girl marked both the end of an era and the beginning of a new one. Despite the fact that some men clearly felt threatened by her, Helen Gurley Brown was a hot commodity. She was invited to take over the failing *Cosmopolitan* magazine and transform it into a self-help manual for sexually active women, which she did with great success. But Helen Gurley Brown was significantly older than the unmarried women and teenagers who were the prime consumers of premarital advice. It remained to be seen how these young women would view the battle of the sexes as they matured into adulthood. Would they be satisfied with Brown's hedonistic philosophy laced with tips on plastic surgery? Or would they demand a far more thorough response to society's sexual ills? Their parents eagerly, yet nervously, awaited the answer.

CHAPTER 2

BEATNIKS AND BATHING SUITS

TWO YEARS AFTER Helen Gurley Brown bared her soul in *Sex and the Single Girl,* a forty-two-year-old fashion designer, Rudi Gernreich, decided it was time for women to bare even more. In June 1964, Gernreich introduced the "monokini," the perfect synthesis of Southern California hedonism, socio-sexual politics, and ready-to-wear wit. Quickly renamed the "topless swimsuit," Gernreich's creation was a standard one-piece suit on the bottom with two delicate straps rising archly between the wearer's breasts. His favorite model, Peggy Moffit, explained to one reporter: "He was trying to take away the prurience, the whole perverse side of sex."[1] It was his personal contribution to the cause of physical freedom.

It was also a brilliant publicity stunt. Only a few thousand suits sold, but the novelty was just the kind of thing that newspaper editors loved. In fact, the *San Francisco Chronicle* featured a photo of a woman in a monokini — her exposed breasts clearly visible — on its front page.[2]

Gernreich's creation caused international consternation. The Soviet government denounced the topless bathing suit as a sign of "barbarism" and social "decay." The pope called it immoral. In New York, police were given strict instructions by the Commissioner of Parks to arrest any woman wearing one of the scandalous suits. Forty evangelicals protested at a department store in Dallas where the monokini was on display. In Chicago, a nineteen-year-old-woman wearing the suit on a public beach was fined $100 for indecent exposure. Even in the South of France — what would eventually become the world's epicenter of topless bathing — the suit was banned. The mayor of St. Tropez instructed officers to keep order via helicopter.[3]

English designers quickly copied Gernreich's idea and created topless evening dresses. Not many women actually dared to go out in public in such

23

a dress, but one woman who did made headlines in Europe and the United States. After arriving at a fashionable restaurant, she removed her fur stole and revealed that she was wearing one of the new dresses. As the patrons stared at her bare breasts, the manager of the restaurant asked the woman to leave.[4]

Gernreich himself loved all the controversy, even if he affected a cool ennui about the whole business. Wearing a snakeskin jacket and gesturing with his favorite prop, a long black cigarillo, Gernreich held a press-conference-cum-fashion-show for the media at a ritzy New York hotel. Barbra Streisand was there, with the editors of the nation's important fashion magazines. The public response to his swimsuit, he explained, was "either funny or horrible, according to how you feel when you get up in the morning." As he told a reporter, the suit expressed "an anti-attitude." Young Americans were bored: "bored by being told what to do, bored by the hopelessness of the atom bomb and by the abstractions of government, bored by sexual discovery in high school."[5]

The abstractions of government had been all too real for the young Rudolf Gernreich, who fled from Nazi-controlled Austria to Los Angeles with his mother in 1938 when he was sixteen. From an early age he knew he was gay and never worked to hide it. For a while he tried dancing, but found he was far more talented as a costume designer. In 1950, Gernreich met Harry Hay, a musician and member of the Communist Party, at a rehearsal for a local dance company. At the time, Hay was toying with the idea of creating a group to champion homosexual rights. When Hay told Gernreich about the idea, the designer was enthusiastic and agreed to help rally support. His childhood in Austria had taught him the importance of organized resistance. Together with three other men they formed the Mattachine Society, named after a troupe of medieval Italian performers who wore masks to disguise their identities, which would become the first successful gay rights organization in the country.[6]

Gernreich was not only openly gay, he was a nudist. He believed that American taboos against public nakedness were unhealthy and puritanical. At the same time that he was organizing for gay rights, he was trying to drum up support for nudism. Gernreich's interest in nudism, like his belief in fighting discrimination against homosexuality, was nurtured during his childhood in Austria, which had been a hotbed of nudist sentiment from the end of the nineteenth century. Many German-speaking Austrians, worried that modern men and women were being corrupted and softened by urban life, espoused a "back-to-nature" philosophy and urged fellow Germans to practice rigorous calisthenics. Nudity, they said, was necessary to strip away the false pretensions of civilized society and inspire communion with nature in all its invigorating glory. Nude gymnastics became the norm in schools throughout the German-speaking world during the Weimar era.[7] But when Adolf Hitler came to power in

1933, he banned all nudism in Germany. For leftists, nudism immediately assumed intellectual significance. If nudism and fascism were incompatible, then freeing people from bodily shame might be an important first step in preventing political repression. In other words, if Hitler saw nudism as a threat, then nudism might be an effective tool in the cause of personal freedom. Gernreich embodied this idea. Every day he swam nude in his Hollywood Hills pool, a fact that was a matter of both pleasure and pride.

Whether Gernreich knew it or not, American nudists had long been fighting their own battles against persecution. For decades, American nudists had attempted to create camps where they could be free from societal regulations regarding dress, but they were inevitably hounded by unsympathetic authorities. When nudists tried to promote their cause through photographic magazines, they met the fierce resistance of the Post Office. Throughout the forties and fifties, the Postmaster General banned nudist publications from the mails. Not until 1958 did the Supreme Court declare that the naked body in and of itself could not be deemed obscene.[8]

A few weeks after Gernreich's topless bathing suit appeared in stores, Davey Rosenberg, the 300-and-some-pound promoter of a failing go-go bar in San Francisco's North Beach district, hit upon the idea of having the go-go dancers wear the monokini to add spice to the club's nightly entertainment. Rosenberg told the owner of the Condor Club his idea and the owner readily agreed to try it. On June 22, 1964, the topless bar was born. The press had a field day and the Condor Club became an instant sensation.

Carol Doda, from Napa Valley and the lead dancer at the club, had the dubious distinction of being the nation's first topless dancer. Doda was also one of the first women in America to use silicone injections to augment the size of her breasts, going from a size 34B to a reputed 44D. With mounds of blond hair, false eyelashes, and little else, Doda danced atop a Baldwin piano, attracting plenty of male customers every night, many of them tourists who'd read about her in the pages of *Playboy*.[9]

At first, the San Francisco police department decided not to press charges against the Condor Club. Their indifference encouraged the rest of North Beach's go-go clubs to follow the Condor's lead. Before long, there were hundreds of topless bars on the West Coast, though San Francisco remained the symbolic home of the topless phenomenon. Tourists poured into San Francisco to visit the "sexually liberated" city and see Carol Doda in person.

Long before the topless dancing craze of the midsixties, San Francisco was known for its relaxed view of vice. From the city's founding in the 1770s, its thriving ports created a large, transitory community of sailors and workingmen seeking adventure. The city exploded during the 1849 Gold Rush, a time when men quickly began to outnumber women. The

Barbary Coast neighborhood near the docks was home to a bustling red-light district, where liquor and sex were always for sale. One newspaper described the Barbary Coast as a "sink of moral pollution" and the center of a "wild sirocco of sin." In 1870, it was estimated that some three thousand prostitutes worked in the neighborhood. According to legend, patrons at the Boar's Head saloon could watch a woman having intercourse with a pig. Many of the women who sold their bodies in the brothels of the Barbary Coast were Chinese and Japanese immigrants, and their ethnicity added an exotic dimension to San Francisco's culture of commercial sex. The Great Earthquake of 1906 and the progressive reform movement in the early 1900s managed to shut down most of the city's brothels, but neither succeeded in curbing the city's permissive reputation, especially since some of the city's streets even bore the name of famous madams.[10]

The North Beach neighborhood where the Condor Club was located had already become a bohemian enclave by the 1950s. Not a beach at all, but a sloping residential area overlooking the city's financial center, it was cheap enough in the fifties to attract a collection of writers, artists, gays, and other bohemians, who made their home amid the working-class Italian families that formed the backbone of the community. In the heart of North Beach stood City Lights, the nation's first all-paperback bookshop. Founded in 1953 by the poet Lawrence Ferlinghetti, City Lights soon became home to a coterie of avant-garde writers. Allen Ginsberg, Jack Kerouac, Michael McClure, Kenneth Rexroth, and other writers who felt disaffected from society and disillusioned with mainstream culture gathered there for readings, dramatic presentations, and late-night philosophical arguments. These "Beats," as they called themselves, pursued sexual experimentation as fervently as they pursued literary experimentation. (The connotations of the term "beat" evolved over time. It was originally black slang for "exhausted" but was later considered short for "beatific" and "beatitude.") Casual sex, open homosexuality, and occasional orgies were essential to the Beat protest against the authoritarianism of American society. By the early sixties, hordes of black-turtlenecked would-be writers, dubbed "beatniks" by the media, were swarming upon San Francisco. These beatniks tended to be sexual exiles in their own country: young men and women who felt constrained by middle-class morality and all its expectations and demands.[11]

Before Carol Doda donned Rudi Gernreich's monokini and danced atop the piano in the Condor Club, the most risqué nightclubs in America were the creation of the man whose name has become synonymous with sex itself, Hugh M. Hefner.

Hefner, of course, was the founder of *Playboy* magazine. The first mass-market magazine to include photographs of nude women (though the photos were carefully framed, cropped, and airbrushed to eliminate any signs of pubic hair), *Playboy* revolutionized American publishing when it was introduced in 1953. Men saddled with domestic responsibilities leaped at the chance to escape their day-to-day concerns in pages filled with soft-skinned, big-bosomed beauties. Hefner had no interest in being branded a pornographer, so he included enough serious material — short stories, interviews, investigative journalism, and cultural criticism by prominent writers — to make his magazine respectable in the eyes of most middle-class Americans.[12]

On February 29, 1960, Hefner capitalized on the growing postwar affluence and the obvious popularity of his magazine (the circulation already exceeded 1 million) by opening the first Playboy Club, in Chicago, his home base. Featuring sixty-three carefully selected waitresses, each dressed as a "bunny," *Playboy* magazine's famous mascot, the club catered to middle-aged businessmen and young urban professionals. The bunnies wore skimpy, tight-fitting, corseted costumes with white collars, black bow ties, black fishnet stockings, high heels, ears, and fluffy white cotton tails. It was, according to Hefner, "high camp." Playboy Clubs were not nearly as racy as the burlesque strip clubs of the 1910s and '20s, but they were the most provocative venues of the post–World War II period. (The burlesque clubs had all but disappeared during the Depression, when purity crusaders forced them out of business.) To avoid prostitution charges, Hefner prohibited the bunnies from dating patrons (except high-level Playboy executives and their friends), and even went so far as to hire undercover agents to test the bunnies' morals. It was a "look-but-don't-touch" (or, more accurately, a "look-but-don't-expect-to-see-much") world. Yet with black jazz performers and cutting-edge comedians also on the bill, the Chicago club was widely considered the most sophisticated nightspot in the world. From a commercial standpoint, the club's formula was brilliant. By the end of 1961, the Chicago club had over fifty thousand members.[13] Three years later there were six clubs in the United States, with a quarter of a million regular patrons.[14] Playboy Clubs soon spread throughout the country, making a mockery of morals crusaders' campaigns to "clean up" society. What could be "cleaner" than a bunny with a fluffy white tail?

In many ways, the beginning of go-go dancing in the early sixties foreshadowed the generational divide that would wrench the country apart by the end of the decade. Inspired by the campy French film *Whiskey-a-Go-Go,* go-go bars spread from Paris to New York, Los Angeles, and San Francisco. At the same time, the first wave of young male baby boomers were just entering their early twenties. They tended to regard Playboy Clubs as tame, stuffy retreats for their fathers, places that were more prudish than provocative. Go-go clubs, by contrast, were more "hip," more "happening." The dancers wiggled and jiggled in short dresses and thigh-high boots. Best of all, compared to Playboy Clubs, go-go clubs were cheap. And when Carol Doda put on a topless swimsuit in 1964, go-go clubs announced the arrival of a new era of heterosexual entertainment. Burlesque, old-timers noted with glee, was finally back.

The topless swimsuit had its origins in a mixture of political protest and bawdy commercialism. Gernreich recognized that taboos against homosexuality and nudity encouraged shame, self-loathing, and the social control of personal behavior. The topless bathing suit was inspired by this quasi-political perspective: It was a champagne cocktail meant to shatter the calm complacency of the status quo. Though Gernreich was an entrepreneur driven by the quest for fame and personal success, he was also a cultural subversive. But the topless-bar phenomenon that emerged in North Beach had virtually nothing to do with Gernreich's more political inclinations. It was a purely commercial phenomenon. Davey Rosenberg and other topless-bar promoters were interested in making money, not changing society. As Rudi Gernreich realized, much of the appeal of the monokini — and, by extension, the topless bar — stemmed from a collective sense of boredom that plagued middle-class Americans in the early sixties. The postwar economic boom of the 1950s had given a greater number of Americans than ever before the opportunity to enjoy the benefits and comforts of bourgeois life. Children born in the late forties and fifties could look forward to lifelong prosperity.[15] As they grew up, they acquired cars, clothes, stereo systems, television sets — all in the pursuit of personal happiness. But by the early sixties, they were indeed bored: bored by everything Madison Avenue had to offer. Men, in particular, were running out of things to consume. Yet they had plenty of money and plenty of leisure time. Davey Rosenberg and his ilk provided the answer: titillating sexual experiences at a price.

The question was: Could a commercialized brand of sexual liberalism inadvertently effect meaningful political and cultural change? Or were commercialism and sexual radicalism inherently at odds? Capitalism depends on the discontent of consumers, who will spend their lives and savings searching for satisfaction through material goods. Sexual pleasure is one of the few forms of pleasure available in a capitalist society that is truly free. Sex satisfies at no cost. In that sense, sex has the potential to undercut the power of materialism. But charge for sex and you turn it into just another commodity. Topless dancing was thus both revolutionary and retrograde.

Carol Doda, the Condor Club's star attraction, told one interviewer that dancing topless was a way "to communicate" with people. "Let's face it," she said, "sex is a part of life and we can't hide it."[16] In interviews, Doda always insisted that stripping was a form of social protest. Was Doda a pawn in the hands of men like Davey Rosenberg? Or was she a new breed of young rebel able to use her own body to make social change? Like countless women before her, Doda exploited men's desires in order to make a living and was willing to be exploited in return, but because she came of age in the midsixties, she had a political vocabulary — borrowed from the civil rights movement and the nascent student movement — with which to justify her vocation.

The topless swimsuit and the Condor Club were both symbols of the early sixties. They embodied the forces of idealism, hedonism, and opportunism. They were not the best that America had to offer, but they helped her secure a new image as a hip, happening nation. The topless swimsuit and the Condor Club were, in a word, "fun." After decades of economic anxiety, world war, and anti-Communist hysteria, a little fun was just what most Americans wanted.

The North Beach bohemians eventually tired of the topless-bar phenomenon. They liked the Condor Club's irreverent attitude, not to mention the sexual stimulation (for the heterosexual men at least) the topless dancing provided. But the beatniks were also repulsed by the club's crass commercialism and the snickering sort of sexual attitudes the club fostered and exploited. In their eyes, topless dancing was only one step removed from the surreptitiously straitlaced mentality of the Playboy Club. The fact that the Condor Club and its imitators drew so many tourists was proof enough that they merely appealed to America's sexually repressed.

Topless bars hardly seem revolutionary today. Usually they are dingy places catering to an unsophisticated crowd or expensive clubs where white-collar males make deals and escape the growing equality of the sexes in the workplace. Today, topless bars stink of sexual repression and reactionary social views. There is nothing, in other words, inherently liberating or progressive about erotic entertainment. But for a brief moment in the early '60s, the cultural climate was so constricting, the simple act of going to a bar to see a woman bare her breasts could seem like a significant social gesture. And the novelty of the experience made it all the more enjoyable.

Ironically, Rudi Gernreich's topless bathing suit and nudist philosophy could have had the real impact on American cultural norms. If Americans had, like Europeans, truly come to accept topless and naked bathing, American attitudes toward the body would have been dramatically altered. But Americans were not prepared for such wholesale cultural change. They settled for the topless bar and left future generations to resolve the rest.

CHAPTER 3

THE PILL: A PRESCRIPTION FOR EQUALITY

I N HIS STATE of the Union address of January 4, 1965, President Lyndon B. Johnson cautiously announced his plans to promote the use of birth control abroad. "I will seek new ways," he told Congress, "to use our knowledge to help deal with the explosion in world population and the growing scarcity in world resources."[1] This statement of support for birth control was not a bold one, but it was the first ever by a sitting president. Johnson knew that by merely alluding to federal financing of contraception, he might anger Catholic voters across the country. And though the president was eager to promote the use of birth control abroad, several states at home had laws against birth control on their books. Johnson's January message suggested it would be a stormy year of controversy and conflict over contraception.

Human beings began using contraceptives thousands of years before the birth of Christ. Archaeologists have found ancient recipes for contraceptive potions using such ingredients as crocodile dung, honey, and sodium carbonate. In the pre-Christian world, evidence suggests that prostitutes used primitive pessaries (spongelike devices) to block sperm from entering the uterus, and men frequently practiced coitus interruptus. Aristotle and other Greek philosophers recommended a range of procedures to prevent conception or abort an unwanted pregnancy. During the Roman occupation of Palestine in the first and second centuries before Christ, Jewish priests recorded various methods known for sterilizing women.[2]

Nowhere does the Old Testament explicitly say that contraception is immoral. It is not mentioned in any of the long lists of crimes spelled out in the Five Books of Moses. The story of Onan, found in Genesis 38, is traditionally cited as a warning against contraception (it has also been used as an injunction against masturbation and homosexuality), but the story has more to do with a son's defiance of his father than with sexual behavior: Onan's father orders him to have sex with his brother's widow in order to impregnate her, but Onan disobeys by "spilling his seed" on the ground, and is then slain by God. Apart from this one story, the Old Testament is indifferent toward contraception. The sections of the Old Testament that catalogue in precise detail the laws of ritual cleanliness and sexual conduct do not say anything about preventing reproduction.

The New Testament is similarly silent on the subject. Various passages emphasize the importance of virginity, marriage, and love, but contraception is never mentioned. Early Christians acquired the notion that contraception was wrong not from the Bible, but from various sources outside Christianity. Not until St. Augustine in the fifth century was the Church's position on contraception fully formulated. According to Augustine, contraception was unconditionally immoral and illicit.[3] Overcome with guilt about his own lustfulness, Augustine was determined to check the impulses of his fellow Christians by restricting sex to procreation.

Throughout the Middle Ages, Christian theologians refined and reaffirmed Augustine's ban on birth control. In practice, however, religious authorities did little to enforce this theoretical ban. European peasants were essentially free to experiment with whatever contraceptive techniques they might devise. Some theologians even gave their official blessing to coitus interruptus. It was not until the end of the eighteenth century, when the birthrate in some Christian countries began to decline, that religious leaders and political officials began to worry about the sexual behavior of married couples.[4]

The Enlightenment led to the first treatises actually advocating birth control and family limitation. Jeremy Bentham, James Mill, and Francis Place encouraged couples to limit the number of their offspring to ensure the maximum amount of resources for every child. Later in the nineteenth century, Robert Dale Owen and Charles Knowlton wrote detailed marriage manuals to teach couples about coitus interruptus and douching. In 1843, the invention of vulcanized rubber led to the creation of modern condoms. Ten years later, however, the Holy Office of the Inquisition ruled that condoms were unacceptable for Catholics.

In the last decades of the nineteenth century, a virtual war raged in English-speaking countries between champions and critics of birth control. In America, Charles Knowlton's practical text *The Fruits of Philosophy: or The Private Companion of Young Married People* (1833) was censored. Anthony Comstock, a Civil War veteran with a sharp sense of moral duty, launched a crusade to ban birth control devices and put abortionists out of business. At Comstock's urging, Congress passed a bill in 1873 making it illegal to mail material advertising "obscene rubber goods." The law also prohibited the importation of any birth control device. Congress authorized Comstock to guard American morals, and guard them he did. He hounded every manufacturer and salesman of contraceptive devices he could find.[5] Meanwhile, many states, driven by the fear that if Protestants continued to use birth control they would soon be outnumbered by Catholics, passed laws making it illegal to use, sell, or display contraceptives. But birth control advocates were equally committed. In 1878, champions of population control in Great Britain formed the Malthusian League to educate physicians about the benefits of contraception. (The group was named after the English pessimist Thomas Malthus, who predicted that population growth would inevitably outstrip food supply, but the group did not endorse Malthus's anti-welfare views.) In America, starting in the 1910s, contraception crusader Margaret Sanger went door to door to teach poor women about condoms and diaphragms. Between 1900 and 1925 international birth control conferences were held in Paris, Liège, the Hague, Dresden, London, and New York.[6]

Over the course of the twentieth century, modernization and secularization helped destigmatize birth control in America. Challenging the Comstock law in court, physicians gained the right to obtain contraceptives through the mail. The U.S. Army spent millions of dollars to supply soldiers with condoms during World War II. One by one, each of the mainline Protestant denominations declared contraception to be a private matter between husband and wife. Margaret Sanger's Birth Control Federation of America changed its name in 1942 to Planned Parenthood and grew until it had thousands of clinics across the country. But state laws against birth control remained on the books. And in a series of papal proclamations in the '40s and '50s, the Catholic Church reiterated its stance against birth control. No matter how hard groups like Planned Parenthood tried to push legislators toward a secular view of sex, politicians, mindful of Catholic votes, refused to repeal nineteenth-century laws against contraception. (It didn't matter to Catholic leaders that those same laws had originally been enacted in order to maintain a Protestant majority.) Such laws did not actually stop women from using contraceptives — Connecticut, which had one of the most stringent laws in the country, also had one of the lowest birthrates — but through the mid-twentieth century timid legislators refused to repeal them.

Laws or no laws, the invention of the oral contraceptive in the late 1950s revolutionized public discourse about birth control. Developed in 1957 and licensed by the Food and Drug Administration in 1960, the birth control pill — which quickly became known simply as "the pill" — gave women a greater sense of sexual freedom than any contraceptive device that had come before. Just as the availability of penicillin in the 1940s had seemed to separate sex from the danger of venereal disease once and for all, the invention of the birth control pill finally appeared to divorce sex from the danger of unwanted pregnancy. It was not that the condom, the pessary, the diaphragm, and the spermicide, all of which preceded the pill, were ineffective, but the pill, a synthetic estrogen taken once a day, at any time of the day, separated the act of intercourse from the use of birth control. With the pill, contraception became "clean."

To midsixties America, the pill was a revolutionary invention, a medical triumph over human biology. Indeed, the pill medicalized contraception at a time when Americans were increasingly turning to medicine to solve personal and social problems. A technological marvel, the pill appealed to America's sense of progress. "In its effects I believe that the pill ranks in importance with the discovery of fire," wrote philosopher Ashley Montagu; others compared it with the invention of the printing press. Montagu theorized that the pill would not only emancipate women and make premarital sex acceptable, it would eliminate the American male's "predatory exploitative attitude toward the female," and allow for the overall "rehumanization" of mankind.[7]

Serious research into a contraceptive in pill form began in 1953 when Katharine Dexter McCormick, who was a former suffragist friend of Margaret Sanger's, and the widow of an heir to the McCormick reaper fortune, gave a major grant to Planned Parenthood to develop an oral contraceptive. The group funded the work of Gregory Pincus, a biologist at the Worcester Foundation for Experimental Biology in Shrewsbury, Massachusetts, who was studying the physiology of conception. McCormick wanted Pincus to develop a contraceptive method that women could control. Pincus teamed up with John Rock, a Roman Catholic gynecologist at Harvard Medical School. Together they developed a synthetic steroid tablet which they tested on women in Puerto Rico. Soon thereafter, the Searle pharmaceutical company agreed to market the first oral contraceptive product in the United States under the brand name Enovid.

Although executives at Searle were well aware that the pill had many potentially dangerous side effects (studies suggested links to nausea, headaches, dizziness, heart problems, and cancer), they marketed the new drug aggressively. An in-house newsletter told Searle salesmen to "weed out all the negative points and convince doctors to get patients started on Enovid TODAY . . . We are making each selected call with one objective: Enovid Prescriptions."[8]

No matter what the motives of pharmaceutical executives may have been, the pill was a major breakthrough in women's emancipation. Women were finally free to control their own reproductive cycles. Not surprisingly, the pill was immediately popular. By 1962, an estimated 1,187,000 women were using it.[9] It took journalists until 1965 to really discover the pill, but once they did, they endorsed it wholeheartedly. As *Redbook* magazine explained, "Since the pill can be taken any time of day, and since it does not involve contact with the genitals, and since it is taken on a regular schedule whether one plans immediately to make love or not, it can be used without full awareness that one is preparing oneself for intercourse." According to *Time,*the pill was "a miraculous tablet." Gloria Steinem, who switched from the diaphragm to the pill in the early sixties, wrote a glowing tribute to oral contraceptives in the pages of *Esquire.* "For one thing, it is more aesthetic than mechanical devices and, because it works chemically to prevent ovulation, it can be taken at a time completely removed from intercourse."[10] The pill's champions insisted that it was entirely safe and, if used properly, 100 percent effective.

American women had been using various forms of birth control for centuries, but once the pill was invented, a kind of cultural amnesia took hold. Other forms of birth control were suddenly considered primitive, even barbaric. One gynecologist claimed, "All women find the diaphragm awkward, or even unpleasant. . . . The pill is easier, less anxiety-producing . . . by a factor of thousands."[11] There was something delightfully modern and pragmatic about the pill, which may have gotten its nickname from a sentence in Aldous Huxley's *Brave New World Revisited* (1958).[12] A woman on the pill could theoretically have worry-free sex any time, any place. The pill promised to erase fear and anxiety, to make sex simple and contraception discreet. The only real reservation anyone expressed about the pill in the midsixties was that it might make women more independent and consequently make men feel more insecure.[13]

When John F. Kennedy, the first Catholic president, was sworn into office in January 1961, the aging Margaret Sanger predicted a new era of sexual repression.[14] A Catholic president, Sanger felt, was sure to oppose birth control. Sanger, of course, was wrong about Kennedy:

Despite his religious upbringing, he believed strongly in the separation of church and state. In fact, as a result of the Cold War, most politicians in Washington, fearing a link between overpopulation and socialism, strongly supported anything that would check the population explosion in the Third World. By the early sixties, former president Dwight Eisenhower was honorary president of Planned Parenthood and a key advocate of federal support for foreign birth control programs. In 1963, Congress allocated $80,000 for population control research.[15] Even if Cold War politicians were operating on questionable assumptions, the Kennedy era witnessed a newly pragmatic approach to family planning.

But it was still illegal for anyone other than doctors to import birth control into the United States. On October 15, 1962, Elly Foote arrived at New York's Idlewild (now JFK) International Airport from Sweden. When she passed through customs, agents searched through her purse and seized her diaphragm. They made her sign a statement granting them permission to destroy it.[16]

Birth control itself was also still illegal in many states in the 1960s. This infuriated William R. Baird, a man who would devote his life to abolishing laws against birth control and abortion. Born in 1932, one of six children in a poor Brooklyn family, Baird was raised to believe it was crucial never to have sex before marriage. When he married in 1953, both he and his wife were sexually inexperienced. After the Korean War, Baird took a job with a pharmaceutical company, which happened to be in the business of manufacturing contraceptive foam. As clinical director, Baird visited a hospital in Harlem in 1963. There he heard the screams of a woman dying from a self-induced, coat-hanger abortion. "She was covered in blood, and she died in my arms." When Baird found out that contraception was illegal in New York, he went to Planned Parenthood to offer his services, but he was snubbed by organization officials. Accepting the role of lone crusader, Baird began going from town to town violating laws against the display of contraceptives. He used a van, which he decorated on the inside like a living room, to bring birth control to poor communities.

I bought an old UPS van, painted it white, put in a fake fireplace and painted fake wood walls and put up drapes. I wanted to create an atmosphere that for twenty minutes you were in Bill Baird's home and could talk about anything you wanted to. That was my shock. I learned about the incredible ignorance of Americans. A woman would come to me and tell me that she used Lysol for douching. To induce abortion, poor people would often use Kirkman soap, which they would chop into little pieces, add water, and introduce into the uterus. They didn't realize that the body could absorb fat from the soap and they could die of a fat embolism.

Or they would use water and salt, which they would insert up into the uterus, but what they didn't know was that it could also cause an air embolism. Women would tell me about how they had thrown themselves down the stairs to cause an abortion. Men would show me how they punched their girlfriends and wives in the abdominal area to terminate the pregnancy.[17]

Almost everywhere Baird went, he was arrested. He was imprisoned eight times in five states. A magazine for African-Americans ran a feature story on Baird and put his phone number on the cover so that women could contact him to find out where to obtain an abortion. Baird was fired from his job at the pharmaceutical company. "The man who had hired me said, 'If you keep on teaching birth control in that van you're going to get fired.' I said, 'Joe, you hired me for my skills and you don't own me. If I want to go bowling after work or go to a movie or teach birth control, it is none of your business.'" Baird took odd jobs and received financial assistance from his friends Abbie Hoffman and Paul Krassner, and he kept on providing birth control to the poor. In 1964, he founded a clinic on Main Street in Hempstead, Long Island, then a predominantly poor, black community.

In the spring of 1965, Baird was operating his van in Nassau County, Republican country. "The police literally pulled me out of the van and handcuffed me, charging me with indecent exposure of obscene objects. . . . Within a few months of my arrest, the state of New York changed the law. Nevertheless, the right-wing district attorney who was running for reelection, William Kahn, announced he would prosecute me anyway. The day after he was reelected Kahn dropped the charges. He was later indicted for double-billing Nassau County."

The following year, Marcus Dailey, the commissioner of welfare in Freehold, New Jersey, announced that he was going to reduce welfare costs by putting unwed mothers in jail. His plan was to charge the women under the state's fornication statute. In response, Baird brought his van to Freehold. He was quickly arrested and sentenced to prison for twenty days.

By 1965, conflict over sexual morality was leading the nation to the brink of a cultural crisis. How could the country that had produced *Sex and the Single Girl*, topless dancing, breast implants, *Playboy*, and the pill still have laws against contraception? The Constitution was vague on matters of sexual morality. The Bill of Rights clearly favored personal privacy and individual autonomy, but nowhere mentioned sexual behavior specifically. If laws against contraception were challenged, the nine justices of the Supreme Court would have to choose between a future ruled by Catholic pro-natalist forces or by Planned Parenthood and its liberal Protestant allies.

The leaders of Planned Parenthood were determined to win this war. They realized, however, that a man like William Baird was too much of a lighting rod for controversy to win support from the courts. They needed a female spokesperson, who would remind judges of their own wives and grandmothers. In Connecticut, the state with the strictest anti-birth control laws in the nation, Planned Parenthood activists found a friend in Estelle Griswold, a Roman Catholic born in 1900. Tall, graceful, and fluent in French, Griswold was the model of a New England matron. She had never even seen a diaphragm when she was asked to take over Connecticut's Planned Parenthood League. At first Griswold had no interest in the job ("It just left me cold," she later recalled), but she soon warmed to the challenge of overturning Connecticut's long-standing anti-contraception statute.

According to Connecticut law, anyone who used a drug or instrument to prevent conception could be fined or imprisoned a minimum of sixty days or both. This meant a married couple could go to jail for using a condom. Furthermore, anyone who so much as assisted another in the use of birth control could be punished as an accessory to a crime.[18] Estelle Griswold thought the ban on contraception in Connecticut was not only a serious invasion of privacy but an example of ridiculously antiquated thinking. Connecticut had one of the lowest birthrates in the nation, evidence that Protestants and Catholics alike were flouting the law. As one observer wrote, "One would assume that the good citizens of the state, regardless of religious persuasion, are heeding the law about as casually as the American public did the Volstead Act [banning liquor] in the roaring 20's."[19] Even Catholic priests were beginning to realize that their flock were straying from the official rules of the Church.

At first Griswold and Planned Parenthood's lawyers simply filed lawsuits on behalf of individual married women who would suffer major health problems if they ever gave birth again. But Griswold was hampered by a lack of money and a lack of organized support. Since it was strictly illegal for Planned Parenthood to open up a clinic in Connecticut itself, Griswold organized trips across the border to New York State.[20] Yet even such trips were technically illegal because they involved aiding and abetting in a crime. In 1960, the Supreme Court upheld Connecticut's 1879 anti-contraception law. But Griswold would not give up. She grew steadily more defiant. On November 1, 1961, she opened an illegal birth control clinic in New Haven, staffed with volunteer doctors. A few patients visited the clinic, including an undercover vice officer.

Four days later, police arrived to shut down the clinic and charge Griswold with a criminal offense. She was delighted. Now she had a strong case to test the law's legitimacy.

Despite Griswold's respectable image, judge after judge ruled against her. Her case wound its way through the courts, climbing the judicial hierarchy all the way to the top. In the meantime, Americans were becoming increasingly concerned about the effects of ignorance on society, a fact exemplified in 1958 by the opening of the play *Blue Denim*, by James Leo Herlihy and William Noble, which told the story of a young man who, afraid to talk to his parents about birth control, gets his girlfriend pregnant. Sexual shame and secrecy, the play insisted, could lead to devastating social consequences. The play, warmly praised by Eleanor Roosevelt in her national newspaper column, reflected the growing public demand for open discussion about sexual issues.

In 1965, the Supreme Court agreed to hear Griswold's plea. At first, the nine justices were divided. Even in the age of Carol Doda and the Rolling Stones ("Satisfaction," a song with sexual overtones, was number one on the charts in 1965), several of the high court judges believed the state of Connecticut had the right to send Griswold to jail for distributing contraception. But on June 7, the court issued a 7–2 decision striking down once and for all Connecticut's ban on contraception. In the majority opinion, William O. Douglas declared that the First Amendment created "a penumbra where privacy is protected from governmental intrusion." Douglas deplored the thought of police officers searching "the sacred precincts of marital bedrooms" and noted that certain rights of privacy were older than the Bill of Rights itself. Both of the judges who wrote dissents in the case agreed that the Connecticut law was illogical and backward, but neither felt the Supreme Court had any right to interfere with the legislation of sexual morality. It was a solid victory for Estelle Griswold and Planned Parenthood and the forces of sexual freedom, though the court's decision in *Griswold v. Connecticut* did nothing to overturn laws in Massachusetts, New York, and other states prohibiting the sale and display of contraceptives. *Griswold* only voided laws against their use.

In the fall of '65, just a few months after the *Griswold* decision, another birth control controversy made headlines. This time, many thought the matter was more serious. National newspapers and magazines picked up a story in the Brown University student newspaper revealing that the campus physician had prescribed birth control pills to two female students, both of whom were unmarried.[21] It was hardly news that college students were having sex, but many were shocked that university administrators were now condoning the practice. In fact, physicians at the University of Chicago and the University of Minnesota had been prescribing the pill to students for some time. But officials at Harvard and other schools publicly deplored the practice and warned that it would have negative consequences. Most physicians in 1965 tended to frown on premarital sex, and school doctors were especially conservative on the subject. "A visit to the infirmary is indeed the best form of birth control," wrote a student at American University to the school newspaper. "The staff has the ability to turn any liberal-minded co-ed into a Victorian prude."[22] The head of AU's health service, James W. Egan, shot back an angry reply, stating that the health service "could not of course prescribe contraceptives for minors without parental permission without serious legal risk." But his concerns were not just legal. "Aside from these considerations, a physician must practice in accord with the dictates of his own conscience and I don't think that putting the stamp of approval on promiscuity by issuing oral contraceptives would be in accord with the standards of the physicians practicing at American University." Egan warned "those adventuresome students who have suffered a complete necrosis of their moral standards" that venereal disease was on the rise.[23]

The pill was particularly in demand on college campuses. College physicians were loath to fit female students with the diaphragm — mainly because the procedure forced the physician to feel personally complicit in the promotion of premarital sex. But the pill let college physicians (almost all of whom were male) avoid penetrating the vagina of a young virgin with his fingers. As historian Beth Bailey writes, "The pill was a wonder drug not simply because of its effectiveness for women, but because of its convenience for those who prescribed it."[24]

Though traditionalists were determined to put up a good fight, the pill gave modernists a decided advantage in the shaping of American society. In some sense, however, the battle lines were blurred. Who was really a liberal and who was a conservative? Support for birth control was strongest in the South, traditionally the most conservative region of the country. Was it because Southern whites were genuinely concerned about the welfare of the poor? Or were they motivated by racism and eager to halt the growth of the black population? Some blacks suspected the latter. They saw dangerous parallels between birth control and involuntary sterilization, a technique favored by German Nazis and American eugenicists. The more social workers tried to bring birth control to poor black neighborhoods, the more left-wing activists fought their efforts. Although Martin Luther King, Jr., was a strong advocate for family planning, even the liberal National Association for the Advancement of Colored People distrusted birth control. In fact, in September 1965 the NAACP opposed a $90,000 federal grant for the dissemination of birth control information in North Philadelphia. The NAACP charged Planned

Parenthood, which had applied for the grant, with attempting to "help Negroes commit racial suicide."[25] Although many blacks believed the pill was a benevolent technological advance, black nationalists tended to regard it as a symbol of genocide.[26] A Planned Parenthood official explained to *Ebony* magazine: "Many Negro women have told our workers, 'There are two kinds of pills — one for white women and one for us . . . and the one for us causes sterilization.'"[27] This kind of paranoia frustrated and angered birth control activists.

The debates over birth control in 1965 reflected deep-seated divisions over the proper relationship between society and the individual. Some believed society had a moral obligation to prohibit the use of birth control; others believed society had no right to regulate such a private matter, and even urged society to take an *active* role in preventing unwanted pregnancies and overpopulation; still others suspected birth control proponents of evil motives. Whatever one felt about birth control, however, the advent of the pill and the decision in *Griswold v. Connecticut* were both major victories for secular humanism. After 1965, of all the major religious denominations only the Catholic Church would continue to oppose birth control. For many women, tradition and fear began to give way to hope and optimism. The terms of the debate had shifted: Opposition to birth control after 1965 would have to be articulated on sociological rather than moral grounds. As sexual pleasure became distinct from reproduction in the public mind, whole new possibilities emerged for both the individual and society.

It is almost impossible to overstate the impact of the pill on American culture. It gave women the freedom to have sex when and where they wished and made contraception palatable to the prudest of the prude. It put birth control on the covers of family magazines and symbolically represented scientific support for the sexual revolution. The pill promised a return to the rationalism and optimism of the Age of Enlightenment.

Paradoxically, however, the pill reinforced American romanticism about sex. It turned contraception into a mysterious, seemingly magical process that partners could avoid discussing with one another. It made it possible to prevent pregnancy without ever touching one's vagina or penis. It was ultimately a technological accommodation to the deepest dualism of Western culture: the belief that the mind is pure and noble while the body is dirty and base. Ironically, the single most revolutionary invention of the 1960s was a tiny, timid little pill, whose appeal derived mainly from the fact that it could be secreted away in a purse or a pocketbook without anyone ever knowing about it. No wonder the pill did little to erase Americans' ambivalence about sex.

CHAPTER 4

LOVE THE ONE YOU'RE WITH

AUGUST IS A cold month in San Francisco. The city has its real summer in September and October. But in August 1965, two young men and two young women tentatively stripped off their clothes and staged a nude "wade-in" off a San Francisco city beach. Imitating civil rights protesters in the South, the four self-proclaimed sexual-freedom fighters disobeyed local laws and customs to make a point about personal liberty. Jefferson Poland, the twenty-three-year-old leader of the group, believed anti-nudity ordinances were a denial of basic civil liberties and, worse, led to sexual repression in society. The founder of the New York League for Sexual Freedom, which by 1965 had evolved into the "national" Sexual Freedom League, Jeff Poland knew that a nude wade-in would capture the attention of the media. He forgot that in August, temperatures in San Francisco often dipped below 60 degrees. The week before the protest, he organized a handful of supporters, mostly North Beach beatniks, and alerted the local press. On the morning of the appointed day, Poland, wearing a swimsuit and a flower behind his ear, arrived with his three friends at the municipal beach known as Aquatic Park. Before cheering crowds and several cameramen, the four would-be protesters entered the icy ocean water and three of them disrobed (the fourth got scared at the last minute). A nineteen-year-old anarchist supporter stood on the shore and waved a banner asking, "Why Be Ashamed Of Your Body?" Other supporters formed a picket line on the beach and chanted, "Sex is clean! Law's obscene!" Reporters, unimpressed with the skinny-dipping stunt but eager for a good story, urged the nude swimmers to return to the shore in order to get arrested. Soon enough they were cited for violating San Francisco's municipal code regulating swimming attire. The two women received suspended sentences and six months' probation. Poland was required to spend five weekends in jail. (It was well known at the time that President Johnson liked to swim naked in the White House pool, a fact that some members of the press thought was indicative of a certain hypocrisy on the part of public officials.) The story made the national news.[1]

Jefferson Poland was one of the first hippies. He was wearing flowers in his hair well before the rest of his generation. He was a beatnik who, several years before it would become a trend, dropped the pretensions of urbane ultrasophistication for the back-to-nature simplicity of Rousseauian romanticism, a long-haired kid who saw the power of combining utopian social protest with over-the-top theatrics while the majority of male college students were still wearing jackets and ties to class.

Born in Indiana in 1942, just before the beginning of the postwar baby boom, Poland was the son of working-class parents. His father was a machinist in an automobile manufacturing plant, his mother a pink-collar worker. As a boy he often wet his bed. His father, determined to "cure" him of this habit, would come into his bedroom every morning and check to see if the bed was wet. If it was, he would tell Jeff to strip and then whipped the naked boy with a belt. Eventually Jeff told his mother about his father's beatings, and mother and son fled to Houston, Texas. They remained on the move. Jefferson attended over twenty schools before going to college. As a result, he perpetually felt like a "newcomer," an exceptionally creative outsider who "retreated into books" and "hardly knew anyone except" his mother.

Jefferson eventually left his mother's home and began hitchhiking his way to California. On one occasion he had sex with a man who gave him a ride; he enjoyed the experience, but also felt an intense sense of shame. He became an itinerant student, drifting in and out of schools, searching for meaning and purpose. By the time he was eighteen, he was having sex with women.[2] He began to question sexual mores, and as an undergraduate at San Francisco State University turned to popular authors like Philip Wylie and Albert Ellis to make sense of his own sexual tastes and the assumptions of American society. Their texts piqued Poland's interest in erotic freedom, but he felt frustrated by the fact that "sexual liberation seemed to exist mainly in books."[3]

Like other young beatniks, Poland moved into a group house to save rent. His roommates were two young women, both of them self-proclaimed anarchists. They taught Poland about "free love," a doctrine of anarchism since the movement began in the early 1900s. Such prominent anarchists as Emma Goldman and her lover Ben Reitman had criticized monogamous marriage as a form of property ownership in numerous articles and public speeches. (In her personal life, Goldman had tried to live according to her beliefs but was consumed with jealousy when Reitman had relationships with other women.) Free love was trumpeted even earlier by Victoria Woodhull, a radical suffragist who, in the 1870s, had several husbands and numerous lovers.[4] By the 1960s, anarchism was all but dead in America, but the idea that monogamy and jealousy were outdated and ought to be abolished had survived among intellectuals and bohemians. Poland was quickly converted to the cause.

Many of the left-wing dissidents of the early sixties congregated at Poland's group house. One was former University of Illinois biology professor Leo Koch, who was famous among radicals for being fired from his teaching position because of a letter he'd written to the student newspaper in defense of premarital sex. Koch had tried to sue the university and, having lost in the lower courts, was still awaiting a decision by the Supreme Court.[*]

[*] Koch had written a letter in 1960 to the campus student newspaper in response to an article written by two male students condemning premarital petting. The students argued that the average college man treated every college woman as "a simple female sex unit" rather than as "a living individual — as an organic complexity of personality and character, emotion and intellect, and passion and reason." (This was some eight years before radical feminists would make the very same claims about the "objectification" and sexual exploitation of women.) But to Koch, such arguments were merely an excuse for conventional moralism. Koch agreed that "unhealthy and degenerative" attitudes were part of campus life, but argued that they were the result of sexual repression and the double standard, not sexual freedom. "A mutually satisfactory sexual experience would eliminate the need for many hours of frustrating petting and lead to much happier and longer lasting marriages among our young men and women," Koch wrote. "With modern contraceptives and medical advice readily available at the nearest drugstore . . . there is no valid reason why sexual intercourse should not be condoned among those sufficiently mature to engage in it without social consequences and without violating their own codes of morality and ethics." Koch's claim hardly represented a radical position in 1960 — twelve years after the first Kinsey Report — but it triggered a near violent response from some members of the university community. The Reverend Ira Latimer denounced Koch as an "animal" and his letter as "an audacious attempt to subvert the religious and moral foundations of America." Latimer charged that Koch was part of a "Communist conspiracy to demoralize the nation." Two weeks after Koch's letter appeared in the *Daily Illini*, the president of the university terminated Koch's contract. The international academic community was horrified (forty-nine academics, including professors from Harvard, Yale, Princeton, Oxford, and Cambridge, formed a Committee for Leo Koch), as were students at the University of Illinois, but the trustees of the university refused to reinstate the botanist. Hugh Hefner considered Koch a martyr for the cause of sexual freedom and wrote a lengthy essay about Koch's case in an installment of "The Playboy Philosophy." Meanwhile, Koch filed a lawsuit against the university, lost, attempted to appeal, lost again, and again attempted to appeal. (*New York Times*, 8 April 1960, 34; 28 June 1961, 13; "The Playboy Philosophy," part five, *Playboy*, April 1963, 66–67; Leo F. Koch, "Academic Freedom at the University of Illinois," *Journal of the Hattori Botanical Library*, December 1960; SFL collection.)

Poland, deeply impressed by Koch's sense of conviction and willingness to challenge moral authority, decided to dedicate himself to the cause of sexual freedom. When comedian Lenny Bruce was arrested on obscenity charges in San Francisco in 1961, Poland participated in protests on Bruce's behalf. At San Francisco State, Poland ran for student office on a platform promising the sale of contraceptives in the school bookstore. Poland lost the election but not his interest in politics.[5]

In the summer of 1963, Poland, like hundreds of other college students, joined the civil rights movement as a volunteer. He endured the summer heat to register voters in Louisiana, where he learned about the growing student movement. In the fall, he moved to New York City in search of work. Two days after the assassination of John F. Kennedy in November 1963, Poland again met Leo Koch. Koch was well connected in Manhattan, and he introduced Poland to the writers of the New York Beat scene. Poland met Allen Ginsberg, who had returned to New York after several years in San Francisco; Diane Di Prima, one of the few women in the Beat community of poets; Ed Sanders, editor of a Beat journal named *Fuck You: A Magazine of the Arts;* and Tuli Kupferberg, a pacifist and songwriter. Poland also met avant-garde actors, directors, and playwrights like Judith Malina and Julian Beck, the founders of the Living Theater, an experimental troupe that used nudity to challenge conventional morality.*

In January 1964, the Supreme Court announced that it would not review Koch's case against the University of Illinois.[6] In response, Poland and Koch decided to form a group to challenge American sexual laws and values. They took the name the League for Sexual Freedom, mistakenly believing it to have been the name of an earlier organization formed in Germany (the organization they probably had in mind was the World League for Sexual Reform founded in 1928 by sexual scientist Magnus Hirschfeld). Such literary luminaries as Beck, Ginsberg, Di Prima, Sanders, Peter Orlovsky, and Paul Krassner were founding members. But Poland, Kupferberg, and a young activist named Randy Wicker were the real leaders of the League.†

Tuli Kupferberg, a so-called "red diaper baby" because he was the son of Communist Party members, was an anarchist and a sexual radical in

---

* In 1963, the year Poland arrived in Manhattan, New York performance artists were already pushing the limits of theater audiences. In a performance that year by Ben Patterson titled *Lick Piece,* a woman was covered entirely in whipped cream, which was then licked off by a male actor. In Carolee Schneeman's 1963 production *Meat Joy,* a maid threw food over a large group of writhing, entangled, barely clothed bodies. (Sally Banes, *Greenwich Village 1963: Avant-Garde Performance and the Effervescent Body* [Durham N.C.: Duke University Press, 1993], 197–98, 216.)

† Wicker was born Charles Hayden, Jr., but when he came out to his family changed his name at his father's insistence.

his own right. Like other anarchists, Kupferberg rejected monogamy as an outdated, bourgeois notion. He and his wife had an agreement that both were free to sleep with other people.[7] In the midsixties, he and Ed Sanders formed a folk-rock band, the Fugs, named after Norman Mailer's euphemism in his war novel *The Naked and the Dead* (1948). Their songs were silly yet provocative, with titles like "Group Grope," "Boobs a Lot," "Kill for Peace," "What Are You Doing After the Orgy?" and "Dirty Old Man." The Fugs appealed to fellow bohemians and the growing number of baby boomers who were seeking alternatives to the sappy lyrics and melodies of pop music.

As soon as Kupferberg and Poland met, they became close friends, sharing as they did an interest in sexual freedom. Kupferberg was a devotee of Wilhelm Reich, the renegade psychoanalyst who believed that sex and politics were deeply linked. Reich had been one of Freud's leading disciples during the early years of psychoanalysis; unlike Freud, however, Reich was a socialist who thought it imperative to combine political activism and sexual theory. Sexual repression, Reich argued, was the cornerstone of totalitarianism, so in order to liberate people politically it was necessary to liberate them sexually first. But Reich was eventually expelled from the Communist Party, rejected by Freud, and ultimately forced into exile by the Nazis. In 1939, he fled to the United States, where he acquired a small but influential group of followers, all of whom subscribed to his notion that sexual repression caused serious psychological damage. In line with his teachings, Reichian analysts taught their patients how to achieve maximum pleasure through intercourse and thereby experience the full release of all pent-up energies. Reich died in 1957 and his library was destroyed by the federal government, but thirty-one Reichian analysts continued to practice his techniques, and his ideas infused the writings of many important intellectuals of the sixties.[8] Kupferberg spent time in Reichian therapy, and Reich's ideas underscored Kupferberg's own beliefs about sexual freedom.

Randy Wicker, the third leading figure in the Sexual Freedom League, was no stranger to sexual politics when he met Jefferson Poland and Tuli Kupferberg in the early sixties. Wicker had been involved for several years with the Mattachine Society, the gay rights organization founded in the fifties in New York by Rudi Gernreich and his friend Harry Hay. In 1962, Wicker had successfully persuaded a New York radio station to allow gay men to speak on the air about their own lives, a first for American radio. In addition, he convinced reporters to write stories on homosexual life for the *Village Voice*, the *New York Post*, and *Harpers*. But when a female friend needed an abortion and could not find a doctor willing to perform the operation (she ended up taking quinine, having a miscarriage, and spending several years in Bellevue mental hospital), Wicker realized that sexual freedom meant more than gay rights. Like Kupferberg, Wicker became a founding member of the New York League for Sexual Freedom in 1964.[9]

At first, the New York League members merely engaged in discussion. At weekly gatherings in Greenwich Village, Poland, Kupferberg, Wicker, and others would meet to debate the meaning of "sexual freedom." The discussions often dwelled on hypothetical situations, lending an abstract, intellectual dimension to the organization's endeavor. They argued the moral merits of prostitution, pedophilia, bestiality (the group decided bestiality was okay if an animal failed to resist), and other controversial sex practices. Wicker recalls that one of the liveliest discussions involved the legitimacy of public masturbation. The group members decided that there was nothing wrong with it so long as a man did not actually hit someone with his semen during ejaculation, which would be a violation of the other person's rights. There were fewer than a dozen core members of the group, but every so often prominent figures in New York's avant-garde would join in the discussions.[10]

Occasionally, group members would stand on the streets of Manhattan and pass out fliers about sexual freedom.* To jaded urban passersby, League members were a mere curiosity. In April 1964, League members held a speak-out at Columbia University, hoping that college students would rally to their cause.[11] Poland and his fellow activists demanded "respect for sexual freedom as a fundamental civil liberty," and called for the decriminalization of interracial marriage, fellatio, cunnilingus, anal intercourse, bestiality, and transvestism. They also attacked censorship laws, laws against public nudity, laws against contraception and abortion, college parietal rules, statutory rape laws, and strict divorce laws. They called for the freedom of "homosexuals and other harmless deviates" from police persecution and for the legalization of prostitution "under conditions which will reduce VD and protect the welfare of prostitutes."

---

* One leaflet explained the purpose of the new organization:

Why organize? Even relatively liberated persons still think of sexual repression as a private rather than a public problem. Having achieved some measure of sexual freedom for themselves, they do nothing for those whose natural desires from infancy to adulthood are being repressed, perverted or even punished by such *social* institutions as the school, the church, the state. They forget that the roots of puritanism are *social* not individual and must be cut first at the *social* level. *THE LEAGUE STRUGGLES FOR* freedom from unreasonable restrictions, legal and societal, on our sexual behavior.

It is interesting to note that League members, Poland especially, saw their mission in political, not simply personal, terms. The notion that sexual matters are political would be picked up by the feminist movement in the early seventies.

League members were as concerned about sexual equality as they were about sexual freedom. "Each person," they announced, "should be free to choose his or her activities and roles without being forced by social pressure or law to conform to rigid masculine and feminine stereotypes."

Taking their cue from the burgeoning civil rights movement, the League members staged a series of demonstrations, some more successful than others. An early protest targeted the New York City district attorney's office after city police arrested filmmaker Jonas Mekas in March 1964 on obscenity charges for showing an underground film called *Flaming Creatures*, which contained close-up images of breasts and genitals, men in drag, and suggestions of masturbation, oral sex, and gang rape.[12] Then when comedian Lenny Bruce was again arrested on obscenity charges in April, Allen Ginsberg and other members of the League organized a committee to fight for his release. Ginsberg issued a press release with the signatures of dozens of important intellectuals. The League also organized a protest in front of the New York Public Library in an effort to bring attention to the library's policy of segregating sex books.[13] On August 23, 1964, the League sponsored a demonstration outside the Women's House of Detention, where a majority of inmates were prostitutes. Jeff Poland, who picketed in front of the building carrying an American flag, attracted the attention of some reporters by calling for the total decriminalization of prostitution.[14] Then, on September 19, Poland and Wicker sponsored the first public demonstration for homosexual rights in New York City.[15] Together they protested the military's policy of investigating and outing "suspected homosexuals" by picketing the city's Armed Forces Induction Center. In October, when Walter Jenkins, an assistant to Lyndon Johnson, was forced to resign over allegations of engaging in homosexual activity in a public rest room, the League adopted a statement in his defense.[16] League members also organized public education sessions at Albert Ellis's Institute for Rational Emotive Therapy. But none of these activities attracted much public notice or galvanized a genuine political movement.

Despite its initial ineffectiveness, the New York League for Sexual Freedom foreshadowed the rise of the hippie counterculture and the radicalism of the late sixties. It brought together a coalition of intellectuals, artists, other bohemians, and sexual minorities opposed to the regulation and zoning of sex. Still, keeping the coalition together was not easy. Wicker wrote to Poland in frustration, "Give up on the homosexuals. . . . Gay kids, by and large, are a bunch of mentally stunted, genitally fixated squares whose sexual interest extends no farther than their next trick's big cock."[17] The League eventually dissolved, and Jefferson Poland moved back to San Francisco.

When Poland arrived in San Francisco in the spring of 1965, students at UC Berkeley were embroiled in a controversy over the politics of profanity. The "filthy speech movement" (so called because it grew out of the "Free Speech movement," which had involved a series of campus protests a few months earlier against university rules about political activism on university property) was forcing nearly everyone in California to reexamine their views about morality and censorship.

In March 1965, a twenty-eight-year-old Berkeley beatnik named John Thomson was arrested by campus police for holding up a protest sign bearing the word *fuck*. The next day four students protested Thomson's arrest. They set up a table with a placard reading "Fuck Fund" and read aloud the final passage from D. H. Lawrence's *Lady Chatterley's Lover*, including lines like "My soul softly flaps in the little pentecost flame with you, like the peace of fucking. We fucked a flame into being. Even the flowers are fucked into being between the sun and the earth. But it's a delicate thing, and takes patience and the long pause." Lawrence's novel, highly regarded among students of English literature, had been granted constitutional protection by a federal court in 1959. Nonetheless, the four students were also arrested.[18]

The campus was divided over the arrests. A senior prelaw student filed a suit against the four students for obscenity.* The student newspaper called for the protesters' expulsion. Tensions escalated when a college fraternity distributed "I Like Pussy" buttons as part of an organized contest. One male student was so offended by the buttons, he filed a complaint against the fraternity. When the university investigated the incident, the fraternity brothers argued that "Pussy" referred to Pussy Galore, a character in the James Bond film *Goldfinger*, and that the buttons had been approved by the dean's office before they were distributed. The fraternity quickly distanced itself from the filthy speech movement, however, "a movement we deplore."[19] In general, there was little support for the use of profanity; even the leaders of the original Free Speech movement wanted nothing to do with the issue. They resented the arrested students for trivializing the issue of free speech. As one of the Free Speech leaders said privately to a university administra-

---

* Because the prelaw student pressed charges, the students were not merely arrested but also tried. They were found guilty on charges of disturbing the peace. The trial was beset by irony. The deputy district attorney prosecuting the four students used the offending word twenty-nine times in his opening statement. Visitors in the courtroom included a group of schoolgirls on an educational field trip; when the district attorney began his opening statement, the schoolteacher quickly ushered her students out of the room (*San Francisco Chronicle*, 9 June 1965). Only John Thomson, the beatnik poet who initiated the controversy, was found guilty of obscenity. (See "UC's Dirty Word Echoes Through Courtroom," *San Francisco Chronicle*, 21 April 1965.)

tor, "Let me begin by stating that I am and forever shall be against the flagrant misuse of speech through the flaunting of obscene language."[20] As journalist Milton Viorst comments, Mario Savio and other leaders of the Free Speech movement "tried to limit [their] involvement in the controversy to a discreet plea for 'due process' for the accused."[21]

Nonetheless, the controversy expanded rapidly. The California Assembly called for the expulsion of the four students who had been arrested. Clark Kerr, president of the university, appeared to be losing his control of the campus and, in a dramatic move, offered his resignation, which was subsequently declined by the faculty. After winning a vote of confidence from the faculty, Kerr suspended, but did not expel, the students who had been arrested. The *Spider*, a campus magazine of political satire, carried an article about the controversy titled "To Kill a Fuckingword," a play on the title of Harper Lee's 1960 novel about racial prejudice, *To Kill a Mockingbird*.[22] Kerr banned the issue. Once again the campus fell into an uproar. Enraged protesters, among them avant-garde filmmaker Kenneth Anger, distributed fliers in support of the student press. As one professor wrote to another,

> This poor ambiguous little word almost toppled the government of the university; it called a thousand professors from class, laboratory, library and study; it seriously troubled the main elective officials of the state; it exhausted the lino-typists of the metropolitan newspapers who set the letters to the editor. The students who used the word did not intend to have this effect: they wanted to show that the adult world was composed of hypocrites. To their amazement and chagrin, they were successful![23]

Despite the desires of the Free Speech activists, the controversy over "filthy speech" could not be ignored.

Jefferson Poland was not directly involved in the filthy speech movement, but he was certainly inspired by the publicity it generated. In August 1965, as the filthy speech controversy finally dissipated, Poland organized the nude wade-in, thereby taking the entire issue of candor one step further. Like generations of nudists before him, Poland believed that there was nothing obscene about the naked body. Laws against nakedness, Poland felt, produced unhealthy attitudes and a cultural obsession with sex. According to the Bible, nudists pointed out, God ordered Isaiah to go naked for three years, while King David danced naked in the town square.

Newspaper and magazine reports of his August wade-in gave Poland a national spotlight.[24] He renamed his group, calling it the Sexual Freedom League (as opposed to the New York League for Sexual Freedom), and invited interested members across the country to form regional chapters.

By now college campuses were bulging with baby boomers. Student populations were larger than they had ever been. These young people knew about the pill; they had read *Playboy* and Helen Gurley Brown in high school. As one sex educator wrote approvingly, "A very real freedom now exists for adolescent couples and for youth in mixed groups to speak openly and frankly about sexual matters."[25] Like Poland many of them had no patience with their parents' hypocrisy: their willingness, for instance, to accept nudity in a titillating magazine like *Playboy* but not on the beaches of San Francisco. Within a year after the wade-in, sexual freedom groups had formed at Stanford, UC Berkeley, UCLA, and the University of Texas. Stanford's Sexual Freedom Forum issued a Statement of Principles, which read: "We view sexual rights as a proper extension of individual civil liberties. We prefer open honest acceptance of varying personal sexual practices to the massive hypocrisy of many parts of our society.... The private sexual activities of consenting adults are sacrosanct."[26] A photo in the *San Francisco Chronicle* showed a handsome young man and two attractive "coeds" handing out leaflets on the college campus. The members of the Stanford Sexual Freedom Forum managed to collect 450 student signatures supporting the distribution of contraception to unmarried women. Students then voted in favor of the measure, 1,866 to 853.[27] The director of Stanford's health service derided the Forum's efforts as "a tragically crude and simplistic approach to an enormously complex and sensitive issue."[28] But as students began selling buttons with the slogan "Make Love, Not War," the link between sexual freedom and student activism was cemented. The slogan expressed the commonly held view that sexual liberation would lead to a decrease in social tensions. "Our capacity for violence," wrote Jefferson Poland and Sam Sloan in *The Sex Marchers*, "is a spill-over, a natural consequence of our repressed sexuality, our caged libidos."[29] As a pithy response to the escalating war in Vietnam, the slogan quickly captured the media's attention.

At the University of Texas in Austin, the Student League for Responsible Sexual Freedom counted fifteen members in 1966, who opposed limiting the sale of contraceptives on campus to married women and sought the decriminalization of homosexuality and the repeal of laws against sodomy. Texas state senator Grady Hazelwood threatened that he would "never vote another appropriation for the University" if the group were not abolished.[30] The day after Hazelwood's threat, the university banned the group from campus. At Merritt Junior College in Oakland, where Jefferson Poland was now enrolled, the Merritt Sexual Freedom Forum, following the lead of their peers at Stanford, succeeded in putting the distribution of birth control on the school ballot in the spring of 1966.

Across the country, Sexual Freedom League chapters took on a variety of issues. At the University of Florida, the school chapter of the Sexual Freedom League vocally opposed miscegenation laws. Members of the Berkeley Campus Sexual Freedom Forum were inspired by this effort and in November 1966 declared in their Resolution on Race and Gender as Sexual Restrictions "each of us must make special efforts to overcome these barriers and find lovers of different races."[31] As the Sexual Freedom League grew, so did the idea that a sexually liberated society would be less exploitative, less tempted by mass-market pornography, suggestive advertising, and other forms of commercialized titillation. When a representative of *Playboy* came to Iowa's Grinnell College to speak in 1965, students, male and female, protested what they perceived as *Playboy*'s pseudo-liberated philosophy by coming to the talk naked.

Like many countercultural groups in the midsixties, the Sexual Freedom League never garnered broad popular appeal. Most college students were too busy experimenting with drugs and sex, listening to the new music, campaigning for civil rights, and marching against the war in Vietnam to devote time and energy to protesting social attitudes about the body. Few saw any real need to demand changes in the law. Though it was still technically illegal to sell or display birth control in some states, students had easy access to condoms, diaphragms, and the pill, so most felt like the sexual revolution was a fait accompli. Many sexually oriented materials could still not be printed or published, but students had little reason to care. Even though a large number of baby boomers had grown up in households where sex was never mentioned or certain sexual activities were explicitly denounced, by the midsixties college students could generally set their own moral standards. They had the money to do as they pleased.

Moreover, premarital sex was a fact on college campuses, and administrators knew they could never punish one student for having sex without punishing hundreds, if not thousands. As a Yale University dean told a reporter in 1966, "We are not interested in the private lives of students as long as they remain private." Ruth Darling, an assistant dean at Cornell, agreed: "We don't ask what they do and don't want to know."[32] In 1965, the Group for the Advancement of Psychiatry, representing 260 psychiatrists, published a report on parietal rules and campus sexual behavior. The report, *Sex and the College Student,* advised administrators to ignore private sexual behavior. "The student's privacy requires respect; sexual activity privately practiced with appropriate attention to the sensitivities of other people should not be the direct concern of the administration."[33] Though controversial, the report had a strong influence on academics and administrators.

Following this advice from the psychiatric experts, college administrators in the midsixties essentially adopted a "don't ask, don't tell" policy on premarital sex. But such a policy could work only if students agreed to draw a sharp line between their private and public lives, keeping their sexual activity secret. The members of the Sexual Freedom League had already shown their unwillingness to pretend that sex was purely a private matter. So long as there were laws regulating speech, dress, and consensual sexual behavior, sex would never be purely private. As far as Sexual Freedom League members were concerned, they were not making sex public, they were merely acknowledging its already public dimension.

Relatively speaking, the Sexual Freedom League was a minuscule movement that was never able to mobilize a significant number of supporters. Few Americans even knew that it existed, and the organization failed to achieve notable political or legal change. But the stories of failed experiments can tell us something about our social structures and cultural values. The Sexual Freedom League failed in part because its founders refused to focus exclusively on the needs of any one particular interest group. Had the League represented solely the interests of gays or women or prostitutes or pornographers or straight males, it would surely have had a larger impact on society than it did. But by attempting to fight sexual repression on every front, the leaders of the SFL never managed to attract a core constituency of supporters. Straights, gays, feminists, free-speech activists, pornographers, sex workers, and the like failed to see the utility of joining a coalition-based movement. Even people who are comfortable with their own sexual desires tend to be squeamish about the desires of others that they do not share.

The Sexual Freedom League also failed because its founders believed they could use political activism to change deep-seated cultural attitudes. Poland did not appreciate the extent of American ambivalence about sexuality. It would take far more than protests or demonstrations to force Americans to recognize the hypocrisy of celebrating American liberty and individualism while prohibiting freedom of sexual self-expression. Moreover, the leaders of the SFL had no vision of the society they were working toward. Without a clear blueprint for the future, they had no hope of ever enlisting major support from college students and other young adults, who already enjoyed unprecedented freedom to have premarital sex. Finally, compared to the serious issues involved in the civil rights movement and the nascent antiwar movement, the mission of the SLF could only seem trivial.

By the beginning of 1966, Jefferson Poland had faded from the national scene. He remained a colorful figure in the Bay Area countercul- ture (going so far as to change his name legally to Jefferson Fuck and then Jefferson Clitlick), but the increasingly dramatic events of the six- ties overshadowed Poland's modest efforts to effect social change. Across the country, thousands of students joined protests against the Vietnam War and thousands more let their hair grow long and began calling themselves "freaks," and later, "hippies." Just as Poland had tucked a flower behind his ear when he stripped in San Francisco's Aquatic Park, hippies worshiped flowers as symbols of peace. They also staged playful stunts to disrupt the daily routines of the somnambulant middle class. As the ranks of the hippies grew, Jefferson Poland and his fellow Sexual Freedom Leaguers faded into the larger tapestry of late 60's America.

CHAPTER 5

OBSCENITY ON TRIAL

WHEN THE PURITANS flocked to the New World in the seventeenth century, they were fleeing the decadence and sexual profligacy of the British middle classes. As far as the Puritans were concerned, most Englishmen were morally corrupt: they might go to church on Sundays, but they remained sinners every other day of the week. In the colony of Massachusetts, the Puritans hoped to establish a base from which they could launch a crusade to save English society, ultimately bringing about a new age of rectitude and virtue. America would serve as a place for the forces of God to organize and plan a strategy to reconquer Europe's soul.

In recent years historians have shown that the Puritans' attitudes about sex were more complicated than classic novels like *The Scarlet Letter* would suggest. Historians have also shown that Puritan leaders were not particularly successful in controlling the sexual behavior of the laymen.[1] Nevertheless, the Puritans left an undeniably powerful legacy of sexual repression. After Massachusetts passed the New World's first anti-obscenity law in 1711, so many books, plays, and newspapers were censored that the slogan "Banned in Boston" acquired a familiar ring and was adopted by promotion men as a tongue-in-cheek advertising ploy. Of course, wealthy white men could always get their hands on erotic material, but Massachusetts officials went to great lengths to "protect" women, children, poor whites, and blacks from erotic influences and their allegedly harmful effects. Puritan elites feared that erotic material would stir up anarchistic impulses among the masses. Censorship, they believed, was crucial to social order.

More than 250 years after Massachusetts first outlawed "obscenity," citizens of the Bay State were still known for their prudery. When William Burroughs's sexually explicit quasi-pornographic novel *Naked Lunch* was published in 1962, hardly anyone was surprised that Massachusetts police immediately arrested booksellers who sold it. And when Grove Press, the book's publisher, appealed an obscenity conviction in 1966, few thought the state's highest court would overturn the decision. *Naked Lunch* was the kind of novel censors loved to hate. It was filled with descriptions of vomiting, urination, defecation, cannibalism, intercourse, oral sex, anal sex, anilingus, strap-on dildos, auto-asphyxiation, rape, drug use, and violence. Simultaneously hailed as social criticism and denounced as self-indulgence ("pure verbal masturbation," according to one reviewer), *Naked Lunch* divided the literary left. Some critics liked it (or claimed to), but many hated it with a passion. In a piece in London's *Times Literary Supplement* titled "Ugh . . . ," John Willett said the book made him feel alternatively nauseated and bored. "If the publishers had deliberately set out to discredit the cause of literary freedom and innovation they could hardly have done it more effectively," he wrote. Another reviewer declared,

> In Burroughs' work, sex is usually violation. It is sterile, inhuman, malevolent. It is a perversion of the life instinct, an organic process turned mechanical. Sadism, masochism, and pederasty prevail; tenderness, love, and knowledge are absent. Sex is simply the obscene correlative of alienation. Despite the elaborate depiction of homosexuality in Burroughs' work, there is no attempt to understand or justify the homosexual.

Naked Lunch was so disturbingly graphic that even the editors at *Playboy*, who prided themselves on their literary liberalism, panned the novel.[2]

The fact that *Naked Lunch* was deplored by so many even on the left of the political spectrum made it all the more astonishing when the Massachusetts state supreme court granted the novel full constitutional protection on July 7, 1966. The judges were hardly eager to defend Burroughs's work. "*Naked Lunch* may appeal to the interests of deviants and those who are curious about deviants. To us, it is grossly offensive," they wrote. But they felt themselves bound by a growing number of U.S. Supreme Court rulings that justified censorship only in the rarest of cases. Thus, the Massachusetts court ruled the book simply could not be declared obscene. The *Naked Lunch* decision marked a critical turning point in the history of American censorship. From that day on, writers and publishers — even in Massachusetts — would have the upper hand in the battle between freedom of speech and public morals. The story of how American censorship law finally collapsed in 1966 involves colorful characters, complex legal theories, strained aesthetic arguments, and a polity torn between a belief in individual liberty and a deeply felt need for social control.[3]

🍃

Since the days of Chaucer and Shakespeare, the English-speaking world has enjoyed bawdy literature, some of it meant to amuse, some of it meant to arouse. Benjamin Franklin wrote lewd verse, as did a member of the House of Commons who supported the American cause during the War of Independence. In 1748, John Cleland, an employee of the British East India Company, penned a lascivious novel, *Fanny Hill: or, Memoirs of a Woman of Pleasure,* which attracted enormous attention for its graphic descriptions of sexual acts between men and women, men and men, and women and women. *Fanny Hill* was wildly popular in both England and America, but in 1821 it was banned in Massachusetts, and the book was forced underground.

So long as citizens are embarrassed by their sexual appetites, democracy is the friend of censors. Throughout the nineteenth century, American states followed the example set by Massachusetts, passing anti-obscenity laws and banning works like *Fanny Hill.* In the 1840s, the federal government began taking steps to block the importation of erotic materials from abroad. In 1873, Congress granted the morals crusader Anthony Comstock broad powers to confiscate erotic materials and arrest pornographers.

In the 1910s and '20s, American culture lost much of its provincial character as new ideas about psychology, society, and sexuality arrived from Europe and were embraced in bohemian and intellectual circles.[4] After reading Freud, social critics concluded that Victorian notions of propriety led to both personal unhappiness and social backwardness. Theodore Schroeder, for instance, was a prominent lawyer, who, after studying Freud, concluded that censors suffered from a strong sense of shame about their own sexuality. Born in Wisconsin in 1864, Schroeder was one of the most prolific legal scholars of the early twentieth century, and he was the first to point out that censorship was a direct violation of the First Amendment. At the time, this was a novel claim: The First Amendment had been all but forgotten by the nation's jurists since the days of the Founding Fathers. In 1911, Schroeder cofounded a Free Speech League to fight the censorship of erotic materials. Most of the books that were being censored at the time were educational texts written to inform women about birth control, so Schroeder became a key figure in the birth control movement. Although Schroeder's Free Speech League collapsed, it was reincarnated in 1920 as the American Civil Liberties Union.[5]

As Freud's influence on Western culture grew, sexual themes became increasingly prominent in avant-garde literature, and censors found themselves fighting more and more books by authors like D. H. Lawrence, Ernest Hemingway, and Henry Miller. In the early 1930s, U.S. customs officers, determined to put a stop to the flood of erotic literature, seized copies of James Joyce's *Ulysses* en route from Paris, where it was first published in 1922. As anyone who has ever read (or tried to read) *Ulysses* knows, it is extremely difficult to decipher, and a person could conceivably get through the entire novel without becoming aware of the sexual references. Still, customs officers feared that the book would have a harmful impact on women and children, so they tried to ban it. In 1933, however, U.S. District Court Judge John M. Woolsey granted First Amendment protection to *Ulysses,* because he did "not detect anywhere [in the novel] the leer of the sensualist." *Ulysses* was "an amazing tour de force" that failed to produce "sexually impure and lustful thoughts" in the "person with average sex instincts." *Ulysses* was not meant to arouse and therefore it was not obscene.[6]

The *Ulysses* case created an important precedent: Only those books that succeeded in arousing readers sexually could be banned. The theory was popular with avant-garde writers who chose to write about sex but nevertheless considered themselves superior to pornographers. They appreciated the fact that the theory drew a distinction between "high art" and "mass culture." D. H. Lawrence, whose novel *Lady Chatterley's Lover* (1928) was censored in the United States until 1959 (and in England until 1960), insisted that he himself would ban "genuine pornography," which he said was "the attempt to insult sex, to do dirt on it." According to Lawrence, French postcards, "dirty" limericks, and anything else that led to "the vice of self-abuse" (masturbation) constituted pornography and therefore did not meet high aesthetic standards or deserve legal protection.[7]

Despite the fact that it suited many writers, the theory developed in the *Ulysses* decision was extremely problematic. Who was to say whether or not a book was arousing? Why was it okay to ban a book simply because it led to masturbation? Nevertheless, the theory served the interests of judges and postal inspectors who believed in banning books but didn't want to seem overly sanctimonious. Accordingly, it was applied in numerous cases throughout the 1930s and '40s.

In the late 1950s, two psychologists, Phyllis and Eberhard Kronhausen, established their professional reputations by refining and reformulating the arousal theory of pornography. The Kronhausens claimed that they could distinguish between two different categories of literature: one noble and uplifting, the other ignoble and degrading. The first category they called "erotic realism." The second they called pornography. Erotic realism deserved legal protection; pornography deserved to be banned, they declared. The only real difference between the two was that pornography aroused while erotic realism did not.

The Kronhausens were modern-minded, secular thinkers, and therefore, in their major study, *Pornography and the Law* (1959), they went to great lengths to show that most of the banned books commonly considered erotic classics were not the kinds of books that should be banned. *Fanny Hill*, for example, was properly to be labeled erotic realism because it was aesthetically superior to the crude pornography consumed by the untutored masses. "In pornography the main purpose is to stimulate erotic response in the reader," the Kronhausens wrote. "In erotic realism, truthful depiction of the basic realities of life, as an individual experiences it, is of the essence"; whereas pornography was psychologically damaging and destructive, erotic realism was benign, even beneficial, for the reader.

Phyllis and Eberhard Kronhausen offered a neat and clean approach to dealing with obscenity. Their academic credentials established their authority as experts. Both held advanced degrees from Columbia University and had studied under the well-known psychoanalyst Theodor Reik. Scandinavian by birth, the Kronhausens considered themselves modern and sophisticated; they possessed a vast personal collection of erotic art from around the world. After the release of *Pornography and the Law*, the Kronhausens were invited to serve as expert witnesses in numerous obscenity cases.

Though the Kronhausens were highly respected in their day, the distinction between "erotic realism" and "genuine pornography" was tenuous at best, meaningless at worst. The same novel might arouse a housewife in North Dakota but put a philosopher in New York to sleep. The Kronhausens assumed that all readers would respond to a given book in the same manner. (It should come as no surprise that some 1960s readers might find *Fanny Hill* unarousing — the novel was written for eighteenth-century audiences.) Meanwhile, the Kronhausens left many questions unanswered. Who was to decide whether "the main purpose" of a book was to "stimulate erotic response" or offer "a truthful depiction of the basic realities of life"? Was every obscenity decision to turn on the judge or jury's evaluation of the author's original intent?

Because the Kronhausens were liberal intellectuals, they could not appear to be endorsing censorship. They therefore added a second element to their argument: The suppression of erotic realism was not only illogical, it was dangerous, because it led people to create and consume more pornography; without exposure to noble depictions of sex, adolescents were sure to turn to the most depraved.

> The denial of basic corporeality can only lead to distortions of the body image, which have been shown to be responsible for the mental states of depersonalization and irreality which mark the more severe emotional disturbances. On the other hand, familiarity with one's body and a relaxed attitude to its natural functions are prerequisites of mental hygiene.[8]

By banning works like *Fanny Hill*, they believed, judges encouraged young men to peruse the worst kind of periodicals.

The Kronhausens carried their logic to its ultimate conclusion. In a healthy society, erotic realism would be freely distributed and freely consumed, while pornography would be anathema. The educated middle and upper classes would have their copies of Ovid and Joyce, but the working classes would no longer yearn for their French postcards. If exposed to the "right" kind of erotic art, they wrote, individuals would be freed of the temptation to "shuffl[e] through a stack of pornographic photographs or magazines in some back-alley tobacco shop or sex shop."[9] One conservative writer mocked this proposed utopia as "an Eden of erotic innocence in which prohibitions will be unnecessary because social relations will be as they should be."[10]

Ever optimistic, the Kronhausens assured their readers that erotic realism in literature could serve "a most useful function in sex education" because it reflected "a basically healthy and therapeutic attitude toward life."[11] But the Kronhausens' theories contained a basic moral dualism between mind and body — the same kind of dualism found in Judeo-Christian morality. Descriptions of the body were acceptable in the Kronhausens' scheme, so long as they did not actually incite bodily responses. While the Kronhausens were highly regarded by liberal thinkers, their simplistic analysis of sexual literature was influenced by their own middle-class biases. Their ideas merely reinforced the right of judges to act as literary critics and censors on behalf of the middle class.

Despite the problems with their logic, the Kronhausens quickly became the nation's leading authorities on pornography. Their book was cited, and praised, by virtually every writer on the subject. Throughout the early sixties, liberal intellectuals agreed that censorship was bad and pornography even worse, but happily, the abolition of censorship would lead to the abolition of pornography. Echoing the Kronhausens, social critic Paul Goodman wrote: "Culturally the greatest curse of censorship is that it produces too many and too trivial art works, all of them inhibitedly pornographic."[12]

The Kronhausens' dualistic scheme had no place for bawdy social satire, which could be extremely crude yet have obvious social importance. It just so happened, however, that in the late fifties, at the same time jurists were turning to the Kronhausens for guidance, a new generation of social critics, angered and disillusioned by McCarthyism, racism, anti-Semitism, corruption, and holier-than-thou sexual attitudes, was coming into its own. This new generation of comics and humorists, led by nightclub performer Lenny Bruce, particularly enjoyed shocking the middle-class public with "vulgar" language and sexual jokes.[13]

These critics aimed their barbs at the moral hypocrisy of the American middle classes. How could people be offended by words describing bodily functions but tolerate the immorality of segregation and poverty? As theater critic Kenneth Tynan explained, Lenny Bruce wanted his listeners to be shocked by the right things: "not by four-letter words, which violate only convention, but by want and deprivation, which violate human dignity."[14] How, Bruce wanted to know, could Americans condemn sex but applaud violence? According to Bruce, his own children were better off watching a pornographic stag film than a biblical epic like *King of Kings*, because the latter ended with the gruesome murder of the messiah. In Lenny Bruce's eyes, American morality made no sense. It was illegal to show sex in movies because children might imitate what they saw on the screen, but it was perfectly fine to show murder.[15]

The authorities did not find Bruce's use of four-letter words amusing or insightful. Nearly everywhere he performed, police arrested him and charged him with obscenity. (Bruce responded by incorporating jokes about police hypocrisy into his routine. Police, Bruce pointed out, were well known for using vulgar language themselves.) In Chicago he was sentenced to a year in jail and a $1,000 fine. (The conviction was eventually overturned by the Illinois Supreme Court.)[16] Needless to say, such controversy only made Bruce more popular as a martyr to middle-class morality, but it also sent a warning to would-be social critics who did not want to spend most of their time in court. For judges, however, Bruce and his ilk created a major headache: Vulgar social criticism could not be classified as either erotic realism or genuine pornography. Bruce was not trying to create art or to stimulate. He was trying to entertain and to provoke. The arousal theory simply didn't apply. It was increasingly apparent to judges that the Kronhausens' simplistic dichotomy between erotic realism and genuine pornography would not suffice in dealing with obscenity.

The eagerness with which Americans tried to ban books in the 1950s guaranteed plenty of legal cases. More often than not, publishers exercised extensive self-censorship over their own products, but when self-censorship failed, police were ready to do the job. Between 1950 and 1952, fifty cities passed censorship laws to block the sale of "pornographic" comic books. In Ottumwa, Iowa, police removed three thousand magazines from newsstands at the request of local ministers.[17] Some towns staged public bonfires, burning piles of offensive comics.[18] In 1953 alone, some ninety attempts were made to ban or burn books around the nation. In Detroit, police officers went after stores selling paperback copies of Hemingway, James T. Farrell, and John Dos Passos. In St. Cloud, Minnesota, a censorship board banned all books listed as objectionable by the National Office for Decent Literature. In Cleveland, police stopped the sale of Freud's *General Introduction to Psychoanalysis,* John Steinbeck's *Wayward Bus,* and Mickey Spillane's *I, the Jury.* The Illinois secretary of state ordered the state librarian to remove six thousand books in state libraries considered "salacious, vulgar or obscene."[19]

Two powerful Catholic censorship groups, the National Office for Decent Literature and Citizens for Decent Literature, published lists of offensive books and magazines to tell Catholics what not to read. Such groups had a chilling effect on local schools and libraries, which were always wary of controversy. Although the American Civil Liberties Union was founded to protect freedom of speech, ACLU officials in the fifties shied away from attacking the censorship of sexual materials. The group's executive director assured critics that the ACLU had never intervened in federal efforts to stop the mailing of "smutty post cards," "strip-tease pictures," or "nudes." As far as he was concerned, the federal government had every right to suppress such literature. As another ACLU official stated, "Nor do we believe that the obscenity laws are interfering with freedom of the press in any way."[20]

In 1957, the Supreme Court agreed to hear an appeal on two obscenity cases, with the recognition that a decision in those two cases would have major implications for the future of American society. One case involved a California couple, David and Violet Alberts, who were in the business of producing bondage magazines and books with a sadomasochistic emphasis. Police had raided the Albertses' warehouse and seized enough books and magazines to fill two trucks and a car. The other case involved Samuel Roth, an Australian-born New Yorker who made his living selling excerpts of banned erotic classics and pirated editions of other erotic novels. Most of what Roth published the Kronhausens would have labeled "erotic realism," but the prosecuting attorney, Roger Fisher (now known for his work on negotiation), sent the justices a box full of the most explicit materials he could find, warning that if Roth were allowed to go free, the floodgates would be opened and the nation would be deluged with hard-core pornography. Fisher's tactic worked, and a majority of the high court ruled that both David Alberts and Samuel Roth should be sent to prison.[21]

Two of three dissenting justices, Hugo Black and William O. Douglas, believed that the First Amendment prohibited all censorship of sexual materials. As far as they were concerned, the fact that sexual materials were controversial made the First Amendment's provisions all the more applicable. But this view was not shared by any of their colleagues. In writing his opinion for the Roth and Alberts cases (the court treated the two cases jointly), Justice William Brennan turned to the Kronhausens' arousal theory, declaring that "sex and obscenity are not synonymous. Obscene material is material which deals with sex in a manner appealing to the prurient interest." But, recognizing the importance of social critics like Lenny Bruce, Brennan added that in order for an item to be declared obscene, it would have to be devoid of "the slightest redeeming social importance."

To some, Brennan's definition seemed like a pragmatic compromise between liberal and conservative views. But even the prosecuting attorney realized that Brennan's formulation left giant legal loopholes. What precisely was "prurient interest"? If a married couple used a magazine to enliven their sexual relationship, did that constitute "prurient interest"? If a teenage boy masturbated to a copy of *Playboy* magazine, was that "prurient interest" or merely healthy adolescent desire? The notion of "redeeming social importance" was problematic too. The concept was actually a tautology: Brennan was saying that a work was legally redeemed if it were redeeming. These ambiguities promised many more years of legal confusion.

Because the *Roth* opinion sent two men to jail, the decision did little to clarify what might actually be considered free speech. But the following year, 1958, the court denied the right of the Postmaster General to prohibit the mailing of the nudist magazine *Sunshine and Health* and thus suggested that nudity, per se, was not pornographic. The publishers of *Sunshine and Health* were granted First Amendment protection because there was nothing explicitly sexual about the magazine.[22] In an even more interesting case, the court ruled that three homoerotic muscle magazines (*MANual, Trim,* and *Grecian Guild Pictorial*, all published by Lynn Womack, who held a doctorate in philosophy from Johns Hopkins) were not obscene because they were not "patently offensive."* Still only Justices

---

* Womack's attorney argued:

If you're going to consider that these photographs were headed for homosexuals, to appeal to homosexuals, then an analysis of these photographs would show that the photographs are no more than the photographs — comparable pin-up photographs — of Marilyn Monroe and the other beauties. . . . [I]f we so-called normal people, according to our law, are entitled to have our pin-ups, then why shouldn't second-class citizens, the homosexual group — if you use that term — why shouldn't they be allowed to have their pin-up? . . . [T]heir pin-up is no worse than our pin-up.

(Quoted in Friedman, *Obscenity,* 93. For the text of the decision, see *Manual Enterprises Inc. v. Day,* 82 S. Ct. 1432 [1962].)

Douglas and Black opposed all anti-obscenity laws on principle. The other seven judges continued to insist that some forms of speech were, by definition, "pornographic," and hence beyond the scope of the First Amendment. They tended to agree with William B. Lockhart, dean of the University of Minnesota law school, who declared in a 1960 law review article that "hard-core pornography" was "so foul and revolting that few people can contemplate the absence of laws against it." A society without such laws, Lockhart wrote, "would be unthinkable."[23]

One man who strongly disagreed with Lockhart's assumption was Barney Rosset. The scion of a rich Chicago family, Rosset had attended a progressive high school where he learned to value innovative literary expression over middle-class morality. As an independently wealthy young man, Rosset bought a dying publishing company, Grove Press, in 1952 and five years later founded a literary magazine to celebrate the avant-garde. After a much publicized obscenity trial in San Francisco in 1957 involving Lawrence Ferlinghetti's City Lights Press edition of Allen Ginsberg's poem "Howl," Rosset devoted his magazine, the *Evergreen Review*, to the work of the Beats.[24]

When it became clear that there was a large audience for provocative literature, Rosset decided to publish the original, unexpurgated version of Lawrence's *Lady Chatterley's Lover*, which had been banned in the United States.[25] Only two days after the book was released on May 4, 1959, the Post Office seized 164 copies. Postmaster General Arthur Summerfield deplored the "smutty passages" and "filthy, offensive and degrading" words. But censorship worked entirely in Rosset's favor. In the first four months of sales, the Grove Press edition of *Lady Chatterley's Lover* sold 161,000 copies, reaching number two on the *New York Times* best-seller list. The more authorities insisted on propriety, the more their efforts backfired.

Rosset's endeavors were appreciated by those who felt ostracized from society as a result of their sexual practices. In January 1960, the gay organization the Mattachine Society presented Rosset with an "award of merit" for his decision to publish *Lady Chatterley's Lover*. The secretary general of the Mattachine Society commended Rosset for his

> courage in bringing to the public print in the United States important works of Erotic Realism in Literature, daring to publish these works in the face of assured acts of censorship and banishment by the prejudiced, the bigoted and the ill-informed, and the announced determination of this publisher to fight this arbitrary denial by authorities of the right of Americans to choose freely what they want to read.[26]

Rosset enjoyed his status as a cultural gadfly. He believed censorship laws were indicative of the nation's moral miasma, and as a savvy businessman, he realized that censorship sold books. Two years after publishing *Lady Chatterley's Lover*, in 1961 Rosset decided to print an American edition of Henry Miller's long-banned autobiographical novel, *Tropic of Cancer*.

In *Tropic of Cancer*, published in Paris in 1934 but banned in the United States, Miller had blurred the traditional line between "literature" and "erotica" to chronicle as realistically as possible his adventures as a young man in Paris. Using every four-letter word known in English, Miller shared with readers all of his own sexual thoughts and fantasies:

> O Tania, where now is that warm cunt of yours, those fat, heavy garters, those soft, bulging thighs? There is a bone in my prick six inches long. I will ream out every wrinkle in your cunt, Tania, big with seed. I will send you home to your Sylvester with an ache in your belly and your womb turned inside out. Your Sylvester! Yes, he knows how to build a fire, but I know how to inflame a cunt. I shoot hot bolts into you, Tania, I make your ovaries incandescent. Your Sylvester is a little jealous now? He feels something, does he? He feels the remnants of my big prick. I have set the shores a little wider, I have ironed out the wrinkles. After me you can take on stallions, bulls, rams, drakes, St. Bernards. You can stuff toads, bats, lizards up your rectum. You can shit arpeggios if you like, or string a zither across your navel. I am fucking you, Tania, so that you will stay fucked. And if you are afraid of being fucked publicly, I will fuck you privately. I will tear a few hairs from your cunt and paste them on Boris' chin. I will bite your clitoris and spit out two-franc pieces . . . [27]

Most contemporary critics agreed that the book contained an important moral message. As John Ciardi wrote in the *Saturday Review of Literature*, "What [*Tropic of Cancer*] praises is the dignity of the individual who will plunge into any experience, and welcome poverty, hunger, and ostracism, so long as he may escape hypocrisy." Others liked Miller primarily because his books were banned. Still others simply found *Tropic of Cancer* erotic. Even Andrea Dworkin, who would later make her name as an anti-pornography activist, found the novel sexually stimulating when she read it as a teenager.[28]

As soon as Grove Press released the unabridged edition of *Tropic of Cancer* in June 1961, police began arresting booksellers who carried it. In New Jersey alone, twenty-eight people were arrested. After a wave of arrests nationwide, many booksellers simply stopped carrying the Grove edition. Although it continued to be sold underground, *Tropic of Cancer* disappeared from bookstores in Los Angeles, Chicago, Philadelphia, and Cleveland. The book was completely unavailable anywhere in Massachusetts or Rhode Island.[29] Grove Press fought obscenity arrests and seizures in trial after trial in state after state. In Brooklyn, the author himself was arrested, an extremely unusual situation. (American authorities had traditionally targeted publishers but spared writers.) Miller and Rosset were charged with conspiracy "to depict and represent acts and scenes wherein the sexual organs of both male persons and female persons were to be portrayed and described in manners connoting sex degeneracy and sex perversion and were to be of such pornographic character as would tend to incite lecherous thoughts and desires."[30] In total, Rosset was forced to defend himself in sixty separate court cases, costing over $250,000 in legal fees.[31]

Theoretically, at least, the Supreme Court had established basic guidelines to determine which material was protected by the First Amendment. According to the Roth decision, a book was obscene if it dealt with sex "in a manner appealing to the prurient interest" and was lacking "the slightest redeeming social importance." But it was becoming clear that the real result of the Roth case was legal chaos. In Chicago a judge ruled that *Tropic of Cancer* was not obscene; only two days later, a jury in Los Angeles decided it was. Did this mean that someone flying on a plane from Chicago to L.A. could not debark with the book in her bag? It was declared obscene in Connecticut, Florida, Illinois, Pennsylvania, and New York but ruled legal in Wisconsin.[32] Once again, the matter had to be settled by the Supreme Court. On June 22, 1964, the court summarily overturned the Florida obscenity conviction. Leery of establishing any major new precedents, the court issued no explanation of its ruling, and in a concurring opinion to another case decided the very same day, Justice Potter Stewart said that it was perhaps impossible to "intelligibly" define the term "hard-core pornography." All Stewart could say was, "I know it when I see it." Stewart's comment summed up the court's intellectual desperation.[33]

Rosset took advantage of his *Tropic of Cancer* victory and published several more books with sexual themes, including John Rechy's autobiographical novel about male prostitution, *City of Night* (1963); Frank Harris's confessional memoir *My Life and Loves* (1963), a five-volume account originally printed in 1923–27 describing the prominent magazine editor's innumerable sexual encounters with young girls of different races; and *The Story of O* (1965), a translation of the 1954 novel by the French female journalist Dominique Aubry (written under the pseudonym Pauline Reage) offering a woman's first-person account of her voluntary descent into a life of sexual slavery and torture.* All three

---

* Harris was not a commoner; he traveled in the same circles as Cecil Rhodes, John Ruskin, and even Queen Victoria. In a review in the *New Republic* (28 December 1963), titled "The Importance of Being Frank," Stanley Kauffmann wrote: "The very amorality of this chronicle gives it a place in moral history." In the *New York Times Book Review* (20 March 1966), Albert Goldman lavished praise on *The Story of O*. He credited the book with a

books shocked the literary establishment but found influential champions and sold vast numbers of copies.

As judges increasingly favored free speech over censorship, social conservatives called more loudly for collective control over the press. In November 1964, the New York Academy of Medicine encouraged President Johnson to use the FBI to combat pornography, which the Academy blamed for the rise of venereal disease and illegitimacy.[34] The same month, the *New York Times* stopped taking ads for Terry Southern's novel *Candy.* "[We] read it and found it to be smutty," said one *Times* spokesman dismissively, despite the fact that the book was on the *Times*'s own best-seller list.[35] In August 1965, New York Mayor Robert Wagner created a special commission to combat pornography.[36]

Despite their best efforts, conservatives could not stem the tide of erotica. In 1963, G. P. Putnam's Sons printed a new edition of *Fanny Hill.* It was immediately seized in Massachusetts. During the initial trial, a variety of English professors from Harvard, Williams, Boston University, Brandeis, and the Massachusetts Institute of Technology testified for the defense. The judge nevertheless declared the book obscene and the decision was affirmed by four of the seven judges of the Massachusetts supreme court.

Putnam's appealed the decision and the U.S. Supreme Court agreed to hear the appeal. *Fanny Hill* had been banned since the 1820s, but by the 1960s it seemed more quaint than dangerous. In 1966, the high court reversed the Massachusetts decision and in the process established three tests of obscenity: To qualify as obscene, a work, taken as a whole, had to "appeal to a prurient interest in sex," had to be "patently offensive because it affronts contemporary community standards," and had to be "utterly without redeeming social value." By so narrowing the definition of obscenity, the court effectively broadened the scope of the First Amendment.[37]

Though a majority of the high court believed it was unwise to continue the ban on *Fanny Hill,* the justices were still hesitant to grant full First Amendment protection to sexual speech. The very same day as the *Fanny Hill* decision, the court upheld the conviction and five-year sentence of Ralph Ginzburg, the publisher of an upscale, expensive, hardcover magazine named *Eros.*

"profoundly religious temperament." In another *Times* article (2 March 1966), Eliot Fremont-Smith declared that the publication of *The Story of O* was "an event of considerable importance" because it marked "the end of any coherent application of the concept of pornography to books." A year after *The Story of O,* Grove published the first English edition of *The Erotic Minorities* by Swedish social theorist Lars Ullerstam. Defending incest, exhibitionism, pedophilia, homosexuality, and other sexual practices, the book had caused a scandal when it was first published in Sweden two years earlier.

The first issue of *Eros*, which appeared on Valentine's Day 1962, was a hardbound, oversize journal containing color reproductions of such masterpieces as Bordone's *Venus and Cupid*, Correggio's *Education of Cupid*, and Niklaus Manuel's *Judgment of Paris*. It also included a translation of Guy de Maupassant's "Madame Tellier's Brothel," never before published in the United States, and erotic poems by John Wilmont, the seventeenth-century Earl of Rochester. There was also an essay on the history of illegitimacy and a reprint of turn-of-the-century advertisements for male grooming and health products, and finally, articles on "The Agonies and Ecstasies of a Stripper" and the risks of heart attacks from intercourse.

Eros was clearly upscale pornography, if it was pornography at all. But Ginzburg knew that to interest prospective subscribers, he would have to make his sales pitch sexually enticing. He sent out 9 million flyers announcing that *Eros* would be "a major breakthrough for the liberation of the human spirit," and hinted that *Eros* would be more suggestive and titillating than any other magazine in print. While *Eros* was not nearly as risqué as Ginzburg had promised, his promotional ploy netted a whopping 150,000 subscriptions.

Despite the expensive, artistic quality of *Eros*, it quickly became the target of political and religious attacks. The National Office for Decent Literature encouraged its members to write the Post Office complaining about the magazine. On December 19, the Philadelphia trial judge sentenced Ginzburg to five years in jail and a fine of $28,000.

The Supreme Court justices based their decision to uphold the conviction on the reasoning that the advertisements and mailing strategies Ginzburg used constituted a form of "pandering" — that is, the exploitation of the weakness of others. (The Court did not like the fact that Ginzburg had tried to mail his circulars from Blue Ball, Pennsylvania).[38] It was a strange decision, not based on any statutory law or precedent, that had legal experts scrambling for their law books to make sense of it. Many considered it a major blow to American liberty. Now even publishers of expensive, high-end erotica could be sent to jail if judges disliked the way such materials were advertised. Some suspected that the real reason the court upheld Ginzburg's conviction was that one issue of *Eros* showed a white man and a black woman in a sensual embrace.[39]

The obscenity issue was a source of endless consternation for American judges, and there was no relief in sight. By 1966, obscenity cases were clogging the courts. Judges throughout the country found themselves desperately trying to interpret vague phrases like "patently offensive" and "contemporary community standards." If one reckoned by the literature available on the local newsstand, the standards of the nation seemed to be growing more lax each year. With the economy at an all-time high, Americans felt good about themselves and their society, so pornographic materials no longer seemed as threatening to social stability as they once had. The ever increasing suggestiveness of mass-media ads for commercial products only added to the confusion. In a commercial for Noxema shaving cream, for instance, a sultry-voiced woman urged men to "Take it off, take it all off." One for Clairol hair color asked coyly, "Does she or doesn't she?" Such ads would have been "patently offensive" to previous generations of Americans, but now they were merely humorous.

As the sixties progressed, judges had other reasons to question the merits of censorship. Televised images of violence against blacks by law-enforcement officials in the South and reports of violence against civilians by U.S. soldiers in Vietnam called into question the real meaning of obscenity. What danger could erotic material pose compared to racism and war? Judges, especially those appointed by Kennedy and Johnson, increasingly viewed state obscenity laws with suspicion. They remembered that the Founding Fathers had distrusted unbridled democracy and tyranny of the majority just as much as, if not significantly more than, they had feared excessive liberty. Legislation drafted by an unenlightened mob, susceptible to religious zeal, was just what the Bill of Rights was designed to prevent. The dangers of a government ruled by the will of the masses was made brutally clear by fascism in Europe and McCarthyism at home. Taking all these matters into consideration, America's leading judges decided it was no longer feasible for them to play the role of literary critics and censors.

In October 1965, the fate of *Naked Lunch* hung on a decision of a Massachusetts lower court. The trial began as most obscenity trials did: The prosecuting attorney handed the judge a copy of the offending book and rested his case. It was believed that the book was so vile, it would incriminate itself.*

The defense presented numerous expert witnesses, one of whom compared the book to Dante's *Inferno* and another who compared it to

---

* According to Burroughs biographer Ted Morgan, prosecutor William Cowan confided in the defense attorney that the state was bringing the case only "because various old ladies are getting on the attorney general's back and insist that he do something about this book or that book." Morgan says Cowan said he wished he could spend his time working on "something more important" but that he felt obliged "to bow to public opinion." (Morgan, *Literary Outlaw* [New York: Holt, 1988], 344.)

St. Augustine's *Confessions* (a notion that outraged the Irish Catholic judge). But the lead defense attorney on the case, Edward de Grazia, says he chose not to put Burroughs himself on the stand because it would have given the prosecutors an opportunity to ask the author whether he had ever taken drugs, sodomized young boys, or killed his wife.[40] Burroughs, one of the more extreme members of the Beat movement, had done all three. He had spent most of his life as a writer in Mexico and Morocco, drunk on whiskey and strung out on heroin. The grandson of the inventor of the adding machine, William Burroughs had grown up with all the advantages and restrictions of wealth. He was eerily thin, and always the outsider (the father of a childhood friend described him as "a walking corpse"), alternatively suicidal and homicidal.[41] Burroughs attended Harvard and fantasized about becoming a psychoanalyst, but settled instead on a career as a writer of surrealist, scatological fiction. Most of his sexual relationships were with men (or boys), but he married twice and accidentally killed his second wife while the two (drunk and stoned) played William Tell with a water glass and an automatic pistol. He wrote *Naked Lunch* in Tangiers, Morocco, high on marijuana (he had just broken his morphine addiction). The first published excerpt of the book was blasted by a Chicago newspaper columnist as "one of the foulest collections of printed filth I've seen publicly circulated."[42] The novel was so dark and dank that even Lawrence Ferlinghetti, the owner of the City Lights bookstore and publishing company in San Francisco, wanted nothing to do with it. When Barney Rosset decided to publish it, *Naked Lunch* was already a cause célèbre.

The prosecuting lawyers did not need to interrogate Burroughs on the stand. The judge had read his book. In his remarks, the judge admitted he saw certain similarities to the *Inferno* but concluded that the book was nonetheless an example of "hard-core pornography" and was therefore obscene. Once again the censors had prevailed.

As they were used to doing, the lawyers for Grove Press immediately filed an appeal. They then sat back and waited. They had little to hope for. This was, after all, Massachusetts.

On July 7, 1966, Massachusetts's highest court, the same court that had upheld the obscenity conviction of *Fanny Hill* only one year earlier, ruled that William Burroughs's excretory novel was protected by the First Amendment. It was a stunning but in some ways inevitable decision. The U.S. Supreme Court had made it clear that a book could be banned only if it was devoid of the slightest social value. Could *any* book really be said to be devoid of the slightest social value? Certainly a book as controversial as *Naked Lunch* was socially significant by virtue of its controversial nature. That glaring discrepancy in the prosecutor's case was simply too much for the Massachusetts high court to ignore:

> As to whether the book has any redeeming social value, the record contains many reviews and articles in literary and other publications discussing seriously this controversial book portraying the hallucinations of a drug addict. Thus it appears that a substantial and intelligent group in the community believes the book to be of some literary significance. Although we are not bound by the opinions of others concerning the book, we cannot ignore the serious acceptance of it by so many persons in the literary community. Hence, we cannot say that *Naked Lunch* has no "redeeming social importance in the hands of those who publish or distribute it on the basis of that value."

In a splenetic dissent, one judge declared: "The book is a revolting miasma of unrelieved perversion and disease. *Naked Lunch,* in truth, is literary sewage." But a majority of the court had found in favor of free speech. The final ruling was delivered in a curt four-paragraph opinion.[43]

When the decision was announced, Americans knew that the battle over obscenity had ended — at least as far as the censorship of books by local police departments was concerned. Writers, publishers, and readers had won. Needless to say, new issues — such as the sale of child pornography, the censorship of hard-core motion pictures, and the use of zoning laws to close down pornographic bookshops — loomed on the horizon. But in 1966, believers in literary liberalism were ecstatic. Secular humanists, eager readers, and those who saw profitable opportunities in publishing erotic books were all equally thankful for the *Naked Lunch* decision. Erotic books had long been available underground, but now they could be sold openly in any store in America. The most repressive legacy of puritanism had been vanquished. The special privileges of wealthy, white men to read what they pleased were extended to all. No court had declared the concept of "obscenity" itself unconstitutional, but "obscenity" was now practically a meaningless term. Many shared the Kronhausens' utopian conviction that the end of censorship would also bring about the end of prurience itself. In 1966, Harry Levin observed, "One of the wholesome results of our hard-won candor is that it could end by driving the pornographers out of business."[44] These idealists underestimated both the extent of American anxiety about sexual "permissiveness" and the determination of pornographers to tap new sources of longing. But their optimism had a powerful effect on the culture. Almost all Americans could now agree on one thing: The nation was undergoing a dramatic change in values and there was no immediate end in sight.

CHAPTER 6

STRANGERS IN A STRANGE LAND: *THE HARRAD EXPERIMENT* AND GROUP MARRIAGE

THE 1966 *Naked Lunch* case inaugurated a new era of literary freedom. The months following witnessed both groundbreaking artistic experimentation and gross commercial opportunism. Bookstores were suddenly filled with everything from provocative poetry to hard-core pornography (often thinly disguised as social commentary). But between these two poles emerged a new middlebrow genre: books meant to titillate readers and, at the same time, teach them about the importance of sexual freedom. Though American laws were slowly catching up with reality — and vice crimes were increasingly seen as "victimless" — critics observed that Americans continued to think of sex outside of marriage as "sinful." The discovery of penicillin, the decline of the double standard, the spread of topless dancing and soft-core pornography, the general acceptance of and easy access to birth control, the rise of the Sexual Freedom League, the growth of the hippie counterculture, and the collapse of censorship had not, many observers lamented, fundamentally changed American attitudes toward carnal pleasure. Many Americans still thought of sex as something dirty. Moreover, they regarded it as somehow unique among physical activities. Why, a growing number of popular critics wondered, did individuals continue to insist on treating sex differently from other pleasurable activities like skiing, swimming, or eating?

Robert Rimmer's novel *The Harrad Experiment* was the archetype of the new sexually utopian narrative, a book that was the very antithesis of William Burroughs's gothic nightmare. One of the most popular novels of the midsixties to early seventies, *The Harrad Experiment*, set in a sexually liberated college, was both an erotic tale and a serious-minded plea for more scientific sexual attitudes. The book's thesis was clear: If individuals took a rational view of sex, there would be no more jealousy, no more monogamy, no more shame — all products of Judeo-Christianity's superstitious anti-sex agenda. From a historical perspective, monogamy was rooted in the concept of women as property. In an enlightened, humanistic world, such a barbaric concept would be abolished. Ultimately, sexually liberated men and women would form happy, enduring group marriages, in which jealousy and secrecy and adultery and divorce would be unknown. In fact, by eliminating shame and self-loathing, sexual rationalism would solve virtually all of society's remaining problems.

In *The Harrad Experiment*, students at a New England college are the guinea pigs in a sociology project to make human sexual attitudes more reasonable. First, every student is paired with a roommate of the other sex. Next, the students learn how to liberate themselves from embarrassment, envy, shame, and other forms of sexual repression. The trick is to abandon the false illusions associated with romantic love and embrace a more scientific approach to sex. Lest the spiritual dimension of sex be forgotten, students read the *Kama Sutra* and other Eastern texts. Only by separating sex and love, however (and rising above possessive inclinations), is it possible to achieve truly meaningful, emotional connection. The students represent "a new sexually oriented aristocracy of individual men and women who [are] free of sexual inhibitions, repressions and hate, and [are] thoroughly educated into the meaning and the art of love as distinguished from the purely sexual relationship."[1] Once the students are freed from false pretenses and sexual repression, they go on to form emotionally, psychologically, and spiritually fulfilling group marriages.

At Harrad College, students discover that heterosexual relationships can be based on full equality between men and women. They realize that most of the differences between men and women (especially the differences in sexual attitudes) are shaped by society, not by biology. In the state of nature, according to the novel, men are gentle and considerate while women crave sexual variety. All extracurricular activities at Harrad are coed and most are done in the nude, such as yoga, swimming, and team sports.

Students also learn that "casual" sex and promiscuity are the products of a repressed culture. For the aim at Harrad is to create "a world where men and women can and must relate their sexual drives and needs for one another into a unified whole so that the act of sex is a perfectly wonderful consummation of a much larger ecstasy and pride and joy and respect for the amazing fact that each of us, man and woman, are human beings."[2]

The novel reflected the upbeat mood and economic vitality of the midsixties. (It also exemplified the segregation still in effect in popular culture: All the characters are white.) All have sunny, buoyant dispositions (at least after overcoming their initial fears and inhibitions); none has any financial worries to speak of. Homosexuality is unknown at Harrad College. As in most utopian novels, conflicts between characters are easily resolved through reason and communication.

Robert Rimmer's vision was of a prelapsarian sexual world, an Eden without guilt or exploitation, where all sex is healthy, friendly, hetero sex. The novel contrasts the Harrad attitude with a cynical and seamy bohemia, where homosexuality, promiscuity, strip clubs, sadomasochism, and rape abound. A visit to an avant-garde strip club featuring male and female dancers disgusts the Harrad students, and the description of the club is meant to disgust the reader. By contrast, on campus rationality and optimism triumph. "Every day we are being shown, and I think convinced, that the individual human being is ultimately good," says one student. Another student explains, "The idea behind Harrad is infinitely larger than pre-marital sexual adjustment. Ultimately, it is a belief that man can take one more step up the evolutionary ladder . . . lift himself by his own bootstraps, and develop a society and culture that is emotionally and mentally in control of itself."[3] In one chapter, Rimmer takes aim at the Sexual Freedom League, which he felt lacked a sense of the nobility of sex. For Robert Rimmer there were "correct" and "incorrect" forms of sexual liberation.

Advertised, to Rimmer's immense displeasure, as "The Sex Manifesto of the Free Love Generation," *The Harrad Experiment* was a blockbuster success when it was published by Bantam Books in 1967.* Within eighteen months it sold over 2.5 million copies and was then translated into Japanese, German, and Italian. Rimmer was personally invited by Betty Friedan to join the National Organizational for Women, which he did, and was asked by the American Association of University Women to write for their journal an article on the cultural construction of gender roles. The president of the American Psychological Association, Abraham Maslow, was a personal fan of Rimmer's novel. The executive director of the American Humanist Association lauded *The Harrad Experiment* as "an important humanist novel."[4]

Thousands of letters flooded in from readers excited and curious about the book. One twenty-one-year-old reader from Pennsylvania wrote to Rimmer, "Since reading the novel, my innermost beliefs and

* It was originally published in 1966 by a small California house, Sherbourne Press.

disbeliefs have been literally changed and organized overnight." Another wrote,

> Initially I picked up your book in the Cal-State L.A. book store figuring it was simply another 'sex book' to help vary an otherwise monotonous routine. . . . But! After thumbing through it I momentarily became aware of its uniqueness — it was much more than just an ordinary book about sex. . . . Your book has actually condensed, clarified and lucidly verbalized many of the beliefs I had but which I could not adequately express.

A female college student wrote, "I never really understood sex. . . . Then I read 'Harrad.' Now I am compelled to write and thank you a hundred times over for your understanding and knowledge." A married woman expressed her desire to "give this option of leading a full premarital life" to her two daughters. The mother of two young children wrote, "I love you! You've made my life so much easier. You've written my book. You've taken my feelings, desires and ideas and presented them in a manner and form more explicit and beautiful than I can relate." Even though *The Harrad Experiment* contains no black characters, a women in an interracial marriage wrote to Rimmer to express her delight with his ideas.[5]

How did Robert Rimmer, a graduate of the Harvard Business School who followed his father into the printing business, become a spokesman for group marriage at the age of forty-nine? A cheerful fatherly figure who lived in the middle-class suburb of Quincy, Massachusetts, with his stay-at-home wife Erma and their two sons, Rimmer disdained the antics of the Beats, especially the ravings of William Burroughs. As many readers were surprised — and often disappointed — to find out, Rimmer's life seemed to be the model of conventionality.

But Robert Rimmer had a secret he longed to tell the world. Twenty years earlier, the Rimmers' marriage had nearly collapsed. Robert had had an affair. When Erma found out, she was devastated, and confided in her friend David, who told her not to be jealous, but rather to accept her husband's sexual drive as a matter of biology. Soon, in fact, Erma and David began having an affair of their own. Though at first Erma and David kept their relationship secret, they eventually conspired to introduce Robert to David's wife Nancy. Their plot worked. Erma was now sleeping with David, Robert was now sleeping with Nancy.[6] At first, they had occasional moments of jealousy, but eventually "sexual and intellectual sharing became a natural way of life" for the foursome. They maintained two separate homes, but otherwise they were inseparable. "We weren't swingers. We never made love as a foursome," Rimmer later recalled. But the two couples traveled together and "were often casually naked together."[7]

For years, Robert, Erma, David, and Nancy kept their personal lives secret. As far as they knew, they were the only ones in America living in such an arrangement. But over time, Rimmer felt compelled to tell the world about the benefits of group marriage. He hated the thought of contributing to social hypocrisy. He desperately wanted to come out of the polygamous closet. Though he chose to use fiction as his medium, Rimmer wrote *The Harrad Experiment* as part of his personal mission to reform American morality.

Rimmer's timing was perfect. Monogamy, more and more Americans were convinced, was outdated and irrational. It was an unrealistic ideal, as scientists like Kinsey had demonstrated, because human beings were not, and never would be, monogamous in practice. How could human beings be expected to obey a moral imperative that contradicted nature? What was the point of trying to be sexually loyal for a lifetime only to fail and feel agonizing guilt? At a time when Americans were being bombarded with the Madison Avenue message "More is better," it made sense that more sexual partners had to be better than one. If one could have as many cars and stereos as one liked, why not as many sexual partners too? For James and Lynn Smith, editors of *Beyond Monogamy,* a collection of scholarly essays, monogamy constituted "a form of emotional and sexual malnutrition," "a condition of sexual deprivation," and "in its own macabre way, a legitimized and normalized form of emotional erotic bondage."[8]

Copies of *The Harrad Experiment* circulated widely on college campuses. "Since I bought my copy, I have seen many people on campus reading it. I no longer know where my own copy is, as it has been passed from hand to hand," one reader complained. Students in graduate psychology courses began using *The Harrad Experiment* as a supplemental text. At Utica College in New York, it was taught as part of a junior seminar. At Lake Erie College, a philosophy professor assigned it in his freshman preceptorial. The professor explained to his students,

> We shall not be concerned in our discussion with determining literary merit, legal standing or author's 'real motives.' Rather, we shall consider the book as presenting a serious proposal to alter our normal social attitudes toward sexual relations before and within marriage to conform more closely (as the author sees it) to more ultimate human values.

An assistant professor at California State College at Long Beach offered a graduate seminar, "Social Interaction," featuring several of Rimmer's books. The professor explained in a letter to the author,

> I read *Harrad* during the summer of 1967 and found, for the first time in my 30 years, that someone had written about all the ideas which I have painfully struggled with for the past ten years ... Your writings, coupled with the

concepts of [educational reformer] A. S. Neill, have had a profound influence on my orientation toward both teaching and my personal life.[9]

But did anyone actually heed Robert Rimmer's injunction to abandon monogamy in favor of group marriage? Linda Price (a pseudonym) did. "*The Harrad Experiment* made a tremendous impression on me," she recalls. "He handled sex like it was the most natural thing in the world. And he made me appreciate that monogamy and marriage were the products of society's sexual repression."[10]

Born in 1945 in Springfield, Oregon, the daughter of farmers, Linda Price grew up believing it was wrong to have sex before marriage. When she was three, her mother caught her masturbating in the bathtub, swatted her across the thigh, and said, "Don't ever let me catch you doing that again." But in the spring of 1967, when Linda was twenty-two and a student at the University of Oregon, she met a seventeen-year-old boy, Scott Bloom (a pseudonym). "The mutual attraction was obvious." Many men had expressed interest in Linda, but she immediately fell for Scott.

At first, Linda, who was still a virgin, was reluctant to have intercourse. One night on a camping trip, the two shared a sleeping bag. "We started out necking and petting and things got really interesting . . . He only had condoms, so I said I wasn't ready because I didn't trust condoms, so we mutually masturbated. Afterwards I was worried because I thought I was becoming a prick tease. I made a decision to get an exam and get pills. I also got a lecture on promiscuity by the doctor, and that really pissed me off."

Linda and Scott began having sex on a regular basis, but after six months, Scott's mother decided she no longer wanted her son seeing Linda. She forbade him to visit Linda or to bring her home. As a result, the two began dating others. "He started seeing a couple of women he was interested in and I started dating people I met at college dances." And while some of the men she dated were less than ideal, Linda found she enjoyed the freedom of an open relationship. Scott, who had read *The Harrad Experiment,* was not jealous. "I felt secure, and when I was secure my jealousy went away. There was a way that Linda made it clear that her sleeping with somebody else was no more a threat to our relationship than her taking up ice skating would be."[11]

One evening Linda and Scott went to a dance club with a woman who lived across the hall in the college dormitory. As Linda recalls: "She was pretty anti-monogamy in her basic attitudes. She had a boyfriend and I think they were not monogamous. Anyway, we went to a dance bar downtown, and we all got really, really drunk. Coming back, one thing just kind of led to another. Scott says I propositioned her. Enough booze and all your inhibitions get stripped away." The three went back to

Linda's room and had sex in her bed. The next day Linda felt "kinda strange." But Linda and Scott continued having threesomes and four-somes. They decided never to get married and to continue having an open relationship indefinitely. (They are still together after thirty-one years).

Americans began experimenting with alternatives to monogamy long before the 1960s. When Brigham Young led his followers to Utah in the 1840s, he made polygamy a key tenet of the Mormon faith. Also in the 1840s, John Humphrey Noyes was teaching his followers to prac-tice "complex marriage" at the Oneida community in upstate New York. Oneida's "complex marriage" was more egalitarian than Brigham Young's polygamy because men and women were allowed to switch partners on a regular basis. Sojourner Truth, the African-American who achieved national fame for demanding "Ain't I a woman?" at a woman's rights convention in the midnineteenth century, was a member of a group marriage known as the Kingdom of Matthias.[12] The idea of reducing the influence of romantic attachments and loosening private emotional bonds to increase collective loyalty goes back at least as far as the Spartans of ancient Greece and was a central theme of Plato's *Republic*.

In the 1960s, *The Harrad Experiment* provided a theoretical frame-work for group marriage for young people who knew nothing of Oneida or had never read Plato. As young adults in the late sixties turned away from the path of suburban domesticity (at least momen-tarily) toward countercultural experiments, they seized upon utopian novels like *The Harrad Experiment* as guidebooks to a better life. In Palo Alto, California, young baby boomers founded a free university, "in order to implement a vision of cultural revolution [with] . . . a new ver-sion of humanity, based on libertarian, democratic and communitarian values," and announced intentions to buy property in order to start a real-life Harrad Experiment. In Berkeley, a group of young men and women founded "Harrad West." "Our basic idea at Harrad West is that perhaps six, eight, or even a dozen or more adults can form 'marriage' relationships with each other as a means of attaining far more than monogamous marriages can offer," the members explained in the mag-azine *The Modern Utopian*. Many wrote to Rimmer to describe their own group marriages inspired by his novel — Rimmer received so many that he published the letters in two separate volumes. The group-marriage movement spread, and by 1970 the *New York Times* could esti-mate that there were at least two thousand group marriages in the United States.[13]

Like Robert Rimmer, science fiction novelist Robert Heinlein acquired a cult following for his books' sharp critique of society's sexual mores. Heinlein, who attended the U.S. Naval Academy before he began writing fiction, was in many ways politically conservative. But his views on sex were far from mainstream: he thought social restrictions on sex outside marriage were based on religious superstition rather than logic. As Heinlein told his editor, who wanted to cut portions of the novel *Stranger in a Strange Land* (1961), in which a Martian comes to Earth and is shocked by Earthlings' obsession with marital infidelity:

> Concerning sex, my book says: sex is a hell of a lot of fun, not shameful in any aspect and not a bit sacred. Monogamy is merely a social pattern useful to certain structures of society — but it is strictly a pragmatic matter, unconnected with sin . . . a myriad other patterns are possible and some of them can be, under appropriate circumstances, both more efficient and more happy making. In fact, monogamy's sole virtue is that it provides a formula defining who has to support the offspring.[14]

In *The Moon Is a Harsh Mistress* (1966), a group of settlers who live on the moon come to realize that when men greatly outnumber women, monogamy does not make sense. Romance, passion, and love — those staples of great literature and popular culture alike — had no place in Heinlein's fantasy worlds.

Charlie Dellin (a pseudonym) discovered Heinlein in high school and slowly absorbed the novelist's critical perspective on American mores. "Scientific fiction," Dellin says, "is the most subversive literature imaginable." When he started college at the University of Minnesota, Dellin was still sexually inexperienced. The day he arrived, he met Lucy, who happened to share his passion for science fiction. More than that, she was adamantly opposed to monogamy. "She'd read everything by Heinlein and Rimmer and thought monogamy was totally irrational," he recalled. Charlie and Lucy took many classes together, became romantically involved, and began having sex.[15]

Dellin was friends with a couple in their thirties, the Kellogs (a pseudonym), who were active, like he was, in the world of science fiction fan clubs. Lucy's best friend Karen took a job working for the Kellogs as a nanny. Karen soon began having a sexual relationship with Jason Kellog, her employer. In the meantime, a male science fiction writer moved into the household and began sleeping with Jason's wife, Mindy. "There was no cheating going on; it was all aboveboard," Dellin says. One night, he and Lucy were supposed to celebrate the anniversary of the first night they had had intercourse. "Instead, Lucy ended up getting stoned and I ended up in bed with Mindy Kellog." Lucy, true to her principles, said she did not mind.

Things did not stop there. "It was pretty much taken for granted by Lucy that Karen and I would be lovers. This was very much the hippie era; I had friends who lived in communes. So very soon I was sleeping with Karen, too." It was not long before Lucy became interested in Charlie's best friend Rick, who was getting his Ph.D. in nuclear physics. But at the same time, she began sleeping with Jason Kellog. Within two years, the Kellog household was a very complex, rather chaotic group marriage.

Robert Heinlein had a particularly strong impact on a young man named Oberon Zell, who in the early sixties founded a religion based on *Stranger in a Strange Land.* As a student at Westminster College in Missouri, Zell was the leader of a large community of science fiction aficionados, who were all fond of Heinlein's novel. Zell lived off campus, and he said his home "became a center for all kinds of outrageous activities, including some wild parties." Zell and his friends also spent time at nearby clay quarries, remnants of the town's extinct brick-making industry. "They were these beautiful pools with luscious colors: greens, blues, turquoises, lavenders. We hung out there and would skinny-dip all weekend and sunbathe and sing songs and party. . . . One weekend we were all out partying by the clay pits; it started to rain and we all went back to our house and it just sort of developed into a very sexual situation." As Zell explains, the party turned into "a major orgy." "The pill had been discovered, so it was a wild time." From that moment on, Zell and his friends began having regular orgies with dozens of people.[16]

Toward the end of college, Zell discovered paganism and decided to form a spiritual movement based on ideas in Heinlein's novels and the principle of pansexual freedom. In 1968, Zell and his followers succeeded in legally incorporating as a religion, the Church of All Worlds. "When we first became public in '68, we rented a large Victorian building in Gaslight Square, the Haight-Ashbury of St. Louis. We were doing 'happenings,' holding [group] weddings in the park, putting out our newspaper, all sorts of things. Pretty much everyone in the church had an open relationship."

Though he was now a religious leader, Zell continued to remain active in the world of science fiction. While attending one science fiction convention, Zell met a young woman, a self-described "hippie witch" who was traveling around the country with her pet boa constrictor. Morning Glory, as she called herself, had left her husband and daughter in Eugene, Oregon, to pursue a life of paganism and witchcraft. Zell was immediately taken with this unconventional young woman, but Morning Glory — who also happened to be a fan of Robert Heinlein — was wary of romantic relationships. "I told him I couldn't be monogamous. I thought he was going to walk away. Instead, he looked at me like he was staring at the Holy Grail."[17] Zell and Morning Glory moved in together and began a series of group marriages.

Nudism was a central tenet of the Church of All Worlds. Zell and Morning Glory spent most of their time at home naked. As Zell's son (by his first wife), who was around nine at the time, recalls, "They were almost always naked at home. It was fine with me, but I didn't really feel comfortable inviting friends to the house. Dad would even answer the door naked." Today, Zell and Morning Glory are still leaders of the Church of All Worlds, based in California. The legacy of their experiment with group marriage is mixed. Zell's son is not a member of the church, but he believes strongly in open relationships. Morning Glory's daughter by her first husband wants nothing to do with her mother or the Church of All Worlds.

It is hard to know exactly how important Robert Rimmer, Robert Heinlein, and other middlebrow utopian writers were to the creation of the counterculture and its sexual values. By the end of 1967, a variety of communes were springing up in cities like San Francisco, Chicago, and New York. The young men and women who came of age in the late sixties had grown up in times of unprecedented prosperity: as a result, they could afford to put aside practical concerns about the future in order to savor life's pleasures and live according to their ideals. Many saw collective living as a rational alternative to "bourgeois capitalism," one that offered an escape from, in Oberon Zell's words, "technocratic, bureaucratic, mechanized, suburbanized, alienated relationships" of the modern world.

Most of the young baby boomers who joined intentional communities also wanted to escape the rigid rules of middle-class morality. They intended to have sex when, where, and with whom they pleased. To them, monogamous marriage simply made no sense. By the end of 1967, group marriage was a prominent element of the counterculture. Yet in order for communes to prevent jealousy and conflict, they often ended up adopting sexual rules that were as rigid in their own way as the behavioral norms of the bourgeoisie.

Art Green (a pseudonym) was a typical sixties hippie who ended up living in communes for both political and personal reasons. He was born and raised in New York; his father owned a mail order company specializing in women's clothing. Both of Art's parents were active Zionists, who taught him about the socialist kibbutz experiments in Israel. His parents were liberals, but sex was never mentioned in the house. "My parents didn't even tell dirty jokes," Art says.[18]

In 1965, he moved to Chicago and took a job with the New Left organization Students for a Democratic Society printing leaflets protesting the Vietnam War. After a year, he quit SDS and began traveling across the country. Everywhere he went, he would set up a printing press and aid the antiwar effort. In each new town he would live in whatever commune would take him.

Eventually, Green moved back to New York. "Things were pretty expensive and I heard about a commune with eight college kids living in a two-room apartment. They said they had plenty of room. I couldn't understand how they could possibly have room! So I went to see them and discovered that they were a group marriage. Then I realized there was plenty of space because everybody was sleeping in the same bed. There was no worry about privacy. People weren't concerned about being seen naked or making love. I remember one meeting of the commune where a couple was screwing right there during the meeting because they didn't want to miss anything. I was pretty impressed by all that. I felt more love right there than I had in any religious community."

The commune members took their group marriage very seriously, and because Art was not an official "spouse," the women were not supposed to have sex with him. This was a typical rule in group-marriage communes. But one day, when the others were out, one of the women agreed to sleep with him so long as he did not tell the others. "It was kind of strange, her cheating on the others," he recalls. What began as a utopian alternative to bourgeois morality had degenerated into a rather conventional situation marked by exclusivity, secrecy, and deceit.

Despite the tensions that were clearly under the surface of the group marriage, the commune members believed strongly in the principle of polygamy and felt they were on a mission to reform society. Sometimes they would go to universities and disrupt classes by passing out "exams" to the students with questions about their sexual behavior. The point was to force students to think about the gulf between society's standards and natural human behavior.

Like many in the counterculture, Green's associates believed there was no reason to be ashamed about being naked. "We were all traveling together in this Volkswagen bus. You can imagine we got pretty dirty. I remember one time we stopped at a college Laundromat and took off all our clothes and put them in the wash. There we were, all of us standing naked. Other students came in and thought it was a new movement, so no one bothered to stop us."

After a while, Green moved to Philadelphia and tried to start his own commune but did not succeed. He was, however, invited to visit the Aloe commune in rural North Carolina, another group marriage. "The rule was you had to be there two weeks before you could have sex with anyone. I didn't have two weeks, only ten days. I was lucky because they made a special exception for me, so I got laid the first afternoon I arrived." Members of the commune worked during the day, either in the fields or in the house. "The custom was that toward evening you would ask someone to spend the night with you. One night I waited too late to ask anyone (after a while you didn't get as horny in the course of the day as you did when you first arrived). There were no triads allowed, so I went to bed by myself. When I woke up in the morning one of the guys I was working with was walking around naked, and, without thinking about it, I just sort of lifted the sheet and motioned to him to come over. He climbed in bed with me and we just sort of cuddled. I realized it was just as much fun cuddling with a man as with a woman. I hadn't seen much bisexuality going on, but I knew it was acceptable." Shortly thereafter, Green's time was up and he returned to Philadelphia. He eventually married, but to this day has an open relationship.

Although Art Green and other hippies saw group marriage as part of a left-wing social movement to transform society and abolish private property, some people who had group marriages were on the far right of the political spectrum. Howard Kolding (a pseudonym), a longtime supporter of Chicago's Mayor Daley and an unabashed opponent of feminism, gay liberation, and drug use, believed the antiwar demonstrators of the sixties should have been "machine-gunned." Nonetheless, Kolding (who describes himself as a "radical conservative") began having a group marriage in the 1950s.

An electrician by trade, Kolding served as a radar repairman during World War II and in the midfifties joined an organization called Technocracy, whose aim was to promote the application of engineering principles to world government. Although Kolding was deeply conservative politically, his outlook on sex was strictly secular. He was suspicious of religious dogma and committed to the construction of a social order along scientific principles. Kolding was married but at one Technocracy meeting he met a young woman he found sexually attractive. "The late fifties were not as repressive as people think they were," Kolding says. "If you were attracted to someone, you made your attraction known and they were either interested or not." Kolding and the young woman began dating. Shortly thereafter, at another Technocracy meeting, his wife Mary met George, a scientist. They too began dating.[19]

Kolding and George had much in common and they soon became friends, even though Kolding knew the other man was having sex with his wife. It was not long before Mary suggested the three have group sex. Because George needed a place to stay, the Koldings invited him to move in with them. He readily accepted the invitation and the three began living together in an arrangement that lasted over a year. George was given his own bedroom, but the three regularly had group sex. (Kolding points out, "It was strictly heterosexual.") As Kolding recalls,

"Sure, it turned me on a little watching him have sex with my wife, but not terribly much. I was a little jealous sometimes, but [the feeling was] not too strong." While George was living with the Koldings, Howard continued to date the young woman he had met previously.

Eventually, George moved out and Howard ended his extramarital relationship with the other woman. In 1960, the Koldings moved to Rockford, Illinois, about ninety miles northwest of Chicago, where Howard befriended a young woman who, like George before her, needed an apartment. She moved in with the Koldings. The woman turned out to be interested in bisexuality. As Howard recalls, "I seduced her and then she seduced my wife. Mary got freaked out and never told me about it, but I found out from somebody else."

In 1967, the Koldings moved to Malvern, Pennsylvania, where John met a local librarian named Betty. They began sleeping together. Soon, Betty left her husband and she and her son moved in with the Koldings. When *The Harrad Experiment* came out, the Koldings discovered they were not the only ones who believed in group marriage. "We all read *The Harrad Experiment* and I wrote a long letter to Rimmer about our relationship that he put in one of his books. I explained that the most difficult thing about having a group marriage was agreeing about money." Though the Koldings were far from hippies, once they read *The Harrad Experiment* they considered themselves part of the vanguard of the sexual revolution. They continued to have an open relationship until they eventually divorced in the midseventies. Today, Howard, age sixty-six, is remarried but says he is no longer much interested in sex.

Group marriage never evolved into a mass movement. Even by the end of 1967, group marriage was a radical proposition. Many Americans may have fantasized about living with several lovers, but only a tiny few ever did so.

Still, the popularity of the books of Robert Rimmer and Robert Heinlein pointed to a growing discontent with the domestic ideals of mainstream culture. And even if group marriage was a fringe phenomenon, those who were involved in group marriages worried surprisingly little about social disapproval. They didn't have to, because two phenomena contributed to a climate of social tolerance: By the end of 1967, most Americans were so well off that they had no reason to worry or be anxious about their future economic well-being; meanwhile, the draft put moral issues in perspective. Together, these two phenomena fostered laissez-faire social attitudes. What one, two, or three people did in private was simply not worth getting upset about. Group marriage hardly threatened to destabilize the social or economic order and was not, by any stretch of the imagination, a life-and-death issue like the draft.

That is not to say that Americans were suddenly comfortable with all types of sexual arrangements. There was plenty of hostility aimed at gay men, lesbians, and interracial couples. The group-marriage phenomenon was largely nonthreatening because most group marriages were strictly heterosexual and rarely involved interracial relationships. Most important, group "marriages" were generally private affairs: they did not demand any sort of legal or public recognition of their existence. Though some advocates (most notably Robert Rimmer) did hope to win official sanction for group marriage, those in communes and other group arrangements tended to regard the state with too much disdain to seek official approval of their activities. And as long as people were willing to be discreet about the nature of their sexual conduct, conventional-minded Americans were content to look the other way.

CHAPTER 7

THE RIGHT TO MARRY: LOVING V. VIRGINIA

TALL, SOFT-SPOKEN, and dark-skinned Mildred Jeter met Richard Loving, a Caucasian brick mason, at a dance in their home town in Caroline County, Virginia, in the mid-1950s. They both knew a romance was taboo, but the attraction was strong. They courted a few years and in June 1958, Mildred and Richard decided to marry. Inter-racial marriages were illegal in Virginia, as they were throughout the South, so the determined couple took a short trip to Washington, D.C., and had their wedding ceremony there. Then they returned to Virginia to start a family.

One morning in October, the Lovings were awakened by the local sher-iff. A grand jury had issued an indictment against them for violating the state's miscegenation law. In the bedroom, the sheriff arrested the young couple and hauled them off to jail. The Lovings spent five days in confine-ment. In January of the new year, the Lovings pleaded guilty to the charge and were sentenced to one year in jail. The trial judge suspended the sen-tence, but only on the grounds that the Lovings leave the state and not return for twenty-five years. "Almighty God," said the judge, "created the races white, black, yellow, malay and red, and he placed them on separate continents. And but for the interference with this arrangement there would be no cause for such marriages. The fact that he separated the races shows that he did not intend for the races to mix."

Forced into exile, the Lovings moved to Washington. But they were not to be defeated. They returned to their home town and lived in fear of arrest for nine years. During that time, they contacted Robert Kennedy, the U.S. attorney general, and asked for assistance. With his help they filed suit against Virginia on the grounds that their constitutional rights had been violated. In 1966, however, Virginia's Supreme Court of Appeals upheld their conviction and the state's miscegenation law. That year the U.S. Supreme Court agreed to hear the Lovings' appeal.[1]

Until World War II, thirty states had laws against interracial marriage. In many states, "miscegenation" (a Reconstruction-era term, from the Latin *miscere*, "to mix," and *genus*, "race," used by racists to deplore the "corruption" of blood lines) could be punished by up to ten years in prison. After 1945, in response to reports of the Nazis' racist atrocities, many states eliminated their miscegenation laws, but as late as 1967, sixteen states still had such laws on their books. Although these laws were not explicitly about sex, they were the product of a culture suspicious of, and frightened by, black sexuality.[2]

From the start, slavery and sexuality were deeply connected. Every American colony in the eighteenth century took legal steps to prevent black men from marrying white women. It was generally assumed that black men were by nature promiscuous and that they hungered for white female flesh. This fear led to the creation of castration laws, which required owners to castrate runaway slaves once they were caught, and to the lynching of black men suspected of having sexual relations with white women. At the same time, it was common throughout the colonies for white men to use their black slaves for sexual purposes. American popular culture was shot through with myths about the sexual ardor of black women, a convenient justification for rape by slave owners.[3] Sex, in other words, was a weapon used to keep blacks in submission.

White fears of black sexuality were not limited to the South. During the New York draft riots of 1863, a white mob protesting Union Army conscription hanged blacks, stripped them, and mutilated their genitals.[4] After the Civil War, there was tremendous fear throughout the country that blacks and whites would begin intermarrying and breeding "mongrel" children. Foreshadowing Nazi practices in Germany, white supremacists passed miscegenation laws to maintain the "purity" of the white race.

Myths about the sexual energy of the black male continued to circulate well after World War II. Even white liberals took it for granted that black men were more virile than white men. In 1957, the novelist writer Norman Mailer, a self-described "libertarian socialist," published an influential essay in *Dissent* magazine titled "The White Negro," which glorified the black male rapist and urged young whites to follow the black man's supposed example. Mailer romanticized the black man's "art of the primitive," his "relinquishing the pleasures of the mind for the more obligatory pleasures of the body." The Negro's music contained "infinite variations of joy, lust, languor, growl, cramp, pinch, scream and despair of his orgasm. For jazz is orgasm, it is the music of orgasm, good orgasm and bad[.]" Mailer took a few drops of Wilhelm Reich's psychological theory, a cup or two of the Marquis de Sade's bedroom philosophy, and a heaping dose of American racism, mixed them together, and produced one of the most extraordinary statements in American letters. Explaining that for the psychopath "orgasm is his therapy," Mailer wrote: "It is therefore no accident that psychopathy is most prevalent with the Negro."

> Hated from outside and therefore hating himself, the Negro was forced into the position of exploring all those moral wildernesses of civilized life which the Square automatically condemns as delinquent or evil or immature or morbid or self-destructive or corrupt. . . . But the Negro, not being privileged to gratify his self-esteem with the heady satisfactions of categorical condemnation, chose to move instead in that other direction where all situations are equally valid, and in the worst of perversion, promiscuity, pimpery, drug addiction, rape, razor-slash, bottle-break, what-have-you, the Negro discovered and elaborated a morality of the bottom.[5]

Mailer was applauding, not criticizing, the black man's alleged "perversion, promiscuity, pimpery," etc., but in the process he reiterated one of America's most destructive myths, repackaged it, and sold it to the generation of young white men who considered him a charismatic leader of their own rebellion against corporate America. Blacks were less impressed.

Most Americans did not need Norman Mailer to teach them about black sexuality; their assumptions and beliefs were already firmly rooted. One white liberal apologized in 1958:

> Being a white man myself I am subject to most of the same fears and complexes that affect the greater part of those of my own race. And I know that the white man feels exceedingly inferior to the Negro male sexually. . . . We white men regard you as an immediate and aggressive danger to our right of sexual expression. We will humiliate you, keep you servile, persecute you — anything to keep you away from our women.[6]

These sentiments were confirmed the following year when school officials in Montgomery, Alabama, banned a children's book titled *The Rabbit's Wedding* because it showed a black male rabbit marrying a white female rabbit. A 1963 Louis Harris poll found that 93 percent of white Americans would be upset if their teenage daughter dated a Negro male.[7]

Sexual attitudes were deeply influenced by the racial double standard. For many young boys in the 1950s, the only pictures of naked females to be found were images of African women in *National Geographic* magazine.

Similarly, Hollywood allowed glimpses of the bare breasts of actresses playing "natives" well before similar shots of white women were allowed. (But *Playboy*, which explicitly emphasized the girl-next-door image of its models, did not introduce a black "Playmate" for ten years. In Hugh Hefner's eyes, presumably, black women were not suitable objects of desire.) All the while, whites suspected that black women were voraciously promiscuous. In 1965, liberal senator Daniel Patrick Moynihan issued a report describing the disintegration of the black family and attributed this disintegration to a culture of promiscuity. The Moynihan Report claimed that the illegitimacy rate among blacks was eight times higher than among whites, though the Report did not acknowledge the higher rate of white abortions.[8]

For all the racial stereotypes, some sociologists in the sixties found that blacks were actually more sexually conservative than whites. A sociologist studying inner-city blacks reported in 1968:

> Contrary to the common expectations of the middle-class that all Negroes are sexually permissive, many Negro parents appear to take a rather negative and restrictive attitude toward the sexual behavior of their children. Compared to most middle-class parents, they are much less likely to permit their children to walk around naked in the house, and they are less apt to appear unclothed in front of their children. Likewise, these families seem more concerned than middle-class parents with preventing masturbation.[9]

Like many black Americans, Nell Painter, who grew up in Oakland, California, and was a student at Berkeley in the early sixties, consciously avoided casual sex in order to protect the image of her race. "I was brought up with a race and class identity that was sexed. You weren't sexually loose. I knew about the sexual stereotypes of black women. I disdained black women who got pregnant." Painter shunned "loose" black girls. "My friend Jackie and I were both bohemians. We decided not to go to the [black] cotillion. We said, 'Those cotillion girls just get pregnant.' That was our way of expressing our class position." Painter did get a diaphragm from Planned Parenthood, but she did not use it for several years. Her boyfriend tried to get her to sleep with him, but she said no. "It was clear to me that sex was a big deal." When she did eventually have sex with a man, she felt compelled to marry him as a result.

Painter tried to be both hip and chaste. The daughter of an academic and now an academic herself, Painter would go to readings by the Beats at City Lights Bookstore in San Francisco, and she read avant-garde books like Henry Miller's *Tropic of Cancer*. People would say 'Oh, you've got to read this, you've got to read that.' And I knew that I had to read those things, to keep up my cosmopolitan front. I knew that I wasn't supposed to be shocked."[10]

Whatever their attitudes toward sexual behavior, blacks, especially poor blacks, had less access to information about birth control options and abortion than white women did. Donna Stanton (pseudonym), who grew up in central New Jersey, recalls, "I didn't have hundreds of dollars to pay for no doctor." Stanton had her first unwanted pregnancy in the early sixties. She performed the abortion herself. "I was in my twenties. I did it myself with a cathartic tube. It's like a tube with a hole on one side which allows the air to open it up and the blood to come out." For her second abortion, Stanton used suppositories that were known as "black beauties." Stanton cannot say how they worked, but she remembers that "there was a lot of bleeding." In the 1950s and '60s, black women who ended up in the hospital after trying to induce an abortion, or who simply went to the hospital to give birth, were sometimes involuntarily sterilized by their doctors.[11]

In the civil rights movement, sex was an especially sensitive, and charged, issue. Early civil rights activists discouraged white women from joining the movement because they feared it would unnecessarily incite violence by angering Southern whites. Northern white women were not actually allowed to participate in the movement until the first "freedom summer" in 1964. Then three hundred young white women from Northern colleges took buses to the South to help register black voters. Since reporters at the time were always eager for stories about college "coeds" defying tradition, the Northern press was suddenly interested in the civil rights movement. Headlines announced that unmarried, white, middle-class girls were traveling to the deep South to aid poor blacks. Civil rights activists realized that sex was helping to sell equality so they encouraged more and more young women to join the cause.[12]

The sight of young white women fraternizing with blacks infuriated many white Southerners, and also perhaps piqued their sexual fantasies. On one occasion in 1964 when Kathy Kunstler, the daughter of famed civil rights attorney William Kunstler, was driving in a car with black civil rights workers, the sheriff of Oxford, Mississippi, stopped the vehicle. In front of a large crowd, the sheriff tried to intimidate the white girl. "Which one of them coons is you fuckin'?" he asked her. "Slut, I know you fuckin' them niggers. Why else would you be down here? Which one is it? If you tell me the truth, I'll let you go. Which one is it?" Of course, Kunstler refused to answer. The sheriff eventually released her anyway. As she and her fellow civil rights workers drove off, he yelled, "Take your white whores and get the hell out of Oxford!"[13] Although civil rights workers were able to get many blacks on the voting rolls and end official segregation, it is not clear that they were ever able to dismantle the South's racist, sexual mythology.

Even within the civil rights movement, sexual tensions ran high. As white female civil rights volunteers arrived in the South, they faced what was known as the "sexual test": repeated sexual propositions from black men in the movement. If women refused the propositions, they were "racist"; if they consented, they were labeled promiscuous, and they also invited the wrath of black women. One white civil rights worker observed, "Every black SNCC worker . . . counted it as a notch on his gun to have slept with a white woman — as many as possible."[14] When a group of white women accused SNCC (Student Nonviolent Co-ordinating Committee) of gender discrimination, Stokely Carmichael responded, "The only position for women in SNCC is prone." The comment may have been intended as a joke, but it provoked outrage from women in the movement.[15]

Civil rights leaders never fully acknowledged the problems of sexual anxiety in the movement, nor found ways to ease the tensions. These tensions grew even more pronounced in the second half of the decade, when civil rights yielded to Black Power. In October 1966, Huey P. Newton and Bobby Seale founded the Black Panther Party for Self-Defense in Oakland. From the beginning, the Black Panthers cast racial politics in sexual terms. In his 1967 autobiography *Soul on Ice*, Panther leader Eldridge Cleaver glamorized black male sexual prowess and mocked the sterility and impotence of the white male.[16] In public speeches, Cleaver urged women to use their "pussy power" to radicalize men, by denying sexual favors to any man who refused to join the radicals (a twist on the ancient *Lysistrata* theme of women withholding sex to force an end to war).[17] Prior to becoming a Black Panther, Cleaver confessed in *Soul on Ice*, he was a rapist. His decision to become a rapist was self-conscious and grew out of his anger toward white women. He "started out by practicing on black girls in the ghetto" and then "sought out white prey" because he saw rape as "an insurrectionary act."[18]

Before becoming a Panther, Cleaver yearned to be sexually desirable. He believed joining the Panthers, donning the paramilitary Panther uniform, carrying a gun, and frightening whites would make him virile, a realization he had the first time he attended a meeting of the Panthers:*

---

* Black feminist critic bell hooks [sic] writes: "The discourse of black resistance has almost always equated freedom with manhood, the economic and material domination of black men with castration, emasculation. Accepting these sexual metaphors forged a bond between oppressed black men and their white male oppressors. They shared the patriarchal belief that revolutionary struggle was really about the erect phallus, the ability of men to establish political dominance that could correspond to sexual dominance." (hooks, *Yearning: Race, Gender and Cultural Politics* [Boston: South End, 1990], 58.)

Suddenly the room fell silent . . . There was only the sound of the lock clicking as the front door opened . . . From the tension showing on the faces of the people before me, I thought the cops were invading the meeting, but there was a deep female gleam leaping out of one of the women's eyes that no cop who ever lived could elicit. I recognized that gleam out of the recesses of my soul, even though I had never seen it before: the total admiration of a black woman for a black man. I spun around in my seat and saw the most beautiful sight I had ever seen: four black men wearing black berets, powder blue shirts, black leather jackets, black trousers, shiny black shoes and each with a gun.[19]

The black nationalist movement tried to exploit rather than challenge sexual stereotypes. But their enemies knew how to do the same. When police officers arrested male Black Panthers, they would often subject them to full strip searches, sometimes in view of television news cameras.[20] Naked black male activists were sure to seem like dangerous predators to middle-class whites.

The exploitation of sexual stereotypes by both blacks and whites increased tension between the races. In August 1965, a white man wrote anxiously to a friend, "I understand that one can now regularly hear young Negro males boast that Negro rights include the 'right' to 'have' a white woman at least one time — and the continual reports of 18-year-old Negro youths raping 70-year-old white women makes sense on no other basis."[21] White fears about black sexuality were as powerful as ever before.

In December 1966, eighteen-year-old Margaret Rusk announced to her father that she intended to marry Guy Gibson Smith, a young black man she had met in college at Georgetown University. Though both of Secretary of State Dean Rusk's grandfathers were Confederate soldiers in the Civil War, Rusk prided himself on his racial liberalism and readily gave her his blessing. But this was 1966, and Rusk knew that the marriage could cause a national scandal. According to reports at the time, he informed President Johnson of his daughter's plans and offered his resignation in advance. Johnson, a keen supporter of civil rights, immediately refused Rusk's resignation. News of the wedding was reported on the front page of the *New York Times*. There was little public outcry, but one white woman, a member of the exclusive Orlando Country Club in Florida, told *Time* magazine, "It will serve the old goat right to have nigger grandbabies." A white Glenview, Illinois, businessman probably spoke for many when he said, "If I were Rusk, I'd be inclined to shoot the guy."[22]

Four months after Margaret Rusk and Guy Smith announced their intentions to wed, the justices of the Supreme Court heard oral arguments in *Loving v. Virginia,* the first case to test the constitutionality of miscegenation laws. Meanwhile, the film *Guess Who's Coming to Dinner* offered a sympathetic portrayal of an interracial romance between Sydney Poitier and Katherine Houghton and featured Spencer Tracy and Katherine Hepburn as Houghton's parents, who slowly learn to accept their daughter's affections for a black man.

The arguments were heated. The attorney representing the state of Virginia claimed that if the court voided Virginia's miscegenation law, it would have to void all laws regulating marriage, including those against polygamy, incest, and the marriage of minors. In response, Chief Justice Earl Warren demanded to know whether states also had a right to prohibit interfaith marriage. The Virginia attorney, realizing he was in trouble, claimed sociological data showed that marriages between blacks and whites were far more harmful than marriages between persons of different faiths. Warren was not impressed with such specious social science.

Two months after oral arguments were heard, in June 1967, the Supreme Court issued its ruling, unanimously striking down Virginia's law. "Under our Constitution, the freedom to marry, or not marry, a person of another race resides with the individual and cannot be infringed by the State," the high court declared. The Lovings had won. An ugly chapter in the nation's history was over. As Richard Loving told reporters the day the decision was announced, "It's hard to believe. Now I can put my arm around my wife in Virginia."[23]

Loving v. Virginia did not end white anxieties about black sexuality. But the case — sparked by one couple's determination to win their rights — eliminated one of the last pillars of Jim Crow and sharply curtailed the power of state governments to restrict sexual unions. The exact same arguments that had been used to justify miscegenation laws would still be used to prohibit same-sex marriages for decades to come; nonetheless, the Lovings' personal victory offered hope to all those who sought to change sexual attitudes in America.

CHAPTER 8

IN LOCO PARENTIS

THE RIOTS AT Columbia University in the spring of 1968 are often remembered as the pivotal protests of the sixties, a series of events that transformed the relationship between American students and university administrators. Columbia students, protesting the construction of a university gymnasium without regard for the well-being of neighborhood residents, occupied the school president's office until police were called in. For students across the country, it was a heady time. But two months before the Columbia riots, a smaller drama was played out across the street, at Barnard College, Columbia's sister school — a drama that would turn out to have far greater implications for the future of student life in America.

Barnard College was known in the sixties as a bastion of tradition and propriety amid the urban jungle of Manhattan. It boasted a student body composed of highly intelligent and well-bred young women from the nation's wealthiest families. Parents sent their daughters to Barnard on the understanding that the school would do its best to shield them from the dangers and temptations of modern city life.

While Barnard administrators were working hard in 1968 to maintain an educational environment suitable for genteel young women, many of the nation's 7.5 million college students, increasingly scornful of school administrators and the status quo, were brazenly flouting convention and flaunting their disregard for campus rules. They were smoking grass, dropping acid, and experimenting with Quaaludes. These disaffected youth, disillusioned with the American dream, listened to folk singers with a social-protest message, such as Joan Baez and Bob Dylan, and to "acid rock" groups like Jefferson Airplane, who celebrated the pleasures of mind-expanding drugs.[1]

Financially secure and certain of future job opportunities if they wanted them, students in the sixties could afford to scoff at rules and regulations that did not suit them. But for decades — indeed for centuries — school administrators had served as foster parents, entrusted with the responsibility of guiding and governing their charges as they made the transition from adolescence into adulthood. Most schools had strict parietal rules, that is, rules prohibiting students from leaving their dormitories overnight or entertaining guests in their rooms. Students caught having sex were certain to be expelled.

A scandal at all-male Yale University in January 1960 showed just what could happen when students were not properly supervised. A local fourteen-year-old girl named Susie had become well known on campus for her willingness to perform oral sex for any Yale student. No one knows how many students Susie actually had contact with, but estimates at the time ranged as high as thirty or forty.

One of the dozens of students who received sexual favors from Susie was David P., a sophomore from Minnesota. Like most of the other young men he knew, David was sexually inexperienced when he arrived at Yale. One night, however, a friend who lived in a nearby suite on the fourth floor of Calhoun College told David that Susie was there and ready to give oral sex to anyone in the dorm. Excited but nervous about his first sexual experience, David went into the room and closed the door. He looked at the girl and thought she was "unattractive and sort of plump," but he unzipped his pants and let her suck his penis until he ejaculated. After she was finished, he went back to his own room and she went on to the next in line.

In mid-January the New Haven police learned about what was going on. Even though she was not charging money, Susie was arrested. Police gave her a copy of the school yearbook, and, presumably afraid of prosecution for committing "crimes against nature," she identified as many students as she could. The investigation quickly made national headlines. Before police even began interrogating suspects, twelve of the students involved withdrew from the university. Eight others were then arrested. A court date was set for the following day. The men were released on $500 bonds.

The trial was very brief. The girl was not present. (Because none of the students had had intercourse with the girl, they were charged with "lascivious carriage," a colonial term for sexual misconduct.) All of the students pleaded no contest. The judge chastised the students and gave them small fines. But the names of all the men were printed in the papers.[2] And each of the students involved in the scandal was suspended for a year. David P. went home to Minnesota and enrolled at the local university, never to graduate from Yale. "It was a very painful time, emotionally," he recalls. As for Susie, she was charged in juvenile court as a delinquent. For decades afterward, rival schools would taunt Yale students at football games by singing, "If I knew Susie, like you knew Susie."

The Yale oral sex scandal made university presidents across the country tremble with fear. If it could happen at an elite Ivy League school like Yale, it could happen anywhere.

In 1962, for example, Cornell University administrators "indefinitely suspended" a male graduate student for cohabiting with a woman.[3] Then in November 1963, the president of Harvard complained that students were abusing the right to entertain women in their rooms:

> We have been badly shaken up recently by some severe violations of our rules of decent standards of behavior . . . Trouble has arisen because what was once considered a pleasant privilege has now for a growing number of students come to be considered a license to use the college rooms for wild parties or for sexual intercourse.[4]

Echoing the president's lament, Dr. Graham Blaine, a psychiatrist for Harvard's health services, issued a warning to school administrators nationwide that they were aiding and abetting illegal and immoral activity.[5] Blaine was unapologetically patriarchal and paternalistic: "From an emotional, physiological and psychological view there are many reasons why the double standard makes sense and in time, we may well see a natural swing back towards it." He blamed the decline of moral standards on women "seeking equality with men in all areas" and suggested a possible return to the nineteenth-century custom of encouraging college boys to have sex with prostitutes in order to protect the chastity of middle-class women.

Although no one paid much attention to Blaine's suggestions for turning back the social clock, other aspects of his report created widespread anxiety. Newspaper editors published numerous exposés about sexual anarchy on American campuses. In the *Ladies' Home Journal,* a Massachusetts judge wrote in 1964: "At too many colleges today, sexual promiscuity among students is a dangerous and growing evil." There was, she cautioned, "abundant psychiatric and medical evidence that illicit sex usually inflicts deep psychic wounds."[6] To prevent the use of dorm rooms for "wild parties or sexual intercourse," some schools began requiring students to keep their doors open any time they were entertaining guests of the opposite sex. (Because the rule generally was that doors be kept open "the width of a book," sly students responded by propping their doors open an inch, the width of a match-"book.") Other schools began insisting on the presence of a chaperone during all visits.

Problems multiplied as universities, for economic reasons, introduced mixed-sex dorms, with men and women assigned to separate floors. The new dorms demanded constant surveillance over student behavior. As one housing director at an institution with mixed dorms wrote in 1964, "I believe there should be a minimum number of entrances to the women's section of the building and that these entrances should be in view of a staffed desk, if possible." The school installed a special alarm system on all doors leading to the women's floors to ring if the doors were opened after curfew. The decline of the double standard meant that women could no longer be relied on to observe the dictates of propriety. As the housing director wrote, "I had counted on the women themselves, to cope with the problem of men on the floor. Needless to say, I was disappointed. People building new halls should not forget to order special double-locking hardware for these doors. Care," the director added, "should also be taken in planning these buildings so as not to have windows leading to the women's wing by a roof or a balcony."[7] As universities grew larger and larger, absorbing the millions of baby boomers graduating from high school, such elaborate architectural schemes were necessarily abandoned, but parietal rules — especially at women's colleges — remained firmly in place.[8]

As late as 1965, a majority of schools still denied students the right to entertain guests of the other sex in their rooms under any circumstances.[9] Married students could rent their own apartments or live in special student housing, of course, but the marriage rate was plummeting year by year. Unmarried students began to realize that it was easier to live off campus than to contend with paternalistic parietal regulations. At Barnard College, however, it was against the rules for a first- or second-year student to live off campus unless she was working part time as a babysitter or housekeeper. Like rules against smoking and wearing shorts in the dining hall, this one was easily ignored. To get permission to live off campus, all a student had to do was lie to the housing office. This is exactly what sophomore Linda LeClair did in 1968 in order to live with her boyfriend, Peter Behr, a Columbia junior. LeClair told school administrators that she was working as a domestic. But her seemingly little white lie ended up landing her at the center of a very big scandal.

It just so happened that in the spring of 1968, a *New York Times* reporter was researching a story about the growing number of students who were cohabiting in college. The reporter found LeClair, who boasted in an interview about how she had lied to Barnard administrators in order to live with her boyfriend. The story did not mention

LeClair's name, but it gave the details of her ploy, and it did not take long for school officials to determine the anonymous student's identity. The university president, determined to protect the honor of the school, called at once for LeClair's expulsion. But angry students protested, and Barnard soon attracted just the kind of national media attention the president had been hoping to avoid. Articles appeared in *Time, Newsweek,* and the *Saturday Review.* LeClair's battle with Barnard College was featured on the front page of the *Times* almost every day for weeks.

At LeClair's request, she was granted a hearing, attended by no less than 250 students and faculty. Many were angry that Columbia men were allowed more freedom than Barnard women — a clear example of the sexual double standard. (By the late sixties, men's colleges had relaxed their parietal rules, in part because an expelled male was immediately eligible for the draft. Expelling a male student was tantamount to sending him to war.) A joint student–faculty Judicial Council then met to discuss the matter and prepare a recommendation for the college president. At the meeting of the council, several testified on LeClair's behalf, including a rabbi and a minister. LeClair herself addressed the council:

> Is the purpose of Barnard College to teach students or to control their private lives? I believe that it is the former. Barnard has no right to control personal behavior. It is solely an educational institution. . . . Barnard's housing regulations discriminate on the basis of sex, age, class in the college, and the distance one's family lives away from the school. Although I am old enough by law to marry without my parents' consent, support myself, which I am doing, live anywhere I want, without parental control, I am not old enough, according to Barnard, to live outside the dorm except as a domestic.

To LeClair the issue was more than simple gender discrimination. "The fact that the rules are discriminatory and the Barnard community is dissatisfied with them is important. However, the most important issue here is the fact that the concept of housing regulations infringes on the rights of some students to live according to their beliefs and of all students to choose their way of living."[10] Feisty and articulate, LeClair argued she had a fundamental right to self-expression.

The Judicial Council agreed. They issued a statement opposing LeClair's expulsion — but banned her from the school cafeteria. The minor reprimand suggested by the Judicial Council reflected widespread support for LeClair and her boyfriend. Nonetheless, the president of the college, Martha Peterson, indignant about the council's response to her initial decision, indicated that she would ignore their vote and exercise her authority to expel LeClair. In response, students staged a sit-in in Peterson's office and gave her a copy of a referendum supporting LeClair, which they said was signed by 850 of the school's 1,800 students.

Letters poured in to the president's office. Some alumni expressed support for LeClair. A fifty-year-old father of three wrote facetiously, "Do not deny the young lady the use of the cafeteria. Rather, brand her as a scarlet woman . . . preferably on the left breast. It is reassuring to know that you are protecting the innocent against such predatory females as Linda. Viva the double standard! Down with liberty — that curious concept of a university." But others saw LeClair's actions as symptomatic of the decline of the American family. One woman stated, "It would be far better to expel or suspend a few delinquents now than to reap later a holocaust of moral misfits[.]" A Presbyterian minister wrote, "Quite frankly and quite bluntly, we had a name for girls like her when I was in school which began with w —." A South Carolina radio station warned that women like Linda LeClair were undermining the "bedrock of the United States. You take sanctity of marriage and the home and the Ten Commandments out of the U.S.A. and you don't have much left on which to hold together a nation dedicated to freedom. Instead you have a people who espouse a principle of the Communist way of life enunciated by Karl Marx."[11]

Linda LeClair was more than just a Barnard student who wanted to live off campus — that is to say, across the street with her boyfriend in his college dorm room. She was a symbol of the sexual revolution, an example to many of all that was wrong with the country. Young women were supposed to fend off young men, not agree to live with them in sin. Why wasn't LeClair worried about her reputation?

Linda LeClair and Peter Behr eventually quit school to join a commune. At the end of the summer, Barnard announced a change in its housing policy: The school would now allow any student to live off campus so long as she had her parents' permission. But this was not enough for the newly radicalized Barnard women. In October 1968, forty Barnard students at one dorm collectively violated college regulations by openly allowing men to stay in their rooms past the weekday 1:30 A.M. curfew. At first the college threatened the students with disciplinary action, but continued resistance to parietal rules ultimately meant the death of Barnard's paternalistic system.[12] Barnard students paved the way for the rest of their generation. At the University of Tennessee in Knoxville, 350 students participated in a rally in February 1969 to demand an end to dormitory curfews for women.[13] Around the country, college administrators, hoping to avoid their own public scandals, quietly extinguished the last remnants of *in loco parentis.* Parietal rules were finally dead.

To careful observers, the Linda LeClair case revealed that college students were beginning to form their own definitions of sexual freedom. The vast majority of American students had no interest in the nudist, panerotic ideology of the Sexual Freedom League, nor in the utopian, polygamous program of Robert Rimmer. Most students did not want to go naked in public or live in group-marriage communes. They simply wanted to be free from the imperative to "save themselves" for marriage.

But even some students who saw no reason for premarital chastity still believed in the principle of monogamy. As journalist Andrew Hacker noted in the *New York Times Magazine* in 1963,

> [W]hen a majority of girls state they would like to have the pill available, it does not mean that they are about to embark on a nymphomaniacal orgy. Quite the contrary, it suggests that they wish to catch themselves a husband and simply desire to have both a sexual relationship and contraceptive protection during the period of engagement.[14]

In 1967, sociologist Ira Reiss reported the results of an extensive study showing that the overwhelming majority of young adults opposed "promiscuity." Though they were more "permissive" than their parents, the baby boomers supported sex before marriage only if it was in the context of a loving monogamous relationship, or what Reiss termed "premarital sex with affection." Reiss concluded that the change in sexual standards over the course of the preceding century had not been a sexual revolution, but rather a gradual and constant process of gender-role readjustment. Other studies, like one reported in *PTA* magazine in 1968, assured parents that college students eschewed casual sex and believed strongly that intercourse should be reserved for potential spouses. In 1968, two sociologists concluded that despite the pill, "we have not had a recent or current sexual revolution in terms of behavior." They noted that "there probably has been some increase in the proportion of women who have had premarital intercourse," but observed that most women having premarital sex were having it only with their "spouses-to be." Young men especially, the sociologists added, were "probably less promiscuous and more monogamous" than ever before.[15]

At Oberlin College and other schools, educators hoped that coed dorms would serve to reduce sexual tensions between male and female students and, in the long run, reduce the desire for sex itself. "As community spirit grows," an Oberlin administrator told *Life* magazine in 1970, "students don't have to pair off as lovers to get to know each other. They form brother–sister relationships, and take on larger groups of friends."[16]

It is hard to determine exactly how many sexual partners the average student of the late sixties had, but by most accounts modified forms of monogamy, not promiscuity, were the norm. Historian Sean Wilentz, who was a student at Columbia during the Linda LeClair controversy, had "six or seven" sexual partners in college, which he says was "higher than average." As he recalls, "There was a lot of fucking going on by couples, but not a lot of promiscuity. People had serious boyfriend–girlfriend relationships. There was a desire for an emotional attachment that was very deep — a desire for stability. Guys and girls felt the same way. The idea of going to a bar every night in order to pick someone up to get laid was not appealing." There was virtually no public nudity or public sex. "I remember once walking into a room and seeing a girl without a blouse on, but that was extremely unusual." Sometimes men and women would live together in the same room, "but it was all very chaste." By his senior year, Wilentz was living with his girlfriend in a monogamous, quasi-marital relationship. "At least half the guys I knew in college ended up marrying their first or second girlfriends."[17]

Valerie Goldberg (pseudonym), who was in the first class of women at Yale, and identified herself as a hippie her freshman year of college in 1971, says promiscuity was never the norm in the counterculture. "Surely it was a whole lot freer than it was before, but I think people had just as much guilt and confusion about sex as they ever did. We had parties where people would smoke too much or drink too much and sleep with their friends, but there were emotional repercussions the next day. Free love is like a free lunch — there's no such thing. I remember traveling, and [multiple couples] would have sex at the same time in the same room, but it wasn't common. Even nudity was rare." Goldberg had had sex with a man for the first time at age fourteen and had several secretive relationships with women in college, but she still obeyed the unwritten rules of the counterculture. "You were supposed to be in a monogamous relationship — serial monogamy, maybe — but monogamy nonetheless. There's only one woman I ever met who really felt like 'anyone at anytime.' I considered her a rogue."[18] (Timothy Leary, a leading guru of the counterculture, was particularly critical of promiscuity and an outspoken proponent of monogamy.)[19]

Though hippies were not necessarily promiscuous, they did pride themselves on their liberated sexual attitudes. As one hippie told a reporter:

I don't know how it started or even when. Our grandchildren will find out from historians. But things sure are changing fast. It's a turned-on generation, and I don't mean pot, although that's happening too, and it's an important part of the whole scene. I mean turned on to ourselves, our minds, our bodies, colors, beauty, living. Our parents are hung up. Hey, they pick a night, some once a week, some once a month, and take their showers and go through a whole ritual, then turn off the lights, do it once and fall asleep. We just find a pad, or a corner of a pad, undress and really get into it — when we want, as often as we want.[20]

For hippies, sexual liberation meant not being preoccupied with sex. "You have to remember," says Jack Gelfand, a professor of computer science who graduated from Rutgers University in 1965, "sex for us wasn't naughty or illicit. It was innocent. Our parents were telling dirty jokes and reading sex manuals. For us, free love was about love, not just sex."[21]

"Make Love, Not War" — it was one of the key slogans of the counterculture. But it was not a rallying cry for casual sex; it was, rather, an almost sentimental plea for harmony and brotherhood. If people would only stop hating and killing one another and instead begin truly loving each other, the world would be a better place. Sex was fine, but "making love" was about far more than sex: it was about being profoundly related to another human being. As Bob Dylan advised *Playboy* readers in 1966, "Sex is a temporary thing: sex isn't love." Love was the central tenet of the counterculture — love of nature, love of life, love of oneself, love of love. Sexual intercourse was merely a way to communicate with, and express love for, another person.

Students in the sixties saw their own sexual relationships in innocent, idealistic terms. This youthful, rose-colored view could be found in the 1966 book *It's Happening: A Portrait of the Youth Scene Today,* by J. L. Simmons and Barry Winograd:

> Each sex feels freer now to have attitudes, interests and tastes which were formerly the exclusive property of one sex or the other. Fewer things are thought "unmanly" or "unwomanly." Men can cook and sew, clean house and iron; women can spout philosophical insights, tinker with woodcraft and fix dirty carburetors. Thus for those with "liberalized" sexual codes, it is positively consistent for a woman to admit forthrightly that she really does enjoy sex and for a man to fall in love and marry somebody who's been to bed with a dozen other men. Some males go further, preferring girls who've had experience with others, shying away from virginity as a possible badge of coldness.[22]

As this passage suggests, hippies were rebels, but they were not quite revolutionaries.* One "square" critic of hippie culture was forced to admit

---

* When Joan Didion was living with, and writing about, hippies in the midsixties she asked them about their sexual values and discovered traces of the old double standard. One hippie told Didion that he was virtually liberated from middle-class moral codes: "I've had this old lady for a couple of months now," he told Didion, referring to his girlfriend, "maybe

that monogamous sexual relationships remained "the ideal" for many hippies. "The hippie ethic of 'make love, not war' has been interpreted by America's dominant culture to mean that sexual practices in the hippie subculture consist of rampant promiscuity . . . As with most impressions of 'deviancy' in the United States, this one is false."[23]

Young adults in the sixties wanted to be left alone. They wanted the freedom to live together and to sleep together. Nonetheless, there was more to Linda LeClair's battle with Barnard than just the desire of two students to cohabit. LeClair was a woman, and the support she received from her fellow Barnard students reflected the growing frustration many women felt about sex roles in America.

As college students formulated their own definitions of sexual liberation, female students often found their sexual values at odds with those of their male peers. Young men did not necessarily believe in promiscuity, but, contrary to the idyllic picture offered by Simmons and Winograd, many young men continued to think of women as potential sex partners first, and friends or classmates or coworkers second. Furthermore, faced with the ever present threat of the draft, some men saw each day in life-and-death terms. "You didn't know when your number was going to be called," says Andrew Wallace, "so you wanted to seize the moment. I remember once I tried to see how many women I could sleep with in one day."[24] Even if most young men ended up being monogamous in practice, plenty harbored fantasies of sexual conquest.

In the radical organizations of the New Left, women found that they were often taken for granted: they were expected to answer phones, cook meals, do laundry, and provide sexual companionship — in other words, to be secretaries, housekeepers, and concubines.[25] Male radicals were often as sexist as their own fathers were. A Students for a Democratic Society brochure stated: "The system is like a woman; you've got to fuck it to make it change." A Black Panther publicly commented, "Superman was a punk because he never even tried to fuck Lois Lane."[26]

---

she makes something special for my dinner and I come in three days late and tell her I've been with some other chick, well maybe she shouts a little but then I say, 'That's me, baby,' and she laughs and says, 'That's you, Max.'" When Didion asked if he would respond likewise, the young hippie equivocated. "I mean, if she comes in and tells me she wants to have Don, maybe I say 'OK, baby, it's your trip.'" The implication was, maybe he did not. Didion also asked him if he was completely free of "his middle-class Freudian hang-ups," and he answered honestly, "Nah, I got acid," explaining that is was only by taking a 250 microgram tablet of LSD every week that he was able to be so "unrepressed." (Joan Didion, "Slouching Towards Bethlehem," *Saturday Evening Post*, 23 September 1967, 25–31.)

One woman remembers that a male fellow-radical suggested that white and black men "ball chicks together to gain solidarity." Another woman who was in the antiwar movement recalls, "The guys in the movement were just awful. They were Neanderthals. They were Neanderthals who'd read too much Hegel and Marx." Male hippies in communes were not much better than their activist counterparts. Former hippie Elizabeth Gipps says, "I remember screaming one day when the men were theoretically meditating while the women were cleaning the floors around them."[27]

Countercultural publications like the *Rat,* the *East Village Other,* and the *Evergreen Review* were filled with erotic short stories, manifestos for sexual freedom, and graphic comics, all from a male perspective. Most erotic material published in the sixties assumed a male audience. In 1966, for instance, the *Evergreen Review* began running translations of Jean-Claude Forest's comic strip "Barbarella," featuring a barely clad, sexually voracious science fiction heroine. Barbarella conquered her enemies by taking off her clothes. Many young women found Barbarella insulting: She was a *man's* fantasy of a liberated woman.

By many accounts, young men in the sixties were indifferent to their female partners' sexual needs. One woman recalls, "Of course, most guys expected you to 'put out' just because they bought you dinner. But every time I had sex I felt like I was dealing with someone from another planet. The guys just didn't get it. They wanted instant gratification — no foreplay. Once I asked a guy to use his fingers to massage my clitoris while we were making love and he looked at me like I was certifiably insane."[28] Says another woman, "The guys fucked like rabbits — in, out, in, out. It was so boring you could die."[29]

The slogans of the era were written by men for men: "Free Land, Free Dope, Free Women"; "Peace, Pussy, Pot." One hippie noted at the time, "Rape is as common as bullshit on Haight Street." He painted a dark portrait of life in San Francisco's hippie capital, the Haight-Ashbury district.

> Pretty little 16-year-old middle-class chick comes to the Haight to see what it's all about & gets picked up by a 17-year-old street dealer who spends all day shooting her full of speed again and again, then feeds her 3000 [micrograms of acid] & raffles off her temporarily unemployed body for the biggest Haight Street gang bang since the night before last.[30]

According to counterculture cartoonist Robert Crumb, "Guys were running around [the Haight] saying, 'I'm you and you are me and everything is beautiful so get down and suck my dick." Artist and activist Shulamith Firestone wrote that a woman who refused to have sex with a man was called a "ballbreaker," a "cockteaser," a "real drag," and a "bad trip."[31] Some hippie men were not ashamed to pressure a woman to have sex as much as conventional society pressured her *not* to.

Young women had begun to feel the expectations of the sexual revolution back in the early sixties. In 1962, Gloria Steinem could write, "The problem is that many girls who are not self-motivated . . . are now being pressured into affairs they can't handle . . . In the fine old American tradition of conformity, society has begun to make it as rough for virgins . . . as it once did for those who had affairs before marriage . . . Chaste girls feel 'out of it[.]' "[32]

In 1968, the year of the Barnard cohabitation crisis, young women in New York City began meeting to discuss the sex and gender problems they felt were plaguing the New Left. The result was a radical feminist movement, one of the major goals of which was to redefine sexual liberation. Real sexual freedom would mean freedom from oppressive sex roles, not just the freedom to "get laid." As Kate Millett, a graduate student at Columbia University, wrote in her dissertation, published in 1970 as *Sexual Politics,* "Coitus can scarcely be said to take place in a vacuum; although of itself it largely appears a biological and physical activity, it is set so deeply within the larger context of human affairs that it serves as a charged microcosm of the variety of attitudes and values to which a culture subscribes."[33] In her dissertation, Millett made it plain that the attitudes and values espoused in the writings of male figures like Sigmund Freud, D. H. Lawrence, Henry Miller, and Norman Mailer were geared toward the subordination of women. These supposed sexual liberals viewed all women as potential whores. Freud treated female sexual desire like a disease; Lawrence, Miller, and Mailer were guilty of eroticizing rape.

Though Millett was critical of the major male sexual philosophers of the twentieth century, she actually shared much in common with the sexual radicals of her own generation. Like Jefferson Poland and other sex radicals, Millett identified herself as bisexual. "A fully realized sexual revolution," Millet wrote,

> would require, perhaps first of all, an end to traditional sexual inhibitions and taboos, particularly those that most threaten patriarchal monogamous marriage: homosexuality, "illegitimacy," adolescent, pre- and extramarital sexuality. The negative aura with which sexual activity has generally been surrounded would necessarily be eliminated, together with the double standard and prostitution. The goal of revolution would be a permissive single standard of sexual freedom, and one uncorrupted by the crass and exploitative economic bases of traditional sexual alliances.[34]

Such sentiments could have been found in any Sexual Freedom League brochure.

Over the course of 1968, numerous radical feminist groups sprang up in New York City. One by one, these groups, such as New York Women's Liberation, New York Radical Women, and the Redstockings, developed systematic critiques of American culture. In small, intimate meetings, young feminists discussed issues that were once reserved for the therapist's office: abortion, birth control, faking orgasm, feeling pressured to have intercourse, lesbianism, bisexuality, pornography, prostitution. These were subjects their mothers might not even have dared to think about, much less mention. The novelist Alix Kates Shulman remembers:

> Some said they felt sexually rejected by their partners, others complained that their husbands never left them alone sexually. Some said they were afraid to tell their partners what pleased them sexually, others said their partners resented being told. Some told about passes they had to submit to at work and on the street, others were bereft because men were intimidated by them and they, the women, were forbidden to make advances themselves. Some spoke about reprisals they feared or suffered as lesbians, others spoke of their fear of lesbians. Some shamefully confessed to having masturbated all their lives, others declared in anguish that they could not masturbate.[35]

In meeting after meeting, feminists decided that young men were unsympathetic to women's sexual needs or, worse, were determined to oppress and exploit women.

Radical feminists never did actually burn their bras, but they did shed them. Seeking a more "natural" and "free" form of dress, young feminists traded their skirts for jeans, their blouses for T-shirts. They refused to wear garters and stockings. Outside the 1968 Miss America pageant in Atlantic City, a group of feminists set up a "freedom trashcan" into which they threw symbols of sexual oppression: bras, high heels, women's magazines, and the like. Although the contents of the trashcan were never ignited, the media created the image of feminists as "bra-burners," and the label stuck.

Young feminists struggled to redefine sexual liberation. Sometimes they ended up defining it as liberation *from* sex. "*I claim that rape exists,*" the feminist theorist Robin Morgan wrote, "*any time sexual intercourse occurs when it has not been initiated by the woman, out of her own genuine affection and desire*" (italics in original). This definition indicted all male desire as criminal. "It must be clear," she stated, "that, under this definition, most of the decently married bedrooms across America are settings for nightly rape." Ti-Grace Atkinson, a New York activist who was one of the founders and first presidents of the National Organization for Women, declared "all sex is reactionary." Atkinson was disgusted by male behavior. "You would go to friends' homes and see guys exploiting women . . . trying to screw their girlfriend's other friend." Many men, Atkinson says, assumed that because she was a feminist she was also a dominatrix. "Men are just more into sex than women," she concluded. But this did not give men the right to expect sexual activity: they had an obligation to "learn to repress their sexuality."[36]

Not all young women — not even all young feminists — agreed with the notion that there was something inherently humiliating about being desirable or desired. As journalist Ellen Willis recalls, "I didn't understand all the outrage about being treated like a sex object. I was angry because I'd always been rejected by men for being too smart, too intelligent. I *wanted* to be a sex object." But plenty of young radical feminists saw sexual activity as a threat to female equality. In a 1968 issue of *No More Fun and Games: A Journal of Women's Liberation,* Dana Densmore, a founder of the feminist group Cell 16 in Boston, repeatedly denounced the sexual revolution and the cultural imperative for women to enjoy sex. Densmore, in fact, advocated celibacy. "Sex is not essential to life," she wrote. "It's inconvenient, time-consuming, energy-draining, and irrelevant."[37] Sexual liberals and feminists did not exactly see eye to eye.

It is fair to say that young people in the sixties were ambivalent about the sexual revolution. There were some, like Linda LeClair, who were willing to fight for their rights. Many, however, took their own sexual freedom for granted and did not see any reason to push for further social change. And some young women who joined the feminist movement believed the sexual revolution itself was to blame for a host of social ills. Though they considered themselves part of the left, some young feminists were so angry about the aggressive sexuality of men, and so unhappy with the status quo, that they often espoused attitudes that were more traditionally associated with the right than with the left.

The ambivalence that young adults felt about sexual freedom was reflected in a survey taken in 1969 at American University in Washington, D.C., which found that almost half the students were opposed to coeducational housing. Only 10 percent of the males and 2 percent of the females said they would want the university to allow men and women to share dormitory rooms. In fact, the most popular housing option among men was separate male and female floors. Among women, the most popular choice was separate male and female dormitory wings. Those students who did want some form of mixed housing were less interested in making premarital sex easier than in having a more "realistic" social environment. Only 9 percent of the students wanted no supervision in the dorms. Many students voiced fears that coed housing would bring about a loss of privacy. One female student expressed a common anxiety about the "confusion" that would be caused by sharing dorms with men. "Frankly, I'm not interested in sharing my bathroom, my sheer night-gowns, or the sight of my hair rollers with 'just any male.' I think the whole idea is ridiculous. We need smaller dorms with less noise, aggrava-tion and confusion — not more so." Indeed, 72 percent of the students surveyed worried that coed housing would come at the cost of privacy.[39]

The AU survey indicates that privacy is a more complicated concept than sexual liberals understood and that the baby boom generation of college students harbored plenty of qualms about social change. At American University, at least, Linda LeClair would have been a nuisance rather than a heroine. Still, by the late 1960s, "traditional" morality seemed bankrupt to students with an intellectual inclination. They were disgusted by the fact that the same men and women who claimed promiscuity violated the Bible could, in the same breath, champion white supremacy. Those who said that homosexuals were going to Hell tended also to condone the killing of women and children in Vietnam. All too often, the very men who deplored prostitution, profanity, and pornography were not above frequenting prostitutes, using profanity, or consuming pornography themselves. In this context, the "new moral-ity" championed by hippies and activists represented a compelling alter-native to the hypocrisy of mainstream society. Whether they defended the rights of the individual (as did Linda LeClair) or the collective inter-ests of the group (as did feminists), student radicals were profoundly committed to building a society consistent with their values. They saw no need for cynicism or resignation, no reason to subordinate their ideals to the demands of the status quo.

In the end, young women in the sixties succeeded in redefining the college experience. College officials abandoned their efforts to police female behavior. Both young men and young women benefited from the new situation. Admittedly, female college students could no longer cite paternalistic parietal rules in fending off unwanted male sexual advances, but this was surely a meager price to pay. No longer was premarital sex ground for expulsion. No longer could parents rely on college administrators as chaperones. No longer were sexually active students forced to regard their teachers as adversaries.

CHAPTER 9

STRANGE BEDFELLOWS: CHRISTIAN CLERGY AND THE SEXUAL REVOLUTION

O N TUESDAY MORNING, July 30, 1968, American Catholics woke up to startling news. The Vatican had proclaimed all forms of birth control (except for the notoriously ineffective "rhythm" method: trying to avoid intercourse during ovulation) immoral and illicit. The pope had effectively declared war against modern science.

The news was startling because in recent years Rome had been moving in a more liberal direction. The Second Vatican Council of 1962 ("Vatican II") had inaugurated a new era of ecumenism. Many therefore had assumed the papacy would come to accept birth control pills as an inevitable part of scientific progress.[1] This assumption was supported by the fact that a panel of leading bishops appointed by the pope himself had recommended in 1966 that the Church adopt a tolerant view of contraception, especially in light of the worldwide population explosion. An earlier pope had even approved the use of birth control pills for certain medical conditions, such as menstrual cramps. Now, in a sudden about-face, Pope Paul VI had issued an encyclical titled *Humanae Vitae* which, in no uncertain terms, instructed Catholics to forswear all forms of "artificial" contraception, including condoms, diaphragms, and the pill.

The pope could not have expected a positive reception in the United States. Studies showed that most married American Catholics (52 percent of Catholic wives) were already using modern forms of contraception.[2] For their part, Protestant and Jewish leaders, concerned about the long-term implications of unwanted pregnancy, were firmly on record in support of birth control. Meanwhile, many American Catholic leaders had come to accept a notion, captioned "the new morality," which held that the Golden Rule, not rigid codes of sexual conduct, should govern human behavior. Accordingly, a large number had come to see birth control as morally neutral.

Several years before the encyclical *Humanae Vitae*, pro-birth control Catholics had begun making news. John Rock, a practicing Catholic and one of the inventors of the birth control pill, believed papal objections to birth control were seriously misguided. In 1963, Rock had published *The Time Has Come: A Catholic Doctor's Proposal to End the Battle over Birth Control*, calling on the Church to accept the pill as progress. The book set off a storm of controversy. One bishop denounced Rock as a "moral rapist, using his strength as a man of science to assault the faith of his fellow Catholics."[3] Others believed he imperiled the future of Catholicism. But Rock knew that many Catholic women were eager to use "artificial" methods of birth control with the blessing of the Church, and he developed complex arguments to prove that the pill itself was a morally acceptable method, stating, for example, that the pill did not function as a contraceptive but rather as an anovulant, which simply regulated the menstrual cycle. He found supporters throughout the country. As one woman wrote: "You are wonderful! Please don't ever get discouraged. You have saved mankind a lot of misery already and for every one who curses you, there must be a thousand who are grateful to you. I just want to be counted among the thousands even though I am forced to lead an absolutely sexless life (my pious husband prefers not to touch me, rather than go against the Church)."[4] By expressing his belief that oral contraceptives were morally legal within the teachings of the Catholic Church, Rock appealed to many Catholics who wanted to practice birth control while remaining faithful to Church teachings.

Given "the new morality" and the appeal of the birth control pill, Catholic officials faced growing pressure from priests and laypersons to approve the use of contraception by married couples. Theologians struggled to find a middle ground. In 1962, the Jesuit periodical *Studi Catholici* suggested — rather ludicrously — that a woman might legally use birth control pills if she were in imminent danger of rape.[5] Others argued that the oral contraceptive might be used by a woman to regulate her menstrual cycle, and thereby make it easier to employ the rhythm method, so long as she did not intend to use the pill explicitly as a contraceptive.[6] Apart from these attempts to elaborate an approach to the pill that would be acceptable to Rome, authorities recognized that

Catholic women were using oral contraceptives regardless of official teaching. A National Catholic Welfare Conference memorandum implored bishops not to deny the sacraments to those who used birth control because it would lead to the exclusion "of one-third of the married faithful from the Church!"[7] This was probably an understatement.

When the pope issues an order, Catholic clergy are expected to fall in line. But in 1968, American Catholic priests were not in any mood to obey *Humanae Vitae*. The civil rights movement and the antiwar movement had taught young Catholics the importance and power of resistance to authority. In a remarkable act of defiance, 87 American Catholic theologians issued a statement against the papal encyclical, declaring it was not morally binding. In the following days, more and more clergy joined the dissent. By August 2 of that year, 172 theologians had signed the statement against the encyclical. A few days later, the number reached 222. By the end of August, more than 600 Catholic clergy members had gone on record opposing *Humanae Vitae*. In community after community, priests issued their own statements in defense of birth control. National polls revealed that a majority of lay Catholics were equally in support of birth control and nearly half (46 percent) even felt abortion was morally neutral. A revolt of serious historical magnitude was under way.

Needless to say, Church authorities were not pleased with the turn of events. The National Conference of Catholic Bishops publicly rebuked the dissident priests and called for order. Four prominent bishops flew to Rome for an emergency meeting with the pope. Administrators at St. John Vianney Seminary in Miami dismissed seven priests for speaking out against the encylical. Cardinal Patrick O'Boyle, archbishop of Washington, D.C., and chancellor of Catholic University, warned local priests that they could face serious penalties if they did not retract their statements against *Humanae Vitae*. When the dissident priests refused to bow down to Church authority, O'Boyle began stripping them of their official duties and privileges.

Washington Catholics were shaken by O'Boyle's actions. One hundred Catholic laymen picketed a Mass being delivered by the cardinal. Then on September 22, two hundred Catholics walked out of St. Matthew's Cathedral in protest when the cardinal began warning parishioners that they would suffer eternal damnation if they violated Church teachings on contraception. Those who remained gave the cardinal a standing ovation. In November, the left-leaning Democratic senator and erstwhile presidential candidate Eugene McCarthy led a demonstration of more than four thousand fellow-Catholics in support of the dissident priests. The American Catholic Church, like the nation as a whole, was clearly in turmoil.

The crisis over contraception eventually ended in stalemate. Some of the priests who had been punished for opposing the pope were restored to full office; others were permanently stripped of their duties. Rome refused to back down; most American Catholics simply chose to ignore Church dogma.

To understand the 1968 contraception battle, one must go back to the early sixties, when "the new morality" was just beginning to make waves in theological circles. At the time, Catholics and Protestants on both sides of the Atlantic were trying to steer a course between puritanism and permissiveness. After World War II, Protestant theologians like Paul Tillich and Reinhold Niebuhr attempted to distill from Christian teachings a core set of ethics, unadulterated by irrational superstitions. They sought to model themselves on the early Christians, who rejected absolute rules in favor of flexible principles. Hoping to invigorate Christianity by making it more rational and less dogmatic, theologians turned to secular philosophers for guidance, particularly existentialists like Kierkegaard and Sartre.

Slowly, a new model of Christian morality emerged. Absolute rules and codes, like the prohibition on premarital sex, were legalisms inadequate for the complex questions of modern life. Every individual had to make moral decisions by evaluating a given situation and the effects of his or her potential actions on other individuals. The New Testament theme of love could serve as a guiding principle for all human relations. If individuals acted out of love for one another, then their deeds could be considered just, even if those deeds did not conform to traditional codes of conduct. This "new morality," otherwise known as "situation ethics," set forth the possibility that premarital sex, sex with contraception, perhaps even extramarital sex might be viewed as moral, given the right situation and the right intentions. By the early sixties, this new wave of Christian thought was transforming theological opinion in the leading seminaries and divinity schools.

To the proponents of the new morality, it was not new at all. It was, rather, a return to the kind of spiritual teachings that Jesus had imparted to his followers. Situation ethics was really the core of Christian theology, with thousands of years of crusty superstition chipped away.

The trend toward situation ethics was underscored by Protestant support for birth control. In May 1960 the General Conference of Methodists decided that "planned parenthood, practiced in Christian conscience, fulfills rather than violates the will of God." And by that same spring, the million-member Southern Presbyterian Church was also on record in support of contraception.[8] On February 24, 1961, the *New York Times* carried the full text of a statement by the National Council of Churches endorsing family planning and advocating population control through voluntary contraception.[9] Contraception, most Protestant authorities now believed, was the technological answer to unwanted pregnancies and overpopulation.

It was not long before Protestants in England began to take on issues even more controversial than birth control. In February 1963, a group of eleven senior members of the British Quakers Church published a critical reevaluation of Christian sexual morality, *Towards a Quaker View of Sex,* which openly rejected "almost completely the traditional approach of the organized Christian Church to morality, with its supposition that it knows precisely what is right and what is wrong, that this distinction can be made in terms of an external pattern of behavior, and that the greatest good will come only through universal adherence to that pattern." *Towards a Quaker View of Sex* challenged Church teaching on premarital sex, extramarital sex, and homosexuality. "There is no reason," the authors wrote, "why the physical nature of a sexual act should be the criterion by which the question whether or not it is moral should be decided." Instead, they emphasized the quality and depth of feeling of a given relationship. "An act which (for example) expresses true affection between two individuals and gives pleasure to them both, does not seem to us to be sinful by reason alone of the fact that it is homosexual. The same criteria seem to us to apply whether a relationship is heterosexual or homosexual."[10]

Towards a Quaker View of Sex was not intended as a manifesto against traditional morality. Far from it. As Francis Canavan later wrote in the Catholic magazine *America,* "[It] would be wrong to interpret the authors of *Towards a Quaker View of Sex* as being anti-moral."[11] Indeed, *Towards a Quaker View* made it plain that "[t]here must be a morality of some sort to govern sexual relationships." But to the authors, the worst kind of sexual sin was "exploitation." They condemned "as fundamentally immoral every sexual action that is not, as far as is humanly ascertainable, the result of a mutual decision." In other words, they restored the Golden Rule to its central place in Judeo-Christian life. At the same time, the Quakers embraced every relationship "where there is genuine tenderness, an openness to responsibility and the seed of commitment" regardless of whether it was sanctified by marriage.[12]

The following month, Anglican leaders joined the fray. An Anglican priest in Great Britain declared during a Sunday sermon, "We need to replace the traditional morality based upon a *code* with a morality which is related to the person and the needs of the person." In the same sermon, he criticized traditional views of homosexuality and mocked the idea that homosexuality is unnatural. "Unnatural to whom? Certainly not for the homosexual himself?"[13] On March 19, English Protestantism was jolted again when Anglican bishop John T. Robinson published *Honest to God,* a book that generated a storm of controversy both in Britain and the United States. The book sold over 350,000 copies in its first year, and Robinson received over a thousand letters within the first three months it was in print.[14] In calling for a personal approach to religion, Robinson argued that the most important Christian doctrine was love. This in itself was not a particularly radical claim, but in teasing out the implications of his logic in a chapter titled "The New Morality," Robinson reasoned

> [N]othing can of itself be labeled as 'wrong.' One cannot, for instance, start from the position that 'sex relations before marriage' or 'divorce' are wrong or sinful in themselves. They may be in 99 cases or even 100 cases out of 100, but they are not intrinsically so, for the only intrinsic evil is lack of love. . . . For *nothing* else makes a thing right or wrong.

Lest the reader confuse his theology as a "license to laxity and to the broadest possible living," Robinson explained that "love's gate is strict and narrow and its requirements infinitely deeper and more penetrating" than the requirements of traditional morality.[15] But readers recognized the revolutionary implications of Robinson's ideas for Christian thought. Robinson's "new" approach to morality was echoed in a July 1963 statement by a medical officer in the British Ministry of Education, who said he saw no reason premarital sex ought to be considered unconditionally immoral.[16]

These British views quickly crossed the Atlantic and prompted discussion about situation ethics and the new morality in America. Ministers and priests were soon calling into question all religious teachings on sexual matters, from premarital chastity to adultery. In August 1963, the Reverend David Wayne, an Episcopal priest and the curate of the Church of the Epiphany in New York City, publicly criticized American churches for discriminating against gay men and women. By this point, the new morality was the hottest topic in theological circles, and mainstream America was tuning in to the clerical debate. In October 1964, *Redbook* ran a story on the new morality, in which Harvard theologian Harvey Cox noted, "We must avoid giving a simple yes or no answer to the question of premarital chastity."[17] A conference on the new morality was held at Harvard in 1965.

At first, the proponents of the new morality were critical not only of censorship and sexual repression, but of the commercial aspects of the sexual revolution. In the magazine *Christianity and Crisis* Harvey Cox reproached *Playboy* for exploiting society's sexual repression. Cox cleverly attacked *Playboy* on its own terms. "*Playboy* and its less success-ful imitators are not 'sex magazines' at all. They are basically anti-sexual. They dilute and dissipate authentic sexuality by reducing it to an acces-sory, by keeping it at a safe distance." Jewish intellectuals were no less critical. Benjamin DeMott wrote in *Commentary* magazine, "In place of the citizen with a vote to cast or a job to do or a book to study or a god to worship, the [*Playboy*] editor offers a vision of the whole man reduced to his private parts." But for the most part, American clergy simply preferred to ignore magazines like *Playboy*. To drum up greater con-troversy, Hugh Hefner sent out thousands of copies of "The Playboy Philosophy" to theologians across the country. His tactic worked. Soon a national debate about the moral significance of the magazine was launched.

As the new morality spread, religious leaders were forced to confront their own inconsistency. Some began smiling benevolently on soft-core pornography. One school chaplain told students at Indiana University that the views expressed in *Playboy* were "more authentically Christian than much that is heard from pulpits today." A pastor at a United Church of Christ in Pittsburgh declared, "The average minister's ser-mons would be more relevant if *Playboy* were required reading." Even-tually, Harvey Cox himself began contributing regularly to Hefner's magazine. The *National Review* described Cox's change of heart the "most remarkable since Saul set out for Damascus."[18]

The new morality had a profound impact on American culture. A 1966 book, *Situation Ethics: The New Morality* by Joseph F. Fletcher, professor of social ethics at the Episcopal Theological School in Cambridge, Massa-chusetts, sold over 150,000 copies in its first two years. In May 1966, the Second North American Conference on Church and Family was devoted to discussion of the new morality. In July 1966, the Esalen Institute, a human-potential retreat in Big Sur, California, held a special seminar titled "The New Morality: Situational Ethics and the New Theology," with presentations by two Episcopal priests. That same year, the National Pres-byterian Council's Office of Church and Society met with a gay rights organization, the Janus Society, which reported in its newsletter:

> The Church members and the Janus members seemed to agree fully that we are gradually, and should be rapidly, moving towards a sexual moral-ity which concerns itself with the extent to which an individual takes pleasure or satisfaction from another with the other's free and compre-hending cooperation, and which places a high value on honesty rather than on compliance with overt codes of behavior.

In December 1967, ninety Episcopal priests in New York concluded that homosexuality was morally neutral.[19]

By the late sixties, proponents of the new morality were describing direct links between eroticism and religious passion. Some clergy echoed the themes of the counterculture. Father Joseph Walsh, a college chaplain, wrote in the Catholic periodical the *Commonweal*, "You find yourself wondering about the meaning of chastity in a technologized, plastic culture where sexuality is most people's only link with the primitive and the ecstatic." Religious leaders began to express support for alternatives to traditional marriage and monogamy. In 1968, Sidney Callahan, writing in the Disciples of Christ magazine *Christian Century*, demanded to know, "If sex is a basically good form of loving communication, why should it be exclusive and why should it be inhibited?" Callahan argued that it was the duty of Christians to "encourage integration of sexuality into the whole personality and into communal life."[20]

On the West Coast, the Reverend Ted McIlvenna was creating actual institutions to reform sexual morality. Born in 1932, McIlvenna was the son of a missionary to the American Indians of the Northwest. As a young man, McIlvenna played professional baseball with the Pittsburgh Pirates and acted on Broadway. After graduating from Willamette University, he followed in his father's footsteps and earned a seminary degree from the Pacific School of Religion in 1958. In 1962, McIlvenna was asked to run the Young Adult Project in San Francisco, a program for runaways sponsored by the Glide Memorial Methodist Church. The church's black minister, the Reverend A. Cecil Williams, had made social welfare a central concern of the church, and McIlvenna soon became involved in the civil rights movement and other forms of student activism.

In the early sixties, McIlvenna received a call from Guy Straight, a member of the local chapter of the Mattachine Society, asking for help on behalf of two gay men who had had their genitals kicked in by police. Horrified by what he saw at the hospital, McIlvenna convened a meeting between religious leaders and representatives from San Francisco's gay rights organizations. After extensive dialogue, the ministers and gay leaders created the Council on Religion and the Homosexual in December 1964.[21]

As its first initiative, the council decided to sponsor a gay New Year's Eve dance. Members of the council notified the local police of the event in advance, believing this would preempt a police raid. They were wrong. Police arrived and broke up the party. Lawyers for the council attempted to stop the police raid, but the officers were determined to show their power and simply arrested three of the lawyers. The vice officers then photographed each of the six hundred individuals present at the dance.[22]

With a grant from the Playboy Foundation, McIlvenna went to Great Britain, where he arranged a meeting of religious leaders to discuss homosexuality. In 1966, the Glide Foundation organized the National Sex Forum and asked McIlvenna to run it.* The forum focused on educating health care professionals about sexuality. McIlvenna then started a program in sexuality at the UCLA Medical School. He had come to believe that the sexual revolution just might save the world.

Given his experiences with the San Francisco police department, McIlvenna was particularly concerned about American attitudes toward homosexuality. Responding to the prevailing psychiatric view of homosexuals as "mentally ill," McIlvenna told the readers of *Playboy*:

> I think it's totally pointless, destructive and narrow-minded to categorize homosexuals in this way and talk of their "disordered sexual development." More and more young people today are trying to teach themselves to love one another regardless of gender, and they're certainly not disordering their development. . . . Men who make love to men and women who make love to women are far, far healthier than people who daren't accept their sexuality at all.[23]

As the sexual revolution's unofficial spiritual leader, McIlvenna was an outspoken champion of personal pleasure.

Other proponents of the new morality joined McIlvenna in pressing for greater and greater change. In a January 1969 article in the *Christian Century* Gordon Clanton wrote: "We must begin to teach that sex is morally neutral," and told readers, "Properly understood and lovingly practiced, sex outside of marriage is indeed a positive good." The following month the same magazine printed an article calling for mandatory sex education for students and teachers, accessible birth control for anyone over fifteen, liberalized abortion laws, and the end of all laws regulating the sale of erotic material. In December 1971, the *Journal of Pastoral Care* printed an article by marriage counselor David Mace endorsing masturbation, adultery, and homosexuality.[24] Around the same time, the United Church of Christ became the first major American denomination to ordain an openly gay minister. Some ministers

---

* McIlvenna alleges that the mainline Methodist denominations in San Francisco initially supported the National Sex Forum financially, but when a minister with a gay son was appointed bishop, he cut off all funding. The National Sex Forum then moved from the basement of the Glide Memorial Church, where it was originally housed, to the local YMCA. Early staff members included Phyllis Lyon, one of the two founders of the lesbian group Daughters of Bilitis; Maggie Rubenstein and Margo Rila, both bisexual activists involved with the Sexual Freedom League; Laird Sutton, a minister; Dick Bennet, a gynecologist; and Herbert Vandervoort, a UCLA psychiatrist.

endorsed secret extramarital affairs, and others encouraged group marriage and open marriage. The Reverend Raymond Lawrence wrote,

> I am increasingly convinced that we are living in a time in which a new form of marriage is in the making. . . . The old marriage of total and exclusive commitment is going to give way to something different in the years ahead. . . . The old idea of one man for one woman, totally and exclusively, is, I believe, basically rooted in insecurity and possessiveness. And for many it is unsatisfying.[25]

Jonathan West (a pseudonym) took such teachings to heart. Born and raised a Catholic, West was an altar boy at his church and "always very spiritual." As a high school student in Baltimore in the early sixties, he found "the whole atmosphere of male–female relationships so stifling" that he and a group of friends created their own "mini Christian counterculture." They organized civil rights protests, drug crisis interventions, and Bible study meetings. But this was a rather unusual Christian fellowship, because the students firmly opposed monogamy. "We did not want any part of the exploitative and oppressive relationships that were the norm around us. Among other things, we emphasized not having exclusive relationships."[26]

West and his friends believed the Bible's sexual tenets had been misinterpreted by Christian clergy throughout the ages. "There is no intellectual support for monogamy or marriage in radical Christianity, and by 'radical' I mean going back to the root. It is quite explicit in the original Gospels that most of the apostles, except for St. Paul, had multiple lady friends. Paul made a big deal about how he was one of the only ones who didn't. And the thing that he opposed the most was marriage, because when you're married, you get tied down and can't preach the Gospels. . . . Nowhere does Paul say 'Don't screw around on the side.'"

West used his knowledge of early Church history and ancient Greek to challenge other Catholic dogma. "Wherever the Bible says 'fornication,' the word does not refer to sex. 'Fornication' refers to having sex with temple prostitutes, which was a form of worshiping a pagan god. . . . Nowhere does the Bible say 'Don't screw around with the girl down the street.' It only says, 'Don't have sex with pagan prostitutes in the Holy Temple.'"

In 1966, West graduated from high school and went to Catholic University. Again, he found a group of friends who were strongly Christian yet disagreed with conventional morality. "We formed relationships that were not exclusive, but with a very strong sense of personal and emotional responsibility. We felt that exclusivity came out of an ownership model of marriage and a sense of scarcity about sex. We were part of the post-pill, pre-plague generation." West and his friends, most of them Catholic, began calling themselves "the Community." Members believed that jealousy represented insecurity. "It was seen as something that happened as the result of clumsiness on somebody's part."

Members of the Community bought a house on Capitol Hill, not far from the university. In the house they set up one bedroom, with one bed, 25 feet by 13 feet. "We got ultra-high-quality foam and special sheets. It worked very nicely because you could accommodate a random number of people on any night." There were private rooms, but the group generally all slept together in the one big bed. "Sometimes people would have sex in the common room. I remember this one time that a woman shrieked in the middle of the night and woke us all up. She and her lover were having sex and she rolled over and got stabbed in the back by his rosary."

Jonathan West was certainly not the norm among sixties Catholics. His view of the Gospels was at odds with that of even the most progressive of ordained priests. But West is interesting because he did not simply renounce the Church; rather, he and his fellow Community members believed they understood the real meaning of Christian brotherhood. They proposed an entirely new vision of Catholic community.[27]

We often assume a simple dichotomy between religion and sexual freedom. It is commonly believed that religious leaders will inevitably value sexual restraint and the irreligious favor sexual liberty. But the relationship between sex and spirituality has always been more complicated. During the sexual revolution of the late sixties and early seventies, the nuances of this relationship were explored. This exploration was possible only because theologians began to recognize the critical distinction between morality and ethics. In many ways, the so-called new morality of the period was neither new nor a morality. It was a return to ancient principles. That so many religious leaders in the late sixties and early seventies hit upon the Golden Rule as the only principle necessary to govern sexual behavior indicates how committed Americans once were to finding a rational basis for the ordering of human society.

CHAPTER 10

PERFORMING THE REVOLUTION

WHEN *OH! CALCUTTA!* opened Off Broadway in June 1969, the scene at the Eden Theater could have competed with the Academy Awards for glitz and glamour. Shirley McLaine, Joe Namath, Julie Newmar, and Hedy Lamarr were among the dozens of celebrities who arrived for the premiere. The show they were going to see was billed as two hours of titillating theater. A play on the French expression "Oh! quel cul tu as!" (Oh, what a nice ass you have), the title gave a taste of what was to come. *Oh! Calcutta!* lived up to its promise: the performance was sufficiently shocking to make many audience members squirm in their seats. The show consisted of a series of vignettes by well-known writers who had been asked to compose something of a sexual nature, among them Jules Feiffer and John Lennon. Though none of the sketches was particularly funny or well written, each contained nudity, four-letter words, and simulated sex.

Every scene in *Oh! Calcutta!* is designed to provoke. In one, the entire cast performs a slow striptease. In another, two mate-swapping couples fumble toward extramarital bliss. In one of the more imaginative, a young man stuns his father by talking casually about his orgasms. ("When I come it's like a river. It's all over the bed, and the sheets and the everything y'know, Pa?") In one of the more confrontational, a man simulates raping a woman after she measures his penis and finds it is shorter than her vagina. The show ends with all ten cast members standing naked on stage. As they strike various poses, the actors speak aloud the possible thoughts of those in the audience: "I mean what is the point, I mean what does it prove? . . . Nudity is passé. . . . She really is a natural blonde. . . . That's my daughter up there. . . . If they're having fun, why don't they have erections?"[1] The show effectively turns the spotlight on the audience, making them part of the spectacle.

The first reviews panned the production. Critic Clive Barnes wrote in the daily *New York Times*:

> Voyeurs of the city unite, you have nothing to lose but your brains. *Oh! Calcutta!* is likely to disappoint different people in different ways, but disappointment is the order of the night. To be honest, I think I can recommend the show with any vigor only to people who are extraordinary underprivileged either sexually or emotionally.

Walter Kerr of the Sunday *Times* was even less kind. "The clumsiest, more labored of jokes are permitted to succeed one another in obsessive monotony. Language no longer matters, structure no longer matters, inspiration no longer matters . . . The people on stage are not engaged in being amusing or pertinent or impertinent or imaginative."[2] Critics worried — rightly — that the use of the theater as part of the campaign against censorship would end up silencing those who supported free speech but still believed in aesthetic standards. But within a few weeks, *Oh! Calcutta!* was getting raves. In the *New York Post* Emily Genauer described the show as "the most pornographic, brutalizing, degrading, shocking, tedious, witless . . . concoction" she had ever seen, yet applauded it as "the most shatteringly effective" show to date.[3] Jack Kroll waxed rhapsodic in *Newsweek*. The show, he declared, made one "laugh, feel and think much more than most current theater," and he assured readers that the pleasures of the production were "the increasingly rare pleasures of sanity."[4] Bolstered by such effusive praise, *Oh! Calcutta!* eventually moved from Off Broadway to Broadway to become one of the longest-running shows in New York theater history, ultimately grossing over $360 million.

The show was originally conceived by Kenneth Tynan, a sharp-tongued British drama critic, whose goal was to expand the boundaries of legitimate theater well beyond what the tastes of the theatergoing middle class normally allowed. Tynan was a self-proclaimed socialist, though his unusual definition of socialism — "progress toward pleasure" — spoke volumes about his brand of politics. Tynan knew just how to play the role of the iconoclast without ever fully alienating the intelligentsia. As a schoolboy in England he had run in a mock parliamentary election on a platform calling for the repeal of all laws prohibiting divorce, sodomy, and abortion. As a professional critic of international renown, Tynan fought vigorously against the censorship of British plays. He could see straight through bourgeois hypocrisies — even in the fifties he realized that the play *Tea and Sympathy,* which many liberals praised for its critique of gender roles, was really a conventional attack on homosexuals disguised as something more benign. Tynan enjoyed hinting in public that he was a man of unusual erotic tastes: he was more interested in a woman's buttocks than her breasts, he liked to dress up in women's clothes, and he enjoyed whipping his female companions on the rear.[5]

In creating his first show, Tynan wanted an erotic event, a display of overt sensuality. He insisted that *Oh! Calcutta!* be choreographed by "a non-queer," and that it include "no crap about art or redeeming literary merit." The show, he announced, would "be expressively designed to titillate, in the most elegant and outré way." The aim was "gentle stimulation, where a fellow can take a girl he is trying to woo."[6] Tynan was the self-appointed champion of sixties hedonism, the official spokesperson for erotica consumers everywhere.

Tynan commissioned sketches from a variety of writers, instructing them to include any kind of fetish or form of eroticism except male homosexuality.* (Tynan opposed the laws against homosexuality, but he was committed to keeping the lines between straight and gay sex perfectly clear.) "The idea," he explained to a friend, "is to use artistic means to achieve erotic stimulation. Nothing that is *merely* funny or *merely* beautiful should be admitted: it must also be sexy."[7] Actors were required to strip during the audition process. As Pamela Pilkenton (a pseudonym), who was in the original Broadway cast, recalls, "I had no idea about the naked stuff. I went to the audition. . . . First I had to dance and I passed, then they asked me to sing, then they asked me to read. Then before I knew it the director was telling me that I had to do this nude audition. It was an improvisation and I had to accomplish removing my clothing during this improv while composing a letter to a friend saying that my book had been published and then I had to put my clothes back on. And I did it, and the director said, 'Okay, you got the job.' And then I went to a coffee-shop and collapsed and thought, "What did I just do?"[8] Pilkenton found herself caught in the confusion of the late sixties — eager to participate in all that was going on, but uncertain about what the consequences of her participation would be.

* Tynan was not consistently heterosexist. In a *Playboy* panel on homosexuality in April 1971, Tynan said: "A health[y] view of sex, by my standards, would be one that permitted any kind of erotic enjoyment that didn't involve coercion or the recruitment of minors."

There was plenty of simulated sex in *Oh! Calcutta!*, but Tynan's original vision was reshaped by director Jacques Levy, a former psychologist who had worked with the Open Theater, an avant-garde group committed to artistic innovation. Levy wanted nakedness, not nudity; sexual frankness, not eroticism. "Tynan had a sort of Victorian idea about what we were doing, you know, the gentleman taking his female companion to an erotic show kind of thing. I saw it more as a way of opening up an area that had been closed off, not only to performers, but to the society in general. I wanted to try to break through to that area, and to set an example for people to be inspired by . . . and to present those aspects that were very much repressed and suppressed in our society." Levy's goal was to show that heterosexual desire was normal and healthy. He also wanted to give audience members the shock of recognition: the sense of seeing themselves on stage. "I wanted the audience to be stunned, delighted, excited, and ready to cheer for what we were doing. There was part of that audience that I wanted to be scandalized — the ones who were against what we were doing. I wanted them to be aware of the fact that this was an affront."[9]

The show's choreographer, Margo Sappington, hoped to blend dance and sensuality. She wanted to free ballet from the constraints imposed on all the arts by bourgeois morality. Her collaboration with Tynan and Levy produced a show that was part camp, part erotic celebration, and part cultural critique.

Whether one went to *Oh! Calcutta!* to be aroused, challenged, or amused, one saw actors and actresses stripped bare and simulating sex. Pilkenton recalls, "People would sit through the first act and part of the second, but at some point they would run out screaming saying, "I can't believe what they're doing up there!,' or they'd hold the program in front of their face and just peek out." Charles H. Keating, Jr., chairman of Citizens for Decent Literature, could barely restrain his fury:

> *Oh! Calcutta!* is pure pornography — a two hour orgy, principally enacted in the nude. It is not possible to verbally depict the depravity, deviation, eroticism or the utter filth of the play. Male and female players fondle each other, commit or simulate intercourse, sodomy, cunnilingus, masturbation, sadism, ad nauseam. This abomination . . . is proposed to be televised live or by video-tape across the nation. . . . Never in Rome, Greece or the most debauched nation in history has such utter filth been projected to all parts of a nation. If there is or ever was any such constitutional prerogative of the American people to have the exercise of the police power in the interests of the public health and welfare, this is it.[10]

Keating wanted the show shut down and the producers hauled off to jail. But the production had been approved by a member of the mayor's office (who came to rehearsals to make sure that there was no penetration or actual arousal on stage), so Keating's demands would never be met. It was simply too late to revive 1950s social standards.

A brazen, if often silly, show, *Oh! Calcutta!* effectively turned sex into spectacle. Despite Keating's tirade, the show found a ready audience. Jack Kroll noted: "With *Oh! Calcutta!* the sexual revolution reaches its middle level — middle-class, middle-brow."[11] Tourists from across the country kept *Oh! Calcutta!* running for an astonishing 1,314 performances. The result was not exactly what creator Kenneth Tynan had had in mind. "The fact that people from the Midwest loved the show shocked everyone except the people from the Midwest," says Jacques Levy. When dramatist Bernard Grossman expressed concern that the trend toward theater nudity might bring down the wrath of conservatives in Congress, who could cut funding for the newly created National Endowment for the Arts, he was all but ignored.[12] *Oh! Calcutta!* was too much of a commercial hit to worry about a future backlash. The show's appeal demonstrated that middle-class Americans were eager to participate in the sexual revolution — or at least observe it from their safe seats in the Eden Theater.

The explosion of on-stage nudity in the late sixties redefined the sexual revolution. It was a clear symbol that times were changing, that puritanical attitudes were disappearing. Theater critics might occasionally fret about the collapse of artistic standards, but for the most part, the cultural elite and the busloads of Midwestern tourists alike welcomed the avant-garde assault on public decorum. Shows like *Oh! Calcutta!* were hailed as proof that backward America was finally becoming liberated. As the editors of *Newsweek* proclaimed in a "special report" in 1969 on sex and the arts:

> In a sense there is no going back. The Victorian age with its hypocrisies and tragic repressions passed, and the Freudian revolution left an irrevocable psychic impetus for self-knowledge and rational freedom. There are still many unexplored continents in the human condition, and the instinct to explore and consolidate new emotional and moral terrains is inescapable. In a mass society, with its omnipresent media that give our nervous system no rest, excesses and vulgarities are inevitable. But the upshot cannot be repression. The law has seen that it cannot work, artists know that it is ugly and dangerous, social thinkers realize that it is reactionary and stifles progressive energies in the body politic, and young people, with their new naïvetés that have replaced the old naïvetés of their fathers, know that it is not fun to live that way. More than ever we need

direction from mature leaders who see the forward energies of their age clearly and can enter into a rational and life-enhancing social covenant with those who will inherit the society.[13]

Newsweek effectively gave its imprimatur to the sexualization of the American stage.

Long before the 1960s, American theater had become associated with sex. The Puritans outlawed theater as a matter of course. Later, vaudeville attracted itinerant actors, who were immune to the moral views of the straitlaced bourgeoisie. Burlesque blurred the lines between art and pornography. Throughout the nineteenth century, actresses stripped off their costumes as often as they put them on. Tableaux vivants — living portraits of notable scenes from paintings and literature (usually paintings along the lines of *The Greek Slave* and *The Birth of Venus*) — featured nude female models in various artistic poses for the benefit of paying spectators.[14] The celebrated actresses of the 1860s, women like Adah Isaacs Menken and Lydia Thompson, appeared on stage wearing next to nothing. To many moralists, there seemed to be only the finest of lines between getting paid to perform on stage and getting paid to perform in the bedroom. Even as vaudeville was replaced by "legitimate" playhouses, theater remained, in the public imagination, guilty by association. Cities established censorship boards to monitor public performances. Playhouses were regarded as unseemly, dangerous places. They were all too often to be found in seedy neighborhoods, surrounded by saloons and boardinghouses. Compromising and uncertain, a life in the theater was out of the question for most middle-class youngsters well into the twentieth century.

Between the 1920s and the 1940s, the American theater was able to improve its reputation. Playwrights pumped out light comedies and cheerful musicals that steered clear of sexual subjects. In the fifties, however, Tennessee Williams began introducing themes such as homosexuality, nymphomania, rape, and impotence. Williams's plays raised important questions about the human condition but rarely offered a sustained critique of society's mores. In the early sixties, avant-garde artists in New York's Greenwich Village resolved to turn theater into a weapon of social protest. Inspired by Jean-Paul Sarte, Bertolt Brecht, Antonin Artaud, and other European intellectuals, they declared war on bourgeois morality, often using nudity on stage to shock audiences out of their complacency.

By the late sixties, a trend toward theater nudity was apparent. On Broadway, actresses regularly stripped off their blouses. Off Broadway, shows like *A Christmas Turkey* and *Tennis Anyone* featured actors without any clothes on at all. Rochelle Owen's *Futz,* about a man in love with a pig, included simulations of oral, anal, and genital intercourse. In Los Angeles, Sal Mineo's production of *Fortune and Men's Eyes,* a play about prison life, starring Don Johnson, shocked spectators with a scene of Johnson being raped by his fellow prisoners. *Dionysus in 69,* staged at a garage in New York's warehouse district, dramatized a Greek orgy.[15] The extraordinarily strong economy of the late sixties created an unusually large audience for theater, even avant-garde experimental theater. More Americans than ever before had the time and money to go to shows, and this made it possible for thespians to explore the limits of self-expression on stage without worry. If some were offended, there would always be others to buy tickets. Stage nudity was so prevalent by the end of 1968 — and so popular — that the editors of *After Dark* virtually dedicated the magazine to documenting the nude male in theater and dance. Playwright Robert Anderson highlighted the trend in *The Shock of Recognition,* a comedy about a writer who desperately wants to put an "average," middle-aged man on stage naked, but is stymied by a reluctant director.

With the arrival of international jet travel in the midsixties, Americans began comparing their own social policies with those of other nations. They soon realized that the Scandinavians were particularly adept at balancing the needs of the community with those of the individual and were apparently immune to the Judeo-Christians concerns about the body. As one woman wrote to her boyfriend in Manhattan while she was vacationing in Sweden in 1967, "The children run naked on the streets of Stockholm. Hard to imagine that on Madison Avenue."[16] Impressed by the well-ordered nature of Scandanavian society, liberal Americans in the late sixties looked to northern Europe for guidance in developing modern laws and public policies. As successful social engineers, the Scandinavians had no rivals. In 1967, Denmark abolished all of its censorship laws; studies showing that the policy led to a decline in sex crimes gave American liberals new cause for optimism. C. L. Sulzberger, chief foreign affairs correspondent for the *New York Times,* articulated the liberal view in 1969. "There is nothing in the least bit either unwholesome or immoral about the Danes, who simply share with Benjamin Franklin, an American never renowned for excessive Puritanism, that honesty is the best policy." To Sulzberger, who was excited by pilot studies showing "a decline in sexual delinquency," the Danish experiment was "admirable for its bold effort to sweep aside shibboleths that have been confusing mankind for centuries."[17]

With the show *Hair,* which opened Off Broadway in 1967 and soon moved to a Broadway theater, Americans had an opportunity to catch up with Danish modernists. An "American tribal love-rock musical" celebrating hippies and their rebellion against mainstream society, *Hair* brought the energy and vitality of the counterculture to the commercial New York stage. The show was popular with the middle-class public, running 1,750 performances. Organized loosely around the struggle for one young man to decide whether or not to comply with the draft, *Hair* was deliberately confrontational. "Sodomy, fellatio, cunnilingus, pederasty. Father, why do these words sound so nasty?" asked the characters early in the show. Audiences were forced to weigh the violence of Vietnam against the innocent playfulness of sex and drugs, to question their assumptions about the significance of such superficial matters as dress and hairstyle, to contemplate the meaning of individualism and liberty. The creators knew how to shock audiences without driving them away. The first act ended with the entire cast facing the audience naked. The sexual revolution had clearly come to Broadway.

Avant-garde artists were excited by *Hair's* mainstream success but were eager to test the limits of New York City's tolerance for theatrical realism. Off Broadway in 1961, the director of *Sweet Eros* had actress Sally Kirkland appear nude on stage for a full forty-five minutes.[18] Several months after *Hair's* Broadway opening, a group of young thespians put on *Che,* a play virtually designed to arouse the ire of authorities. In *Che,* a political satire with the tagline "Don't Bite the Cock that Feeds You," actors spent most of their time on stage nude simulating various sex acts. According to the *New Republic* magazine, the play's unambiguous message was "that power is a question of who literally . . . screws whom."[19] Before the opening-night performance, the four members of the cast, all "in costume," piled into a limousine, drove around the city, returned to the theater, and then climbed out and walked naked through the backstage door. The twenty-one-year-old actor who played the U.S. president recalls, "I loved it. I was young and proud of my body and I guess I was kind of an exhibitionist." Audience members were encouraged to participate in the quasi-pornographic performance. This was all too much for city police, who busted the show on opening night, just as the cast members were taking their bows. When the officers began arresting the actors, the show's naked star, Larry Bercowitz, announced to the departing audience members that the real performance was only beginning. A police officer instructed Bercowitz to put on some clothes, but he looked at the officer and said, in his loudest voice, "Take me naked or don't take me at all," and then began lecturing him about the real meaning of obscenity. "I let him know that killing and violence are OBSCENE, not Art or Love, or simulated Love," Bercowitz wrote that night in jail.

The ten prisoners were charged with consensual sodomy, obscenity, and public lewdness. The cast members felt the arrest was groundless (all of the sex acts on stage were simulated) and a violation of their civil rights. As Bercovitz wrote behind bars,

> As far as I'm concerned the obscenity in the world is the situation in which Richard C. Hot Lips is standing in a field in Viet Nam while bullets are flying over his head reporting to us so that we can see that the WAR really exists, so that we can determine whether or not we are winning. Man, WAR is OBSCENE!!! Violence is what is obscene and we enact violence on stage in "Che," the play, to show people to themselves. . . . Frustration and repression leads to violence. Lack of love mental and physical leads to violence, then to war. . . . MAKE LOVE NOT WAR!!!

The cast members were released after one night in jail. A three-judge panel was convened to hear the case. Since much of the sex in the play was homoerotic — and homophobia was still rampant, even in the theater community — few were willing to come to the show's defense. Famed Broadway producer David Merrick testified against the cast, saying that *Che* was anything but art. The judges acquitted the ten defendants on the sodomy and obscenity charges but found them guilty of public lewdness.[20] *Che* reopened, but the show was toned down to avoid further prosecutions.

Oh! Calcutta!'s extraordinary success was due in part because it struck a balance between the idealism of *Hair* and the audacity of *Che*. But it would never have made it to Broadway if other aspects of American culture had not been changing as rapidly as the New York stage. The evolution of the motion picture, in particular, reflected and encouraged the revolt against reticence. Between 1967 and 1969, movies underwent a marked transformation as barriers against four-letter words, nudity, and sexual subject matter came tumbling down. Movie producers and directors, like their counterparts in the theater, realized that American audiences were eager to be titillated and would pay to see "racy" material, so long as it did not transgress certain unspoken limits.

More than any other mass medium, motion pictures had long worried authorities. Movies were believed to have a powerful and immediate effect on those segments of the population most "susceptible" to pernicious influences: women, children, blacks, the poor. Ever since the earliest days of cinema, self-appointed guardians of the public morals had fought to keep producers in line. (Early films, after all, had contained a good bit of nudity and overt sexuality.) After a series of sex scandals and threats of congressional intervention, Hollywood producers in the 1930s had agreed to a policy of self-censorship. Still, watchdog organizations like the Catholic Legion of Decency, formed in 1934, maintained constant surveillance over Hollywood to protect the innocent from explicit sex. For decades, the Legion of Decency used the threat of nationwide boycotts to force film producers to comply with its standards for family fare.

The transformation of the film business in the midsixties made it economically impossible for Hollywood to continue the policy of self-censorship, and it directly undercut the power of the Legion of Decency. The rise of independent distributors and theaters, the influx of foreign films, and the growth of a minor industry in "sexploitation" pictures rendered the Hollywood studio system practically obsolete. As Hollywood studios gave way to independent producers, the rules regarding sex on the screen were rewritten.

Cheaply made, widely distributed "sexploitation" films managed to capture a large segment of the teenage market. Russ Meyer's *Immoral Mr. Teas,* (1959), a film without dialogue or plot but with plenty of bouncing bare breasts, cost $24,000 to make and generated over $1 million in gross profits. Meyer's *Vixen* (1968), with a scene in which a woman rubs a fish over her body, cost $76,000 and grossed $6 million.[21]

With tastes expanding and the economy booming, art houses opened in most of the nation's big cities. These small theaters screened the homoerotic underground films produced by Andy Warhol, Jack Smith, and Kenneth Anger. In most of Warhol's films, the camera lingered over Joe Dallesandro's lean, muscular, naked body. A hustler willing to have sex with anyone, male or female, as long as he was going to get paid, Dallesandro was the model of a new sexual antihero. Needless to say, authorities tried their best to close down theaters showing Warhol's films.[22] Ironically, Warhol's director, Paul Morrissey, was actually eager to show the damaging effects of the sexual revolution, not to glorify erotic liberation. He wanted to document the dehumanizing nature of prostitution and casual sex. But audiences and authorities alike assumed that Morrissey's films were a celebration of sexual freedom.

Foreign filmmakers played a key role in defining the motion picture as a modern art form. To European writers and directors, the finest movies stayed true to life, allowing, as theater did, for the shock of recognition. In 1967, the British film *Ulysses,* based on the Joyce novel, became the first in which an actor uttered the word *fuck.*[23] *Georgy Girl* (1966), another British import, showed nude male actors from the rear. Since sixties audiences were always hungry for the "new," these foreign made films had a clear advantage over more traditional Hollywood fare. Sometimes, however, the threat of embargo by customs officials was so strong that foreign films were edited for the American market. British director Lindsay Anderson, for instance, made two versions of his film *If* . . . (1968), both of which included a shower scene at a boys' school. In the version shot for European audiences, the boys were naked. In the American version, the boys were draped in towels. Increasingly, however, filmmakers refused to bow to official morality. British director Ken Russell's adaptation of D. H. Lawrence's *Women in Love* showed two male actors wrestling in the nude in what amounted to a lengthy overtly homoerotic scene.

Foreign films even began to suggest intercourse. In 1969, the Swedish import *I Am Curious (Yellow)* became a cult classic after customs officials attempted to ban the film. Distributed by anti-censorship crusader Barney Rosset, *I Am Curious (Yellow)* was primarily political in content, with a meandering, hard-to-follow plot, but it contained numerous scenes suggesting heterosexual intercourse.

The movie follows the adventures of a young blonde named Lena, who divides her time between socialist politics and sexual exploration. With the help of marriage manuals, Lena and her boyfriend make love in various positions and locales. In one scene, they have sex on the balustrade of the royal palace while a guard looks on. In another they attempt to have intercourse in the lotus position. At one point, Lena even kisses Borjë's penis ("small, light, childishly contented kisses," according to the screenplay).

Full frontal nudity, suggested acts of intercourse, and the depiction of fellatio led to the seizure of the film by U.S. customs officials in 1968. During the initial trial, many critics, including several clergymen, came to the film's defense, but the jury nevertheless agreed with the government that the film was obscene. The obscenity ruling only generated more interest in the picture, and when the decision was overturned on appeal, *I Am Curious (Yellow)* became one of the most discussed films of the decade. Thousands waited in long lines to see the picture, despite its tedious pace and the fact that it consisted mostly of banal commentary on Sweden's political neutrality.[24] Men may have landed on the moon, but to many *I Am Curious (Yellow)* was *the* event of 1969. Nancy Surek, who was in her early thirties and a mother of two at the time the film opened, felt like she simply "had to see it." There were lines around the block at the Cinema 57 in Manhattan. Even former first lady Jacqueline Kennedy Onassis attended the film. Liberal critics, continuing to insist on a distinction between "erotic realism" and "pornography," assured themselves that *I Am Curious (Yellow)* was the former and not the latter. As *New York Times* film critic Vincent Canby wrote, "[The scenes are] explicit, honest and so unaffectedly frank as to be nonpornographic. . . . By acknowledging the existence of genitalia and their function in the act of love, the movie salvages the depiction of physical love from the scrap heap of exploitation, camp and stag films." (Not everyone was so sanguine. On June 6, 1969, a theater showing *I Am Curious (Yellow)* in Houston was deliberately set ablaze.)[25]

Throughout the late sixties and early seventies, film after film explored the dynamics of human sexuality. *A Clockwork Orange, Midnight Cowboy,* and Pier Paolo Pasolini's version of Boccaccio's bawdy fourteenth-century classic *The Decameron* abolished the last remnants of cinematic reticence. On April 7, 1969, Justice Thurgood Marshall issued the majority opinion of the Supreme Court in the case *Stanley v. Georgia.* Police had raided an Atlanta man's home and seized three rolls of 8mm film; when the movies turned out to be hard-core stag films, the man was arrested, convicted, and sentenced to a year in jail. The high court declared that American citizens had the right to enjoy whatever sexual materials they pleased in the privacy of their own home; police officers had no business seizing pornography out of a man's dresser drawer. In *Stanley v. Georgia,* erotic consumerism found official recognition. It seemed to many that censorship was about to disappear forever.

The theater and film of the latè sixties can be understood only when placed in the context of the time. The anti-establishment sentiment stirred up by the war spilled over into the leisure activities of many Americans. A significant number of young people experimented with marijuana and psychedelic drugs. Every week, millions of viewers were tuning in to *Laugh-In,* a TV comedy sketch show with a bawdy sense of humor that was breaking all the rules of network television. *Screw,* a tabloid weekly devoted entirely to sex, was on the newsstands throughout New York. In almost every city, the local alternative paper carried the raunchy cartoons of R. Crumb.

At the same time *Hair* was playing Off Broadway, the sexual revolution was reverberating throughout the youth culture. Rock concerts had become vast outdoor gatherings, where drugs, music, sex, and politics all blurred into one. Jim Morrison of the Doors, whose trademark "young lion" image included a mane of unruly hair, a bare chest, a thin beaded necklace, and skin-tight black leather pants, recognized better than anyone else the erotic dimension of rock concerts:

> When we perform, we're participating in the creation of a world, and we celebrate that creation with the audience. It becomes the sculpture of bodies in action. That's politics, but our power is sexual. We make concerts sexual politics. The sex starts with me, then moves out to include the charmed circle of musicians onstage. The music we make goes out to the

audience and interacts with them. . . . so the whole sex thing works out to be one big ball of fire.[26]

Morrison called himself an "erotic politician." At a 1967 concert in New Haven, he ran into conflict with the police. First, an officer found him "making out" with an eighteen-year-old girl backstage. Not recognizing Morrison, the officer instructed the two to desist. According to Morrison's biographer, he "grabbed his own crotch and told the cop 'eat it!' " After several more antagonistic movements, the office sprayed Morrison with Mace. Later, during the performance, Morrison accused the police of brutality. He then went on to sing "Back Door Man":

> Oh, I'm a back door man
> I am a back door man
> Well, the men don't know;
> But the little girls understand.

Morrison was arrested and charged with lewd behavior. Most sixties music was not sexually explicit — drugs and politics, not sex, were the major themes of the day — but the link between rock and sex was clear. Rock concerts were becoming scenes of Dionysian disorder. At a 1969 concert in Miami, Morrison encouraged the audience members to strip off their clothes. "Man, I'd love to see a little nakedness around here . . . grab your friend and love him. Take your clothes off and love each other." As the drugged-out crowd shed their clothes, Morrison teased and taunted them. "You wanna see my cock, don't you? That's what you came for, isn't it?"[27] (It is unclear whether Morrison did expose himself on stage. But many at the time believe he did, and Morrison certainly encouraged the belief.)

The era itself was a highly theatrical time. Hippies, artists, and activists were all, in a sense, "on stage." Their activities were constantly photographed, their every utterance tape-recorded, their doings discussed in the pages of national newspapers and magazines. It was nearly impossible to live through the sixties without experiencing a sense that one was part of a significant moment in the drama of history.

The theatricality of the sixties extended to the act of participating in the sexual revolution. A vicarious way to participate was to attend a show like *Oh! Calcutta!* or a film like *I Am Curious (Yellow)*. And, consciously or unconsciously, urbanites went to the theater to be on stage themselves. The very act of going to a risqué show was a performance, which one could expect to be discussed, examined, and reviewed by the mass media. Article after article, news broadcast after news broadcast commented on the men and women who were "liberated" enough to sit through a show like *Oh! Calcutta!* The cultural spotlight was aimed directly at those who visited smoky art houses to view Warhol films or waited in lines to see the latest Swedish import. When Jacqueline Kennedy Onassis went to see *I Am Curious (Yellow)* in Manhattan, photographers waited outside the theater. (She left early and got into a brawl with one of the photographers, an event that was then covered by all the major newspapers.)[28] In fact, audiences received nearly as much attention as the shows they went to see. Some audience members, like Cynthia Albritton, better known as Cynthia Plaster Caster, who made plaster casts of rock stars' erections, knew that their backstage boldness would draw the media's focus, but even less celebrated consumers of popular culture found themselves the subjects of intense speculation. As Jerry Talmer wrote in the *New York Post* about the opening night of *Oh! Calcutta!*, "The audience was more interesting than the show."[29] It is no accident that when a film version of the show was made, it began with shots of audience members filing into the theater.

There was an art to the performance of sexual liberation, even if it was only for the benefit of one's next-door neighbors.[30] Men wore their shirts open at the collar, exposing their chest hair and perhaps the hint of a gold chain. Some wore colorful scarves, signifying both fashion consciousness and a sophisticated sensuality. Tight pants accentuated the buttocks and the genitals. Young women wore leather miniskirts and thigh-high boots. Rudi Gernreich's topless swimsuit opened the door to body stockings and see-through clothing.

No one worked harder at performing the role of the sexually liberated person than Hugh Hefner, the publisher of *Playboy*. Hefner carefully crafted his public image, always appearing in costume: his signature silken smoking jacket. The lead character in his own personal drama, he surrounded himself with a supporting cast of beautiful young women and threw lavish parties where the rich and famous made cameo appearances. He had cameras installed in his bedrooms so that his sexual encounters could be filmed for later viewing. For a while, Hefner appeared as the host of his own television show, *Playboy's Penthouse.*

The performative quality of the sixties in general and the sexual revolution in particular found its ultimate expression in "happenings," semi-spontaneous, quasi-artistic events that were a form of street theater designed to wake the Western world from its slumber. Though happenings did not always involve nudity or sex, often enough male and female spectators, eager to demonstrate their liberatedness, shed their clothes to participate. At some happenings, participants covered their bodies in paint. At others, they actually had sex with total strangers. As Al Hansen, a leader of the happenings movement, explained,

Anyone can be a performer in a happening. The challenge is for the creator of the happening to choose people who will do a good job, i.e., do exactly as they are told and yet transcend that. The role each person is given to play in my happenings is a limitation that they are expected to surmount . . . I want the performers to surprise me and they usually do.[31]

At an early sixties happening at Cornell University, female participants took off their blouses, waved them over their heads, and sang rock songs while the male participants hurled red smoke flares into a trash heap. At a happening titled "Soap" that took place at Florida State University, participants first urinated on articles of their own clothing, then divided into couples. One member of each couple stripped naked, to be covered in jam by his or her partner.[32] By the end of 1969, nude happenings were taking place from coast to coast. Not every happening had a sexual component, but spectators were always entitled to defy bourgeois morality by stripping off their street clothes and joining in the event. The happening became the model for all theater in the sixties; in fact, it became the model for demonstrations, rallies, rock concerts, and "participatory democracy" writ large. As director Jacques Levy says, *Oh! Calcutta!* was itself a happening.

The overwhelming success of *Oh! Calcutta!, Hair,* and *I Am Curious (Yellow)* suggested that many were eager to participate in the production of a new, sexually liberated society. They were willing to wear the costumes, speak the lines, and follow the stage directions of the sexual revolution. But the more Americans joined in the collective performance of sexual freedom, the more frustrated some felt. In an article in the *Saturday Evening Post* in 1968, writer Arno Karlen declared his disappointment with the superficial changes he saw taking place:

> Four-letter words and miniskirts don't mean people act very differently in bed. Anyone who thinks the most basic sexual values have changed might try . . . announcing publicly that he is currently enjoying adultery or homosexuality. . . . We need a real [sexual revolution] badly — a real one that will allow people to live healthy, expressive sexual lives without legal penalties and social obstacle courses. As in another emotion-laden issue, the black man's fight for progress, the smug cant of progress lets people evade the need for deep, difficult change.[33]

For Karlen, the sexual revolution was about much more than nude shows on Broadway. It was about translating the principles of secular humanism into significant social reform. If one really wanted to transform society, one would have to abolish all obstacles to personal self-expression.

The celebration of nakedness in the late sixties could be seen as a direct assault on the "power structure." By allowing society to gaze upon the naked human form, artists hoped to topple the entire social order. If every man from the chief justice of the Supreme Court down to the local police sergeant, if every woman from the first lady to one's own younger sister, could be revealed as Shakespeare's "poor, bare, forked animal," then all of society's illusions would be open to inspection.

The sexual revolution, as Karlen (any many others) saw it, was a revolution against shame. Shame kept people from being honest with one another. Shame kept people from enjoying themselves. Shame kept people from resisting laws they opposed in private. Shame kept people from being fully alive.

But abolishing shame was no easy matter. It was not nearly as simple as eliminating censorship or promoting contraception. Western culture was shot through with shame about sex. As a result, children were taught to be ashamed of their bodies and their desires from the first moments of cognition. They carried this shame into adulthood and learned never to admit their fantasies and fears. But to root out shame would require an attack on one of the most basic tenets of bourgeois morality: the prohibition of "self-abuse." So long as individuals were afraid to admit to the practice of masturbation, the rest of sexual revolution amounted to a sham. As the patrons filed out of the Eden Theater after the opening-night performance of *Oh! Calcutta!* in June 1969, which one of them was willing to confess to a desire to go home and masturbate to the memory of what was shown on stage?

CHAPTER 11

STICKY FINGERS

W HEN TREVOR LAKE (a pseudonym) was growing up in 1940s Indiana, there was nothing more shameful or secretive than masturbation. "My father caught me when I was twelve. I was jerking off in my room. Boy, there was hell to pay. He told me I was a pervert. He used a belt on my behind." Trevor's father was a Baptist, though the family went to church only on Easter and Christmas, and sex was a highly charged issue in the Lake household. "He caught me a couple of times after that and every time, he whipped me with the belt." Terrified of his father's wrath, Trevor tried to stop masturbating, but he says, "I couldn't help myself." One reason he did not stop was that he and his buddies would masturbate together. "We would play games. You know, we'd try to see who could shoot first or shoot the farthest." Still, his father's attitudes and actions took their toll: As an adult, Lake would suffer from impotence nearly every time he tried to have sexual inter-course with a woman.

Actor Jack Lemmon recalls his own experience growing up in the 1930s.

> Once my mother . . . came in and sat on the edge of my bed as I was lying down to go to sleep. I was around thirteen. And she said, "Do you ever play with your thing?" — or whatever she called it. I'm sure she didn't say cock or something like that. And lying, I said, "No. Why?" And she said, "Well, that's good, because it can make you crazy."

When famed pediatrician Benjamin Spock was a young boy, his mother took a similar tack. "She would come and sit on the side of the bed, after

I'd gone to bed, or take me into the den, and say, 'Now, Bennie, you will keep yourself pure, and I hope you will keep pure thoughts. You do want to have normal children and be worthy of a fine wife, don't you?'"[1]

By 1969, masturbation was one of the few sexual practices that was still taboo. To acknowledge that one masturbated was to admit to a personal failing, a weakness of will, an unhealthy obsession. One observer noted in 1974:

> [A]side from pubescent boys . . . most people who masturbate remain more or less guilt ridden about it, and nearly all of them are extremely secretive about their masturbating and would be horribly embarrassed to have anyone know the truth. In speaking of the act, practically everyone is jocular, condescending or scornful, thus tacitly implying that it is something he or she could never stoop to. Even though any reasonably well-informed single young man or woman knows that nearly every other single man or woman masturbates at least occasionally, almost no one will admit, even to an intimate friend, that he or she does so. It is far easier to admit that one does not believe in God, or was once a Communist, or was born illegitimately, than that one sometimes fondles a part of his own body to the point of orgiastic release.[2]

Masturbation, in other words, remained a source of intense anxiety.

Alfred Kinsey had reported in the late forties and early fifties that most men and women masturbated, but Kinsey's sociological conclusions were just that: cold academic observations without the kind of personal testimony needed to give them life. Throughout the early sixties, psychologists and sex educators tried to dispel the many myths surrounding masturbation, but the general reluctance to concede that one personally engaged in autoeroticism precluded popular enlightenment.

It was not until Philip Roth's 1969 novel *Portnoy's Complaint* that Americans began to acknowledge the practice. *Portnoy's Complaint* was nothing less than a signed confession of guilt for years of sexual self-stimulation. The author had spent over five years in psychoanalysis, and his book was written as a single monologue by a patient to his analyst. Though it was fiction, the first-person narrative voice gave *Portnoy's Complaint* an autobiographical feel. Alexander Portnoy, the neurotic hero of the novel, unburdens himself by sharing his deepest, darkest secrets:

> Then came adolescence — half my waking life spent locked behind the bathroom door, firing my wad down the toilet bowl, or into the soiled clothes in the laundry hamper, or splat, up against the medicine-chest mirror, before which I stood in my dropped drawers so I could see how it looked coming out. Or else I was doubled over my flying fist, eyes pressed closed but mouth wide open, to take that sticky sauce of buttermilk and

Clorox on my tongue and teeth. . . . Through a world of matted handkerchiefs and crumpled Kleenex and stained pajamas, I moved my raw and swollen penis, perpetually in dread that my loathsomeness would be discovered by someone stealing upon me just as I was in the frenzy of dropping my load.

Once, when his own fist would not do, Portnoy tells us, he "banged" a "purplish piece of raw liver" he borrowed from his mother's refrigerator. "Now you know the worst thing I have ever done," Portnoy admits with unrelenting candor. "I fucked my own family's dinner."[3]

Portnoy's Complaint was an instant best-seller. There were waiting lists at New York City libraries to borrow a copy. Philip Roth, then teaching literature at the University of Pennsylvania, had single-handedly (so to speak) transformed the American literary landscape.[4]

Almost all male mammals masturbate to the point of orgasm. Some male primates, like chimpanzees and rhesus monkeys, even practice auto-fellatio.[5] It is a truism among sociologists of sex that all men masturbate at some point in their lives. So how did human beings come to regard masturbation as a form of sin and "self-abuse"?

As with many Western taboos, the notion that masturbation is morally wrong originated with Judaism and became a central tenet of Christianity. During the Middle Ages, masturbation was regarded by church authorities as a violation of God's law, but little was done to stamp out the practice. Opposition to masturbation on "medical" grounds did not emerge until the eighteenth century, and only then by an accident of history. The manufacturer of a powder meant to cure individuals of the desire to masturbate published a promotional pamphlet titled *Onania, or the Heinous Sin of Self-Pollution,* which declared that masturbation led to gonorrhea, blindness, insanity, and other crippling conditions. Although *Onania* was just an advertising gimmick, readers assumed it was a serious scientific treatise. By the late 1700s and early 1800s, authorities were doing everything in their power to stop children from masturbating. Rousseau urged eighteenth-century educators to maintain constant surveillance over their young male wards. "Do not leave [a boy] alone during the day or night; at least sleep in his bed . . . If he once knows that dangerous supplement, he is lost indeed."[6] In the United States, doctors recommended the circumcision of all male infants, as a means of reducing the temptation to "self-abuse."[7]

Various devices were developed to make it impossible for a young man to have so much as a nocturnal emission. One such device included a metal strap designed to fit around the penis. The strap was attached to an electrical source that would emit an alarm if the strap expanded. Presumably, the person wearing the device would be jolted from his slumber and his erection would subside.[8] Other devices possessed straps with sharp spikes that stabbed the penis if it began to become erect. If these machines did not work, some doctors recommended cauterizing the urethra. In the nineteenth century in the United States, health reformer Sylvester Graham was so worried about masturbation that he invented dry crackers to soak up young men's sexual desires. In the early twentieth century, sex educators stressed that masturbation would both weaken men physically and deplete them of the kind of moral strength necessary to succeed in a competitive society.* C. S. Lewis's 1941 novel *The Screwtape Letters* contained an explicit warning to children about the dangers of masturbation.[9]

Before 1969, it was practically impossible for a young man to grow up in America without hearing about the "dangers" of masturbation. Many boys first learned of such dangers from the Boy Scout Handbook, which said in no uncertain terms that masturbation was wrong. Rumors circulated that masturbation caused pimples, warts, fatigue, insomnia, weak vision, stomach ulcers, mental illness, impotence, and a host of other unwelcome conditions. Cartoonist Al Capp recalls,

> I had an innocent upbringing, and yet I felt terribly depraved. We were all terrified and believed without any question that masturbating would soften our brains and dim our eyesight. We all knew that it was a dreadful, destructive thing to do, and anytime any of us did it we walked around hangdog and shamefaced, knowing we would never grow up to be quite the men we ought to be.[10]

American institutions did not treat masturbation lightly. The official policy of the United States Naval Academy at Annapolis during the first half of the twentieth century was to refuse admission to any candidate if the examining surgeon could detect "evidence" of masturbation. Patients in mental institutions caught masturbating were often put into straitjackets or otherwise physically restrained.[11] A 1959 study of medical students showed that 50 percent of medical school seniors in

---

* Many explanations have been put forward to account for the rise of pseudo-scientific claims about the dangers of masturbation. Some argue that industrial capitalism, which was just beginning to emerge in the early modern period, demanded an ethic of delayed gratification. Others argue that doctors, educators, and like-minded experts were attempting to assert their authority over sexual matters as a way of gaining professional power. Still others claim that early moderns were eager to promote sociability and that masturbation was symbolic of antisocial tendencies.

Philadelphia believed masturbation led to insanity, a view that was shared by a significant number of faculty members as well.[12]

The American aversion to masturbation reverberated throughout the culture. Before 1969, even commercial forms of sexual titillation aimed at men (such as burlesque, pinups, skin magazines, and topless dancing) carefully shunned any association with masturbation. Burlesque, for instance, styled itself as light entertainment. Men took their wives — and sometimes even their daughters — to burlesque shows. No man would have dreamed of masturbating in the back rows of a burlesque house. In the 1940s, pinups were not to be confused with pornography: they were meant merely to make soldiers think fondly of the girls back home. And they were certainly not meant to encourage masturbation, which, military commanders believed, would weaken the fighting spirit. In the fifties, *Playboy* and other men's magazines portrayed themselves as serious literary journals, or as lighthearted escapes from the pressures of work and marriage. *Playboy* was something to toss on the coffee table, not to keep in a bedroom drawer. Likewise, Playboy Clubs and topless bars were coded as casual retreats from everyday life. At the most, men might gawk at the waitresses or dancers, but masturbation was strictly forbidden. No matter what the form of commercial eroticism, masturbation was either never acknowledged (as in the case of pinups and men's magazines) or was expressly prohibited (as in the case of burlesque, Playboy Clubs, and topless bars). A healthy man might want to look at naked women, he might enjoy sharing the experience with his buddies, he might choose to subscribe to a "girlie" magazine, but when it came time to satiate his sexual desires, he found an actual partner. To admit to "jerking off" was to admit to being less than a man.

If as late as the 1960s American men felt shame and guilt for engaging in masturbation, it is hard to imagine how women felt. Most young girls growing up before the sexual revolution knew little about their own genitals. Country singer Loretta Lynn says that when she was twenty-six, a doctor "told me about this little deelybob we women got on the outside. I didn't know anything about this little deelybob, and it's funny that my husband didn't know about it either."

Actress Sally Kellerman recalls, "Every time I masturbated, I said, 'Oh, God, I'm never going to do this again.'"[13] The Victorian notion that women were not supposed to have sexual desires shaped attitudes toward masturbation well into the twentieth century.

When Alfred Kinsey interviewed women in the 1940s about their sexual practices, he found that many believed masturbation caused poor posture, ovarian cysts, cancer, appendicitis, sterility, headaches, kidney problems, hormone imbalance, and heart trouble. Freudian psychoanalysts added their own items to the list. Not infrequently, psychoanalysts told their female patients that masturbation would consign them to a lifetime of frigidity and psychosexual immaturity.[14]

Though less is known about masturbation among female mammals than among male mammals, it has been shown that female squirrels, ferrets, horses, cows, elephants, dogs, baboons, monkeys, chimpanzees, rabbits, rats, and even porcupines stimulate their own genitals. Though Kinsey's statistics should by no means be used uncritically, he reported in 1953 that 58 percent of all American women masturbate to orgasm at some point in their lives.[15]

No matter how universal masturbation may be, women who masturbated in the 1960s, or had masturbated as young girls, usually felt intense remorse and self-loathing. Betty Dodson, who grew up in Wichita, Kansas, in the thirties and forties, began masturbating at age five. As an adult, she said, "I was made to feel that masturbating meant there was something wrong with my sex life, that I should get my sexual pleasure from the man's penis only, not from my clitoris by myself." When she was still a girl, Dodson used a mirror to look at her genitals. "I looked at my sweet little child's cunt and was instantly horrified!!!," she wrote in *Liberating Masturbation* (1974). "I was obviously deformed. I happen to have the style of genitals that has the inner lips extended and when I saw them hanging out . . . I thought I had stretched them like that from masturbating. . . . I swore off masturbating [immediately]." As she grew older, Dodson's worst fears were confirmed by others. "Coming from the 'Bible Belt' in Kansas, I knew very well where the Church and conservative moralists stood. But even supposedly liberal friends put down masturbation and made it clear that it was a second-rate sexual activity. My only source of sex information in those days was dreary marriage manuals and random bits of male-oriented Victorian psychiatry. When I finally made it to the couch, therapists were mainly Freudians. . . . So masturbation, especially in women, was considered to be either compulsive or infantile behavior."[16]

Partially as a result of "the negative sex conditioning" she received, Betty Dodson spent most of her first marriage sexually frustrated and emotionally distraught. "Quite typically my marital sex got down to once a month and, when it did happen, my husband would come too fast. I wouldn't come at all. We would both be embarrassed, depressed and silent." After her husband went to sleep, Betty would masturbate under the covers. "I did it without moving or breathing, feeling sick with frustration and guilt the whole time."

Dodson eventually divorced her husband and began having an affair with another man. They were able to communicate more openly and honestly, and he admitted that he too felt guilty about masturbating. Once again Dodson studied her own genitals in the mirror. This time she realized that her sense of shame was misguided. She also began watching herself masturbate.

Dodson had moved to New York City in the 1950s to study illustration. Like many artists, she frequently drew nudes. In the years after the breakup of her first marriage, however, Dodson began painting nudes actually having sex. She began doing, as she put it, "huge magnificent drawings and paintings of humans celebrating physical love."

In 1968, Dodson had her first solo exhibition at a New York gallery next door to the Whitney Museum. Before the exhibition opened, she worried about "irate citizens throwing rocks" and authorities closing down her show on charges of obscenity. But in the wake of the *Naked Lunch* decision, the Barnard College controversy, and the storm surrounding *Humanae Vitae*, New Yorkers were prepared for anything. Eight thousand people came to see Dodson's images of "life-size, heroic figures fucking behind huge bright-colored sheets of plexiglass." Because the images were in the gallery windows, every passerby could see them. A New Jersey newspaper article from the time gives a sense of the scene at the Wickersham Gallery. "Even the 'Inner Sanctum' at Pompeii, into which only males are permitted, couldn't reveal anything more intimate or shocking in the realm of bedroom sexuality than the subject matter flagrantly exposed to the general public promenading on Madison Avenue."[17]

For her second show, Dodson decided to include four images of women masturbating. "When the drawings arrived at the gallery the day of the opening, all hell broke loose. The director refused to hang the four masturbation drawings as planned, so I threatened to pull out the entire show of thirty pictures." Dodson and the director reached a compromise and two of the masturbation drawings were included in the show. One was a six-foot drawing of a female friend: "legs apart, clitoris erect, approaching orgasm with her vibrator." Dodson soon discovered that such images made men and women alike extremely uncomfortable.

Dodson was horrified by the extent of sexual repression in American society. For women to liberate themselves from such repression, Dodson felt, they needed to practice masturbating on a regular basis. Many women knew nothing about masturbation; others were so ashamed of their bodies that they never touched themselves; still others tried to masturbate but were unable to experience orgasm. She was convinced that "sexual liberation was crucial to women's liberation, and that masturbation was crucial to sexual liberation and the destruction of paralyzing sex roles." To jump-start the revolution, Dodson created a slide show of photographs of female genitalia. She showed these slides during a session titled "Creating an Esthetic for Female Genitals" at a conference on sexuality sponsored by the National Organization for Women in October 1974. Dodson also began holding classes for women in autoeroticism. Stressing the importance of being what she called "cunt positive," Dodson self-published a book celebrating the diversity of female body types. *Liberating Masturbation: A Meditation on Self-Love* featured full-page drawings of female genitalia and gave detailed instructions on masturbatory techniques, such as using vibrators and exercising pelvic muscles. "Sex is like any other skill — it has to be learned and practiced," she wrote.

Gloria Steinem recalls meeting Dodson at a coffee shop on the East Side of New York. "She was from Kansas, she was completely like a cheerleader. We're sitting in Chock Full of Nuts and she's describing to me the joys of masturbation. And she's telling me about her mother and how her mother learned to masturbate. And the people around us were electrified."[18]

Dodson's books and drawings were utilized by women's groups throughout the country. In Atlanta, Georgia, for example, the Atthis Collective, which specialized in sex therapy for lesbians, ran workshops featuring Dodson's photographic slides of women's genitals.[19] One twenty-one-year-old woman who began masturbating the year she read an article by Dodson wrote to her, "Since I have begun masturbating I have found it easier to accept myself and other people as well. I have found though that women are afraid to discuss their bodies, especially genitals, with one another because I think they are afraid they will be attracted to each other." Another woman wrote, "I thought your article . . . was fantastic. After reading it I had my first self-induced orgasm! I'm very grateful." A woman who masturbated with a vibrator and dildo "was sure no other woman in the world was so sexually maladjusted that she had to revert to such perverse instruments for her gratification"; then one day she saw a drawing by Dodson of a woman masturbating with a vibrator. "Ever since I saw your drawing I've felt better about myself — not so guilty, not so alone, not so weird after all. . . . Pretty soon orgasms came easier and I began to be really glad I had the vibrator."[20]

Betty Dodson was not the only one to see that women were disempowered by social attitudes toward masturbation. In 1972, the Reverend Ted McIlvenna of the National Sex Forum in San Francisco published "Getting in Touch: Self Sexuality for Women." A guide to masturbation, "Getting in Touch" included close-up photographs of the female genitalia, images of a middle-aged woman masturbating with a vibrator, and written exercises. As the title indicated, the book encouraged women to explore their own bodies ("Get a good look at your clitoris, you inner and outer lips, your vagina. Look at and feel the inner and outer lips near your vagina; your anus; and the area between the anus and the vagina"), but the authors were careful not to make universal claims about female sexuality or privilege certain activities over others.*

$$\clubsuit$$

Despite their best efforts, neither Betty Dodson nor Ted McIlvenna was able to banish anxiety about masturbation from America's shores. Superstition and ignorance persisted. *Sexual Behavior,* a study by journalist Morton Hunt published after both *Liberating Masturbation* and "Getting in Touch" and funded by the Playboy Foundation, illustrates how deeply entrenched the fear of masturbation was in American culture. Hunt insisted on the differences between "healthy" and "unhealthy" types of masturbation to such an extent that his supposedly empirical study read something like a nineteenth-century treatise on the dangers of self-abuse:

> The few compulsive masturbators among our interview subjects all boastfully accounted for their masturbation as necessitated by their unusually powerful sexual desires and capacity — but in truth they seemed more driven than desirous, more sated than satisfied by their masturbating, and without exception they had only shallow and brittle relationships with their sexual partners.

Hunt singled out feminist proponents of masturbation like Betty Dodson for special denunciation:

> Certain militant feminists, denigrating the nature of heterosexual interaction, have urged women to use vibrators or their own fingers for sexual relief, and have waxed rhapsodic over the fact that a woman can give herself numerous orgasms in a single uninterrupted session. But while this kind of performance results in total sexual satiety, it yields none of the complex emotional satisfactions, and none of the replenishment of the ego, produced by loving, heterosexual intercourse.

In a nod to science, Hunt acknowledged that researchers had found no evidence of physiological or psychological risks associated with masturbation, but he insisted on the emotional dangers of the practice:

---

* "Getting in Touch" did have its prescriptive side, however: "Practice [masturbating] as often as you want, but at least three times a week." Indeed, the authors warned, "You have to want to work on it. You have to be willing to get in touch with your own body and feelings. You have to take the time to work on it. You have to provide yourself with a learning environment. . . . You have to be selfish and take the time for yourself. Good sex takes time and energy." With such instructions, "Getting in Touch" threatened to turn sex into manual labor.

> [I]t is only fair to add that there is some danger involved in the total and
> uncritical acceptance of masturbation. It can be misused by — and prove
> hurtful to — certain persons with special psychosexual problems . . . The
> immature, the self-doubting and the socially inept; men who are afraid of
> or hostile to women, and vice-versa; husbands and wives who are in con-
> flict — all these and others can use masturbation as a neurotic and dam-
> aging solution to their problems. The likelihood of doing so has surely
> been increased by the fact that some enthusiasts of sexual freedom have
> said, without qualification, that masturbation is categorically good.[21]

Hunt claimed to be on the side of science and sexual liberation, but his analysis was clouded by the myths of masturbation's ill effects.

But by the summer of 1969, Americans, at least those in New York and San Francisco, had been exposed to a less judgmental view of the prac- tice. The public display of pictures of women masturbating and the publication of pamphlets exhorting women to study their own genitals were surely the culmination of the sexual revolution. Many thought that such sexual freedom would finally eliminate real "perversions," such as homosexuality. Weren't gay men and lesbians, as psychologist and self-proclaimed sexual revolutionary Albert Ellis asserted, simply "repressed" heterosexuals longing to be freed from their neuroses? Wasn't homosexuality a symptom of repressive Judeo-Christian moral- ity, just like pornography was a symptom of censorship?

As modern-minded Americans comforted themselves with the thought that the sexual revolution would have untold psychological benefits for "perverts" and "deviants," police patrols across the country were raiding gay bars and hauling gay men off to jail. It was a practice that had been going on for decades. Most straight sexual revolutionaries were too busy liberating themselves from their own hang-ups to take notice. In June 1969, a group of gay men at a bar in Greenwich Village realized it was time to fight back on their own.

CHAPTER 12

GAY LIBERATION

I T WAS A warm Friday night, June 27, 1969, at the Stonewall Inn, a
seedy but popular gay bar on Christopher Street in Greenwich Village.
The city was pulsating with the energy of the student movement and
the counterculture. The bar was packed as usual, dozens of men milling
about, all looking for love, or at least a little fun. The music was loud
and the lights were dim.

There were all sorts of men at the Stonewall that night. Students bitter about the draft, businessmen excited that the stock market had
reached an all-time high, young hustlers hoping to make a quick buck,
high-heeled drag queens lamenting Judy Garland's recent death. Morty
Manford was there, a Columbia sophomore at the time. Suddenly, as
Manford tells it, "some men in suits and ties entered the place and
walked around a bit. Then whispers went around that the place was
being raided." The lights were turned on, the doors were locked. The
plainclothes police announced a bust.[1]

The Stonewall, like most gay bars in the sixties, was owned by the
Mafia. When the Mob refused to pay off the police, there was almost
always trouble. In New York, as in many cities, gay bars were technically
illegal. This came in handy for politicians in an election year: an incum-
bent mayor could always call for a raid to boost his popularity. Raids
were standard affairs. The police arrived, hauled the patrons off in
paddy wagons, and put the men in jail for the night. The following
morning the names of the "guilty" would be printed in the papers. An

unlucky fellow could lose his job and, if he led a double life, his wife and children. Professionals had the most to lose: a doctor could be stripped of his license, a lawyer disbarred.[2]

That night at the Stonewall Inn, no one suspected this raid would be different from any other. The police waved their badges; the paddy wagons waited outside. Most of the customers would be released: the police planned to arrest only the bartenders and the drag queens. As the raid proceeded, and men were let outside, a crowd gathered in front of the bar to watch and commiserate.

But then something happened. A patron was clubbed on the head by a police officer. A handful of pennies were thrown. Rocks were tossed at the windows of the bar.

A police officer waved a gun and tried to quell the crowd. Anger was in the air.

Manford remembers, "Somebody took an uprooted parking meter and broke the glass in the front window and the plywood board that was behind it. Then somebody else took a garbage can, one of those wire-mesh cans, set it on fire, and threw the burning garbage can into the premises."

As the fire blazed, New York's paramilitary Tactical Police Force arrived. Hundreds of blue-uniformed officers poured into the streets, beating gay bystanders with billy clubs. Someone sliced the tires of the paddy wagon. More windows were broken; blood splattered on the pavement.

The riot lasted the weekend. Thousands filled the streets of Greenwich Village. The demonstration was practically ignored by the *New York Times* ("Four Policemen Hurt in Village Raid" was the headline on page 33) and was mostly mocked by the *Village Voice*. But it didn't matter. Gay liberation was born.

Americans have always prided themselves on their individualism and tolerance. But before Stonewall, homosexuals were deemed unworthy of such tolerance. They were too "different," too "queer," too "abnormal," too "deviant," too "perverted," too "inverted," to be granted social equality. Although every gay person's experience of society's homophobia was unique, almost all had experienced the sense of terror of being discovered by the wrong person, be it a parent, a sibling, a schoolmate, a coworker, a boss, a police officer, or a spouse. Those few who were "out" were always the butt of jokes in the straight world. Unlike the black child or the Jewish child, the young gay person could not look to his or her family for support or strength in confronting prejudice. Gays could pass in the straight world, but this was a mixed blessing. It meant for most a life of lies and fear.

Sodomy — sex between two men — has always occupied a unique place in Judeo-Christian culture: generally feared, denounced, criminalized, and fraught with symbolic significance. The man who allows himself to be penetrated has traditionally been particularly reviled. But it was not until the modern era that social scientists developed the notion of sexual identity as fixed and unchanging, based on exclusive preference for one gender, and fundamental to one's personality. By the middle of the twentieth century, cadres of experts were hard at work cataloguing the characteristics of homosexuals in order to make it easier to identify, prosecute, and "cure" them. In popular culture, homosexual men were derided as "faggots," "pansies," "queers," "fairies," "fruits," and "queens." Homosexual women were ridiculed as "dykes" and "bull-dykes." To be gay was to be pathetic and weak, but it was also to be threatening and dangerous, since homosexuals were believed to be child molesters and recruiters for Satan. At the same time, homosexuality was thought to be a disease — contagious and debilitating.[3] Few straights ever thought about these contradictions critically.

Life started to become especially difficult for sexual outsiders in America during the Depression. The repeal of Prohibition seemed like it would introduce a new era of personal freedom, but instead it gave government officials the opportunity to regulate bars and nightclubs. They often used this power to shut down gay establishments and keep those that were allowed to remain open under close scrutiny. During World War II, the military employed "scientific" methods to identify homosexuals in an effort to keep them out of the service.[4] Meanwhile, the nation's sudden transition from a rural to an urban society — and the social dislocation this process caused — only exacerbated homophobia. This social dislocation sparked concerns about juvenile delinquency and adolescent sexuality and ignited fears that children might fall prey to evil influences. In the public imagination, these amorphous, ill-defined evil influences were projected onto the figure of the homosexual. Once the postwar baby boom began and many parents had more children than they could easily supervise, the irrational fear that homosexuals might be waiting in dark alleys, ever ready to seduce the innocent, consumed the nation.[5]

Rapid urbanization and modernization also aggravated the situation by complicating gender roles. Twentieth-century American men found themselves searching for ways to prove their masculinity. The modern man, who was expected to eschew violence, dote on his children, be a model companion, commute diligently to work, and eagerly consume new products, had to struggle to assert his independence, authority, and sexual prowess. Hoping to seem more virile, heterosexual men eagerly mocked "pansies." As long as a straight man could feel superior to homosexuals, he could feel confident about his own place on the social ladder.[6]

After World War II, during which many young male and female soldiers discovered their interest in members of the same sex and came to accept the label "homosexual," returning soldiers established gay enclaves in port cities like San Francisco and New York. But discrimination and prejudice remained strong. In the paranoid climate of the Cold War, anti-homosexual attitudes reached a fever pitch. Panic about political deviants overlapped with panic about sexual deviants. Like Communists, homosexuals seemed to lead shadowy, secretive lives. They were apparently invisible, yet allegedly everywhere. Both were dangerously "un-American" because they failed to conform to societal norms.[7] Many films of the fifties and early sixties, notably those of Alfred Hitchcock, portrayed Communists and criminals as effeminate, unmarried, or otherwise unmanly men.[8]

Police, educators, and other professionals agreed that it was crucial to deter people from becoming homosexuals. In 1959, a psychiatrist warned female inmates at the Framingham Reformatory in Massachusetts, "Homosexuality can never be accepted by the world at large. If all people were to become homosexuals there would be no further reproduction. The world would end more slowly but just as surely as by the atom bomb . . . [I]n the long run, lesbianism is a sick way of life and . . . it is an unhappy way of life."[9] Psychiatrists were wont to use a variety of invasive and ineffectual methods in the attempt to eradicate homosexual desires: hormone injections, electroshock therapy, and nauseating fluids meant to make a person vomit every time he or she looked at a nude picture of someone of the same sex.

In Tampa, Florida, officials fired thirty educators on the grounds that they were homosexual — even though none had actually been arrested for particular conduct.[10] Employers went to great lengths to root out gays from the workforce, and a minor industry even developed to assist in this effort. Private investigation firms offered their services to spy on employees during their off-hours. The president of one such agency warned companies of the presence of homosexual employees: "The problem of homosexuality seems to be increasing. Frankly, it's a difficult thing to establish. I like to go on the rule of thumb that if one looks like a duck, walks like a duck, associates only with ducks, and quacks like a duck, he probably is a duck."[11]

Every so often, a mainstream newspaper or magazine would comment with a combination of condescension and horror about the size of the local gay community. In December, 1963, for instance, the *New York Times* ran a front-page story on "the growth of overt homosexuality" in the city.

"The overt homosexual — and those who are identifiable probably represent no more than half of the total — has become such an obtrusive part of the New York scene that the phenomenon needs public discussion," the *Times* wrote. In January 1966, *Time* magazine declared: "[Homosexuality] deserves no encouragement, no glamorization, no rationalization, no fake status as minority martyrdom, no sophistry about simple differences in taste — and above all, no pretense that it is anything but a pernicious sickness." When one of *Time*'s reporters, Andrew Kopkind, was arrested for having sex with a man in Griffith Park in Los Angeles, in 1964, the publishers of the magazine told him he would have to "become straight" or he would lose his job. They sent him to a psychiatrist who tried to teach him how to meet women on airplanes.[12]

In June 1964, *Life* magazine devoted a feature story to the homosexual subculture of San Francisco, noting:

> [T]oday, especially in big cities, homosexuals are discarding their furtive ways and openly admitting, even flaunting, their deviation. Homosexuals have their own drinking places, their special assignation streets, even their own organizations. . . . This social disorder, which society tries to suppress, has forced itself into the public eye because it does present a problem — and parents especially are concerned.

The story, like other articles of the time, presented homosexual life as inherently dismal and depressing, a "sad and often sordid world."[13]

Still, the *Life* article did inspire many gay men to move to San Francisco, a city the article described as "the gay capital of the world." One professor of English at an Ivy League school recalls, "I remember reading about San Francisco being a den of iniquity in *Life* magazine, and thinking, that's where I want to be." Similar articles helped fuel a migration to the growing gay ghettos in other cities as well. But as neighborhoods like San Francisco's Castro, Greenwich Village, and West Hollywood became recognized zones for openly gay men and women, mayors and police chiefs brandished their power to close gay bars and keep gays in constant fear. In New York, the liquor authority began revoking the licenses of bars believed to attract gay patrons. In 1962 alone, city police closed thirty gay bars.[14]

Though gay life before Stonewall was undeniably difficult, gays did manage to forge relationships and communities amid the persecution and public hysteria. Playwright Donald Vining, for one, had a happy and long-standing relationship with his lover Ken, whom he met in a New York steam room in the 1950s. The relationship, though not monogamous, was romantic and lasted several decades. Vining was "out" to his mother and friends. He and Ken did not live together, but that was only because, according to Vining, Ken feared that cohabitation "would limit his sexual opportunities." Vining kept a diary in which he recorded his daily activities, including his sexual encounters. The diary reveals how "cruising" for sex was a common part of gay urban life, even if most heterosexuals were unaware of it. In the spring of 1955, he wrote:

> I decided to go up to Central Park West. In front of the Museum of Natural History . . . I met a nice youngster. . . . There was no leering and no sex talk save that when three extreme queens went by, he said, "That's too much. Too much. They spoil it." When I made ready to leave, he invited me to his room and when we got there he wasted no time and said, with perfect relaxation, "Shall we take off our clothes?" Tho only twenty, he was what can only be called a sexual natural, being utterly relaxed and uninhibited, and at the same time thoughtful and pleasant in bed, both during and after sex.

On another occasion, Vining wrote: "For an hour and a half [a friend] regaled me with stories of a month he spent in . . . the army. . . . [H]e took full advantage of the rampant gay life going on among the several thousand isolated service men, who weren't allowed to fraternize with the natives. He said that within two hours of arrival, he was in bed with a sailor." Contrary to the stereotype of the frightened, persecuted homosexual, Vining was all but blasé about gay life. "If I cruise and don't at least get to talk to somebody new, I feel guilty later, not for having cruised but for having wasted my time."[15]

Before Stonewall, a young man could always find sexual partners at private parties, public restrooms, or the local YMCA. In Boston, men sometimes met in the bathrooms of the Harvard Square subway station. George Mansour met Joe Santa Maria in the subway bathroom in 1958; they eventually moved in together and remained lovers for over four decades. In New York, men met at the Everard Baths, among other places. Kenneth Pitchford attended weekly orgies in the early sixties at a friend's apartment in Greenwich Village. "Every Thursday we would go to his place. He would spread sheets out on the floor and provide plenty of Vaseline. We would fuck like dogs."[16] Of course, every major city had its share of discreetly gay bars.

Although hard-core gay pornography was difficult, if not impossible, to find before Stonewall, there were several "muscle magazines" with intentionally homoerotic overtones. For instance, Bob Mizer's *Physique Pictorial*, which was published from 1951 to 1990, featured drawings of muscular men in jockstraps bathing, boxing, or wrestling. In 1964, the homophile Janus Society, with the intention of creating a "gay *Playboy*," began publishing *Drum*. Unlike most gay-oriented publications, which steered clear of overt eroticism, the purpose of *Drum* was to put "the 'sex' back into homosexuality."[17] The January 1966 issue, in fact, contained a full frontal nude centerfold. The publishers were charged with obscenity, but with the help of the ACLU, free speech eventually won in court.[18]

Still, for many young gay men and women in the days before the liberation movement, life was filled with pain and despair. It was hard not to feel alone, inferior, worthless. Many fantasized about suicide or actually took their lives. Even someone like the writer Allen Young, who managed to find a sexual partner in college, was nearly destroyed by self-loathing.

> Our fear and shame were the keys to our survival. I became editor in chief of the college paper; he became managing editor. We took all of the same classes. We ate our meals together, and we became roommates. To all our friends, and even in our own minds, we were just college buddies. No one "suspected." We knew no other gay people — that was the last thing on our minds. The passion we knew in bed at night was always muffled by our inability to say "I love you" to each other, by the awareness that the whole world which was rewarding us as men was saying "no" to our homosexuality.

Ultimately, they stopped having sex and "got girlfriends" to affirm their heterosexuality. Throughout, Young thought about suicide. His onetime boyfriend eventually became "a kind of hermit," a schizophrenic, until his mother had him committed to a mental hospital. It was typical for colleges up through the 1960s to expel students suspected of having homosexual relations. "It is rather well known," wrote one student to the American Civil Liberties Union in 1966, "that from time to time colleges in Texas and elsewhere simply dismiss a student from school on the basis of a mere complaint, or even anonymous letters, stating that the student has been seen in 'bad' company or that he looks or acts 'queer.'"[19]

Like the civil rights movement, which began long before the Freedom Summer of 1964, the gay rights movement developed over the course of several decades. In the 1950s, during the height of anti-Communism, Harry Hay and Rudi Gernreich's Mattachine Society, the first American "homophile" organization, was soon joined by ONE Inc., as well as by the Daughters of Bilitis, an organization for lesbians. Chapters of these three groups were formed across the country, helping to create a small but significant gay rights movement.

Although the early founders of the movement were members of the Communist Party, over the years the movement became less and less militant. Instead of demanding immediate social change, activists focused on forging ties with the psychiatric community. In fact, gay activists often accepted unquestioningly the pronouncements of psychiatric "experts."[20]

Through the fifties and sixties, gay activism had relatively little impact on the national culture. Most Americans never learned of the Mattachine Society or ONE Inc., and few gays saw fit to join the cause. The biggest event happened in Great Britain in 1957, when the Wolfsenden Report effectively decriminalized all homosexual contacts between consenting adults. The situation began to change in the late sixties, when gay college students, accustomed to the radical tactics of civil rights demonstrators and the don't-tread-on-me attitude of hippies, started to speak out against prejudice and persecution. In 1967, Bob Martin, a freshman at Columbia University, was kicked out of his room by his suitemates after he hung sexy pictures of men on his walls. Angry but resilient, Martin sought refuge in his schoolwork. He decided to study the history of homosexuality in America and found a friend in Jim Shenton, a professor in the history department, who became his adviser and confidant. Adopting the pseudonym Stephen Donaldson, Martin founded the nation's first Student Homophile League. Younger and less conservative than most gay activists, Donaldson was not afraid of drawing down the wrath of the straight world. When the *New York Times* ran a piece in December 1967 about same-sex friendships, Donaldson took the straight world to task in his letter to the editor. "It must be evident that the contemporary fear of possible homosexual implications of close emotional relationships between persons of the same sex is itself unhealthy and even paranoid."[21]

Seven months earlier, the *Times* saw fit to print an article about Donaldson's new Columbia group, the existence of which was shocking to most middle-aged New Yorkers.[22] No one was more upset than the president of the university, Grayson Kirk. "This episode is deeply distressing to me," he wrote to one alumnus. "This episode is extremely distasteful," he wrote to another. Alumni, meanwhile, were outraged. One Boston neurosurgeon declared in a letter to Kirk:

> It is still the opinion of a great many physicians that homosexuality is a mental disorder, and that the difference between homosexuals and heterosexuals is not simply analogous to that between Republicans and Democrats, as the homosexuals would have us believe. Frankly, I can find no more justification for a Student Homophile League than for a Student League of Schizophrenics or, perhaps, of Sadists.

Kirk tried to comfort alumni by telling them that the Student Homophile League was a "little tempest" and "a thing of the past." As he wrote to one alumnus, "After extensive counseling from the Chaplain of the University, little more, if anything, will be heard from them, I am confident." But straight Americans were not so easily assuaged. Realizing that he had a public relations nightmare on his hands, Kirk insisted that the group was not a problem because it was academically oriented and was not a social club (that is, it would not lead to gay sexual encounters). He wrote to the *Los Angeles Daily Journal*:

> I need not tell you that even if the group had been organized for a social purpose, such purpose would not be allowed to be perpetrated on this campus. The League has been formed for the purpose of study and discussion of the problems of homosexuality to promote greater understanding of the extent and significance of the homosexual problem in our society, and to help secure educational, legal and social rights to which homosexuals are entitled as members of a free society.[23]

Though Kirk tried to make the Student Homophile League sound like a polite debating society, Donaldson had no intention of running a timid organization like those already in existence. He denounced "the sexual repression and other undesirable features of heterosexual middle-class value systems." As far as he was concerned, sexual liberation was a crucial element of the struggle for gay equality. His defiance inspired students at Cornell, New York University, and Stanford to form similar homophile leagues.[24] Before long, there were homophile leagues at schools across the country.

The same year Stephen Donaldson created the first student homophile league, on the other side of the country Richard Mitch, a Los Angeles writer who went by the pseudonym Dick Michaels, was arrested in a bar raid. It was a typical sort of raid and it cost Michaels $600 to defend himself in court. Afterward, Michaels was so furious he joined a small organization named PRIDE (Personal Rights in Defense and Education) and then took over the PRIDE newsletter and turned it into a newspaper for the gay community, the *Los Angeles Advocate*. Like many other underground newspapers, the *Advocate* began as a mimeographed pamphlet. But it was infused with Michaels's anger and determination. "Homosexuals," the first editorial declared, "more than ever before, are out to win their legal rights, to end the injustices against them, to experience their share of happiness in their own way."[25]

Despite the sudden spurt of activism in the late sixties, the vast majority of gay men and lesbians continued to live their lives as they always had. "We're faced with a kind of cruel alternative," explained activist Arthur Evans. "If we deny our emotions, don't show them in public and appear to be straight, then we can have a career; but if we're open, and show our affections the way heterosexuals do, and lead an open sexual life, then our careers are ended."[26]

Gay characters began popping up with increasing frequency in movies and theater, but often these characters died or ended up in prison, a reminder to gay audiences that they lived in a hostile and fearful culture. The 1968 film *The Detective,* for instance, linked homosexuality to psychopathology and murder. *The Killing of Sister George,* another 1968 film, suggested that lesbianism led to terrible misfortune. *The Boys in the Band* opened Off Broadway that same year and was made into a movie in 1970. Though its author, Mart Crowley, was gay, it was still a dark portrayal of gay life. "Show me a happy homosexual," one character says to another, "and I'll show you a gay corpse."[27]

The more visible gays became, the more critics worried about the decline and fall of American society. Medical experts continued to insist that homosexuals were sick, and until 1973 homosexuality was listed in the American Psychological Association's Diagnostic and Statistical Manual (DSM) as a mental disorder. Even those who considered themselves "progressive" on such issues as birth control and premarital sex often saw homosexuality as an illness or a symptom of poor parenting. In 1967, Mary Steichen Calderone, the founder of the Sex Information and Education Council of the United States (SIECUS), cited preventing boys and girls from becoming homosexual as a reason to include sex education in the public schools. "Homosexuals are made, usually by puberty, not born or seduced." As far as Calderone was concerned, "the 'making' of a man or a woman should no longer be left to chance, nor to the instincts of parents."[28] The editors of the academic journal *Medical Aspects of Human Sexuality* frequently published articles on gay sex that had no trace of scientific credibility. One 1968 article, for instance, alleged:

> Although it is quite clear to both partners [in a homosexual encounter] that a man is having a sexual relationship with a man, the simulation of a heterosexual experience is required. Mutual sharing of the pretense that one partner is a female is a necessary component for a satisfactory sexual experience. It cannot be simply that sexual experience is sought for the pleasure involved, because masturbation alone or the same sexual act with a woman, which would be at least physiologically gratifying, is specifically to be avoided . . . There is a need to deny at some level of consciousness that one has sexual interest in women.[29]

Though doctors were supposed to be scientists, they tended to reflect the biases and prejudices of their cultural milieu. Worse, they packaged these prejudices in the language of medical authority, often making categorical, and unproven, claims.

If anything, hostility toward homosexuals probably intensified in the sixties because gay men and women were becoming more visible. For instance, when Grove Press published John Rechy's *City of Night* in 1963, Alfred Chester, in a piece titled "Fruit Salad" in the *New York Review of Books,* blasted Rechy for trying "to boil every last drop of poetry out of pederasty."[30] But as the decade progressed, and demands were increasingly being made for women's liberation, workers' liberation, third-world liberation, and Chicano liberation, it was only a matter of time before gays began demanding gay liberation. In January 1969, Marvin Garson called for "Queer Power" in the pages of the underground paper the *San Francisco Express Times*: "Remember when it was impolite to suggest that a Negro gentleman might have black skin? Now it's 'Say it loud, I'm black and I'm proud.' Maybe in a few years the queers will be saying something like, 'Don't keep trying to rise above it — kiss me, darling, I'm queer and I love it.'" Garson argued that there ought to be an openly gay man or woman on the Supreme Court. In April, Craig Shoomaker, a Columbia University undergraduate dissatisfied with what he believed to be the reformist approach of the Student Homophile League, started his own radical organization called "Homosexuals Intransigent!" Shoomaker flatly rejected the public–private distinctions of bourgeois morality. "Sex is just sex, whether in public or in private. It is not wrong anywhere, except perhaps in the subway during rush hours, when it might obstruct traffic."[31] Though Shoomaker never attracted more than a handful of followers, his bold ideas on sexual morality would soon be echoed throughout the gay world. Only two months later, the Stonewall riots showed that homosexuals were indeed becoming intransigent.

Political movements are not born fully formed; they require numerous acts of small-scale resistance. As noted, the Stonewall riot was preceded by many years of activism; without this prior activism, Stonewall might never have occurred, or rather, it might never have been turned into a symbolic event of major importance. Moreover, gay life before Stonewall was just as varied and complex as it was after. Gays found creative ways to resist heteronormative social codes throughout the decades.

That said, Stonewall marked a turning point in the consciousness of the community.* Shortly after the Greenwich Village protests, a group

---

* Although the term *community* was frequently used in the sixties and seventies, it is an imperfect concept. As Michael Warner writes, "Although it has had importance in organizational efforts . . . the notion of a community has remained problematic because nearly every lesbian or gay remembers being such before entering a collectively identified space, because much of lesbian and gay history has to do with noncommunity, and because dispersal rather than localization continues to be definitive of queer self-understanding ('We Are Everywhere'). Community also falsely suggests an ideological and nostalgic contrast with the atomization of modern capitalist society. And in the pluralist frame it predisposes that political demands will be treated as demands for the toleration and representation of a minority constituency." (Warner, Introduction, *Fear of a Queer Planet* [Minneapolis: University of Minnesota Press, 1993], xxv). I use the term aware of these limitations.

of angry young radicals formed the Gay Liberation Front, a Marxist group modeled on other organizations of the New Left. A few months later, disagreements within the GLF led to the creation of a splinter group, the Gay Activist Alliance. Under the banner "Gay Is Good," activists staged rallies, organized protests, and picketed newspaper offices and television stations. In their constitution, Gay Activist Alliance members declared "the right to make love with anyone, any way, anytime," and "the right to treat and express our bodies as we will."[32] Students were emboldened by Stonewall as never before. "We regard established heterosexual standards of morality as immoral," one radical group announced, "and refuse to condone them by demanding an equality which is merely the common yoke of sexual repression." They further called for "the removal of all restrictions on sex between consenting persons of any sex, of any orientation, of any age, anywhere, whether for money or not, and for the removal of all censorship."[33]

After Stonewall, the national media were forced to acknowledge gay activism, though news articles were often less than sympathetic. In a friendly nod to gay readers, *Time* warned in October 1969 that homophobia was often produced by "innumerable misconceptions and oversimplifications." The magazine also declared "the case for greater tolerance of homosexuals is simple." But unable to practice tolerance itself, *Time* offered a denigrating list of categories of gay males, including "the catty hair-dresser," "the lisping, limp-wristed interior decorator," and "the desperate" who are "pathologically driven to sex but emotionally unable to face the slightest strains of sustaining a serious human relationship[.]" *Time* assured readers that one-third of all "confirmed adult inverts" could be "helped to change," while an even larger number of "prehomosexual children" could be "treated successfully" with psychiatric counseling. Finally, the magazine's editors raised the question of "to what extent homosexuality and acceptance of it may be symptoms of social decline."[34]

Such thinly disguised derision in the media, however, only fortified the resolve of gay activists. After *Harper's* magazine published an article by Joseph Epstein in September 1970 that offered an apologia for his own homophobia ("There is much my four sons can do in their lives that might cause me to anguish, that might outrage me, that might make me ashamed of them and of myself as their father. But nothing they could ever do would make me sadder than if any of them were to become a homosexual"), activists staged a sit-in in the magazine's offices.[35] One of them recalled:

> In the reception area one group of us set up a table with coffee and doughnuts, others spread out and leafleted every desk in the company. As people came to work, we walked up to them, offered a handshake, intro-

duced ourselves, saying "'Good morning, I'm a homosexual. We're here to protest the Epstein article. Would you like some coffee?'"[36]

Throughout the spring of 1970, chants of "Gay Power!" could be heard in the nation's cities. Activists organized a giant "gay-in," a sort of mass coming-out party, in New York's Central Park. Tens of thousands of men and women gathered for a day of celebration. "Muscular male bodies, stripped naked to the waist, wrestled playfully in the shade," the newspaper *GAY* reported. "Striking women, beautiful without makeup, kissed in the sunlight." Many believed a revolution was at hand. Students at the University of Minnesota founded an organization called FREE (Fight Repression of Erotic Expression). Members of the Gay Liberation Front participated in an antiwar rally in Washington, D.C., by chanting "Suck cock, beat the draft" and — five years after Jefferson Poland's nude wade-in off the coast of San Francisco — tore off their clothes and waded naked in the Reflecting Pool by the Lincoln Memorial. A gay-in like the one in New York was held in Los Angeles's Griffith Park.[37] In June 1970, parades were held across the country, commemorating the Stonewall riots of the previous year. "Welcome to the first anniversary celebration of the Gay Liberation movement," announced the organizers of the New York parade in a flier.

> We are united today to affirm our pride, our lifestyle and our commitment to each other. Despite political and social differences we may have, we are united on this common ground: For the first time in history, we are together as the Homosexual Community . . . We are gay and proud. No one can convince us otherwise.[38]

Stonewall gave young gays the sense they were participating in a true revolution that would lead to the overthrow of the bourgeois, patriarchal, heterosexist power structure. Stonewall had shown the gravity of the gay struggle: If gays resisted their oppression, the state would use its full force to keep them in line. Gay liberation, therefore, represented a declaration of war. One 1969 flier asked, "Do You Think Homosexuals Are Revolting?" and answered "You Bet Your Sweet Ass We Are!"[39]

Most of the books written about the 1960s either elide or altogether ignore gay liberation. Given the marginalization of gay life in American culture, this should come as no surprise. Nor should it come as a shock that most of the books written about gay liberation pay scant attention to the larger sexual and social changes of the era. But this historiographic divide demands careful scrutiny. Was the gay liberation movement entirely outside the more mainstream sexual revolution? Were the goals of gay activists particular to gays themselves and therefore irrelevant to the rest of Americans? Or was there a subtle, dialectical relationship between gay liberation and the broader sexual revolution?

These seemingly simple questions are hard to answer. Certainly gays and straights lived in two separate social worlds. Straight singles went to bars, beaches, dance clubs, parties, and resorts that catered to straights. Gay singles went to bars, beaches, dance clubs, parties, and resorts that were almost exclusively gay. A pornographic magazine was aimed either at heterosexuals or homosexuals, but never both.

The split between heterosexuals and homosexuals extended to the youth movement. Some radicals thought gay liberation was a CIA plot to undermine the credibility of the New Left. The Socialist Workers Party refused membership to all homosexuals on the grounds that homosexuality was a symptom of "bourgeois decadence." In the early women's movement, *lesbian* was a dirty word. Gays themselves were divided about whether or not to align with the larger youth movement. A few believed gay liberation was one component of the larger struggle to overthrow the imperialist, corrupt, bourgeois state. Most, however, believed that socialist revolution could wait until after gay rights had been won.[*]

For straights, "sexual liberation" often meant personal, psychological transformation — freedom from hang-ups. For gays, personal liberation required social and cultural change — the elimination of repressive laws, the abolition of damaging stereotypes, the relaxation of taboos on public displays of homosexual affection (like holding hands and kissing).

Although they were supposedly determined to root out hypocrisy, ignorance, superstition, fear, and shame, straight sexual revolutionaries did not necessarily think supporting homosexuality would help the cause. Self-appointed spokesmen for the sexual revolution, like Norman Mailer and Robert Rimmer, had few kind words to say about homosexuality. More often than not, they portrayed homosexuals as paragons of sexual repression. Sexual liberation, in their eyes, involved liberation *from* homosexual inclinations. Mailer, for one, trumpeted an aggressive brand of heterosexuality based on rigid gender roles that left no room for homoerotic alternatives. In an essay published in 1966, Mailer gave left-wing legitimacy to homophobia:

> I think there may be more homosexuals today than there were 50 years ago. If so, the basic reason might have to do with a general loss of faith in the country, faith in the meaning of one's work, faith in the notion of oneself as a man. When a man can't find any dignity in his work, he loses virility. Masculinity is not something given to you, something you're

---

[*] This tension was reflected in the split between GLF and GAA. The former was a standard socialist group, the latter a single-issue organization.

born with, but something you gain. And you gain it by winning small battles with honor. Because there is very little honor left in American life, there is a certain built-in tendency to destroy masculinity in American men. The mass media for instance — television first, movies second, magazines third, and newspapers running no poor forth — tend to destroy virility slowly and steadily.[40]

For those who did not consciously deplore homosexuality, it remained largely irrelevant. Most of the men and women who participated in "the swinging sixties" thought of homosexuals as a breed apart.

Conservative critics of the hippie generation often played on society's homophobia to attack such things as long hair on men and pants on women. In the March 1965 issue of *Esquire,* Helen Lawrenson bemoaned young women's makeup and clothing styles. "Although these are beautiful young girls, far from appearing sexually provocative, they are enough to paralyze men into permanent impotence." Lawrenson was appalled by the idea of "unisex" fashions. "Can you imagine a cocktail party with both sexes in similar tailored suits? It would look like a fag-bar hangout." According to Lawrenson, the new fashions were "anti-sex." She was extremely anxious about androgynous clothing and her fear betrayed a deeper anxiety about the fragility of heterosexual desire. "I cannot help thinking that it is sort of nice for girls to look like girls and men like men. If I am wrong, then we may at last be entering an era when equality of the sexes could threaten to end in cancellation of the race."[41] In 1969, newspaper columnist Harriet Van Horne said that men who wore "frilly Edwardian clothes" were of "dubious masculinity"; they were "the wrong men . . . who do not understand the way to a woman's heart."[42] In a 1968 article, sociologist Charles Winick worried that the depolarization of sex roles (what he called the "bleaching of differences") would lead to massive social confusion that "might ultimately prove to be almost as hazardous as the rigidities of authoritarianism." Like other social theorists, Winick attributed the "neutering and role-blurring" of "the beige generation" to the absence of fathers during World War II.[43] Those who condemned long hair on boys conveniently forgot that the Founding Fathers had worn wigs. When journalist Dan Wakefeld grew sideburns and let his hair grow long in the late sixties, he was "sneeringly called a hippie by strangers": "My manhood and my patriotism were questioned on streets and in stores."[44] In retrospect, it seems that beneath all the anxiety about clothing styles lay a deeper fear that most heterosexuals were never very heterosexual to begin with.

Gay activists, for their part, tended to disdain straights and to ignore the quest for heterosexual liberation. Apart from the occasional call for pansexual freedom, gay activists were too busy fighting for gay rights to consider other issues. Homophobia was so ingrained in the culture and discrimination was so pervasive that the task of transforming public opinion was truly monumental. Some gay activists concluded that separatism and supremacism were the only viable answers. Craig Shoomaker, the founder of Homosexuals Intransigent!, aspired to create a self-governing all-male gay district within Manhattan. Not only did Shoomaker have no interest in sexual liberation for straights, he attacked bisexuals because he believed they stood in the way of gay liberation:

> [Bisexuality] is not a sign of "health" but more often of shame on the part of homosexuals who must for their psychological peace pretend they are really bisexual — that is, partly "normal." . . . It's time we stopped thinking it a virtue to be non-judgmental regarding people or cultures . . . I hold it against a man's tongue that it has slithered over a clitoris; I hold it against his penis that it has gotten itself coated with the sebaceous lubricant of a vagina and the copious effluent of female orgasm . . . Just as I regard a vagina as a thing I would not want to get near myself, I find revolting the idea of vicarious heterosexual sex through a bisexual. So bisexuals, fuck off. Stay out of my life. You view me with disdain, but I view you with disgust.[45]

Like Shoomaker, many gay men saw straight men, straight women, and bisexuals as enemies with whom there was no hope of ever aligning for common aims. At the far extreme of the gay male separatist movement, a group of white gay men founded the National Socialist League, a neo-Nazi organization aimed at resurrecting fascism and the German cult of male beauty in a twisted version of gay power. (Needless to say, traditional Nazi groups and gay Jews were none too pleased.)

Apart from such extremist views, gays often felt sorry for straights who blithely accepted the restrictive morality they inherited from previous generations. Playing on Betty Friedan's notion of the "feminine mystique," Peter Fisher captured this sense of pity in a book he published in 1972 to help heterosexuals understand homosexuality.

> Some gays [are beginning] to see heterosexuals in much the same light that heterosexuals have viewed homosexuals for years. A new "straight mystique" is arising in which the stereotypical heterosexual appears as a tragic, self-defeating, sexually inhibited individual, hiding his sexuality in the closet, while the media exploit his fascination with sex and his need to live up to society's roles. Can heterosexuals ever really be happy?[46]

Fisher was being facetious, but underneath his humor lay a serious critique of the hypocrisy he saw in the straight world. It was common for gays to chant, "Two, four, six, eight, gay is twice as good as straight!" "This slogan," explained Allen Young at the time, "reflects our understanding of homosexuality as a superior way of life to heterosexuality as we experience it. Heterosexual relationships are encumbered by notions of how men and women are supposed to behave. It is a system which has male supremacy built in."[47] In 1969, the activist and social critic Paul Goodman extolled gay promiscuity as a democratizing force:

> In my observation and experience, queer life has some remarkable political values. It can be profoundly democratizing, throwing together every class and group more than heterosexuality does. Its promiscuity can be a beautiful thing (but be prudent about VD). I myself have cruised rich, poor, middle class, and petit bourgeois; black, white, yellow and brown; scholars, jocks and dropouts; farmers, seamen, railroad men, heavy industry, light manufacturing, communications, business and finance, civilians, soldiers and sailors, and once or twice cops. There is a kind of political meaning, I guess, in the fact that there are so many types of attractive human beings.

Goodman recognized that some might criticize promiscuity for offering "an appalling superficiality of human contact," but he argued that promiscuity had to be better than "the usual coldness and fragmentation of community life" found in the heterosexual world.[48]

While gays and straights did not unite in a common cause of universal sexual freedom, the gay liberation movement did emerge within the context of the sixties and, more specifically, within the context of the sexual revolution.* It is fair to say that without the climate of activism generated by the student movement, the public furor aroused by the pill, and the general optimism inspired by the decline of censorship, gay liberation would never have exploded onto the scene when it did in the summer of 1969. The fact that college students were challenging the U.S. government about the war in Vietnam, demanding the right to cohabit in college, that actors were willing to be arrested in order to perform plays like *Che,* that society matrons were challenging state laws against birth control, made it that much easier for gays and lesbians to find the courage to forge their own grassroots movement. The sexual revolution gave gays and lesbians confidence in their own political project because it validated the importance of self-expression and underscored the possibility of wiping out ignorance, superstition, hypocrisy, shame, fear, and self-loathing.

The sexual revolution also paved the way for gay liberation by forcing heterosexuals to question their own assumptions about sexual morality. As gay playwright and AIDS activist Larry Kramer states, "Hugh Hefner

---

* It is interesting to note that Carl Whitman, who wrote *The Gay Manifesto* in 1969, was one of the founding members of Students for a Democratic Society.

did more for gay liberation by creating *Playboy* than any other single person did." It is not so much that *Playboy* promoted the discussion of gay issues or endorsed gay rights (though it occasionally did do so) as that the magazine legitimized sexual desire outside of marriage.* In a similar way, the pill, by separating intercourse from reproduction, pointed to the possibility of sex purely for pleasure. If one was willing to accept sex as a matter of pleasure alone, than one could no longer object to homosexuality on the grounds that sex was "supposed to be" procreative.

Sometimes sexual revolutionaries and gay revolutionaries did recognize their common aims. The Sexual Freedom League was especially conducive to cross-fertilization. Jefferson Poland, the founder of the League, identified himself as bisexual, so he insisted the SFL acknowledge the importance of gay rights. (Poland, always a nudist, wanted to strip off his clothes at the first gay pride parade in Los Angeles, but the head of ONE Inc. asked him not to do it because it might lead to police harassment.)[49] As we saw, Poland's colleague Randy Wicker abandoned the homophile movement for the sexual freedom movement because he felt the first was too narrow in its aims. Pete Wilson, an SFL member, was so inspired by Jefferson Poland's iconoclasm, he went on to become one of the original founders of the Gay Liberation Front.[50]

Some gay activists actually challenged the very categories "gay" and "lesbian" because they believed in an expansive definition of sexual liberation. "[T]he vision of liberation that I hold is precisely one that would make the homo/hetero distinction irrelevant," Dennis Altman wrote in his 1971 book, *Homosexual Oppression and Liberation*. "The artificial categories 'heterosexual' and 'homosexual' have been laid on us by a sexist society," wrote another activist. Likewise, the Gay Liberation Front declared "homosexuality" and "heterosexuality" to be "false categories."[51] After Stonewall, many activists believed such simplistic,

---

* The Playboy Foundation gave limited financial support to homophile groups. Ursula Enters Copely, of the Homosexual Information Center, writes: "Although we argued some . . . Playboy shared our efforts to revise American laws so as to exclude all private sexual activity between consenting adults — a cause we assumed everyone would willingly join regardless of their sexual proclivities. . . . [T]here is no question that the right of privacy was one of the principal links between the 'heterosexual revolution' and the 'homophile movement'" (letter to author, 22 January 1996). *Playboy* editors were consistently critical of homophobic attitudes. For instance, when a letter writer asked, "If the laws and mores in America are changed to accept homosexual behavior, who is going to protect me, the average American male, from homosexuals and perverts? When I'm in a public rest room, who is going to keep the homosexual's hands off me?," the *Playboy* editors replied, "Legalization of homosexual acts in private between consenting adults and public acceptance of such behavior does not automatically means that sexual assault, in public or in private, will also be accepted. . . . [We] believe you exaggerate the threat to the average American male, who should be perfectly capable of discouraging unwanted propositions without resorting to 'barbarism.'" ("Defenseless Male," Forum, *Playboy*, May 1968, 61.)

binary labels on the brink of extinction. They perceived the gay liberation movement as only one component of the larger sexual revolution.

There were other ways that sexual freedom and gay liberation overlapped. *Screw,* a New York sex newspaper with a mainly heterosexual male audience, included a column about gay life by Jack Nichols and Lige Clark, two Greenwich Village hippies. They used their platform to appeal to straight men for support for gay liberation. In one particularly biting piece that ran in 1969, consisting of an imaginary dialogue between a vice officer and his son, Nichols and Clark scored the hypocrisy of so-called morals squads:

BOY: Daddy . . . What kind of policeman are you? Why don't you wear a uniform like other policemen?

DAD: I'm a vice-cop, son.

BOY: What do you do all night, Daddy?

DAD: I stand in smelly public rest rooms, son, and play with my diddler.

BOY: But, Daddy, that's what you once gave me a spanking for.

DAD: Yes, son, but you were just having useless fun. I do it for money.

BOY: What else do you do?

DAD: If I see a queer, I wave my diddler at him and show him how big it is. . . .

BOY: What's a queer, daddy?

DAD: A queer is a guy who likes to play with other men's diddlers. I arrest men like that and put them in jail.[52]

Al Goldstein and Jim Buckley, the publishers of *Screw,* used money from the newspaper to finance *Gay* and *Gay Power* magazines.

The connections between gay liberation and the sexual revolution were not many, but they were important. Sexual revolutionaries who wanted to stamp out superstition realized the necessity of changing attitudes toward homosexuality. Men like Barney Rosset, owner of Grove Press, and Ted McIllvenna championed gay liberation because they wanted Americans to be less fearful about sex in general. By the same token, Rosset's *Evergreen Review,* with its controversial literary content and erotic illustrations, was an inspiration to young gays like Michael Bronski and Charlie Shively, who, as teenagers, devoured any countercultural materials they could find. As adults, Bronski and Shively became two of the founders of a radical gay collective in Boston.[53] Indeed, most gay liberationists — exceptions like Craig Shoomaker aside — welcomed those legal and cultural changes that allowed straights to print and purchase sexually explicit materials, live together, and enjoy sex outside of marriage. The more open and extroverted straights became about their own sexuality (admitting to an interest in such practices as oral sex and anal sex), the more freedom gays expected they would have to do the same.

From Stonewall through the end of 1970, American liberals were supportive of gay liberation. In fact, it looked to many as if the gay revolution could be accomplished with few angry words. The legacy of John F. Kennedy, the rise of secular humanism, the influence of the New Left, and the extraordinary economic vitality of the era contributed to a national mood of tolerance. Shortly after Stonewall, the *Los Angeles Times* ended its long-standing ban on the use of the word *homosexual* in advertisements. A county court in Denver told local police to end the harassment of bathhouse patrons. The University of Nebraska approved a course in gay studies. Huey Newton, then leader of the Black Panthers, expressed public support for gay liberation, arguing that gays "might be the most oppressed people in our society." The Teachers Advisory Council of Minneapolis granted permission to the Guthrie Theater to show a play about homosexuality to over a thousand high school students. KRLA, a Los Angeles radio station, bought a full-page advertisement in the *L.A. Times,* pleading for gay rights. When the mainstream Fifty-fifth Street Playhouse in Manhattan began showing Wakefield Poole's pornographic gay film *Boys in the Sand* in December 1971, the entertainment paper *Variety* and many other mainstream newspapers gave the film positive reviews.[54] Many Democratic politicians in New York warmly embraced gay rights.[55]

The strongest support for gay rights came out of the religious community. Laud Humphreys, a graduate of the Seabury-Western Theological Seminary who served as an Episcopal minister for fourteen years and then became a sociologist, gave his approval to public gay sex in 1970. He was a married man and an untenured assistant professor of sociology at Southern Illinois University when he published *Tearoom Trade: Impersonal Sex in Public Places*. Humphreys's book challenged common assumptions about the "harmful" effects of sex in public bathrooms ("tearooms" = "T rooms" = "toilet rooms") and advised communities and police officers to ease up in the surveillance of rest room activity.

Humphreys suggested that it was police persecution and the social control of homosexuality that drove men to engage in rest room sex; if society accepted semi-public gay sex, it would actually become less common. Humphreys's book caused a major controversy when it was published — not, notably, for his recommendations for social policy, but because it seemed to many to be an invasion of privacy: that is, an invasion of the privacy of those who engaged in public sex.*

Although straight sexual revolutionaries and gay liberation activists often had their differences, the energy and excitement in the air in 1969 and 1970 had less to do with identity politics than with large-scale social transformation. Young radicals believed they could change the world. As a member of a gay collective in Boston declared, "If cock-sucking could bring down Rome, think what we might do to Capitalism and the American system of imperial terror. Down with Production; Up with Pleasure."[56] The members of the collective were all socialists and belonged to Students for a Democratic Society. They subscribed to a four-point program of social change: public sex, prostitution, pornography, and promiscuity. The goal was not simply gay rights or gay acceptance, it was the wholesale reconstitution of the social order.

But while long-haired twenty-year-olds were plotting to topple thousands of years of Judeo-Christian dogma and establish a dictatorship of the sexually liberated, a generation of middle-class, middle-aged adults were still struggling with the sort of anxieties that were more appropriate for the therapist's couch than the revolutionary's soap box. Many married couples looked upon the sexual activities of the younger set with envy and frustration. A man couldn't take advantage of the new climate of sexual freedom if he suffered from impotence. A woman couldn't very well wave the banner of sexual liberation if she wasn't orgasmic. Fortunately for straight middle America, Masters and Johnson were ready to come to the rescue.

---

* After observing tea-room encounters, Humphreys followed his subjects home and later, in disguise, returned to interview them about their attitudes toward politics, sexuality, and the like. His major critic was Nicholas Von Hoffman ("Sociological Snoopers," *Washington Post*, 30 January 1970).

CHAPTER 13

THE GOLDEN AGE
OF SEXUAL SCIENCE

OPIES OF *Human Sexual Inadequacy*, a 467-page sober-looking tome in dark green, unillustrated dustjackets, by sex researchers William Masters and Virginia Johnson, went on sale April 27, 1970. The event was marked by stories on the front page of dozens of newspapers, including the *Washington Post* and the *Boston Globe*. The authors were lauded by journalists, fellow scientists, doctors, educators, religious leaders, and other professionals. Three hundred thousand copies were bought within two months.[1] In dense, difficult prose, *Human Sexual Inadequacy* examined a range of distressing sexual problems, from impotence to inorgasmia. More important, the book offered simple solutions for long-term ills. In fact, Masters and Johnson claimed that by using their techniques developed in the laboratory they could cure 60 percent of all chronic impotence cases and 74 percent of all cases involving occasional impotence. Even more striking, they reported 98 percent success in treating men who suffered from premature ejaculation. As for female "frigidity," the sex therapists reported 83 percent treatment success in cases of chronic inorgasmia and 77 percent success in cases of "situational orgasmic dysfunction."[2] Four years earlier, their groundbreaking *Human Sexual Response* had disproved Freud's theory of the vaginal orgasm and been an international bestseller.

Reviewers could barely find enough adjectives to praise Masters and Johnson's book. As Richard Rhodes, who would go on to write his own sex treatise, *Making Love: An Erotic Odyssey*, twenty years later, exclaimed:

For heterosexual men and women, *Human Sexual Inadequacy* completes the sexual revolution. It offers substantial hope to the sexually disabled. It provides authoritative guidelines to those who would like to bring greater intimacy to their marriages. But, beyond these medical goals it proposes by implication a bill of rights for both men and women in our still repressive society. It proposes the sexual and personal equality of women, the release of men from the burden of mechanical performance, the promise of intimate communication, the possibility of sexual ecstasy. In a society which changes partners faster than it changes toothpastes, such a bill of rights must seem a revolution to which all but the most irreparably damaged or permanently embittered can pledge allegiance.[3]

In a similar vein, sex educator Harold Lief asserted: "Masters and Johnson are doing more to bring about the fusion of love and sex, to enrich sex with loving feelings, and to enrich love by appropriate means of demonstrating and sharing sexual pleasure, than anyone else" in the field. According to an article in *Life* magazine, Masters and Johnson were "exquisitely professional" and "totally dedicated sex researchers."[4] The reviews were so positive, and they received so much free publicity, the two became household names whose faces were instantly recognizable to millions of Americans across the country.

William Masters, born to a wealthy Cleveland family in 1915, studied at Hamilton College and the University of Rochester School of Medicine and Dentistry. His mentor at Rochester was George Washington Corner, a professor of anatomy and one of the key supporters of sex researcher Alfred Kinsey. Masters hoped to follow in Kinsey's footsteps, but Corner insisted that Masters first establish himself as a scientist in a field other than human sexuality in order to be taken seriously. After medical school, Masters served as an intern in obstetrics and gynecology at St. Louis Maternity Hospital, then held an internship in pathology at the Washington University School of Medicine, also in St. Louis which he followed with an internship in internal medicine at Barnes Hospital. During these years, he published several papers on human hormones and aging. In 1947, he took a position at Washington University, where he was promoted to associate professor of clinical obstetrics and gynecology. Not until 1954, at the age of thirty-eight, did he begin to work directly on sexuality, by interviewing male and female prostitutes about their sexual histories and making empirical studies of his prostitute subjects during sexual arousal. The following year, he established the Reproductive Biology Research Foundation in St. Louis to promote this physiological research. At the suggestion of one of his female subjects, Masters hired a female coworker in 1957, Virginia Johnson, born Virginia Eshelman in 1925. Though she had no scientific training, Johnson soon became Masters's collaborator and co-researcher.[5]

In 1966, they issued the first modern study of the physiology of desire, *Human Sexual Response*. Although few of the book's research methods or conclusions were actually original, the book itself was viewed as a major step forward in the journey toward sexual knowledge. The very scope of the book's project — a study of sexual response in 694 individuals — seemed breathtaking. The book was hailed as a sign of scientific progress, and almost every review was complimentary.[6] Quickly reaching number two on the *New York Times* best-seller list, the book was nearly as popular as the two world-renowned Kinsey studies had been. For those who wanted a more accessible version of the text, Ruth and Edward Brecher published *An Analysis of "Human Sexual Response,"* which sold more than 500,000 copies.[7]

Human Sexual Response seemed altogether groundbreaking. Using cameras, tape recorders, and specifically designed electronic equipment, Masters and Johnson observed hundreds of heterosexual couples having intercourse. They probed and measured human genitals. The notion of scientists studying the most intimate matters with such clinical detachment and high-tech hardware was startling yet comforting. Their research was widely regarded as reassuring evidence of America's scientific advancement.

At a time when large numbers of Americans were consciously rebelling against puritanism and provincialism, simply owning a copy of *Human Sexual Response* was a guaranteed mark of sophistication. Masters and Johnson, however, were wary of being seen as popularizers. Masters, in fact, admitted that "every effort was made to make this book as pedantic and obtuse as possible," adding, "may I say, in all modesty, I think we succeeded admirably." Indeed, historian Paul Robinson has described *Human Sexual Response* as one of "the worst written books in the English language."[8] The authors cultivated their images as the quintessential scientists, wearing white lab coats and speaking in medical jargon whenever possible. Johnson, who did not complete four years of college, always referred to Masters in public as "the doctor." Midsixties Americans, thoroughly entranced by empirical science, saw Masters and Johnson's work as the coup de grâce to Victorian mysticism and romanticism.

Although one could argue that it did more to obscure the discussion of sex than to clarify it, Masters and Johnson's work did serve as a direct attack on the double standard. And the publication of their book led to hundreds of articles in mainstream publications about such subjects as clitoral orgasm, masturbation, and penis size. Journalists, in fact, seized on the book as an opportunity to discuss sexual topics in print.

By far the most significant aspect of *Human Sexual Response* was Masters and Johnson's research discrediting Freud's theory of the vaginal orgasm, a theory American psychoanalysts had long treated as gospel. For decades, women had been told by analysts and popular psychologists that the pleasures of the clitoral orgasm were spurious compared to the superior experience afforded by the vaginal orgasm. In her book *Female Sexuality* (1953), psychoanalyst Marie Bonaparte had even recommended surgery to move the clitoris closer to the vagina for inorgasmic women. In unqualified terms, Masters and Johnson declared that the vaginal orgasm did not exist. Using electrical monitors and internal lights, the researchers had studied the walls of the vaginal canal and showed that they were incapable of erotic excitement. Only the stimulation of the clitoris could lead to climax. With the publication of *Human Sexual Response,* countless women were freed from feelings of inadequacy and abnormality.

Many doctors, however, continued to insist on the existence of the vaginal orgasm. In 1968, psychoanalyst Helen Wagenheim asserted that the clitoral orgasm was more often than not a consequence of "simply masturbation," which tended to be accompanied by "reflections of inadequate personality development."[9] Some doctors opposed all sex research. In response to an article about Masters and Johnson in 1970, one physician wrote to *Medical World News:* "I find it unbelievable that our profession will stand still for promotion of moral degradation in our patients."[10] Meanwhile, psychoanalysts like Theodor Reik continued to claim that most women suffered from "penis envy" and other unproved Freudian phenomena. [11]

Although their work was hailed by many feminists, Masters and Johnson themselves were politically conservative. Masters voted for Richard Nixon in 1968 and Johnson recoiled from the label "feminist." She told a reporter, "I've grown up in a man's world and loved every minute of it. I've been given so much consideration by men, both professionally and personally." To Johnson, "lady liberationists" and "emancipated women" presented a danger to society by making men feel inadequate; feminism threatened to cause the sort of "sexual dysfunction in the male that the Victorian woman so often contended with herself."[12] In 1970, Johnson's views on feminism were printed in *Redbook,* a magazine aimed at housewives:

Any woman who demands the right to her sexual climax the way she demands equal job rights is simply ignorant of sexual physiology. In achieving equality she must preserve those aspects of herself as female that the male has learned to value . . . She has to give, as he has to give, if together they are to get the pleasures they both seek.[13]

Although both Masters and Johnson were divorced (Johnson three times) at the time they began their sex research, they both viewed marriage as the proper domain of sexual expression, and in 1971, they married each other. (They divorced in 1991.)

In the tradition of Enlightenment rationalism, Masters and Johnson's work was infused with a strong sense of free will: With the proper training, any individual could exercise control over his or her own sexual "response." Masters and Johnson intentionally avoided all discussion of the unconscious in their work. Their goal, in fact, was to develop an alternative to psychoanalysis for the treatment of sexual problems. For Masters and Johnson, Freud was a fraud, his theory of psychosexual development little more than superstition mixed with bad science. Their approach was based on a medical model: isolation of a specific problem and direct intervention to eliminate it. At their Reproductive Biology Research Foundation, they intended to quickly and painlessly aid women who were unable to achieve orgasm and men who suffered from such problems as premature ejaculation and impotence. Unlike psychotherapists, who treated individuals in isolation over the course of several years, Masters and Johnson worked strictly with married couples — "marital units," as they chose to call them — and promised to cure these couples of their sexual dysfunctions within a matter of days. Numerous couples shelled out the $2,500 fee for three weeks of sex therapy at the Foundation, discussing and then demonstrating their sexual practices in order to receive expert coaching in erotic technique. (At first, Masters and Johnson supplied surrogate sex partners for individual patients who needed help, but after a lawsuit by a man who claimed Masters and Johnson paid his wife to be a sex surrogate, they ended the practice.)[14]

Most of the techniques Masters and Johnson recommended to unhappy couples were actually rather banal. To stop premature ejaculation, they suggested squeezing the penis just prior to orgasm. This was an old trick used by prostitutes, which Masters had learned during his early research. To cure impotence and inorgasmia, they encouraged couples to engage in sensual massage. Such a suggestion might have been helpful to some, but it was hardly a groundbreaking recommendation. There were, moreover, many gaps in *Human Sexual Inadequacy*, questions left unanswered about their research and therapy. The authors never precisely defined what they meant by therapeutic success; nor did they indicate whether success was determined by the patient or by the therapist. Furthermore, it was not stated in the text how many applicants for treatment were rejected, a statistic that might have been crucial to interpreting their results. Masters and Johnson explicitly attempted to divorce sexual functioning from any social, psychological, or political context. But this raised questions of its own. No information was given about any patient's views on sex, marriage, or career. Were the patients happy in other areas of their lives? Did they feel they had equality in their relationships? Why did they choose to see a sex therapist? How might self-selection bias have affected the research?

These many questions notwithstanding, Masters and Johnson's research was widely accepted as official wisdom on human sexuality. In many ways, however, Masters and Johnson were less scientists than they were marriage counselors. (It is no accident that they never considered a pharmacological approach to impotence.)[15] Part of the mission of the Reproductive Biology Research Foundation was to train pairs of male and female therapists who would function as marriage counselors with special expertise in the area of sex. To further this aim, Masters and Johnson recruited the Philadelphia marriage counselor Emily Mudd and the psychologist Raymond Wagoneer. Mudd and Wagoneer built a program to train the male–female therapist teams, and by 1971 scores of therapist pairs were being certified by the Foundation.[16] Soon similar training programs were in operation across the country. Thousands of middle-aged, middle-class married couples began consulting "professional" sex therapists. The result was a highly profitable industry that marketed quick and easy solutions to sexual problems.

Eunice and Trevor Lake (pseudonyms) of Peru, Indiana, typified many of the couples who sought out the advice of sex therapists. In 1974, the Lakes consulted a husband-and-wife team of therapists in order to treat Trevor's case of chronic impotence. Over the course of three months, their therapists prescribed a variety of techniques. The Lakes were assigned "homework" that progressed from verbal communication and nonsexual massage to nude play without intercourse. Eunice Lake recorded her thoughts about this homework in a private journal. One entry describes an attempt at "genital massage," which she found to be a taxing procedure with limited results:

> I am not sure what was supposed to happen but if it was erotic response, it didn't. First, I felt like some kind of specimen on an examination table (even though we were in the proper position). Most women, including myself, find themselves in this position only when being examined by a doctor and from experience develop a mental turn-off to sexual arousal. The touching felt good but I could tell that I wasn't the least bit lubricated and could sense that this turned Trevor off, but I wasn't able to do anything about it.[17]

Ultimately, according to Eunice, this sort of therapy did help cure Trevor of his impotence. But in the process it transformed sex into a gynecological exam for her.

Masters and Johnson acknowledged this problem and recognized that their techniques could actually aggravate conditions like impotence. They called the tendency to monitor one's own state of arousal "spectatoring" and noticed that it led directly to "performance anxiety." Yet they failed to offer a way to avoid such critical awareness. As Masters noted, "Most people have difficulty with sex because when sex goes wrong, they *work* to make it better. You can't do that with a natural function — so one of our jobs is to discourage working at it."[18] As one self-help book based on Masters and Johnson's techniques conceded, "No doubt much of this sounds hopelessly self-conscious and here we are suggesting that self-consciousness is part of your problem."[19]

Ignoring all forms of social analysis, Freudian, feminist, or otherwise, Masters and Johnson encouraged couples to treat sex as something completely separate from other life experiences. The idea of designating a set time for sexual "homework" assumed a distinction between sexual contact and other aspects of an intimate relationship that was sure to aggravate, rather than alleviate, sexual tensions. Masters and Johnson made no attempt to teach people about their bodies or thoughts outside the bedroom (or laboratory). Whereas Freud tried to show how society shaped sexual desires and how sexual desires shaped society, Masters and Johnson intentionally tried to sever this link.

Their unwavering focus on laboratory observation of sexual behavior blinded them to the need for an awareness of the social context of human sexuality. Might a woman not suffer from inorgasmia, for example, because she spent the entire day changing diapers and scrubbing floors? Might a man not suffer from impotence because advertising and pornography fed him images of the ideal female body that no real woman could live up to?*

Masters and Johnson were brave but sloppy scientists writing for a curious but undemanding public. Tending to be a bit careless about their statistics, they claimed that half of all married couples suffered from some form of sexual "dysfunction," a figure that was quickly accepted and widely repeated by the media. Having done no sociological studies of any kind, Masters and Johnson could not possibly have possessed the kind of knowledge they claimed to have.[20]

All too often, Masters and Johnson assumed that their own scientific research in one area qualified them to speak as authorities in other areas.

---

* Of course, the invention of Viagra has shown that impotence is often a physiological condition that can be treated chemically.

For instance, they attacked the idea of sex outside of a monogamous male–female relationship. In their eyes, heterosexuality and monogamy were sacrosanct. They dismissed open marriages and group marriages as unworkable, and they gave plenty of hints that they believed homosexuality to be a form of sexual dysfunction.[21] It is not that they were wrong to hold such opinions, but they did not have any scientific evidence to support their case. Their proclamations came ex cathedra. Unfortunately for the history of sexual science, Masters and Johnson ended up believing in their own public image as America's official sex doctors.

Still, they deserve much credit for having attempted to study bodily processes objectively and scientifically. There were plenty of self-appointed experts running around in the late sixties and early seventies willing to make claims about sex without having done any research whatsoever. For instance, following the overwhelming success of Masters and Johnson's books, and the subsequent flood of newspaper and magazine reports about sex therapy, medical experts discovered "The New Impotence," a supposedly high incidence of men reporting the problem. In October 1972, *Esquire* magazine quoted a member of the New York Community Sex Information telephone help line: "You get the feeling that every man in the city is impotent or suffers from premature ejaculation."[22] The journal *Medical Aspects of Human Sexuality* published a roundtable discussion on the subject in its October 1971 issue, in which four out of the five experts on the panel concurred that rates of impotence were increasing. The clinician credited with discovering the problem, George Ginsberg, associate director of psychiatric services at New York University Hospital, cited one major cause for the trend: the new sexual assertiveness of women. "When we explored these sexual failures, we found a common male complaint: Newly freed women demanded sexual performance." Apparently, sexually assertive women threatened men's sense of masculinity. Accordingly, women bore the responsibility for mitigating the impact of their newfound strength.

> Unconscious transmission of feminine revenge by an aggressive manner and over-assertiveness may enhance a man's castration anxiety with consequent fear of the vagina. This must be seen in an adaptational and social framework rather than as a purely psychological and particularly intrapsychic phenomenon.

The New Impotence caused Ginsberg and fellow experts to reevaluate the sexual revolution. "Although for some the new 'sexual freedom' may indeed be liberating, for others it merely induces different symptoms rather than improved mental health."[23]

Ginsberg was only one of many doctors who regarded feminism with suspicion and the sexual revolution with disdain. Strangely enough, when it came to sex, the medical establishment as a whole was often willing to settle for ignorance and superstition instead of rigorous thought and concrete facts. Masters and Johnson were far from model scientists, but compared to contemporaries like George Ginsberg, they had much to offer the cause of sexual freedom. If nothing else, they gave journalists the opportunity to write about important aspects of human sexuality without euphemism or vulgarity. Whether their own research was objective or not, Masters and Johnson increased the scientific credibility of the idea of separating fact from opinion in the study of sex.

CHAPTER 14

MEDICINE AND MORALITY

THE INTELLECTUAL DISARRAY of the medical establishment regarding sex, typified by the work of George Ginsberg, paved the way for one of the most inaccurate and misleading "sex education" books of all time, *Everything You Always Wanted to Know About Sex . . . But Were Afraid to Ask.* It was also the hottest book of 1970, staying on the best-seller list for eighteen weeks. Copies of the book were so hard to come by, one branch of the New York Public Library had a 39-patron waiting list for Reuben's book.[1] After a glowing review in *Life* magazine, *Everything You Always Wanted to Know* became a publishing phenomenon, and the book's author, a New York psychiatrist named Dr. David Reuben, attained instant celebrity status. Reuben, with his nerdy glasses and sheepish can-you-believe-I'm-telling-you-this smile, made the cover of *Newsweek* and was invited to appear on *The Dick Cavett Show, The Merv Griffin Show,* and *The Tonight Show.* (For the last, Reuben garnered a stunning 53 percent of the ratings.[2]) He was the self-styled Robespierre of the sexual revolution, supposedly charging forward with brutal honesty where others feared to tread.

But Reuben's collection of unscientific claims and recycled myths was like Robespierre's guillotine, far more dangerous than anyone at first imagined. It was replete with the very sort of misinformation Alfred Kinsey and Masters and Johnson had worked hard to discredit. "It won't be long," Reuben pronounced without citing any supporting evidence, "before almost everyone in the United States has venereal disease." Manufacturing statistics out of whole cloth, Reuben claimed that

80 percent of Americans engaged in oral sex. In a section on birth control, he recommended douching with Coca-Cola:

> Long a favorite soft drink, it is, coincidentally, the best douche available. A Coke contains carbonic acid which kills the sperm and sugar which explodes the sperm cells. The carbonation forces it into the vagina under pressure and helps penetrate every tiny crevice of vaginal lining. It is inexpensive (ten cents per application), universally available, and comes in a disposable applicator.[3]

Reuben failed to mention that such a procedure could cause salpingitis, peritonitis, or a fatal gas embolism.[4]

Reuben devoted many pages to "explaining" homosexuality, presenting his opinions on the subject as statements of fact. "One penis plus one penis equals nothing," he wrote. "There is no substitute for heterosex — penis and vagina." Reuben discoursed at length about how male homosexuals inserted inanimate objects into their rectums. "Some of the more routine items that find their way into the gastrointestinal systems of homosexuals via the exit are pens, pencils, lipsticks, combs, pop bottles, [ladies'] electric shavers, and enough other items to stock a small department store." He claimed that "nearly every intern in the emergency room of a large city hospital" had seen gay male patients with objects lodged in the anus. According to Reuben, a doctor told him: "It usually happens like this: Two fags are having a big time on Saturday night, you know, drinking and whooping it up. The queen rolls over and waits for his boy friend to give him the works, only he slides in the first thing he has in his hand, usually the whiskey glass." The anonymous doctor described how he once operated on a man who had a flashlight inside his rectum.[5]

The book was packed with factual errors. "Cancer of the penis occurs only among *uncircumcised* men," Reuben wrote, a statement that is simply untrue. "Erection of the nipples always follows orgasm in the female," he alleged. "In spite of heaving hips, lunging pelvis, passionate groans — no nipple erection, no orgasm. It is an accurate mammary lie detector — for those who insist on the truth."[6] Reuben, unfortunately, insisted on anything but the truth. Gore Vidal denounced Reuben in the *New York Review of Books*, pointing out the utterly unscientific nature of his claims. But who was going to listen to Gore Vidal, a self-identified bisexual novelist, over a well-known doctor? Even *Screw*, the raunchy New York newspaper, called *Everything You Always Wanted to Know* "the most insane book in the history of psychiatric theory."[7]

When challenged on the validity of his statements, Reuben was unshakably smug. "In psychiatry everyone is entitled to his own opinions based on his own experience."[8] No matter how shoddy his science,

Reuben was embraced by fellow doctors as the official spokesman on sex in the seventies. At the University of Pennsylvania, for instance, *Everything You Always Wanted to Know* was assigned to students taking a course sponsored by none other than the school's Sexual Counseling Service.[9] Reuben was, without a doubt, America's favorite sex guru in the early seventies.

As the story of *Everything You Always Wanted to Know* reveals, the sexual revolution was a much more complicated phenomenon than most accounts suggest. The materials hawked to cash in on the revolution sometimes contained nothing more than village superstition in modern dress. The liberationist fervor of the late sixties and early seventies did not preclude the persistence of older ideas and assumptions. Indeed, the sexual revolution sometimes merely gave those ideas and assumptions a new gloss of pseudo-scientific certainty. It was not long after Reuben's book was published that an urban legend was born: Many Americans began believing that they knew someone who knew someone who knew a doctor who had extracted a rodent from the rectum of a gay man. The nineteenth-century criminal sodomite, who had become the turn-of-the-century invert with castration anxiety, who had became the postwar child molester, was now the disgusting hedonist in a morality tale about deviance and decadence in an age of too much tolerance.

How could Americans in 1970 — some twenty years after the first Kinsey Report — swallow Reuben's fallacies and outright lies? Why didn't the medical establishment tear him down and defend the honor of the profession? There is no simple answer to this last question, but when it came to sex, physicians frequently sacrificed scientific objectivity for moralism and superstition. Psychiatrists — given virtually free rein to invent their diagnostic claims — were particularly guilty of forsaking the scientific method in favor of personal prejudice. Through the sixties and well into the seventies, the medical establishment clung to Victorian attitudes about human sexuality but draped those attitudes with the mantle of modern science.

Until the sixties, American doctors had subscribed to a cult of reticence, avoiding all mention of sex. In 1960, the year the pill was licensed by the FDA, only three medical schools in the nation offered courses in human sexuality. Such reticence had its costs. As noted in chapter 11, a 1959 study of medical school seniors in Philadelphia found that half of them believed masturbation caused insanity. One 1962 study showed that 283 out of 514 doctors felt they lacked the training to deal with "marital problems."[10] The American Medical Association did not even acknowledge the possible legitimacy of contraception until 1965, two decades after "family planning" was accepted by the middle class and some fifty years after Margaret Sanger began her initial campaign for birth control. (Prior to 1965, the AMA actively opposed the dissemination of "propaganda" intended to promote contraception.)[11] Unlike the American Law Institute, which began endorsing abortion law reform in 1959, the AMA objected to even limited reform efforts until 1967.

Throughout the sixties and seventies, doctors — especially psychiatrists — allowed moral assumptions to color their thinking. Many, if not most, insisted on treating sex as something more sacrosanct than a set of biological and psychological processes. Not all doctors were moralistic, of course, but professional organizations like the AMA and the American College of Obstetricians and Gynecologists were so leery of social reform, they sacrificed their credibility as scientific associations. It is no accident that in the sixties the vice president of the National Organization for Decent Literature was a physician. Almost entirely white, wealthy, male, and married, the medical profession had the most to lose from social change.

Looking back, it is hard to believe how many late-twentieth-century doctors subscribed to nineteenth-century views of sex. "Rape," claimed Karl Rugart of the University of Pennsylvania Medical School in 1968, "is a tricky label for something that may result from a girl's subconscious seductive impulses." Rugart doubted that rape might ever diminish a woman's subsequent capacity to enjoy sex.[12] Judd Marmor, a physician at Cedars-Sinai in Los Angeles, warned in 1971 that sex without love was "unhealthy" and argued that sex ought to be more than just a "biological discharge."[13] Throughout the sixties, the magazine *Sexology*, published by physicians to provide the general reader with information about sexuality, was shot through with unscientific moralism. Articles in *Sexology* frequently condemned sex outside of marriage and warned against "excessive" masturbation.[14] Some doctors actually recommended feigning a nonjudgmental attitude toward patients while subtly suggesting restrictive moral codes. Gail Anderson, a gynecologist at the University of Southern California School of Medicine, urged physicians to provide an "atmosphere for a free discussion of what the sex act means," all the while leading the patient to a realization of "what the consequences of a so-called liberal attitude toward sexual activity may be."[15]

Doctors sometimes seemed far more progressive than they really were. In 1964, a group of physicians founded the Sex Information and Education Council of the United States. The organization's mission was to make information about sex education available to school administrators. SIECUS certainly seemed like it was at the forefront of sexual enlightenment. Most of the physicians on the board were either associated with Planned Parenthood or were involved in sex research. In fact, some right-wing groups denounced SIECUS as part of a Communist conspiracy to undermine American life.[16]

Yet being respectable was more important to SIECUS than taking a strong stand on sexual issues. The organization's founder, gynecologist Mary Steichen Calderone, born in 1904, was extremely wary of seeming like an advocate for social change. As Calderone wrote to one left-wing critic in 1970, "I am quite pleased that people . . . are accusing SIECUS of being 'bourgeois latent puritans.' It is very refreshing, and indicates to me that we are on the right track."[17] Like Virginia Johnson, she refused to identify herself as a feminist ("I think some of these [feminist] organizations are shrill and anti-female," she told *Playboy* in 1970, "and I am not a crusader for women's rights. Women don't have rights — as women only. They have human rights. That's what I crusade for"), and she considered abortion "immoral." Calderone readily admitted her "really profound belief that sex belongs primarily in marriage," and her view of promiscuity as "sad." As she explained, "I'm not looking forward happily to a widespread acceptance of casual sex. . . . I look upon casual sex as being purely for pleasure, with no regard for the relationship of the partners."[18] Despite her medical and scientific training, Calderone was never one to separate sex and religion. "The attitude to be conveyed is that sex is an exalted, wonderful, exciting gift from God and that it is probably most rewarding within an enduring relationship such as marriage."

As noted in chapter 12, Calderone often encouraged sex education on the grounds that it would prevent children from growing up to become homosexual adults. Such positions lost SIECUS potential supporters. In fact, some gay organizations actively opposed sex education, fearing that school programs would inevitably include an anti-gay agenda.[19]

Still, SIECUS did represent the liberal wing of the medical profession. Doctors generally disassociated themselves from sex education altogether. One psychoanalyst, Dr. Eunice Lorand, and a family psychiatrist, Dr. Gerald Sandson, began a campaign in 1968 against sex education in the public schools, arguing that it interfered with the "latency period" described by Freud.[20] Possessing only the most rudimentary understanding of Freudian theory, these doctors worried that SIECUS and other sex education groups might corrupt young children's minds. Howard Hoyman, a physician and faculty member at the University of Oregon, was outspoken in his opposition to teaching students about birth control, "sex techniques," and methods of venereal disease prevention (other than abstinence). "The formal, ideal sexual standard in our society," Hoyman told his colleagues, "is that sexual intercourse is for marriage — and that it should be based on mutual love and fidelity in family life." Hoyman strongly urged premarital chastity and rejected the privatization of sexual morality. In 1966, he wrote: "Human sexual behavior is only partly a personal and private matter; it is also a matter of public concern because sexual behavior has important social, ethical and religious implications and outcomes."[21] Any mention of venereal disease prevention, Hoyman argued, "would be an open suggestion to all teenage boys and girls that they could engage in illicit sex relations." As far as the classroom discussion of homosexuality was concerned, Hoyman insisted that teachers ought not "cater to morbid curiosity" or "go into details that might cause normal boys and girls to develop neurotic fears that they might be sexual perverts." To Hoyman there was a fine, yet critical, line between moral education and "genital education."[22]

Such attitudes infuriated public health officials who took a strictly humanist approach to social problems. As one Chicago public health officer told the members of the Illinois Institute for Sex Education:

> Germs cause venereal disease. Sexual activity is only the mode of transmission. Eradicate the germs and venereal disease will be eradicated. That, after all, is the goal of VD education as we in public health understand it. If your goal is making the myth of a virginal-monogamous society a reality, please label your efforts properly so you don't confuse those who think the eradication of VD is your goal.[23]

For many years, doctors were reluctant to discuss sexual matters at all. It was not until 1967 that American physicians finally introduced a professional journal devoted to sexual issues. But the journal they created, *Medical Aspects of Human Sexuality*, was focused more on promoting heterosexuality and monogamy than on advancing the cause of medicine. In psychiatric jargon, contributors condemned promiscuity, homosexuality, and other forms of "deviant" behavior. A typical article, "Sexual Promiscuity as a Symptom of Personal and Cultural Anxiety," asserted:

> Sexual promiscuity is one form of pathological self-enhancement by which an individual seeks relief from tension when his sense of security and personal esteem have been disturbed. The incidence of promiscuity may increase dramatically at times when there is widespread cultural anxiety. It is particularly likely to assume epidemic proportions when the culture seems to default on its responsibility to provide available and reliable institutions by which the individual may achieve meaningful future gratifications.[24]

Needless to say, such claims were presented without any supporting evidence.

In 1970, the American Medical Association published its very first series of sex education books, *Approaching Adulthood*. For decades, the medical profession had left sex education to parents, religious authorities, and poorly trained schoolteachers. The *Approaching Adulthood* series, intended for fifteen-to-twenty-year-olds, reflected the medical community's fervent disapproval of masturbation and premarital sex. "There is something counterfeit about sex satisfaction that is not a part of the love of two persons for one another," the authors wrote regarding masturbation. "Also," they noted, "masturbation is a solitary practice which, if continued over a long period of time, sometimes makes difficult the cooperative sexual relationships of married life." No empirical study had ever reached such a conclusion. The authors then went on to warn teenagers to "take responsibility for keeping away from situations" where "heavy petting" might occur. *Approaching Adulthood* staked out a clear and unambiguous position on premarital sex: "Unmarried persons have more to lose than to gain by trying to enjoy the sexual aspects of married life before they can assume the responsibilities." As for prostitution, the authors commented: "The whole business seems sordid and disgusting." Homosexuality did not even merit mention in the book.[25]

While the AMA preferred to ignore the existence of homosexuality, some psychiatrists were pursuing an active approach to "curing" men and women of their same-sex desires. Many used crude behaviorist techniques, such as aversion therapy, whereby patients were shown homoerotic images and then subjected to putrid smells and other unpleasant sensory experiences, and electroshock therapy. Some psychiatrists advocated excising brain tissue, while others took the less drastic approach of giving patients drugs or encouraging males to visit female prostitutes.[26]

Given the attitudes of the medical profession, a clash between liberationists and physicians was inevitable. But by the early seventies, with so many different definitions of sexual freedom in the air, it was often hard to tell who was really on the side of the sexual revolution.

Through the sixties, the American College of Obstetricians and Gynecologists (ACOG) was the leading champion of the birth control pill. Since the Catholic Church still officially opposed contraception, ACOG appeared to represent the principles of secular rationalism. But by the end of the sixties, even many non-Catholics suspected that the pill was less benign than its proponents claimed. Feminists, in particular, did not think the pill was quite the wonder drug its makers and advocates advertised.

Early research on the pill had revealed numerous risks associated with its use. Clinical trials in Puerto Rico in the 1950s had shown that the pill could lead to breakthrough bleeding, deformations of the cervix, and death. Before the pill was approved by the Food and Drug Administration for use as a contraceptive in the United States, only

123 women had used it under medical observation for longer than a year. Enovid, the major manufacturer, was well aware by 1961 that the pill was linked to thrombosis and embolism. In fact, company executives knew that at least eleven women had died from pill use.

Original versions of the pill contained very high doses of synthetic hormones: four times more estrogen and ten times more progesterone than necessary. There were several press reports about frightening side effects, from simple bloating to heart attack. These stories caught the attention of a young journalist named Barbara Seaman, who covered health issues for women's magazines like *Good Housekeeping* and *Ladies' Home Journal* and was the ghostwriter for Dr. Joyce Brothers's nationally syndicated column, "On Being a Woman." Seaman had had an abortion at nineteen and had written several controversial articles on sex in the past — two of which had been banned in Boston — and she began doing research on the pill. She quickly became concerned that the 8 million or so American women taking the pill were at serious risk. Pill use appeared to be correlated with everything from arthritis to urinary tract infection.

In late 1969, Seaman published her findings in a book titled *The Doctors' Case Against the Pill*, which warned women that oral contraceptives were far more dangerous than most people suspected. It infuriated the leaders of Planned Parenthood, who believed that concerns about the pill were being exaggerated by their political and religious enemies to keep contraception use down. A copy fell into the hands of U.S. senator Gaylord Nelson, who was deeply disturbed by what he read. In 1970 he convened a series of hearings to determine whether the pill was in fact unsafe.

None of this would have been out of the ordinary, but ACOG, which was called upon to testify about the pill, vehemently defended the drug, in the face of extensive evidence about its dangers. Both ACOG and the AMA opposed proposals to require inserts informing patients of possible side effects. ACOG, which had close ties to the pharmaceutical industry, sided with industry interests over patient education. Meanwhile, pharmaceutical companies used an argument to defend the pill that was similar to the one used by cigarette manufacturers: There simply was not enough evidence to prove the product was unsafe.

If the AMA and ACOG had had their way, Congress would never have succeeded in requiring pharmaceutical companies to include printed inserts with side-effect information in all drug packaging. Strangely enough, the medical profession preferred to keep patients in ignorance than to let them make educated choices on their own. But a group of women from D.C. Women's Liberation, angry about ACOG's position, organized protests outside the Senate hearings. They demanded access to information about the dangers of synthetic hormones, and contended that the diaphragm could be just as conducive to sexual liberation as the pill. They asserted that their aim was not to limit women's sexual freedom but to ensure that women were well informed of the physiological effects of this seductively easy form of birth control. Their campaign garnered enough media attention to undercut the combined influence of the AMA and ACOG. The package-insert bill was passed into law and pill use declined sharply. (The dosage was eventually reduced to a safe level.)[27]

Revelations about the intra-uterine device, or IUD, caused even greater damage to the reputation of the medical establishment than the controversy surrounding the pill. At first, liberal doctors trumpeted the IUD as the final instrument in female emancipation. A coil that could easily be inserted in the uterus and left in place for months, the IUD required far less effort on the part of women than the pill did, which had to be taken every day to be effective. Then, in 1974, studies revealed that the IUD was especially dangerous.

The contest over the pill reflected the growing split between feminists and the medical profession. In Boston, radical feminists founded a women's health collective to provide an alternative perspective on sexual issues. The book they published in 1973, *Our Bodies, Ourselves,* transformed the discourse of female physiology. Like other books of the time, *Our Bodies* showed readers how to examine their own sexual organs and assured women that there was nothing unhealthy or dangerous about practices like masturbation and lesbianism. But unlike other books, *Our Bodies* gained a vast readership.

What did sexual liberation really mean? What was the ultimate goal of the sexual revolution? What was the secular and humanistic approach to issues regarding sexuality? When *Everything You Always Wanted to Know About Sex . . . But Were Afraid to Ask* appeared on bookshelves in 1970, many thought David Reuben was the prophet who would answer these questions. But if Reuben's book represented the best the medical establishment had to offer, the nation was out of luck. Ignorance and superstition would remain the order of the day.

CHAPTER 15

WHY DO THESE WORDS
SOUND SO NASTY?

ERHAPS MORE THAN any other issue associated with the sexual revolution, pornography rankled authorities. By the end of the sixties, erotic books and magazines were available in abundance. In addition to revising cultural norms, the judicial retreat from censorship gave publishers, purveyors, and purchasers of graphic sexual material the confidence to exercise their full freedoms under the First Amendment. Adult bookstores were now popping up in cities from coast to coast. Mainstream movie theaters had begun showing features like *I Am Curious (Yellow)* and, increasingly, hard-core films disguised as documentaries about sexual practices in Scandinavia. Across the land, pundits railed at the "flood" of pornography (a favorite metaphor) they believed to be "deluging" the nation.

Although some politicians may have been genuinely concerned about the effects of commercial sex on American culture, others surely clamored about pornography to distract attention from the war in Vietnam. In 1968, President Lyndon B. Johnson appointed a task force to report on the problem of pornography. Johnson expected that a committee of solid citizens, charged with investigating the whys and wherefores of "smut," would reach the conclusion that stronger censorship laws were necessary.

Like the president, Congress had grown ever more frustrated with the Supreme Court's unwillingness to endorse obscenity laws. By the time the findings of the task force were due to be made public, legislators had sent two hundred bills to the floor of Congress, all designed to increase restrictions on sexual material. These legislators hoped, nay, assumed that the report of the task force would support such bills.

Nearly all of Washington was taken by surprise when details about the report of the first Presidential Commission on Obscenity and Pornography began to circulate in the fall of 1970. For the majority of the members of the commission had reached the striking opinion that pornography was harmless, perhaps even beneficial. The commission had voted to recommend the repeal of all laws intended to prohibit consenting adults from purchasing or consuming sexually explicit material. After consulting a wide range of scholars and conducting their own empirical investigations, the commission members had become convinced that government concern about sex in books and movies was misguided. Noting that sexually explicit materials served "to increase and facilitate constructive communication about sexual matters within marriage" and that "the most frequent purchaser of explicit sexual materials" was a college-educated, married male, in his thirties or forties, of above average socioeconomic status, the majority of the members of the commission had concluded that obscenity laws, not pornography, were detrimental to society.[1] Before the report ever reached Congress, President Richard Nixon, who had replaced Johnson as chief executive during the commission's tenure, denounced the report's findings and blasted the members of the commission. To Nixon's immense frustration, scientists, the true priests of modern society, had sided with free speech and sexual liberalism against "common decency." Americans rushed to buy copies of the controversial report.

The Presidential Commission on Obscenity and Pornography was created by an act of Congress in 1967. Although even conservative estimates showed that federal and state agencies were already spending roughly $10 million to $15 million each year fighting pornography, Congress still considered the traffic in pornography to be "a matter of national concern." At Johnson's behest, Congress authorized the commission to study the matter for two years and then report their findings to the American people. "After a thorough study, which shall include a study of causal relationship of such materials to antisocial behavior," the commission would "recommend advisable, appropriate, effective and constitutional means to deal effectively with such traffic in obscenity and pornography." If enough scientific evidence could be gathered to show the dangers of pornography, it was hoped, the Supreme Court would no longer overturn every obscenity conviction on its docket.

The commission members were appointed by Johnson in January 1968. Though their identities were supposed to be kept confidential, news reports revealed that the panel included a Methodist minister, a rabbi, a Catholic priest, a state attorney general, an English teacher, a professor of psychiatry, a professor of sociology, a child psychiatrist, a juvenile court judge, and other lawyers, social scientists, and writers. William B. Lockhart, dean of the University of Minnesota Law School, was appointed chair. Prior to joining the commission, Lockhart had presumed that a society without any restrictions on sexual speech would be "unthinkable."

At first, commission members reviewed the existing scientific literature on pornography. Finding little of substance, they decided to embark on their own program of research designed to provide quantitative data on the effects of pornography on the public.

The commissioners certainly had their work cut out for them. Although, as they noted, the size of the porn industry was much, much smaller than law enforcement officials were wont to suggest, there was still plenty of material to study. By the spring of 1970, 830 adults-only bookstores, 1,425 bookstores with adults-only sections, and 200 theaters showing silent but hard-core 16mm stag films were in business nationwide. An estimated 45 million pieces of sexually oriented material were sent through the mails each year. Studies showed that roughly 80 percent of American boys and 70 percent of girls had seen visual depictions or read textual descriptions of sexual intercourse by the age of eighteen.[2]

To find out just who was purchasing erotic materials, the commission sought out the assistance of several sociologists. For six days in August 1969, one team of sociologists observed 2,477 men as they entered two adult bookstores in Denver. It turned out that 89 percent of those pornography consumers were white, 74 percent were between the ages of twenty-four and fifty-five, and 26 percent wore suits and ties. Another team of social scientists spent fourteen hours observing ten adult bookstores in Boston. Of 493 male patrons and 1 female patron, 95 percent were white, and 51 percent wore business suits. Both studies noted that a majority of the men were wearing wedding rings. Other teams stationed themselves outside bookstores in San Francisco, Los Angeles, Manhattan, Chicago, and Detroit. All found similar results. The average consumer of adult materials was a white, male, middle-aged, married professional. The stereotype of the "dirty old man" in a trench coat was clearly a myth.[3]

As the commissioners discovered, the only thing that was new about pornography in the sixties was its wide distribution — hard-core pornography had long been available for those who could afford it and were willing to risk prosecution to obtain it. In the 1800s, "French postcards" — photographs of men and women fornicating — circulated on both sides of the Atlantic. As soon as motion pictures were invented, "stag films" were made showing full penetration. Eight-millimeter stag films were frequently screened at "smokers" held by men's clubs such as the Elks. The 1920s and '30s saw a proliferation of sexually explicit comic books, called "two-by-fours," which featured copulating cartoon characters. Underground bondage magazines were highly profitable in the 1950s, as were cheap paperbacks about rape, sodomy, incest, and lesbian love.

The fifties, in fact, was hardly the decade of innocence it is so often remembered as. In 1950, novelist James Jones wrote to his editor: "It is . . . 'cunt' that us American men of the lower classes . . . are interested in. It isn't love; the love only comes later, if at all."[4] Pornography was part of American life. At one 1950s stag party in Washington, D.C., 197 boys, ages eleven to seventeen, gathered to watch erotic films (the party was organized by the father of one of the boys). By the midfifties, hard-core films featuring the actress Candy Barr were so famous, Barr was considered a stag film star. Police complained frequently that advertisements for erotic films and magazines were sent to children, boys and girls alike. Sometimes teenagers also got into the business of selling pornography. A sixteen-year-old boy in Washington, D.C., made $3,000 selling what police described as "extremely pornographic" material.[5] Pornography was so prevalent in fifties America that some people felt it posed a greater problem to society than either Communism or narcotics.[6] A forty-one-year-old Franciscan priest from upstate New York testified before Congress in 1955 that he was so worried about the issue of pornography that he conducted a personal investigation of the extent of the problem. He asked two boys, both fifteen, to "go out and buy" him "some real filthy literature," not the kind "that can be bought on newsstands," the "real filthy" kind. The boys came back with dozens of books and magazines.[7]

Publishers of sadomasochistic books and magazines operated throughout the country in the 1950s. Irving Klaw and his sister Paula were typical pornographers of the fifties. The Klaws, based on New York's Lower East Side, published the deceptively titled *Cartoon and Model Parade*. Paula tied up the models and took the pictures, while Irving handled the business.[8] Police estimated that the magazine, which sold for fifty cents a copy, grossed $1.5 million each year.[9] No matter how many times men and women like the Klaws were arrested and thrown in jail, market demand for erotic material drew them back into the business.

Pornography was apparently so ubiquitous in the 1950s that FBI director J. Edgar Hoover believed America to be in a state of moral turpitude. On January 1, 1960, Hoover sent out a message to all law enforcement officials: "The morals of America are besieged today by an unprincipled force which will spare no home or community in its quest for illicit profits." Hoover cited rising rates of forcible rape as proof that the nation was in decline. The problem, he stated, was pornography. "[S]ex crimes and obscene and vulgar literature often go hand in hand. The time for half-hearted, oblique action against dealers in depravity is past." To combat pornography, Hoover called for stricter censorship laws and stronger efforts by law enforcement officials.[10] To fight an apparent rise in child sex abuse, he proposed fingerprinting every teacher and school employee in the nation.[11] Hoover longed for a more innocent time.

> It is . . . a grievous fact that drugstores and "sweetshops," pleasant meet-ing places for past generations, now display publications which a few years ago would have a place in only the bawdiest of gathering places. These signs of moral decay, tolerated by adults, cannot help but debase the thinking of our impressionable teen-agers.

Without defining pornography, Hoover claimed it was a $500-million-a-year business.[12]

Given the amount of money spent to combat pornography over the years, the commissioners appointed by Johnson in 1968 wanted to determine what Americans actually thought about the stuff. After sur-veying 3,255 individuals, they discovered that only 2 percent of Ameri-cans believed pornography was one of the two or three most serious problems facing the country. Sixty percent of Americans believed that there should be no restrictions on the sale of erotic materials to adults. (Those who supported restrictions on sexual material also tended to believe in prohibiting newspaper articles criticizing the police, books criticizing the government, and speeches against God.) It also turned out that an overwhelming majority of social workers and child guid-ance counselors did not believe that pornography played a significant role in causing juvenile delinquency. A full 80 percent of psychologists were forced to admit that they had never experienced a case in which pornography had led to antisocial behavior. Studies showed, in fact, that while the amount of available erotic material had increased dra-matically between 1960 and 1969, the number of arrests of juveniles for sexual offenses had gone down.* In Denmark, the number of reported rapes had plummeted after censorship was eliminated in 1967 and had continued to drop as sexually explicit materials filled the nation's book-stores and movie theaters.[13]

Much of what the commission discovered contradicted conventional wisdom. Studies showed that the average person had much greater ex-posure to erotic materials during adolescence than sex offenders had.

---

* The number of juvenile arrests for forcible rape had gone up 86 percent, but this figure was explained by the demographic effects of the baby boom.

In one study, incarcerated rapists were asked at what age they had first viewed images of heterosexual intercourse. It turned out that the mean age of first exposure for rapists was eighteen, while the mean age for the general population was fifteen.[14] "Research to date," the commissioners concluded after reviewing dozens of similar studies, "thus provides no substantial basis for the belief that erotic materials constitute a primary or significant cause of the development of character deficits or that they operate as a significant determinative factor in causing crime and delinquency."

The commissioners initially suspected that exposure to pornography might result in "callused attitudes" toward women. (In fact, well before the rise of the feminist anti-pornography movement, 41 percent of the American males and 46 percent of the females they surveyed believed "sexual materials lead people to lose respect for women.") But after several years of research, the commission members were convinced that such fears were "probably unwarranted."[15]

Taking all these findings together, the majority of the commissioners agreed that "empirical research designed to clarify the question has found no evidence to date that exposure to explicit sexual materials plays a significant role in the causation of delinquent or criminal behavior among youth or adults." As a result, the majority of the commissioners recommended that *all laws regulating the sale of erotic material to adults be repealed*. They agreed that laws regulating the public display of erotic material and the sale of such material to minors deserved to be maintained. (Two commissioners dissented, believing even those laws designed to keep erotic material out of the hands of children and away from public display should be repealed.)

The majority of the commission concluded that sexual silence and shame were far worse than pornography.

> The Commission believes that much of the "problem" regarding materials which depict explicit sexual activity stems from the inability or reluctance of people in our society to be open and direct in dealing with sexual matters. This most often manifests itself in the inhibition of talking openly and directly about sex. Professionals use highly technical language when they discuss sex; others of us escape by using euphemisms — or by not talking about sex at all. Direct and open conversation about sex between parent and child is too rare in our society. Failure to talk openly and directly about sex has several consequences. It overemphasizes sex, gives it a magical, non-natural quality, making it more attractive and fascinating.[16]

The majority view was summed up by a commissioner who was a Methodist minister:

I consider the birth and ensuing work of this Commission to have been a milestone in the history of human communications — the first time in history in which men cared about the problem enough to seek the truth about it through the best methods known to science. . . . I have long been concerned that the burden of blame and the therapy of re-education be focused on the true sources of the sexual crimes and maladjustments which plague our country and its citizens. If certain kinds of books or films had been proven the cause, then I was quite willing to join in the crusade against them. However, it has been very adequately shown through our research that the roots of such behavior lie in the home and in the early years of familial and sibling relationships.

It was a remarkable statement, but one that failed to move any of the nation's legislators.[17]

What claims have not been made about pornography? It has been blamed for the degradation of modern society. It has been derided as banal, boring, and repetitive. It has been variously condemned for causing homosexuality, inspiring rape, instigating hostility toward women, promoting promiscuity, and weakening the aesthetic faculties. It has been labeled sexist, racist, inherently degrading, and sacrilegious. It has been defined in innumerable ways, each less precise than the next. It has been said to include such works as *Madame Bovary* and the "Wonder Woman" comic strip. It has been said not to include photographs of a man wearing leather chaps penetrating himself with a bullwhip. It has been said to exist purely in the eyes of the beholder. It has been said to be the work of the devil.*

The concept of pornography as a distinct category did not exist until the nineteenth century. It was first used in English in the translation of a German art history book to describe the many sexually explicit works found among the ruins of Pompeii. Archaeologists had been shocked to discover that the ancient Romans had decorated the walls of their dining rooms, bedrooms, and common areas with depictions of men and women in the act of copulation. Vases, lamps, and other everyday objects were decorated with images of the god Priapus, his giant penis always

---

* Personally, I am taken with Alex Comfort's 1959 comment, "Pornography is easily definable by observation — it is the name given to sexual literature which someone wishes to suppress" (Comfort, "The Traffic in Pornography," *Guardian*, 19 March 1959). My own definition of pornography is any material produced for the purpose of masturbation. This definition is flawed, of course, because one can never know the original (or true) intentions of an artist, author, photographer, or filmmaker, but it serves well in theoretical contexts.

erect. The French, who oversaw the original excavations of the city, did not quite know what to do with the disturbing relics, so they placed them all in a secret museum in Naples, off-limits to women and children. The curators of the museum called the objects under their control "pornography," from the Greek *pornographos*, "writing about prostitutes."[18]

It is hard to understand why the modern West has always been so much more troubled by sexual images than by violent ones. Murder has always been illegal in the West, but the representation of murder has rarely inspired the kind of hue and cry generated by the depiction of adults having sex. Those who claim that pornography will impel children to engage in sexual conduct seem not the least bit concerned that war stories and Westerns will encourage children to kill their neighbors. For all the talk of "sex and violence" on television, no one seems to blink at the amount of blood spilled in a boxing match, but one can only imagine the outcry that would follow if a similar amount of semen were shown in a bedroom scene of a daytime soap opera.

Ever since the Victorian era, pornography has troubled the conservative, the liberal, and the radical, but for three very different reasons. The conservative fears that pornography will undermine the social order, encourage juvenile disobedience, turn innocent women wanton, and diminish respect for marriage and religion. The conservative attributes to pornography terrifying power: the power to destroy civilization. For the conservative, censorship is the only answer.

The liberal is committed in principle to freedom of speech, yet for the liberal, pornography is a reminder that reason cannot always triumph over instinct, nor nurture over nature. Pornography's powerful sway over the body mocks the Enlightenment dream of a world of rational beings, each imbued with free will. In a similar vein, the fact that more men seem to enjoy visual pornography than women do underscores the possibility that there might be psychobiological differences between the sexes — a notion that is anathema to the liberal. Accordingly, a good number of liberal intellectuals have tried to argue that gender differences in reactions to pornography are primarily the result of sociocultural influences. Some liberals conclude that under the right circumstances, all women would enjoy erotic materials; others conclude that under the right circumstances, no man would. No matter how much the liberal may trumpet the benefits of free speech, he or she will always flinch at the thought that the appetite for pornography might be an inevitable part of the human condition.

The radical's reaction to pornography is less predictable than that of the conservative or the liberal. Some radicals embrace pornography, seeing it as a handy weapon with which to break down the pillars of oppressive orthodoxy. These radicals will talk eagerly of "transgression," "self-expression," and "sexual liberation." (It is almost never clear what sort of world the pro-pornographic radical hopes to create. One finds it hard to believe that the radical simply wants pornography everywhere, at all times of the day and night.) Other radicals eschew pornography entirely, believing it to be a cynical product of those in power, designed to distract the exploited and oppressed: In Orwell's *1984*, pornography is mass-produced to keep the proletariat from rebelling against the Party. The downtrodden worker who is perpetually sated from consuming pornographic images will never recognize his real chains of oppression, nor rise up in revolt. Marxists, in particular, distrust pornography because it is the quintessential symbol of the cash nexus and because it represents the ultimate in human alienation.[19]

Clearly, pornography unsettles most, if not all, of the grand designs of modernity. It upsets virtually every assumption we have inherited from the Renaissance, the Reformation, the Enlightenment, and the Romantic era. Pornography reminds us how little we have progressed since the dawn of civilization, when men first carved images of copulating couples into cave walls. We remain slaves to our desires, and our desires remain banal and predictable. No matter how many adult bookstores are allowed to flourish, no matter how much sexual content is allowed to appear in film and on television, no matter how many skin magazines are allowed to be sold on newsstands, the modern world will not relinquish the flicker of hope, the pang of faith, that pornography will one day disappear forever. The conservative is content to rely on the power of the police, the liberal believes that the right kind of sex education will do the trick, the second type of radical assumes that revolutionary fervor will dry up demand. All, however, share the same sense of yearning. (Indeed, pornography might be defined as that which creates two longings: the longing for orgasmic release and the longing to abolish pornography itself.) To be resigned to pornography's presence in the public square, to allow pornography into the children's nursery is to turn oneself into a pariah, a psychopath, a villain. Our attitude toward the representation of sex serves as the sharpest reminder of our unbridgeable distance from the world of the ancients we otherwise so admire.

When word was leaked that the Presidential Commission on Obscenity and Pornography planned to tell Congress to strike down all restrictions on the sale of pornography to consenting adults, there was widespread outrage. Even before the report was made public, one psychologist denounced it as "a gross mixture of truth and error, part science fiction, and certainly a travesty of a scientific document."[20] Politicians from both parties denounced the conclusions of the report. The Democratic Senate whip, Robert Griffin of Michigan, urged that the government tighten rather than relax the nation's obscenity laws, and Democratic senator Robert Byrd of West Virginia said, "This outrageously permissive commission shows how far this nation has traveled down a road of moral decadence." In fact, the Senate voted 60 to 5 to reject the report entirely.[21]

Anti-smut crusader Charles H. Keating, Jr., the leading dissident member of the commission and the only one appointed by Nixon, filed suit in an attempt to block publication of the report. If the majority of the commission would not endorse broad censorship, Keating would censor the majority of the commission. Keating withdrew his suit when he and the other two members of the commission who advocated stricter censorship laws were given the opportunity to write a dissent that would be included in the report. Their dissent, shaped with a little help from conservative ideologue Patrick Buchanan, denounced the majority report as "a Magna Carta for the pornographer." Unable to marshal any scientific evidence in support of their view that pornography leads to "moral corruption," the dissenting members disavowed science itself. "We believe," they wrote, "it is impossible, and totally unnecessary, to attempt to prove or disprove a cause–effect relationship between pornography and criminal behavior."[22] They so much as admitted that it would be "virtually impossible to prove that one book or one film caused one person to commit an anti-social act or crime" and that if one demanded such proof in order to justify obscenity laws, it would lead logically to the repeal of all such laws. Instead of stressing facts, the dissenting commissioners stressed their beliefs. "We believe pornography has an eroding effect on society, on public morality, on respect for human worth, on attitudes toward family love, on culture." They called for a full-scale war on pornography, urging all fifty states to set up film boards to review and license motion pictures, to establish anti-pornography teams in every state attorney general's office and every state police headquarters, and to amend their laws to broaden the definition of obscenity.

Charles Keating added his own personal reflections to the minority report.

> For those who believe in God, in His absolute supremacy as the Creator and Lawgiver of life, in the dignity and destiny which He has conferred upon the human person in the moral code that governs sexual activity — for those who believe in such "things," no argument against pornography should be necessary.[23]

As for the scientists who prepared the reports on which the commission's final conclusions were based, Keating blasted them as "academicians with ivory-tower views, who have little or no responsibility to anyone or anything, excepting their own thought processes which go unhoned by the checks and balances of a competitive, active, real world." If nothing else, Keating (or Buchanan) had a flair for the rhetorical flourish: "Credit the American public with enough common sense to know that one who wallows in filth is going to get dirty. This is intuitive knowledge. Those who will spend millions of dollars to tell us otherwise must be malicious or misguided, or both."

As good liberals, the majority members of the commission did not simply resign themselves to a future full of pornographic books, magazines, and movies. The majority members urged Congress and the states to bolster sex education programs for children:

> Sex education, straightforward and adequate, begun in the home, continued in school, and supplemented by community agencies such as religious, medical and other social service institutions, can reduce interest in pornography as a source of information and can assist in developing a healthy attitude toward sexuality.

But conservatives were hardly interested in relying on sex education to stamp out "unhealthy" attitudes. In fact, the right-wing John Birch Society had been waging a war against sex education for years. On August 22, 1970, Attorney General John Mitchell declared that the Nixon administration was pledged to opening "a new front against filth peddlers." President Nixon gave his response to the commission's report during a speech to a working-class audience in Baltimore. "So long as I am in the White House," Nixon declared, "there will be no relaxation of the national effort to control and eliminate smut from our national life." Nixon invoked a haunting specter of social disorder: "If an attitude of permissiveness were to be adopted regarding pornography, this would contribute to an atmosphere condoning anarchy in every other field — and would increase the threat to our social order as well as to our moral principles."[24]

The dissenting members of the commission claimed that the majority had played fast and loose with their statistics. The dissenters grossly overstated their case, but they were correct in one regard: The majority report did play down public concerns about pornography. The majority, citing a survey they commissioned, claimed that only 2 percent of Americans rated "erotic materials" as one of the most serious problems facing the country. The survey results may have been accurately reported, but the survey itself was cleverly worded to elicit a tolerant

Playboy Club, New York, 1962. The waitress is dressed in the club's famous "Bunny" outfit, complete with fluffy white tail. The clubs were considered hip when they opened, but they soon became symbolic of both the double standard and the snickering sexual attitudes of the 1950s. By the midsixties, Playboy Clubs faced competition from topless bars like the famous Condor Club in the North Beach section of San Francisco. (Corbis/Bettmann-UPI)

Bill Baird (right) *and fellow protesters campaigning for the legalization of birth control.* The use of birth control was illegal in Connecticut until 1965 and remained illegal in Massachusetts and many other states until the landmark U.S. Supreme Court decision in *Eisenstadt v. Baird* in 1972. Baird, a former pharmaceutical company employee, devoted himself to the birth control cause after witnessing a woman's death from a botched abortion. (Courtesy of Bill Baird)

William Masters and Virginia Johnson listening to couples having sex. Famed for their use of direct observation and electronic recording devices to study sexual arousal, Masters and Johnson were the premier sex researchers of the 1960s. Their 1966 bestseller *Human Sexual Response* demonstrated the importance of the clitoris in female sexual pleasure, discrediting Freud's theory of the vaginal orgasm, and showed that women were capable of multiple orgasms during a single sexual encounter. Ironically, Virginia Johnson was highly critical of both the women's movement and the sexual revolution she helped foment. Though Johnson had no formal scientific training, she and Masters always wore white lab coats to emphasize their legitimacy as researchers. (Courtesy of Virginia Masters)

Still from the film Flesh, *1968, written, produced, and directed by Paul Morrissey, presented by Andy Warhol.* Morrissey's goal was to demonstrate the pathos of prostitution and the emptiness of casual sex by making a tedious film featuring plenty of nudity and sexual subject matter. But when police seized copies of the film and called it obscene, it was heralded by the avant-garde as a tribute to sexual and artistic freedom. The film appealed to both gays and straights because its strikingly handsome star, Joe Dallesandro, was nonchalantly bisexual. (Courtesy of Paul Morrissey)

Still from the Broadway performance of Oh! Calcutta!, *1969.* An instant smash, *Oh! Calcutta!* was the brainchild of British theater critic and outspoken sexual enthusiast Kenneth Tynan. Tynan had originally intended to create a teasing, titillating revue for sophisticated gentlemen, but the show's director wanted a more countercultural sensibility. The resulting compromise was an evening of profitable, provocative entertainment that let audience members believe they were participating directly in the sexual revolution simply by watching a performance. (Santi Visalli Inc./Archive Photos)

Still from Bob and Carol and Ted and Alice, *1969.* In the midsixties, couples across the country began experimenting with "open marriage," and so-called swing clubs began popping up in towns from coast to coast. In the swinging world, jealousy and possessiveness were considered symptoms of social backwardness. Some couples formed "group marriages" that were meant to provide sexual variety in the context of long-term companionship. With *Bob and Carol and Ted and Alice,* Hollywood eagerly exploited these efforts. Needless to say, producers were never going to allow a happy, romantic ending for this foursome. (Corbis/John Springer)

Young baby boomer couple at Woodstock, 1969. Many believed that the sexual revolution, by sweeping away centuries of shame and secrecy, would result in a new erotic Eden, in which relations between the sexes would become more innocent and playful. This optimistic view was an essential element of the hippie counterculture and had one of its most public airings at the Woodstock arts festival in the summer of 1969. It also infused the writings of both popular authors like Robert Rimmer and Robert Heinlein and serious intellectuals like Herbert Marcuse and Norman O. Brown. (Archive Photos)

Two drawings by Betty Dodson, 1970. Artist Betty Dodson became the unofficial spokeswoman for masturbation in the late sixties and early seventies after her work was shown at the Wickersham Gallery on New York's Upper East Side. Dodson represented an early strand of feminism that emphasized the importance of female sexual pleasure for personal liberation. She held group sex parties in her Manhattan apartment and offered workshops in self-arousal. (Courtesy of Betty Dodson)

Encounter group members watching two men wrestle in the nude. The emergence of the sexual revolution corresponded with the rise of the human potential movement, whose proponents argued that taboos against nakedness and touching kept human beings emotionally immature and alienated from one another. At "growth centers" like the famed Esalen resort in Big Sur, California, participants often played games to break through their psychological barriers about same-sex physicality. (Courtesy of Mother Boats)

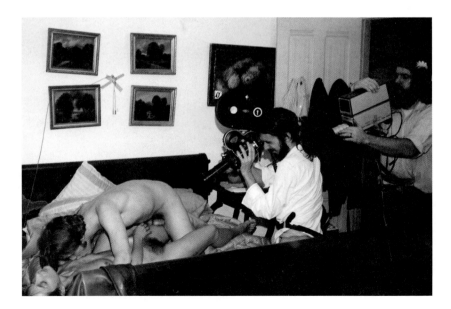

Hippies making a porn film. Homemade sex films were a convenient way to make money in the early seventies. Actors could easily be found through ads in alternative newspapers like the *Berkeley Barb* and the *East Village Other*. At first, sex films played in art houses catering to a bohemian crowd, but erotic movies proved so popular and profitable that many of the theaters stopped showing art films entirely and began playing porn exclusively. (Courtesy of Mother Boats)

Gay pride in New York, early 1970s. In 1969 patrons of the Stonewall Inn, a bar in Greenwich Village, fought back during a routine police raid, a protest that gave a burst of energy to the fledgling gay liberation movement. In the years following, activists organized memorial marches throughout the country, forcing the nation to recognize the gay liberation movement. Many early gay activists saw their own movement as part of a larger sexual revolution that would liberate everyone from sexual repression — note the all-inclusive language of the banner "Freedom of Sexual Expression." This would later be replaced with a narrower, more strategic emphasis on gay rights. (Archive Photos)

Woman in handcuffs after having an abortion. From the 1930s to the Supreme Court's decision in *Roe v. Wade* in 1973, getting a legal abortion was extremely difficult, time-consuming, and expensive. Obtaining one required petitioning a hospital board and demonstrating that the procedure was medically necessary for health reasons. Even more expensive illegal abortions were often dangerous and could lead to uterine damage or even death. This woman was arrested in Tallman, New York, after having an illegal abortion in 1971. (Mort Haber/Archive Photos)

Students streaking at Columbia University, 1974. Streaking, the practice of running nude through a setting where nudity was not the norm, marked the end of one era and the beginning of a new. It was not motivated by any commitment to social change or even a true belief in hedonism. It was, rather, a way to attract attention, prove one's courage, and have a little fun without taking any real risks. In some cases, streaking was a way for male students, responding to coeducation and the rise of feminism, to reassert their power and authority through an overt display of male unity and virility. (Archive Photos)

Women Against Pornography march, Times Square, 1977. By the midseventies, with the economy stagnant, crime and drug abuse on the rise, and porn theaters and prostitution spreading, the sexual optimism of the prior decade quickly faded. Though a few radical feminists continued to champion personal pleasure, many targeted pornography, claiming it inspired men to harm women. To the dismay of other liberals, the organizers of Women Against Pornography were so intent on fighting sexual "filth" that they were willing to work with the leaders of the Religious Right to do so. (Corbis/Bettmann-UPI)

Lesbian activist, circa 1973. At first, lesbian activists tended to work within feminist and gay political groups. But many lesbians felt ostracized from the feminist community and were disgusted by the casual sex and commercialism of the gay male subculture. Eventually lesbians formed their own organizations and began making their own demands. (Archive Photos)

Man at San Francisco gay pride event, 1980. By the early eighties, gay leathermen and -women were demanding recognition as a minority within a minority. In most cities, leather bars offered "tops" and "bottoms" the chance to meet. Some provided dimly lit spaces to engage in practices like fisting, whipping, and cbt (cock and ball torture). The enthusiastic acceptance of pain as a path to sexual pleasure dashed the hopes of sexual optimists, who had believed a new age of greater gentleness and humanity in sexual relationships was on the horizon. (Archive Photos/Fotos International)

TIME magazine cover, 1982. In the pessimistic climate of the late 1970s, the discovery of a new, incurable, sexually transmitted disease was widely interpreted as a sign that the sexual revolution was defunct and that the promiscuous would inevitably be punished for their activities. The media helped fuel the backlash against sexual liberalism; this backlash would influence the nation's response to AIDS in the 1980s and eventually result in the "culture wars" of the early 1990s.

response. Throughout the country, citizens' groups and angry mayors were mobilizing to enforce censorship laws and rewrite zoning laws. In Los Angeles, police were actively fighting strip clubs, in Chicago they were raiding bookstores, in San Francisco they were seizing copies of underground papers like the *Berkeley Barb*. The tactic of playing down the public hunger for censorship was doomed to backfire because it left liberals with a false sense of confidence about the strength of the First Amendment.

Although they were occasionally willing to twist survey results to support their case, the majority members of the pornography commission represented the liberal conscience of a generation that held fast to the dream of a society shaped by trained experts and scientific authorities. Unfortunately, sharp divisions in society no longer allowed for the simple solutions of such a paradigm.

The Report of the First Presidential Commission on Obscenity and Pornography never had the impact its authors hoped for.* For the most part, however, it didn't matter. So long as the nation's leading jurists refused to enforce vague obscenity statutes, the statutes could remain on the books without having a serious chilling effect on publishers or booksellers. As the nation entered the seventies, those on Capitol Hill spluttered about the demise of Western Civilization, while the American people quietly adapted to the realities of erotic expression in a free society.

* A second, more notorious presidential commission on pornography was assembled in 1985 under Attorney General Edwin Meese. That commission was an occasion for Christian Fundamentalists and anti-pornography feminists to wage war against the First Amendment. The hearings were so politicized that the commission lost all possible respect from the academic, scientific, and legal communities.

CHAPTER 16

(ID)EOLOGY: HERBERT MARCUSE,
NORMAN O. BROWN,
AND FRITZ PERLS

IN MANY WAYS, the sexual revolution of the sixties was a product of demographic and physiological forces. There was an extraordinary number of teenagers and young adults relative to the rest of the population. "We're talking about a time when hormones were raging," says one former hippie. "As far as I am concerned, much if not most of the energy driving the counterculture, the protests, the activism was just from kids trying to get laid." The late sixties were marked, in some sense, by a critical mass of mating urges, a sort of collective libidinal overload. But the sexual revolution also had a more interesting, intellectual component. Students were not merely seeking out sexual experiences; they were talking about, writing about, and reading about the meaning of sexual freedom. It was a time when ideas mattered, and ideas about sexuality mattered a great deal.

For young radicals, the ideas in Herbert Marcuse's *Eros and Civilization* (1955) were the cornerstone of the revolution. Marcuse, a Jewish academic who fled to the United States from Nazi Germany in 1934, was a member of the Frankfurt school of critical theory. In the United States, he taught first at the New School for Social Research in New York, then at Brandeis and finally at the University of California at San Diego. For many years, Marcuse was regarded as just another long-winded philosophy professor. But over time, he acquired a vast following of eager young aspiring intellectuals who were attracted to his unique synthesis of Marx and Freud. By 1970, the *New York Times* could proclaim Herbert Marcuse "the most important philosopher alive."

Indeed, everywhere Marcuse spoke, hundreds, sometimes thousands, of students gathered to hear his thoughts on social reform and erotic liberation. As social historian Theodore Roszak noted in 1968, "The emergence of Herbert Marcuse . . . as [one of the] major social theorists among the disaffiliated young of Western Europe and America must be taken as one of the defining features of the counter culture."[1]

What made Marcuse's critique of bourgeois attitudes so timely was his reevaluation of a key statement Freud had made in the 1930s about human nature: that sexual repression was necessary for civilization to survive. Without a certain number of restrictions, Freud had suggested, human beings would live in constant anarchy. To his contemporaries, such a claim made perfect sense. The Austrian economy had collapsed in the 1920s, the German economy had followed suit, the American Depression had set in shortly thereafter, and, by the beginning of the thirties, the entire Western world was in financial ruins. Depression-era thinkers heartily agreed with Freud that civilization depended on delayed gratification, and some even concluded that the moral laxity of the Roaring Twenties was to blame for the financial disaster of the thirties. But in the prosperous 1960s, such pessimism no longer seemed logical. The endurance of civilization — at least from an economic standpoint — was assured. The issue by 1970 was what *kind* of civilization would continue. Did the future hold in store only greater and greater materialism, more and more violent wars, an endless spiral of corporate greed, personal alienation, and environmental decay? Or was an alternative available? A future defined by love, friendship, and peace?

Born in 1898, Marcuse was old enough to be a grandfather to most of the young men and women of the New Left. But this did not stop students from worshiping his ideas. In *Eros and Civilization,* worn copies of which were passed from hand to hand on college campuses, Marcuse showed that Freudian theory could be stripped of its pessimistic implications. He introduced the notion of a utopian world in which the entire body would become "eroticized" and all physical activity would turn into sexual "play."

Marcuse offered a unique reading of Freud's *Civilization and Its Discontents* (1930), in which the founder of psychoanalysis had insisted on the eternal opposition between sexual desire and society. The infant, Freud had declared, is "polymorphously perverse" or, to put it another way, the entire body of the infant is capable of erotic sensation. For the infant, nursing, cuddling, urinating, defecating, and masturbating are all indistinguishably pleasant activities, hence they can all be described as erotic. At the same time, most adult activities, Freud argued, are sublimations of erotic energy. Everything from building a house to painting a portrait to forging a friendship involves a channeling of libidinal impulses. Civilization, Freud had concluded, requires sexual repression for its very survival. The adult must experience erotic sensation only through genital intercourse. If adults were to continue in the polymorphously perverse state, civilization would crumble. If workers were to gratify their immediate desires, houses would not be built, cars would not get made, the economy would inevitably collapse.

Marcuse took issue with Freud's ahistorical reading of the human condition. According to Marcuse, the opposition between society and sexuality was not eternal at all, but rather historically and economically contingent.

Marcuse conceded that periods of scarcity require basic sexual repression to maximize the productivity of workers. In periods of scarcity, workers must delay their own gratification for the sake of the society as a whole. Furthermore, the day is necessarily divided between "work time" and "leisure time," and only during leisure time is eroticism allowable. Likewise, in periods of scarcity, eroticism must be channeled into genital, procreative sexuality. The common good demands it. And as a result, most of the body is de-eroticized.

Unlike Freud, however, Marcuse rejected the argument that such repression was universally necessary. "The excuse of scarcity" that had been used to justify "institutionalized repression since its inception" lost its force when "man's knowledge and control over nature" made possible "the means for fulfilling human needs with a minimum of toil." In other words, Marcuse implied, the booming economy of the United States in the late twentieth century eliminated the need for sexual repression. Given the surplus created by postindustrial capitalism, one could unleash the libidinal instinct from its historical repression without fear of economic ruin. "The culture of industrial civilization has turned the human organism into an ever more sensitive, differentiated, exchangeable instrument, and has created a social wealth sufficiently great to transform this instrument into an end in itself," Marcuse wrote. If human beings did transform themselves into "ends in themselves," the result would be a new civilization, in which pleasure and play would be central to daily life.

In Marcuse's view, erotic liberation would mean a return to the polymorphously perverse state of the infant, that state prior to the division of the body into specific zones for working, eating, genital intercourse, and the like.

No longer used as a full time instrument of labor, the body would be resexualized. The regression involved in this spread of libido would manifest itself in the reactivation of all erotogenic zones and, consequently, in a resurgence of pregenital polymorphous sexuality and in a decline of genital supremacy.

In the end, both society and the self would benefit. Competitive capitalism and corporate greed would disappear as pleasure replaced performance in the hierarchy of values.

> The body in its entirety would become an object of cathexis, a thing to be enjoyed, an instrument of pleasure. This change in the value and scope of libidinal relations would lead to the disintegration of the institutions in which the private interpersonal relations have been organized, particularly the monogamic and patriarchal family.[2]

Clearly, *Eros and Civilization* was not light reading. Herbert Marcuse was not another Helen Gurley Brown or Robert Rimmer. Marcuse's ideas were embedded in dense, polysyllabic, Germanic prose. But it is a testimonial to the intellectual aspirations of students in the sixties and seventies that they grappled with Marcuse's writings. They did not just read his books because they were in vogue; they tried to live his ideas into practice. At the University of Wisconsin, for instance, leftist students seriously entertained the notion of building a polymorphously perverse workers' paradise infused by the pleasure principle; several of those students became nudists.[3] Gay students at Columbia University passed out leaflets with selections from Marcuse's writing to passersby, in the hope that they would recognize the need for cultural transvaluation. Perhaps most important, his ideas were picked up by Shulamith Firestone, a radical feminist, who incorporated them into her 1970 bestseller *The Dialectic of Sex.* Firestone helped to popularize the notion that sexual liberation meant freedom from "the tyranny of the genital."

Just as they devoured Marcuse, students voraciously read the works of Norman O. Brown. They particularly studied *Life Against Death: The Psychoanalytical Meaning of History* (1959), Brown's first major treatise on Freud. "Now, with 50,000 copies in print," wrote *Time* magazine in 1966, "it ranks . . . as one of the underground books that undergraduates feel they must read to be with it."[4] Like Marcuse, Brown, born in 1913, was much older than his followers, and, as a classics professor at Wesleyan University, he was deeply immersed in the world of academic thought. Short, with a round face and awkward smile (he was known by his friends as Knobby), Brown made up in passion for sexual freedom what he lacked in physical charm. He shared Marcuse's determination to discredit Freud's thesis that civilization requires sexual repression. In *Life Against Death,* Brown declared: "[T]he question confronting mankind is the abolition of repression[.]" While Marcuse reexamined Freud in light of Marx's economic materialism, Brown drew on traditional romantic thinkers for his rereading of psychoanalysis.[5] He too borrowed from the early Marx, but relied more heavily on Blake, Wordsworth, Goethe, Nietzsche, and several Eastern mystics. Brown even drew on the language of Christian theology to describe his vision of sexual salvation: "the resurrection of the body."* Like Marcuse, Brown believed in a reunified self, one that was "polymorphously perverse," and liberated from "the tyranny of the genital."

Life Against Death urged readers to abandon the path of sublimation favored by Freud and embark instead on a journey toward psychosexual liberation. To do this, they would have to chose "the life instinct" over "the death instinct.": "The life instinct, or sexual instinct, demands activity of a kind that, in contrast to our current mode of activity, can only be called play. The life instinct also demands a union with others and with the world around us based not on anxiety and aggression but on narcissism and erotic exuberance." Like Marcuse, Brown hoped to resexualize the entire body. "The abolition of repression would abolish the unnatural concentrations of libido in certain particular bodily organs . . . The human body would become polymorphously perverse, delighting in that full life of all the body which it now fears."[6]

It is hard to appreciate how popular both Marcuse and Brown were among students in the sixties and seventies.[†] They have now been all but forgotten by intellectuals, but in the communes of the sixties, they were household names. They redefined the notion of "the good life," one of the most important categories in Western thought, in a manner that appealed directly to the sexual revolutionaries of the younger set. Both philosophers gave intellectual credence to ideas that were already circulating in the counterculture. They showed that one could respect the seriousness of scholarly inquiry and, at the same time, the importance of sexual pleasure and play.

While Marcuse and Brown were busy reconstructing academic discourse to make room for the erotic, psychotherapist Fritz Perls was hard at work transforming the language and practice of psychotherapy. The founder of Gestalt therapy and a leader of the human potential movement, Perls believed all therapy should lead toward sexual self-expression.

Born in Germany in 1893 and trained there as a physician and a classical psychoanalyst, Frederick "Fritz" Perls spent time in analysis with Karen Horney and Wilhelm Reich, two of Freud's most famous students. In the early thirties, Perls fled from Nazi Germany to South Africa, then moved to the United States in 1946. Like several other of Freud's dissident disciples, Fritz criticized psychoanalysis for overemphasizing the role of the unconscious in human life.[7] Perls believed psy-

---

* The idea of the "resurrection of the body" as a sexual transformation of human consciousness is alluded to in D. H. Lawrence's *Lady Chatterly's Lover*.

† Cultural critic Camille Paglia, a paragon of the sixties bohemian, cites Brown as one of her "most important influences." Interview with Camille Paglia by the author, telephone, 17 February 1997.

chotherapy should give human beings a sense of free will, not make them feel resigned to the awesome power of the unconscious. In 1952, he formed the Gestalt Institute of New York.* Perls's version of Gestalt therapy drew from Zen Buddhism, psychoanalysis, and existentialism. It challenged individuals to exist entirely in what Perls called the "here and now" without dwelling on either the past or the future.[8]

Perls was, according to one account, a "man whose involvement in sex was so consuming it was staggering."[9] One of his biographers writes, "Two of Fritz's outstanding qualities were the strength of his sexual drive and the range of his sexual interests."[10] He had sexual encounters with both men and women, and often, in fact, with his patients. In New York during the 1940s, Perls had intimate relationships with Paul Goodman, Julian Beck, and Judith Malina, all three of whom were actively bisexual and critical of prevailing mores.[11] To Perls, honesty with oneself and a willingness to experience life to the fullest were the fundamentals of happiness.

By the late sixties, Perls and Gestalt therapy had a large following. Perls had become a nationally known figure, and individuals were traveling from across the country to meet with him at the Esalen Institute in the cliffs of Big Sur, California. Esalen was a refuge for those who rejected mainstream society and its emphasis on acquisition, productivity, and efficiency. At Esalen, one could take classes in yoga, Eastern mysticism, group marriage, massage. There, surrounded by greenery, sulphur baths, and a spectacular view of the Pacific, Perls's followers were encouraged to take off their clothes and give up their fears of being seen naked. Almost always naked himself, Perls taught eager visitors to overcome their own inhibitions. "Be here now!" the white-bearded philosopher enjoined his disciples, urging them to appreciate the sensual, physical experience of everyday life.

Perls believed in immediate gratification and brutally honest communication. Counterculture philosopher Alan Watts remembers: "Once [Perls] saw a particularly beautiful girl sitting in the baths at Esalen. He looked at her for a long time, and then went over to her and said, 'You vant [sic] to suck my prick.' And by God, she did."[12]

Perls's hedonistic philosophy and his charismatic personality won him renown as the prophet of a new era of human potential. Perls biographer Martin Shepard describes his first meeting with him in 1968, two years before his death. "By then Fritz's reputation for extraordinary therapeutic skills preceded him wherever he went. If you can imagine the thrill of a groupie waiting to meet Mick Jagger or a commoner the Queen . . . you

---

* *Gestalt* means "whole" or "holistic." Perls's version of gestalt therapy had little to do with the gestalt school of analysis that already existed in Europe.

might just begin to appreciate the attraction" Fritz held. "To work with this bearded, brilliant, unpredictable, rascally old marvel offered the hope of nirvana, of cure, of coming to Lourdes on a stretcher and being able to leave by foot. It was akin to being touched by the blessed spirit."[13]

The three philosophers of the sexual revolution — Herbert Marcuse, Norman O. Brown, and Fritz Perls — provided followers with the tools to examine Freud's legacy in America. They offered a sustained critique of Freud's statements on sexual repression. They also showed that social criticism and idealism were not only compatible, the first led ineluctably to the second. As men who had come of age in the 1920s, they revived the sexual enthusiasm of the Jazz Age and gave it a philosophical foundation. In retrospect, however, it becomes clear that all three fell short of their own ideals. Marcuse, Brown, and Perls were symbolically significant for the sexual revolution, but in their own personal lives they were far from revolutionaries.

Marcuse was surely the most respected of the three. His ideas were unconventional yet palatable to other academics. They were, it is important to note, also grounded in middle-class notions of personal identity and sexual morality. Whereas Freud saw human beings as pained, complex creatures ruled by aggression, lust, and a desire to die, Marcuse assumed that they were rational beings with basically gentle, friendly dispositions. (Marcuse himself loved stuffed animals, particularly hippos. His stepson Osha Neumann recalls, "He felt a particular kinship with hippos, not as they actually shit and fight in the forest, but as some teddy bear version. . . . He would sit with this one stuffed hippo in his lap and project this image of a non-aggressive, non-genital sexuality."[14]) Marcuse endorsed a view of erotic liberation as sanitized as *Playboy*'s. In effect, Marcuse took the sex out of sexuality. Never discussing actual bodily activities or erotic desires, Marcuse's prose remained ethereal and esoteric. His writings never referred to gender, to sexual orientation, or to actual sexual behaviors. Feminist theorist Camille Paglia recalls, "I thought he was boring, bland."[15] As another sixties philosopher, Marshall McLuhan, would say, his medium betrayed his message.

Marcuse went out of his way to show that his ideas would not lead to "a society of sex maniacs." He felt very strongly, and tried to make clear, that there was a distinct difference between his own vision of "libidinal transformation" and the mere "release of constrained sexuality" he saw taking place around him:

The latter process explodes suppressed sexuality; the libido continues to bear the mark of suppression and manifests itself in the hideous forms so well known in the history of civilization; in the sadistic and masochistic orgies of desperate masses, of "society elites," of starved bands of mercenaries, of prison and concentration-camp guards.[16]

Marcuse was anything but a hedonist. He accepted the necessity of "basic" sexual repression for the benefit of civilization. His only goal was to eliminate "surplus repression," the repression rendered unnecessary by the West's economic vitality. (Marcuse left it unclear how one was supposed to go about distinguishing between "basic" and "surplus" repression.) While he wanted to abolish traditional patriarchal morality, his aim was to replace it with "maternal libidinal morality," which would recognize the value of pleasure but be able to distinguish it from the "blind satisfaction of want."[17] His use of the term *maternal* is revealing. Underneath Marcuse's rationalist program of social reform was a vision of the Earth Mother gently holding humanity in her bosom.

Indeed, Marcuse turned out to be more of a romantic than a social reformer. He rejected sex education and sexual guides for couples. "I may be wrong but I feel that a human being has to learn some things by himself," he told *Psychology Today* in 1971. "If someone has to study a textbook on sexual behavior in order to learn how to make love to his wife or girl, something is wrong with him."[18] According to his son, Peter, Marcuse never talked about sex at home, and subtly recommended waiting until marriage to have sex.

After his first wife died, Marcuse, who could not drive or cook for himself ("He was enormously inept in the physical realm," Osha Neumann recalls), moved into the home of his friend Franz Neumann, who was married and had two sons. Soon Marcuse began having a secret affair with Franz's wife, Inge. Apparently, other members of the Frankfurt school counseled Marcuse against such behavior, but he did not listen. When Franz died, Marcuse and Inge married. Several years later, Marcuse began having an affair with his favorite graduate student, Erica ("Ricky") Sherover. When Inge found out, she banned Sherover from the house, but that did not put an end to the relationship.[19]

Marcuse was a man of many contradictions. Osha Neumann remembers, "In terms of his sexual relationships, everything was very covert, very traditional." The house was "very repressive. Herbert in terms of his personal life insisted on a level of distance and a level of bourgeois order in his life that was protective of him. I remember him telling me very approvingly about Thomas Mann, who, at least according to Herbert, would get up every morning and put on a jacket and a tie and then sit down at his desk and write books about people led by passion. It was a little complicated for a kid to digest."

Marcuse was intensely private and secretive. "Insofar as [he had] a carnal, genital, sexual drive, it was concealed," Neumann said. "It was there certainly in terms of his affairs, but it was always concealed."* As a boy, Neumann felt like Marcuse was far too Germanic, distant, and ironic to be a father figure. "It was very difficult for me and my younger brother," says Neumann. Like the radicals he so inspired, Marcuse was ambivalent about putting sexual freedom into practice.

If Marcuse's view of sexual freedom was more intellectual than sensual, Norman O. Brown's conception of erotic liberation was candidly mystical. On the surface it sounded radical: Like rock star Jim Morrison, Brown espoused the Dionysian over the Apollonian, the orgiastic over the organized. But because Brown never provided any specifics about the Dionysian life, his philosophical commitment to "sexual liberation" was deceptive. In the end, Brown would disappoint his most passionate followers by arguing, in a second book titled *Love's Body* (1966), that the path to Dionysianism was through nothing more carnal than writing poetry. For Brown, as for Marcuse, the actual demands of the human body were insignificant when compared to the realm of the mind. Both men seemed to be sexual radicals challenging the dualism of Judeo-Christian civilization, but were merely conventional intellectuals coming down on the side of the soul.

Fritz Perls was perhaps the most hypocritical of the three. He was an anti-intellectual, in the literal sense, seeing more value in physical experience than in analytical thought. He called all intellectuals "mind-fuckers" and derided psychoanalysis as an illness pretending to be a cure. This was probably his greatest appeal, given the sterile academicism of psychoanalysis in the 1950s, but it was also his greatest failing, because he never developed a system of ethics to guide human behavior. Like Wilhelm Reich before him, Perls attacked authoritarianism and the repression of emotions. Yet his style of therapy was often sexually prescriptive. As one of his female patients later recalled, "He told me I should fuck around. It was really a crazy thing to tell me. He created problems I didn't really want. I'm 'supposed' to fuck around because my therapist tells me that." In his own fashion, Perls was didactic and authoritarian. His goal was to get his patients to "express" themselves without concern for those around them. Perls did so himself. Another patient remembers, "I've never seen a man who could be so sarcastic, so

---

* Both Marcuse's son and stepson were extremely reluctant to talk to me and felt like they were betraying Marcuse's sense of privacy.

belligerent, so nasty, and get people so frustrated that they would be ready to assault him."[20]

Without a theory of social relations, Perls had no perspective on power, on the relationship between authority and sexuality, or on the dynamics of gender relations in society. Though he stayed married to his own wife, Laura, Perls encouraged divorce for the sake of change and "growth," without considering the economic and emotional implications for couples and their children.[21]

Although they were not always as radical as they claimed to be, Marcuse, Brown, and Perls did give Americans hope in the possibility of personal liberation. Vastly important social critics in their own day, they bridged the gulf between the generation of postwar intellectuals and the generation of student protesters. They took classical psychoanalysis out of the hands of professional experts (who had already managed to twist Freud to serve their own sexist and heterosexist ends) and gave new social theories to the idealistic young. Marcuse, Brown, and Perls may not have succeeded in supplying their followers with workable philosophies, but their efforts to articulate coherent programs of sexual freedom helped to give the early seventies a searching, if not entirely satisfying, dimension.

CHAPTER 17

NO PRIVACY PLEASE: GROUP SEX IN THE SEVENTIES

THE NOTION OF sexual privacy that we take for granted today did not truly emerge until the nineteenth century. In colonial America, bedrooms did not have doors. In eighteenth-century France, aristocrats received guests in their bedrooms, blurring the lines between physical and social intercourse. It was not until the Victorian era that modern norms of sexual privacy truly took hold. It was then that — at least in theory — sexual behavior was relegated to the bedroom, and the bedroom was defined as off-limits for other forms of socializing. (In fact, of course, the Victorian era was a time in which public sex was prevalent and prostitution flourished. For the poor, who often lived seven or eight to a room, middle-class strictures regarding sexual privacy were simply unrealistic and irrelevant.) But even as the modern regime of sexual privacy gained sway, small groups of rebels continued to engage in communal forms of sexual activity. In early-twentieth-century New York, for instance, the mystic Pierre Bernard was notorious for sponsoring all-night orgies that attracted rich society men and women.[1] Over time, however, bourgeois notions of sexual privacy became so much a part of American "common sense" that group sex became practically unthinkable. It was not until the 1960s and '70s that cracks began to appear in the wall of sexual privacy. As those fissures grew, group sex once again emerged as a legitimate possibility.

In 1971, the *New York Times* ran a story on the front page of the "Food, Fashions, Family, Furnishings" section headlined, "Group Sex: Is It 'Life

Art' or a Sign That Something Is Wrong?" The headline might have been a nod to conventional morality, but the body of the article showed that both conventions and morality were in flux. Hippies were not the only ones experimenting with sexual freedom. Among New York's society set, group sex was becoming commonplace. There were monthly "swing parties" by invitation only, casual get-togethers for the uninhibited, and spontaneous sensual massage sessions that turned into orgies.

The article featured several couples who insisted on the aesthetic and psychological benefits of collective copulation. A few psychiatrists were invited to weigh in with their "expert" opinion. Today, the article serves as a revealing artifact, a remnant of a different world, when a certain segment of the upper middle class saw group sex as simply another sort of entertainment and was not the least bit ashamed to admit it.

Before group sex became chic, "swinging" hit the suburbs. The origins of swinging are obscure (some say the modern style of "wife-swapping" began in 1957 after an article about the practice appeared in the men's magazine *Mr.*), but by the midsixties, couples across the country were switching partners for an evening at a time. [2] A series of articles in the *Chicago Daily News* in 1967 helped spread the word about swinging throughout the Midwest.

By all accounts, most swingers were white, upper-middle-class, college-educated adults in their late twenties and early thirties who were bored with the amusements offered by suburban life. They were architects, professors, accountants, housewives, and they made every effort to keep their sexual lives from spilling over into their professional worlds. It certainly would never have occurred to the suburban swinger to think of sex in political terms — the two were as unrelated as lawn chairs and Frigidaires. Often very conservative in politics and dress, swingers tended to establish and follow strict rules in their sexual experimentation. Swing parties generally began at nine P.M. and were over by one A.M., so that neighbors would not suspect strange goings-on. At a swing party, one could expect to find half a dozen or so white heterosexual couples — blacks and homosexuals were almost never invited. (It was an unwritten rule that male homosexuality activity was forbidden at swing parties; women, however, were always allowed — and frequently encouraged — to indulge in lesbian activity.) Swing parties were as exclusionary as the rest of suburban life. Sometimes dress codes were specified: women were told to wear "baby doll" negligees, the men boxer shorts. In the first few hours, the couples would drink and mingle, all the while meeting potential sex partners. At a certain time, the sexual activities would begin, and the new pairs would disappear behind closed doors (although some swingers' groups did keep the doors open and even condoned group sex). After the frolicking was finished, the couples would regroup in the living room for coffee and dessert. In some sense, the swing party was merely a twist on the conventional Kaffeeklatch, an opportunity for couples to bridge the gulf of alienation created by the privatization of modern, domestic life.

Some swingers started formal groups to facilitate mate-swapping. The Golden Sphinx club, for instance, held socials every other month and charged $10 for admittance. Electronics engineer Bob McGinley and his wife Geraldine organized Club Wide World, which met every Saturday night with a $5 entry fee. Others subscribed to specialized magazines or correspondence clubs. In August 1970, swingers organized a convention in Chicago that attracted 184 couples.[3]

In whatever form, swinging was a much discussed phenomenon in the late sixties and early seventies. John Updike's 1968 novel *Couples* was a dark portrayal of mate-swapping in a quiet New England town. In 1969, the Hollywood film *Bob and Carol and Ted and Alice* brought open marriage to movie theaters across America. Sociologists made a minor industry of studies on swinging. At least one was funded by the National Science Foundation.[4]

Some of these studies showed that suburban swingers, unlike their fellow hedonists the hippies, tended to be preoccupied with hygiene and cleanliness, scrubbing and polishing their homes to eliminate every possible germ before guests arrived for a sex party.[5] They treated sex like any other form of suburban recreation, sometimes even inventing party games to help new participants overcome their anxieties.

Eunice and Trevor Lake were typical Midwestern swingers, he a family physician, she a full-time homemaker. They considered extramarital sex part of their leisure activities. Some couples shopped for new furniture, others liked to learn new sports, the Lakes enjoyed seeking out new sex partners. Their attitudes about sex reflected the unique milieu of the suburban swinging set. For a long while, Trevor wanted a traditional housewife, not a woman devoted to sexual self-improvement. "These have been agonizing years watching Eunice read hour after hour her 'trashy sex journals' and 'how-to-do-it' books totally oblivious to the myriads of menial tasks in a house filled with clutter," Trevor wrote in 1975 in a brief essay about his marriage. "Arriving at our present lifestyle has been a long, tortuous and traumatic experience both for Eunice and me. Nevertheless, I am indeed grateful for having done so." Eunice Lake was particularly concerned about dirt and germs; she was reluctant to have sex with her husband unless he showered first. (Trevor had similar concerns, so he was unwilling to touch his wife's anus.) Eunice spent much of her time "making the house look more inviting for loving."

It was Eunice who originally recommended that the Lakes try swinging, but it was also Eunice who was most torn between swinging and monogamy. "We have free choice on so many things in life," she wrote in her diary on one occasion in 1975. "Our loves, our likes, our marriages, our occupations, our hobbies, the way we raise our children — but when it comes to sex there is supposed to be no choice!! If we really are all unique human beings, no two alike, then how in the hell can we all want the same thing when it comes to love and sex?"[6]

Unlike the flower children of the hippie generation, Trevor Lake believed group marriage was ridiculous, and he had, in his wife's words, "an aversion to queers." Eunice had little interest in career or politics. She never joined the women's movement. She divided her time between raising her children, keeping house, working on improving her sexual relationship with her husband, and reading self-help books. But the couple did, on occasion, smoke marijuana and have the communal erotic experiences more readily associated with the East Village than with small-town Indiana. After one such experience with their friends Bill and Sarah, Eunice wrote:

> There is just simply nothing bad, dirty, evil or wrong — it was good, it was happiness. Rationalization? Maybe! Probably! But I don't care. I just have a feeling that our friendship with Bill and Sarah will always be a warmer one. . . . All I know is that I am happy that it did happen and feel very good about myself, about Trevor, about our marriage, about loving and touching in general. The "don't touch me" society we are living in is such a sham. It's sad but I'm not. I feel so open to life — to living — to being. And I still want to love and be loved — to touch and be touched.[7]

Eunice was not always so sanguine about her extramarital encounters, but she was consistently critical of the "monogamy is the *only way*" point of view. In fact, she declared, "I've come too far to ever again accept the patriarchal, double-standard, closed definition of what many espouse marriage should be for all participants. Happiness is conformity?? No way!!"[8]

In cities like New York and Los Angeles, swingers were the laughingstock of the sexual revolution. They were everything urban elites disdained: politically conservative, anti-intellectual, provincial. But urban elites, no matter how status conscious, did not want to be left out of the fun. In fact, they were willing to go a step beyond swinging to group sex.

To justify their own excursions into the world of mate-swapping, they invested it with cultural significance, turning it into everything from high fashion to "life art" to a surrealist brand of socialism.

When we look back at the group-sex enthusiasts of the early seventies, we see three distinct groups. The sophisticated insisted that sexual morality was a "private" matter, but went out of their way to seek publicity for their group-sex activities. For them, publicity was a means of acquiring what social theorists call "cultural capital," the power and influence that come from fame. Just as the sophisticated looked down on the suburban swingers, left-wing activists looked down on the sophisticated. Left-wing activists did not care about publicity per se, they wanted to "smash monogamy" as a way to destroy the institution of private property. For them, privacy and private property were inextricably linked. Finally, there were the reformers, who didn't want to change society economically but who honestly believed that sexual freedom would eliminate social problems like war, hate, and human suffering. These three groups — sophisticates, activists, and reformers — all struggled to define the boundaries between public and private life.

In an orgy, the gulf between self and other — that source of psychological alienation and spiritual loneliness which has troubled philosophers throughout the ages — momentarily disappears. Collective fervor and communal pleasure erase the typical boundaries between individuals. An orgy allows participants the opportunity to explore every aspect of human sexuality, to translate fantasy into reality. Orgies satisfy both our voyeuristic and exhibitionistic desires, and at an orgy, the lines between heterosexuality and homosexuality inevitably blur. An orgy reflects human beings' social nature — it engages them in communal activity for their collective gratification — and their animalistic past. Orgies, the ultimate expression of the ecstatic, have often been linked to religious rites and spiritual undertakings.

The orgy is one of the oldest of human rituals, a key element of ancient Greek life, though we know only a few facts about when they occurred and what took place. We know, for instance, that there were regular orgies at the temple of Aphrodite at Byblos. We also know that at Megara, boys participated in a public kissing contest each spring. The boy who kissed another with the most sensuality won the annual prize. In Thessaly, lesbian orgies were part of the festival of Aphrodite Anosia. And though we know little about the Eleusinian Mysteries, an autumnal ritual that lasted nine days, we do know that they involved orgiastic activities.[9]

The Romans were even more partial to orgies than the Greeks were. The cults of Cybele, Isis, and the Bona Dea all involved orgiastic rites. Roman baths were places for homosexual and heterosexual group sex. According to a contemporary report by Athenaeus of Naucratis, the Etruscans were particularly keen on orgies as a form of entertainment.

> When [the men] get together for companionship or in family parties they do as follows: first of all, after they have stopped drinking and are ready to go to bed, the servants bring in to them . . . sometimes female prostitutes, sometimes very beautiful boys, sometimes also their own wives; and when they have enjoyed these the servants introduce lusty young men who in turn consort with them.[10]

Roman emperors were notorious for throwing orgiastic banquets that involved not only group sex but rape, forced sodomy, ritualized torture, and other cruelties.*

Though orgies may have gone out of fashion during the later Middle Ages (at least, few records exist to show they occurred), they were all the rage in the 1660s, during the English Restoration. English rakes prided themselves on having sex with as many partners at one time as feasibly possible. One such libertine, Lord Chattleman, ended up in court for having sex with two of his manservants and forcing those same servants to rape his own wife. "The Earl," said one of the servants in a court deposition, "took delight not only in being an Actor, but a specta-tor while other men did it." In eighteenth-century England, orgies were no less popular. Charlotte Hayes, a madam of a well-known London brothel, arranged a special evening during which twelve young boys cop-ulated on the floor with twelve young girls for the visual benefit of twenty-three paying guests (eleven of them allegedly members of the House of Commons). The ceremony was based on a legendary Tahitian ritual for the deflowering of virgins known as the Feast of Venus.[11]

If any two people embodied New York sophistication in the late sixties and early seventies, it was Howard Bellin, a successful plastic surgeon, and his wife Christina Paolozzi, an Italian countess-cum-fashion-model. They were the envy of the Upper East Side. He was twenty-eight, already successful, and a registered Conservative when they met in 1963.

---

* Of course, the fall of Rome has been blamed on such behavior, but as Burgo Partridge writes in *A History of Orgies,* indifference to matters of state, not sexual indulgence itself, led to the downfall of Rome. "What we have to decide is whether . . . the Empire would have col-lapsed just as surely if the Romans had, for example, spent too much time playing golf."

She was a well-known model who appeared regularly on the covers of magazines like *Harper's Bazaar* and *Vogue*. "At the time we met," Bellin recalls, "she was dating an influential senator and a major Broadway producer." But after their first date, they had sex, and after their second, she gave Bellin a toothbrush and key to her apartment. After the third date, Christina told Howard she wanted him to marry her. "She was a very powerful woman," says Bellin. "Our engagement picture was on the cover of the *New York Daily News*. That's how well known she was."[12]

Bellin and Paolozzi married and then settled into high-society life. She went back and forth to Europe, doing fashion shoots and making the social rounds. After one trip to Rome, Bellin says, she came home and casually told her husband that she had had an affair with another man. "I went crazy," says Bellin. "And that's when she said to me, 'Don't be so bourgeois, darling. You should enjoy yourself, I should enjoy myself. We're still in love, but it's important to have a little adventure.' If she were alive today she might tell you otherwise, but the truth is she talked me into it."

At first, like other swingers, they had certain rules. "We were not supposed to have affairs when we were together in New York, only when one of us was traveling." But the rules soon relaxed. Before long, both Bellin and Paolozzi were spending most nights of the week having sex with others. "I remember one night, I was in bed with Christina. I got a call from my friend Bob. It was two-thirty in the morning. He said he had two girls at his place and he was too tired but they wanted more. He wanted me to come over. I said, 'Bob, I can't. I'm here with Christina.' She overheard the conversation and said 'Don't be stupid. Go, have fun. Don't stay home on my account.' So I went and made love to these two women."

Bellin and his male buddies had sex parties that lasted all night long. "It's really quite mind-boggling. It was crazy. Just every kind of promiscuity. Nothing kinky, I mean . . . mostly just raw sex. Once I had six women in the same bed at the same time. . . . It wasn't wonderful. How do you keep six women focused on sex all at the same time? Maybe three at one time, but the other three would be talking." Was it hard to find women for such orgies? "Not at all. You just called a girl up and invited her over. I think Quaaludes played a major role in all of it. The sexual openness, the lesbianism. Quaaludes really got the girls going." Bellin says he probably had sex with over a thousand women.

Bellin and Paolozzi were open about their open marriage, which was the talk of the town. When Barbara Walters asked if she could interview them for a television special on swinging, they readily agreed. Bellin, for his part, began writing a book about his sexual experiences, though he never finished it. Neither Bellin nor Paolozzi shied away from publicity, for publicity guaranteed them status as ultrahip socialites.

John and Mimi Lobell were another Manhattan couple who chose fame over anonymity. Even more than Bellin and Paolozzi, they sought out publicity and were eager to be identified with the sexual revolution.[13]

The Lobells, both architects, began experimenting with open marriage and group sex in the late sixties. They had met as students at the University of Pennsylvania. Mimi was from a Midwestern, Republican, Anglo-Saxon, "pre–sexual revolution family. I knew I was supposed to be a virgin when I got married." She lost her virginity at eighteen with a young man she was dating. "I had a terrible time because I had slept with him and I thought, Now if I don't marry him I'll be a slut." Though the young man agreed to marry her, Mimi's parents insisted she break off the engagement because they felt she was too young to marry. "It was very hard to go ahead and let myself have sex with a second man. I thought, Oh, now I'm really a tramp. . . . But then I remembered a roommate saying that a woman who has sex with two men at the same time is a slut, and I thought, 'Well, I don't do that.'"

It was not long before Mimi would do just "that." When Mimi and John met, they developed an intensely close relationship. "We would go for three days in his room, barely coming out for food." They began talking about group sex almost immediately. "He used to read Victorian pornography, books like *The Pearl,* so we would lie in his bed and read scenes to each other. The passages often involved more than two people, so they were fuel for our fantasies."

The Lobells moved to New York in 1966. "We were very, very social when we first got to New York," says Mimi. They happened upon a copy of a book called *The Housewife's Handbook on Selected Promiscuity* (1962), written by Arizona housewife Rey Anthony. It was the subject of a major obscenity trial in Philadelphia. "We started talking again about what it would be like to have another person in bed with us. I remember definitely [on my wedding night] I already felt that sex was not as exciting because it was no longer illicit. I think I've just always been a genuinely polyamorous person," says Mimi.

John describes the swirl of sexual activity in New York in the late sixties. "We saw the sexual revolution going on. We were going to avant-garde movies, happenings. We were very involved in all the energy around New York, which included sex. Eventually we said, 'Hey, why not get involved in this?'" John was teaching at Hunter College when the Lobells had their first threesome. John had a female student he thought might be interested in group sex. When he invited her to the house, she accepted the invitation. Mimi remembers the evening well. "It took forever and forever and forever for anything to happen. We were just too nervous; we didn't know how to break the ice and say, 'Well, let's have sex now!' Finally we did and it was wonderful and we felt fantastic and in love with the world."

Though they were older than most hippies, drugs were so much a part of late-sixties life that John and Mimi began dropping acid. "We were really like flower children," says Mimi. "At one point we said to each other: Why should we miss the sexual revolution just because we're married?" Mimi decided to take a male lover. She met a man from John's architecture firm whom she found "very good-looking. I went to his place. He was a very elegant bachelor from a wealthy family. His apartment was beautiful, with fine art all around. He [served] chilled lobster and wine. He was virtually in a smoking [jacket]."

The Lobells were friends with another couple, Dean and Carol Brown, two artists on the cutting edge of New York's art scene. Dean was a photographer who specialized in landscapes. "They were in their thirties, a little bit older than we were. Somehow the idea came out that it would be a very good thing to have a photographic portrait of us making love, almost like a landscape." The Lobells agreed to be photographed having sex. "We ended up having three different shoots. The first was just John and myself. The second one was John and an old girlfriend. The third was of me with a man that I was interested in."

John recalls how they began to "come out" about their sexual activities. "I had a friend from high school who got married and moved to Long Island. He was our 'suburban friend,' a conservative, straight businessman. He was an athlete, a real serious type. One time he was over and we sort of brought up the subject to see if we would be totally ostracized. You know, were we totally weird? We knew about wife-swapping in California, but we didn't think of ourselves as swingers. . . . Suddenly this guy says, 'I think I know where you guys are headed. I've been having sex with my friends for six months.'"

Soon, the Lobells went public about their group-sex activities. A photo of Mimi having sex with another man appeared on the cover of the avant-garde art magazine *Culture Hero*. John wrote an article for *Screw* on male orgasm; the article was accompanied by pictures of John masturbating. "The week the article came out, I was up for tenure at Pratt [Institute, the prestigious design school]. But it was no problem. At the time, the culture was supportive of being adventurous." The culture was so supportive, John and Mimi wrote a book about their group-sex activities, *John and Mimi: A Free Marriage* (1972).

"We thought of ourselves as politically, spiritually engaged people," says John. "We really freaked if anyone called us swingers. We felt the same way as the hippies. The idea of people who lived in the suburbs and had organized get-togethers with all sorts of rules — open rooms or closed rooms and afterwards you sit around and have coffee or poundcake — that was not us, we did not identify with that, and we were upset when people used the term 'swinging.'" Like the Lobells, George and Nena O'Neill published a book about the joys of open marriage, entitled simply enough, *Open Marriage.*

The Lobells didn't consider themselves bisexual, but both had experiences with members of the same sex. With gay liberation in the air, bisexuality took on multiple dimensions. There was a certain amount of encouragement within the counterculture to broaden one's sexual horizons, and that "pressure" could serve as an excuse for someone who wanted to experiment with bisexuality without admitting to homosexual inclinations. One of John's first experiences with a man was with countercultural icon Abbie Hoffman. "Abbie heard about our book and came to visit us. At some point he said, 'You know, it's really politically necessary for me to have some bisexual experiences.' So we went to his family's place in the Hamptons and did everything, and he said, 'So, did you convert?' and I said, 'No, I still like girls,' and he said, 'Me too.'" (John says that Abbie tried to introduce the Lobells to John Lennon and Yoko Ono, but the famous couple did not want to be associated with group sex.)

Sex, Mimi says, is like food. "You may want good French food most of the time, but now and then you want a pizza." John uses a similar analogy. "If a woman is married to a dull farmer and they have a family, does that mean if she wants to go to the city and go to a museum once in a while she should get a divorce? If you watch sitcoms, does that mean you should never read Gide or vice versa? That's what an affair is."

As we look back at the phenomenon of group sex in the early seventies, we do so through our own specific set of lenses. We are influenced, of course, by the fact of AIDS and by the prohibitions against promiscuity that are so much a part of post-AIDS culture. We are also inclined to assume that a connection exists between the rise of open marriage and the rise of divorce — that jealousy will inevitably destroy an open marriage. Anecdotal evidence on this subject has served as a substitute for scholarship. One woman says, "Everyone I knew who had an open marriage ended up divorced. The whole thing was a disaster." Such claims have come to sound true through force of repetition. Perhaps most important, we live in a time when sexual behavior is understood in terms of "identity" rather than inclination. It may now be acceptable to "be gay" in educated circles, but it remains utterly unacceptable for heterosexuals or homosexuals to want partners of both sexes at the same time.

Living, as we do, in the age of AIDS, it is hard not to be shocked by what was considered relatively innocent in the early seventies. It is impossible to understand the enthusiasm for group sex without appreciating how insignificant sexually transmitted diseases seemed to be at the time. Penicillin was known to cure gonorrhea and syphilis way back in the 1940s. By 1971, those diseases seemed trivial, almost laughable. What did a dose of the clap mean when it could be cured with a simple shot of antibiotics? To many, a case of crabs was no more serious than the common cold. Though epidemiologists knew that venereal disease rates were on the rise, the fact was irrelevant to anyone who considered him- or herself sexually liberated. Artist Margo Rila recalls:

> I'd say like once a year . . . there might be one [group sex] party with a V.D. epidemic. . . . We had sign-in sheets at parties, so we knew everybody and since they were members or friends of members we knew how to contact them. . . . People were very responsible about this in group sex situations — the minute somebody [got] V.D., they usually call[ed] the party organizer or someone else involved and people call[ed] everybody. I heard that one morning at the Oakland V.D. clinic there were 15 or 20 people there from the party and they were all sitting around talking and laughing. They were just as social as they had been at the party.[14]

In the gay male world, rates of sexually transmitted disease were particularly high. One gay guidebook stated, "VD is a fact of life. For every gay who has never had a venereal disease, there is a gay who seems never *not* to have had one."[15] But sexually transmitted diseases were so easy to cure, few considered them worth worrying about. As disease rates rose rapidly, many singles, straight and gay alike, began consuming antibiotics on a regular basis as preventive measure (which may have actually increased the chances of infection by weakening the immune system).[16] Since penicillin did work effectively against most types of VD, and no type was known to be incurable or life-threatening, it is not surprising that many Americans considered a case of "syph" a minor matter, or perhaps even a badge of honor.

While swingers were not worried about venereal disease, they *were* worried about jealousy.[17] Jealousy was the bane of the movement's existence. Eunice Lake, for example, tried very hard to rid herself of moralistic assumptions, a process she called, aptly enough, mental "housecleaning." But, she admitted, the process was not easy. "I do have a problem that I must come to terms with — something I used to think was not part of my nature and at least now is — jealousy." As she wrote on another occasion, "Being alone or trying to carry on a normal conversation while your husband is fucking someone else calls some deep down emotions up to the surface. And not very nice ones at that." Two months later she wrote in her diary about her "jealousy phase": "I have had lots of time to think and really see what a negative emotion jealousy is. It produces nothing good — no smiles, no laughs, much misery (self-induced) but even with all of that, I think it was necessary to experience it myself."[18]*

According to Mimi Lobell, her husband was never jealous of her sexual encounters with other men, but she had a hard time with jealousy at the beginning of their open relationship. She "had too much pride and self-esteem," however, to think it was okay to be jealous.

Some open marriages — like all marriages — did end in separation or divorce. Howard Bellin and Christina Paolozzi eventually separated, but they continued to live under the same roof. "We split the apartment into thirds," says Bellin. "One third for me, one for her, and one for the kids. We had the terrace in common and the kitchen in common, but otherwise we kept to our separate areas. We stayed in this arrangement for two years. We were no longer sleeping together [and] we were both having other people over to the apartment." They got divorced, then remarried each other; Paolozzi died of a brain tumor shortly thereafter. Today, Bellin is single and says he no longer believes in open marriage. He recalls the sixties with a mixture of nostalgia and regret. "The bottom line is, it didn't work. I never thought my kids knew, but they did and they resented it. In a way, I regret it. If we had really worked to stay together and not done all this craziness, it would have been better for the relationship." It is hard to know, however, to what extent this sort of self-analysis is influenced by the contemporary cultural prohibition on promiscuity.

Could the divorce rate's rapid rise after 1960 be linked to the spread of swinging? It is very unlikely. Swinging was never widespread enough to have that kind of impact. It was always a form of statistically deviant behavior (as opposed to adultery, which may be statistically normal). In terms of anecdotal evidence, for every open marriage that ended in divorce, there is one that survived intact. The Lobells, for instance, "slowed down" their swinging activities in the midseventies and were monogamous for some fifteen years. In 1995, they began meeting other couples on the America Online computer network. (Since the invention

* Apart from jealousy, Eunice often felt pressure from other men to engage in extramarital sex. At times she wanted to tell those men, "Hey look, I just can't hack your feelings of genitally oriented contact for me. I can accept you as a unique human being and you are free to relate to anyone on your basis that you want." But she found it hard to be so direct.

of the Internet and its chat groups, swinging of the highly regulated, suburban, exclusionary variety has enjoyed a virtual renaissance. It is now possible to locate thousands of couples with open marriages within a few seconds.) Today, they once again have a full-fledged open marriage. Eunice and Trevor Lake are still happily married, and although they no longer mate-swap, they remain friends with many of the couples they used to swing with. "Swinging," says Eunice, "brought us all much closer together than we would have been otherwise."

One of the most powerful influences shaping our view of the group-sex movement of the early seventies is also one of the hardest to recognize. We live today in a time when sexuality is understood in terms of identity: straight or gay, for instance.[19] A person is allowed to take a same-sex lover because he or she "is" gay — it is part of the person's essential identity, something over which he or she has no control. (The gay rights movement did not invent the notion of sexual identity — homosexuals were branded as fundamentally different from straights long before the movement got going — but the movement did help secure the notion as a fixture of late-twentieth-century liberalism.) At the same time that "being gay" has become normalized (at least in liberal circles), a craving to have sex with multiple partners has become stigmatized. The net result is that the swingers of the seventies seem, in retrospect, immoral, decadent, or, at the very least, ridiculous. Their promiscuous impulses have no justification in the world of sexual identities. In order to accept swinging as "normal," one would have to adopt an entirely new worldview, one shaped by an existentialist rather than an essentialist view of human behavior. One would have to consider the possibility that every human being might have a different sexual identity, given not by the past but by the future. That is to say, perhaps one constantly reinvents one's sexual "identity" as each new possible sexual encounter presents itself. Perhaps one's desires are not fixed and immutable but always open to change. Perhaps past desires are not, as we so often assume, reliable indicators of future desires. In other words, perhaps it is not appropriate to characterize one's sexual orientation until the end of one's life when one is no longer able to choose to have any additional sexual encounters. We can distinguish, then, between two different paradigms: sexual identity (given by the past) and sexual self-invention (given by future possibility). As we look back at the 1960s and '70s, it is important to keep this in mind. If we assume that one's sexual identity is given by the past, then swinging seems foolish, ridiculous, bizarre. If we assume, however, that one constantly reinvents one's own identity through the choices that one makes, each of which is given by future possibilities, then swinging, celibacy, and monogamy seem like equally valid options.

Today, secular Americans take the idea of sexual identity for granted. It is always already present in our culture in the way we talk about desire. Sexual identity is the dominant mode, or epistemological framework, for interpreting erotic experience. We are quick to classify ourselves and others as heterosexuals, homosexuals, lesbians, transvestites, transsexuals, sadomasochists, pedophiles, fetishists, "breast men," "butt men," "tops," "bottoms," "size queens," and so on.* Each of these identities is assumed to be given by the past. The fact that the one "identity" we are least willing to accept *as* an identity is bisexuality shows how unstable the entire system really is. We are reluctant to accept bisexuality as an identity because it does not serve as a predictor of the future based on the past. Indeed, bisexuality is not an identity at all, it is a statement of possibility. To be bisexual is to be, in sexual terms, existentially free. To conceptualize the notion of bisexuality, one has to step outside the entire framework of sexual identity and step into the framework of sexual self-invention.[20]

In 1971 it was not clear which direction Americans would go in — toward the paradigm of sexual identity or the paradigm of sexual self-invention. Even in the gay liberation movement, as we have seen, there was significant resistance to the idea of heterosexual and homosexual labels. It was possible to operate in either world, to interpret the present as a function of the past or as a function of future possibilities. Americans were at a fork in the road of human self-understanding. They were living in a moment of paradigmatic pluralism. Not surprisingly, it was a heady, confusing time.

Most die-hard leftists either took sexual liberation for granted ("I was getting laid every day," one former activist recalls) or looked down on those who elevated sexual politics above civil rights and socialism. But those to the farthest left of the political spectrum, a small group of student activists who called themselves the Weatherman, believed sexual liberation was an essential element of political revolution. The group, which took its name from a Bob Dylan lyric ("You don't need a

---

* Other "identities" are imaginable: men who get turned on by pornography, men who do not get turned on by pornography, women who get turned on by pornography, women who do not get turned on by pornography, people who like sex with the lights on, people who like sex with the lights off, women who like men with tattoos, men who like women with pierced nipples, etc., etc. If one were to expand this list to its logical conclusion, it would become readily apparent how contrived the notion of sexual identity really is. Granted, identitarianism is strategically useful in combatting discrimination, but as a coherent epistemology it is sorely lacking. On identitarianism, see Warner, Introduction, *Fear of a Queer Planet*, vii–xxxii.

weatherman to know which way the wind blows"), was formed in 1968 at Columbia University, the intellectual capital of Students for a Democratic Society, when three SDS activists — Mark Rudd, John Jacobs, and Bernadine Dohrn — organized their own faction.* It consisted mainly of white students from wealthy backgrounds who were disillusioned with the privileges of money. Rejecting the pacifist principles of SDS and other New Left organizations, the Weatherman advocated the violent overthrow of the United States government — backing the Black Panthers' efforts in that direction — and the total rejection of private property. The leaders of the Weatherman exploited the erotic energies of radicalism in a way no one else had before. Jacobs wore tight jeans, a leather jacket, and a gold chain with a lion's tooth. He kept his hair slicked back in retro-fifties fashion. "His style was street-corner stud, intended to clash with that of the earnest student radical," wrote two chroniclers of the sixties. Dohrn was the true celebrity of the three. Her uniform consisted of a black miniskirt, leather boots, and a button reading "Cunnilingus is Cool, Fellatio is Fun."[21] Since they believed that radically reshaping sexual norms was essential for the destruction of "bourgeois" hegemony, their political program led logically to specific sexual practices. Monogamous relationships and the nuclear family were, in their eyes, an inevitable impediment to true socialism. In September 1969, Bernadine Dohrn and other female Weather leaders began a campaign to "smash monogamy." Members of the movement were instructed to abandon monogamous relationships and told to have sex with as many partners as possible. In some cases, men were told to sleep with men and women to sleep with women. The goal was carnal Communism, loyalty to the movement instead of to one's lover. "In line with the principle that the building of communism begins with the remaking of people, the conquest of bourgeois limitations and values [is] considered part of the process of making the revolution," one Weatherman member explained.[22] Weather women saw the anti-monogamy campaign as a crucial step in women's liberation, since monogamy was so clearly a patriarchal institution. "Our monogamous relationships broke up because we simply didn't need them any more," one woman wrote in defense of the group. "We began not to have to identify ourselves through men and could become total human beings. Women began digging each other; jealousy and competition were not necessary any more because our point of existence was the revolution; and the old way of life became intolerable to us."[23] Whether it was for group cohesion or

* The name was singular, to emphasize the unity of the group, but in the media it often appeared as *Weathermen*. In the midseventies the group became known as the Weather Underground.

militant feminism, Weatherman organizers attempted to integrate politics and pleasure at a "national orgy" in Cleveland, Ohio. As one who was there later recalled,

> There were people fucking and thrashing around all over. They'd sort of roll over on you, and sometimes you found yourself spread over more than one person. The room was like some weird modern sculpture. There'd be all these humps in a row. You'd see a knee and then buttocks and then three knees and four buttocks. They were all moving up and down, rolling around.[24]

To the Weatherman members, the very existence of monogamy was an impediment to social progress. Orgies were an opportunity to fashion a new basis for society, built literally on the pleasure principle.

The Weatherman was not the only pro-sex political group in the early seventies. Some radicals left the United States and moved to Amsterdam, where socialism and sexual liberalism already had popular support. One group of expatriate hippies decided to create a sex-radical collective there, which they called "Suck." To support themselves, and to promote the revolution, they published an English-language newspaper by the same name. Andrea Dworkin, who spent several years as an expatriate in Amsterdam before she became well known as a feminist theorist, felt the images of fellatio and cunnilingus in *Suck* would help liberate men and women from sexual repression. "[T]he emphasis on sucking cunt," she wrote, "serves to demystify cunt in a spectacular way — cunt is not dirty, not terrifying, not smelly and foul; it is a source of pleasure, a beautiful part of female physiology, to be seen, touched and tasted." What Dworkin especially appreciated was that *Suck* treated "sucking as an act of the same magnitude as fucking. That attitude, pictures of women sucking cock, men sucking cunt, and all the vice versas, discussions of the techniques of sucking, all break down barriers to the realization of a full sexuality."[25] Dworkin was strongly opposed to the privatization of sexual experience.

A former prostitute and abused spouse, Dworkin endorsed cunnilingus and fellatio as inherently political acts.

> Given the selective enforcement of the laws, the shame that attaches to forbidden acts, and the fact that acts of oral lovemaking represented in words or in pictures are generally deemed obscene, sucking must be seen in and of itself as an act of political significance (which is certainly wonderful news for depressed revolutionaries).[26]

As much as Dworkin appreciated the contents of *Suck,* she felt the magazine was ultimately undermined by its sexism.

The pages of *Suck* have, sadly, nothing to do with sexual liberation — there is no 'counter' to the culture to be found anywhere in them. They are, instead, a catalogue of exactly those sexist fantasies which express our most morbid psychic sets. They chart the landscape of repression, a land- scape that is surprisingly familiar.

Dworkin envisioned a world of group sex even more "liberated" than that portrayed in the pages of *Suck*: a world of "androgynous pansexu- ality" free of all taboos on incest, adult–child sexual contacts, same-sex contacts, and human–animal contacts. "The object is cultural transfor- mation. The object is the development of a new kind of human being and a new kind of human community."[27]

Germaine Greer, a witty and outspoken Australian activist with a Ph.D. in English literature, was also a member of the Suck collective. Greer combined a knack for cultural criticism with a willingness to reveal intimate details about her own sexual life: "I myself did not realize that the tissues of my vagina were quite normal until I saw a meticulously engraved dissection in an eighteenth-century anatomy textbook," she wrote in the best-selling book *The Female Eunuch* (1971), where she also encouraged women to taste their own menstrual blood and accept their own bodily odors.[28] Realizing that young girls were often pressured to engage in sexual acts, she stressed that sexual libera- tion required personal strength and the ability to say no. But she felt the ability to say yes was equally crucial to women's well-being. "Women are not by nature monogamous," she declared.

In 1970, Greer helped organize the Sexual Egalitarian and Libertarian Fraternity (SELF), which sponsored a "Wet Dream Festival" of erotic films in Amsterdam that year. As Greer described it:

Our goal is sexual liberation. Our tactic the defiance of censorship. Thus expressed our aims are political, for the patterns of sexual interrelation- ship are created by and in turn support the other social structures. The approved sexual relationship in all western societies is exclusive, posses- sive, colonizing, exploitatory [sic], sex is recognized as intimately con- nected with violence, for the power of the one over the other must be enforced and enforceable.[29]

For Greer and other members of SELF, sexual liberation meant free- dom from "exclusive, possessive, colonizing" sexual relationships. The Wet Dream Festival, which attracted over 400 people, was part movie screening, part Roman orgy. A *Rolling Stone* reporter was so shocked by the scene, he left before the real orgy even began, but one woman saw the festival as the beginning of a "New Civilization" based on pansexual freedom: "This was the first sex party I had ever attended where there was equal representation of heterosexual, bisexual, homosexual. Everyone was making it in every possible combination. Gay guys balling with women, lesbians making it with guys, straight and gay men together, straight and gay women, everyone doing his or her own thing as well as everybody else's thing! . . . The flow from person to person was easy, as it was from group to group. . . . I had many thrilling and intimate human contacts. I was fucking with a beautiful young guy in Position C (dog fashion) when I felt his rhythm change. I looked back and saw my gay friend Arnold fucking him from behind. My partner was bisexual, and it really turned me on. He was sandwiched between a cock and a cunt, and we were all grooving together." The festival was a "bacchanal indeed," she continued, "the ancient ritual of celebrating life and offering thanks to the Great Goddess and her Earthly Priestesses . . . It was a great experience being in a room filled with so many sex-positive women. That's the real base for social change: women saying 'yes' to their sexuality, pleasure and joy with no bargaining."[30]

Ultimately, Greer was disappointed with SELF, just as Dworkin was disappointed with *Suck*. Most of the films shown at the Wet Dream Festival were, in Greer's opinion, "commercial porn films, made to exploit the misery of the deprived and the perverted, at minimal cost, badly shot, worse played by the unhappy actors blackmailed by force or lack of money, dingy, murky, spotty, choppy, film sex without dialogue or soul or body"; the others were underground films, which either "celebrated sex in narcissistic and 'artistic' ways or they offered a sort of commentary on decadent social mores." Bodil Joensen, for example, showed *A Summer's Day*, a film depicting her own sexual activity with pigs, dogs, horses, and other animals. "I like animals in all ways," she explained in an interview,

> not only as pets as most town people who have a dog or cat, because animals can be used in so many ways and we have so much use and pleasure from them. . . . What is so wonderful to me is the fact that animals, or rather certain animals, are able to get my hot feeling going.[31]

Greer was most disturbed by the "infantile and sadistic" films of Otto Muehl. Muehl served in the German army during World War II and made his name in the postwar European avant-garde art scene by filming himself urinating, defecating, and masturbating in public. He then began making violent films that included everything from bestiality to coprophilia.[32] Reflecting on the festival, Greer wrote:

So all the members of SELF were poisoned. We sickened and slumped incapable of bridging the gaps between each other. We saw our hideous impotence so clearly that it seemed that the Festival had betrayed revolution and had driven it into another world. We were guilty with each other. By the end of the third day we could barely hear each others' voices.[33]

Greer did not give up hope. Determined to carry on the sexual revolution, she wrote: "We must commission films, make films, write, act, co-operate for life's sake. The battle against sadism and impotence is more desperate than we ever believed."

The politically engaged projected elaborate systems of meaning onto human sexuality. The Weatherman believed that group sex would abolish private property and usher in a new age of socialist harmony. Dworkin and Greer hoped that group sex would dethrone patriarchy and lead to more humane social relations. For these left-wing activists, group sex was goal-oriented, a way to get beyond bourgeois morality in order to begin the process of building a better society.

Somewhere between the activists of the New Left and the swingers of the suburbs fell couples like Iris and Ken Brent (pseudonyms). Eager to reform society but uninterested in politics, the Brents saw group sex as an end in itself. They espoused pleasure for pleasure's sake. For them, the orgy was the supreme expression of human relatedness. Group sex, they believed, could eliminate everything from racial prejudice to militarism.[34]

A middle-class Chicago couple, the Brents were far from hippies. "Ken and I, and the swingers we know, are not advocates of communal possession-free living," Iris observed in the early seventies. "We are not drop-outs from the economic establishment. We have simply opened our lives to include others in intimacy. We feel that we have benefited from such expansion."[35] As part of their expansion, both of the Brents had bisexual encounters, and Iris once had sex with five black men. She described her memories of this interracial orgy in an autobiographical account, published as *Swinger's Diary* (1973):

> I would be lying to claim that I remember everything that happened. All I can be sure of is that we built no barriers. Speech, vision, hearing, taste, touch, all were brought to play in this abandonment to pleasure. Time melted, absorbed in a multitude of orgasms.
>
> I was aware of the visual and tactile pleasure of Roger's black penis entering my vagina. . . . Then George slid his penis between my breasts, grasping the softness of them and pressing them about his shaft. Roger

immediately applied his tongue alternatively to nipples and penis, flicking back and forth as he continued his masterful in-and-out movement in my vagina. . . .

I think we all came together. . . . As their semen spurted out over my body, and Roger's began to drain out of my vagina, I felt drowned in sex. . . . . I felt like a princess who had just been anointed queen—like the center of the universe, warm, happy, and oh, so very satisfied.

My body wasn't the only contented part of me; my mind was equally satiated. I was in a state of euphoria totally new to me. It was like floating or flying. I hadn't known that sexual abandonment could bring on such a wonderful condition.[36]

For Iris Brent, interracial sex was the first step to racial harmony. "I sincerely believe that our society would be more integrated, more happy and less oppressive if sexual freedom were permitted our children and young people." Like gay liberationists who urged fellow gays to make themselves known, Iris Brent urged other swingers to come out of the closet of monogamy: "It behooves those of us who have personally tried some of the different forms of living to speak up so that others will know how these ideas work in our society. For it is one thing to know that primitives in a South Sea Island practice sexual permissiveness, and another to learn how such behavior works in modern America."[37]

Determined to live true to her principles, Iris Brent left her children with her husband, Ken, in Chicago, moved to California, and took a job with a nudist magazine. But she published *Swinger's Diary* under a pseudonym, Brent, in order to protect her children.

California was a magnet for seekers like Iris Brent who decided to devote themselves full-time to the cause of sexual freedom. On a fifteen-acre hilltop outside Los Angeles, John and Barbara Williamson established the veritable capital of the sexual revolution, the remarkable Sandstone Retreat, in 1969. As those who visited the retreat in the early seventies discovered, Sandstone represented the ultimate in heterosexual liberation. Every weekend, hundreds of couples traveled from across the country to copulate with complete strangers on Sandstone's shag rugs and sofas. Sandstone was more than just casual sex, however. It was the promise of a new world of physical freedom.

With a strong, charismatic personality, John Williamson seemed to one observer to be a veritable "messiah of sex."[38] He and his wife and a small group of fellow swingers lived year-round at Sandstone, spending most of their days and nights in the nude, regularly swapping partners. Outsiders were invited to visit the club on weekends for a fee. They could roam about the estate nude, participate in group sex in the "ballroom" of the main house (its floors covered in plush brown carpeting) or take a dip in the large pool. Sandstone offered a whole new dimension in voyeurism, exhibitionism, and liberation from jealousy.

Many of the club's regular visitors were high-profile professionals, like journalist Max Lerner, football-star-turned-actor Bernie Casey, and government critic Daniel Ellsberg. Not surprisingly, the retreat attracted enormous publicity: articles about it appeared in the *Los Angeles Times, Esquire, Penthouse,* and *Playboy.* Barbara Williamson appeared on *The Dick Cavett Show.* Sandstone was also featured in several books. Tom Hatfield and Gay Talese interviewed Sandstone members extensively for *The Sandstone Experience* and *Thy Neighbor's Wife,* respectively. In a 1975 article for *Oui* magazine, writer Herbert Gold offered a taste of the Sandstone experience:

> The large water-bed domain has a cathedral ceiling. . . . A sign says: PLEASE, BEYOND THIS POINT, SPEAK ONLY SOFT WORDS OF LOVE. It seems to be an injunction that is observed by the faithful. Clothes disappear into the cloakroom. The ballroom beyond, a nook of linked foam mattresses, seems assigned to serious individual and group voyeurs, while the couples couple in the water-bed chapel, heated to 80 degrees; a rhythm of water beds, the water-bed peace that passeth understanding and maketh inner space. Bath oil, massage oil, incense smells. Punk smells rising over the evening. Soft words and murmurs and mirrors so everyone can share.[39]

Sandstone's leaders considered themselves at the forefront of the sexual revolution. They believed they could transform the world. The revolution would begin not, as socialists believed, with the abolition of private property, but with the abolition of privacy itself. A sign at Sandstone introduced visitors to the club's philosophy:

> Why don't we believe in privacy? Privacy means you see the environment as hostile. You're an animal vulnerable to attack. But here, there are no doors on the bathrooms, the environment is gentling. Lovemaking is not a paranoid and threatening gesture that you have to hide from the world. It is tribalized. You are in the community. You do your thing; it is yours. Others may want to watch, learn, comment, even laugh. But they are of your tribe; the laughter is not hostile. Here, you trust the spectators. You trust yourself. You're not working for a grade. You're not even working for a peak experience. You have your own soul, a kind of privacy, within a semipublic world that supports you, helps you, cares for you, shares with you.[40]

It was an adult-centered world. Children under eighteen were forbidden. Sandstone was not part of the youthful hippie counterculture, it was a counterculture unto itself.

Sandstone enthusiasts, though they were part of a minority, did not feel it necessary to embrace the language or the logic of minority politics. They did not even have a term (like "gay" or "lesbian") to describe themselves. Rather, they viewed sexual liberation in universalist terms. Ultimately, they believed, every heterosexual couple would discover the benefits of open marriage and group sex. Not expecting any political or legal opposition to their activities, middle-aged sexual reformers never gave much thought to strategies of resistance. They were white, married, middle-class professionals, who assumed that the world would accept them as they were and follow in their free-and-easy footsteps.

But reality soon came crashing in. In 1970, the Los Angeles County Public Welfare Commission decided to shut down the retreat by denying Sandstone a "growth center" license. A costly court battle ensued, which forced the Williamsons to sell the club. An appeals court eventually overturned the Public Welfare Commission's ruling and the club was reopened in 1974 by Paul Paige, a former United States Marine and marriage counselor. Paige shared the Williamsons' idealistic belief in group sex, but he also saw the need to make money. Paige instituted annual dues of $740.[41] The worlds of commercialism and social change were converging. From then on, sexual liberation would almost always come with a price tag.

CHAPTER 18

THE JOY OF SALES: THE COMMERCIALIZATION OF SEXUAL FREEDOM

THERE IS SOMETHING remarkable about the fact that the most intense form of pleasure known to human beings is available to practically all of us at any time of the day or night. Orgasms are not scarce or precious resources; they don't need to be rationed or hoarded. A healthy adult can have at least one a day, sometimes many more. If no partner is available, one's own hand will do the trick (many, in fact, prefer masturbation to intercourse). Fantasies come to us — whether we like it or not — free of charge. Yet we live in a society in which people feel compelled to spend vast sums on sex. We organize life in such a fashion that sex *becomes* a prized commodity. We accept the notion that there might always be a bigger and better orgasm — it will just cost more. We may have to pay for more pornography, or pay for another prostitute, or pay for a more expensive dinner, or pay for more therapy, or pay for better makeup, or pay for softer sheets, or pay for a babysitter, or pay for plastic surgery, or pay for another romance novel, but we are resigned to the fact that we must pay for pleasure.

Paying for sex is not new. What was new in the early seventies was paying for sexual freedom — that is, paying for the opportunity to experience the wonders of sexual liberation, to be part of the sexual revolution. It was clear from the start that many Americans did not want to be left out. Shrewd entrepreneurs saw an easy way to make a quick buck.

Playboy and *Sex and the Single Girl* were early — and successful — forays into the commercialization of sexual freedom. But the process of commodification took on a whole new dimension in the early seventies as product after product promising sexual liberation entered the market. The new line of goods was typified by *The Joy of Sex* (1972), which sold 3.8 million copies in the first two years.[1] The book would become a bible for countless Americans seeking initiation into the sexual revolution. Its author, Alex Comfort, was a utopian in the strictest sense of the term. A British obstetrician who was also an anarchist and pacifist, Comfort, born in 1920, came to the United States in 1969 as a senior fellow at the Center for the Study of Democratic Institutions in Santa Barbara, California. Back in England he had written several polemical books, including *Sexual Behavior in Society* and *Barbarism and Sexual Freedom: Lectures on the Sociology of Sex from the Standpoint of Anarchism.* A respected poet, a songwriter (he wrote lyrics for Pete Seeger), and an expert on aging, Comfort was not your ordinary sexologist.

Perhaps better than any other sex book of the period, *The Joy of Sex* mastered a certain nonchalance about its subject matter. Comfort may have begun his career as an idealist, but by the time he wrote The *Joy of Sex,* a certain amount of cynicism had seeped into his view of sexual relations. The book strikes a note of bemused boredom, both with the hang-ups of conventional society and the overeagerness of recent converts to sexual freedom. "The people who go to Masters and Johnson are getting over hangups so basic that in past generations the folk tradition would have taken care of them," Comfort explains in the introduction, titled "On Advanced Lovemaking." The book's art is in its understatement. ("Vibrating hotel beds, operated by a coin-in-slot timer, are also well spoken of, but are apt to run out at the critical moment, or make you ill.") At times *The Joy of Sex* reads rather like a book of household hints. The section on semen notes:

> There is no lovemaking without spilling this, on occasions at least. You can get it out of clothing or furnishings either with a stiff brush, when the stain has dried, or with a diluted solution of sodium bicarbonate. If you spill it over each other, massage it gently in — the pollen-odor of fresh semen is itself an aphrodisiac, which is why the smell of fresh grass or thalictrum flowers turns most people on.[2]

No matter why one actually bought it, owning *The Joy of Sex* became a not-so-subtle symbol of urbane style. Comfort described it as "the first explicitly sexual book for the coffee table." It was, in other words, the perfect product for the status-conscious who wanted to keep up with their sexually liberated neighbors. It was no accident that the book's drawings showed a couple who defied traditional middle-class standards of beauty. Her underarm hair and his unruly beard and uncircumcised penis were meant to suggest a couple more "in touch" with their own bodies than the "uptight straights" of middle America were. In fact, Comfort told readers that armpit hair "should on no account be shaved," while he approved of shaving pubic hair. As for deodorant, the *The Joy of Sex* stated that it was "banned absolutely."[3]

The Joy of Sex was, as it claimed to be, a marriage manual. Like all marriage manuals, it gave information and advice to the heterosexual couple hoping to increase their erotic enjoyment. But it was also handy for those who needed a flashlight to venture down the dark alleyways of the sexual revolution. There were thus detailed instructions on everything from frottage to anal sex.*

Comfort's publisher, eager to capitalize on the success of *The Joy of Sex*, did not wait long to release a sequel, titled, appropriately enough, *More Joy*. Both represented the taming of the sexual revolution in the early seventies. Hippies did not need lessons in creative copulation, but their parents and older siblings did. Sara Evans, who was in her early thirties by the time the sexual revolution was in full swing, recalls: "I had gotten married in 1966, so I felt a little envious that I was missing things. I didn't have any strong wish to change my situation, but I was aware that there was this experimentalism going on and that if I was younger, things might have been different."[4] *The Joy of Sex* and *More Joy* helped those who were older than the baby boomers feel like they too were part of the action.

But as consumer products marketed for the suburban middle class, Comfort's books were not exactly cutting-edge. Though Comfort stressed the natural bisexuality of all human beings (a truism of the time), he nevertheless counseled readers "it's probably not a good idea for straight males . . . to rush out and realize all their bisexual potentials, simply because they might, unless they're very hardy, find it disturbing themselves," and warned that "gay solidarity" was deceiving men into thinking they were exclusively gay. He considered himself a proponent of sexual equality, but his feminism often fell short of the mark. "Don't get yourself raped," he advised his female readers, "i.e., don't deliberately excite a man you don't know well, unless you mean to follow through." In a section giving instructions on bondage, Comfort noted matter-of-factly: "The expression of erotic astonishment on the face of a well-gagged woman when she finds she can only mew is irresistible to most men's rape instincts." As for prostitution, Comfort declared: "[T]he commonest motive for becoming a streetwalking pro is an active dislike of males."[5] Such gross generalizations and unsupported claims

---

* "With the woman kneeling, head well down, carefully lubricate your glans. . . . Put the glans to the spot and press gently and steadily, while she 'bears down' to let you in. At first she will close up tight. Then after a few moments she will begin to open. Go in slowly, never more than glans deep, and take your friction on the pull rather than the push." (150).

were passed off as fact. But who was going to question such clichés of "common sense"? Comfort's books sold well, in part, because they barely challenged conventional wisdom.

Even more than Comfort, the many publishers of men's magazines in the early seventies were motivated by the possibility of profit and knew how to sell sexual liberation. Bob Guccione's *Penthouse,* which was the first mass market magazine to show women's pubic hair (others included only airbrushed photographs) when it was launched in April 1970, was a purely commercial venture. While living in London, Guccione saw the success of *Playboy* and realized that he could get rich by pushing the bounds of the printable. With a clever initial advertising campaign ("We're going rabbit hunting," read the copy, accompanied by a drawing of the famed Playboy mascot in the crosshairs of a rifle) and pictorials featuring male–female couples, *Penthouse* blasted its way into the American market.[6] It was received with enormous enthusiasm. Dick Clark, wholesome record-spinning icon of mainstream American youth, raved about the magazine. "Having read the first American edition of *Penthouse,*" Clark wrote in a letter to the editor, "I can only say that . . . one can expect the very best from [it]. All in all, *Penthouse* is here to stay. My congratulations for a job well done."[7] But *Penthouse* was more than just another skin magazine. It promised to keep the reader on the front-lines of the sexual revolution. Guccione made a virtual pledge to his readers that he would forever do battle against the forces of repression. This was an essential element in the magazine's extraordinary appeal.

Guccione, like Hefner before him, exploited middle-class aspirations to European sophistication. Other magazine publishers, however, found they could successfully appeal to working-class interests. In one magazine, photographs of a model named Mandi were accompanied by text suffused with class consciousness:

> Mandi is a lovely girl, prone to fantasize at length about the men she has encountered throughout the day. Things have a tendency to go up and down a great deal at the brokerage firm where she works. Up and down of course refers to the stocks and bonds she deals with. But the men seem so stuffy! It's hard to visualize them personally as capable of getting it up and less going down, down, down!

The magazine quoted Mandi herself: "The men I work with are such terrible bores they don't know what a girl hankers for!" In case the reader failed to understand Mandi's desires, the editors explained, "At the moment, her principal fantasies involve strong men — laboring men with firm bodies."[8] Working-class men, in other words, were as entitled to the benefits of the sexual revolution just as surely as their middle-class bosses were.

If men would pay to be sexually liberated, why wouldn't women? This was the philosophy behind *Cosmopolitan,* the magazine Helen Gurley Brown took over in 1965 after her phenomenal rise to celebrity status with *Sex and the Single Girl.* Brown found that female readers were eager for a magazine that encouraged them to be sexually expressive. With readers came advertising revenue. Financially savvy, Brown realized that the decline of the double standard could translate directly into dollars. Under Brown's direction, *Cosmopolitan* began featuring centerfolds of nude males. In April 1972, a much publicized picture of actor and former football player Burt Reynolds, who was then at the height of his Hollywood fame, lying nude (though discreetly posed) on a bearskin rug caused *Cosmo* sales to skyrocket. For Reynolds, it was a chance to make a statement about sexual liberation.

> The only kick I got out of the whole thing was that I was sending up *Playboy,* which I hate desperately. It's a masturbatory magazine under the guise of being a very sophisticated male journal. A man can buy *Playboy* and stroll out with his head held high, and go to his john and jerk off and nobody thinks anything. But that same man goes in and says, "Let me have a copy of *Boob,* or *Crotch,* or *Screw,*" and he has to put them into a brown paper wrapper or buy a copy of *House Beautiful* to wrap them in.[9]

Whatever his reason, Reynolds's decision to bare his buttocks for the camera had everyone talking. The issue practically sold out within two days. When he appeared on the Johnny Carson show shortly thereafter, the show's ratings reached a record high.

The sensation created by the *Cosmo* centerfold sent a message to magazine publishers. A New York publisher soon introduced *Playgirl* magazine, which featured a monthly male centerfold, and Bob Guccione tried his hand at the women's market with a short-lived magazine named *Viva.* (Guccione seemed to think that women would prefer to look at images of clothed men cuddling naked women than images of naked men themselves. As a result, *Viva* could hardly claim to be at the forefront of the sexual revolution and it died almost as soon as it began.) As always, the goal was to create the allure of sexual radicalism in order to maximize profits.

But magazines were costly to start and always entailed great financial risk. Eager entrepreneurs found that sex films were fairly cheap to make and, with independent theaters proliferating across the country, easy to distribute. "In those days," television producer Susan Baerwald recalls, "everyone who owned a camera tried making a porn film."[10] The industry got its start in San Francisco, where attitudes were generally lax and hippies were willing to take off their clothes for a few dollars an hour. Theaters specializing in "blue movies" started popping up in the Bay

Area in the late sixties. By 1969, San Francisco boasted twenty such theaters. In July of that year, two brothers, Jim and Artie Mitchell, began showing hard-core films at the O'Farrell Theater in the city's sleazy Tenderloin district. Other theaters quickly followed suit. Sex films were effectively decriminalized in San Francisco in 1970, when juries in several trials failed to find them obscene.[11]

Like other aspects of the sexual revolution, the first wave of sex films combined idealistic aspirations with more mundane financial considerations. Films like *Censorship in Denmark* (1969), made by Alex de Renzy, contained an implicit critique of American mores. Acting in sex films could amount to a form of personal protest against bourgeois morality. Mary Rexroth, a Stanford University faculty member and the daughter of Beat poet Kenneth Rexroth, acted in at least half a dozen pornographic films as a rebellion against sexual repression in society. Operating an X-rated theater could be cast in sociopolitical terms, though it sometimes required a large stretch of the imagination. At one San Francisco theater, African-American owner Bob McKnight showed films depicting interracial sex. To McKnight, such films served the purpose of "shooting down myths and stereotypes about black people." Arlene Elster, the operator of San Francisco's Sutter Cinema, believed her occupation was a direct contribution to society. In December 1970, she helped organize the First International Erotic Film Festival. The festival and the films shown there were detailed and generously praised in the pages of the *San Francisco Chronicle.*[12]

The intelligentsia delighted in the trend toward the explicit. John Money, a biologist at Johns Hopkins, believed erotic films encouraged valuable social change.

> They are defining new possibilities in arbitrary sexual relationships, breaking down the stereotypes as to what is male, what is female. This is the first generation of humankind which can separate its recreational sex from its procreational sex, and I find it very valid that people of this generation claim the freedom to expand their sexual horizons. Expansion beyond their parents' standards is a normal step. For the first time in history, young people are teaching lessons to the older generation, and that is what these movies are really about.[13]

In the *New York Times,* Foster Hirsch offered a veritable tribute to erotic films.

> For the first time in the history of this country, pornographic films are openly available to adults (21 and over). And I think this state of permissiveness is a sign of health rather than sickness, of hope rather than despair. It can be liberating and therapeutic for people to have easy access

to the visual depiction of sexual fantasies. Pornography needn't be degrading for the performers or the viewers — at its best, it can be a celebration of human sexuality. Watching pornography in a public theater can be a purgative social event, a means of easing inhibitions, of alleviating hypocrisy and fear, of freely acknowledging that we are all sexual beings.[14]

Hirsch articulated a new ideal of the public sphere, the pornographic theater, where individuals would share the experience of sexual communication. Such grandiose claims were surely lost on the majority of filmgoers. But the very fact that the good gray *Times* would print Hirsch's paean to pornography suggests how rapidly American society was changing in the early seventies. Whether these changes would last was a different question.

At first, sex films represented a small and relatively insignificant segment of the motion picture market. But in 1972, Gerald Damiano's *Deep Throat* demonstrated that Americans from all walks of life would pay to participate — at least vicariously — in the much talked about sexual revolution. The film combined a counterculture sensibility with hardcore footage of heterosexual penetration. In the opening sequence, psychedelic music plays as a man performs cunnilingus on Linda Lovelace, who looks bored. Taking out a cigarette, she asks, "Do you mind if I smoke while you eat?" With this dry sense of humor, the remainder of the film follows the desperate attempts of Lovelace to find sexual pleasure, which eludes her because she does not know that for some unexplained reason her clitoris is located in her throat. Her condition is discovered by Harry Reems, playing a mad doctor. When Lovelace performs fellatio on Reems, she is cured of her inorgasmia, and the film cuts to a scene of bursting fireworks. The movie was praised and publicized by Al Goldstein in his tabloid *Screw,* and an estimated six thousand customers paid to see it in its first week at the World Theater in New York's Times Square.[15]

Critics applauded the arrival of the hard-core feature film. Newspapers ranging from the trade magazine *Variety* to the Wilmington, Delaware, *Evening Journal* lavished praise on *Deep Throat,* and the movie made an astonishing $25 million. It was shown in first-run and art house theaters in seventy-three U.S. cities, including such upscale communities as Princeton, New Jersey. The film drew not only male viewers, but heterosexual couples and groups of single women. Film critic Arthur Knight applauded *Deep Throat* as the "first film of this genre to acknowledge the importance of female sexual gratification." In response to *Deep Throat's* tremendous popularity, a few television newscasters began reviewing pornographic films.[16]

Attempts *were* made to ban *Deep Throat,* A New York judge forced the World Theater to stop showing the film.* Prosecutors, desperate to find experts who would support censorship, turned to the medical profession for help. Psychiatrist Max Levin, a witness for the prosecution in the New York trial, testified that the film was harmful because it denied the importance of the vaginal orgasm described by Freud. Psychoanalyst Ernest van den Haag claimed the film was dangerous because its hedonistic ethic would pave the way toward fascism.[17] In a thirty-five-page decision, Judge Tyler ruled that *Deep Throat* represented a "feast of carrion and squalor" and the "nadir of decadence." "This is one throat that deserves to be cut," the judge declared.[18] But the decision was eventually overturned, and theaters specializing in X-rated films soon opened throughout America, from the cities to the suburbs, from the East Coast to the Midwest. Despite the attack by Judge Tyler, juries in conservative towns across the country, like one in Binghamton, New York, a town with a population of only 64,000, ruled that *Deep Throat* was entitled to First Amendment protection. By the end of 1972, *Deep Throat* was one of the nation's most popular films.[19]

Deep Throat proved that pornography was profitable. After it paved the way, San Francisco theater owners Jim and Artie Mitchell began making their own films, including *Behind the Green Door.* Featuring an extended orgy (with multiple men having intercourse with the same woman), interracial sex (a black man penetrating a white woman), and a slow-motion close-up of a man ejaculating into the air, *Behind the Green Door* offered audiences the sense of participating in a world of "far-out" sexual fantasies. (In a strange twist of events, the film's star, Marilyn Chambers, a onetime model, happened to appear on boxes of Ivory Snow as a young mother holding a baby just as the film opened. This, of course, led to numerous jokes on television talk shows and boosted ticket sales immensely.)

The commercialization of sexual freedom worked just as well with gay audiences as with straight ones. In San Francisco, Joe and Sam Gage produced *Kansas City Trucking Co., El Paso Wrecking Co.,* and *L.A. Tool and Die,* three films with explicit gay sex. *Score* (1969), a film by Randy Metzger, featured both straight and gay sex. Gay pornographic magazines and books took advantage of the fact that gay men, like their straight counterparts, were more than willing to pay for pleasure, no matter how fleeting.

---

*Police used a variety of tactics to crack down on pornographic films. In some cases, they would use licensing laws to shut down theaters. In New York police attempted to enforce such licensing laws even after they were ruled unconstitutional by a federal judge. (See *New York Times,* 28 December 1972.)

In a 1973 U.S. survey, one quarter of the respondents said they had seen an X-rated film in the prior twelve months.[20] But films offered only what might be described as voyeuristic liberation. New Jersey entrepreneur Steve Ostrow hoped to capture those consumers ready for the real thing. His vision: a commercial sex club catering to that segment of the New York City population in search of the ultimate in polymorphously perverse pleasures. An investment banker from the suburb of Matawan married to a Scarsdale debutante, Ostrow was an unlikely spokesman for sexual liberation. But by turning the Continental Baths into one of the world's most notorious nightspots, he joined the growing ranks of sexual celebrities in early-seventies New York.

For most of his adult years, Ostrow lived a conventional, middle-class, married existence. One night, however, he had a secret sexual encounter at a seedy gay bathhouse in lower Manhattan, one of a handful that had been around since the early part of the twentieth century.* Ostrow found the experience so liberating, he decided to tell his wife about his sexual attraction to men. Though she was upset by his revelation, she elected to stay with him in an open marriage. Ostrow, however, was not content merely to come out or to continue exploring bisexuality. Recognizing a potentially profitable business opportunity, he decided to open a commercial sex club of his own. Displaying a flair for the dramatic, Ostrow began his project in 1969 by renting the basement of the elegant Ansonia Hotel, in the heart of New York City's mostly residential Upper West Side. The Ansonia, a giant wedding cake of a building at the corner of Broadway and West 74th, was built at the turn of the century as a private apartment house for New York's wealthiest eccentrics. Ostrow converted the basement swimming pool and lounge area into the 20,000 square-foot Continental Baths. His aim, apart from making money, was to create a public space where sexual expression would be celebrated. Ostrow hoped that men would visit the club to experience sexual freedom openly without shame or guilt or secrecy.

The Continental Baths, unlike any bathhouse in New York history, combined public sex with cabaret-style entertainment. Ostrow hired a variety of musicians, singers, and comedians. Still, police raided the club, arresting men for having sex.[21] Then a peculiar event occurred. Bette Midler, who performed regularly at the Continental Baths, mentioned her experiences during an appearance on *The Tonight Show* in 1970. As a result, the Continental became a public sensation. Heterosexual couples from the suburbs began commuting to the city to hear con-

---

* Gay bathhouses had existed in New York City since the end of the nineteenth century, but in the years after Prohibition they became secretive enclaves of nighttime sexual activity, their presence generally ignored by the city's media. (Chauncey, *Gay New York,* passim.)

certs at the club. These couples mixed and mingled with the gay men draped in towels who pursued sex in the Continental's back rooms.

Eventually, as more and more women came to the club, they began participating in the sexual activities. Slowly the Continental Baths evolved into a commercial sex club for both men and women, a fact that delighted Ostrow. He saw his club as the vanguard of a new "pansexual" utopia. As he told a reporter from *Rolling Stone* in 1976:

> We're close now to total sexual liberation here, but I wish everybody in the world could have witnessed the first awakening down there, the dawn of the revolution, the first girl turning on to the beautiful boys in towels, the first straight guy who did, the first gay guy turning on to the naked women! Will this sound excessive? That the Continental has grown full with love, like my life! The world comes here now to feel the release of decades of pent-up sexuality, all those years of inhibition are splattered, if you will, against my walls! Enough semen has been excrecated [sic] here to populate the world to infinity!

The club was so popular, Mayor Abraham Beame and Congresswoman Bella Abzug visited to give campaign speeches. On Broadway, a comedy titled *The Ritz* (1973) was set in a steam bath. Ostrow, who began giving talks at the New School for Social Research on "Being Your Authentic Self," saw the bathhouse as the model of American life for the future. To promote racial harmony, he took out advertisements in the city's black newspapers and invited blacks to come to the Continental for free. Ostrow brought his own children, a son age six and a girl age twelve, to the Baths in 1976. "The kids are very hip, very happy, very healthy. I tell them they've begun life in an era without labels, in which they can just be sexual people. They think I'm the greatest father who ever lived." He hoped to create a self-enclosed sexual paradise, where women and men could come to eat, drink, sleep, and be sexually satisfied. Inside the club he established a VD clinic and offered private therapy sessions for "those still sexually unsure."[22] One woman who went to the Baths remembers, "People got used to seeing each other parade around. It was surprising to see so many well-known people naked. . . . It was all in trying to have the most excitement you could. Everyone was looking for stimulus. People had private parties too. They would play games, where they would turn out the lights and then grope around. I was turned on by seeing other people make love. There was freedom in the air."[23]

With so many straights now coming to the club, the Continental Baths fell out of favor with New York City gays in the midseventies, but Ostrow's enterprise succeeded in bringing bathhouse culture into public view. The bathhouse was bought in 1977 by Larry Levenson and Mike Ross, who changed the name to Plato's Retreat and began catering to heterosexual couples exclusively. The $25 entry fee (a little less than the price of a Broadway theater ticket) included an "all-you-can-eat" buffet of bagels and lox, chicken salad, shrimp, wine, and scotch. Levenson and Ross installed a steam room, a pool table, and a "mat room" for orgies, and they posted a sign above the front door emblazoned with the slogan "Make Love, Not War." Plato's Retreat was soon a world-famous experiment in heterosexual relations. Movie stars, models, and rock stars visited the club. Howard Bellin remembers: "I was at a party with a great friend and this party turned into an orgy. I distinctly remember being in a bedroom with two women making love when my friend walked in and said 'Come on, forget about this, we're going to Plato's Retreat.' I said, 'What, are you crazy?!' Plato's Retreat had only been open about three weeks. I was furious. But let's just say I wasn't sorry we left the party. Plato's Retreat was unbelievable. I had never in my life seen anything like this and probably never will again. I mean, thirty, forty couples all making love at the same time, it was amazing, you cannot believe it. Ahhh, those were the days. . . . It was out of the Roman Empire, everything except the vomitorium."[24]

According to *Time* magazine, over six thousand men and women visited Plato's Retreat each month in 1977.[25] A disco song in honor of the club was recorded by Joe Thomas. Plato's Retreat was even favorably reviewed in the middle-class consumer magazine *New York* in 1977.[26]

Meanwhile, owners of gay bathhouses began advertising in the gay press and made efforts to improve their industry's image. A former owner of the Club Baths in Manhattan describes the transformation in the early '70s:

> We made the baths beautiful and clean and treated our customers as special human beings and made them feel good about themselves. We gave them pink spotlights and real plants and numerous facilities for anonymous sex. For a year we operated a free venereal disease clinic at the Club. We turn[ed] away drunks and people on drugs. . . . We brought respectability to the baths.[27]

The Club Baths expanded into a chain of thirty-seven independently owned bathhouses around the country. By 1977, there were at least 129 openly gay bathhouses in the United States, from Charlotte, North Carolina, to Hammond, Indiana. In San Francisco, the Sutro Baths offered a range of options. Sunday nights only women were admitted, Tuesdays only men, and on Wednesdays and Saturdays only heterosexual couples. Friday evenings, advertised as "hot and nasty," the club was open to everyone — gay, straight, and bisexual.[28] As commercial spaces, where a variety of sexual transactions were available in one convenient location, bathhouses were the erotic equivalent of the modern department store, a "naked Bloomingdales."[29] "For sheer efficiency," wrote Charles Silverstein and Edmund White in the *The Joy of Gay Sex* (1977), "the baths can't be bettered."[30] Playwright Larry Kramer recalls, "The baths were wonderful. I used to go every night after writing. They were a very efficient means of getting laid."[31]

For gay men who liked their sex rough, liberation and commercialization went hand and hand, because together they allowed sadomasochism an unprecedented visibility. Although a handful of s/m clubs had existed in San Francisco in the early sixties, it was not until the seventies that ritualized s/m became a popular and high-profile form of expression in the gay community. In 1969, Fred Halstead and Joey Yale made *L.A. Plays Itself*, the first feature-length, hard-core gay sex film with spanking and bondage. In 1970, *Born to Raise Hell*, directed by Roger Earle, opened in Los Angeles. It showed s/m sex in all its permutations. Numerous s/m novels, now considered classics of the genre, were published in the early seventies, including *The Young Master* (1970) by William Lambert III, *All or Nothing* (1971) by Dick Vaden, and *Run Little Leather Boy* (1971) by Larry Townsend. In 1972, Townsend published the first guidebook to living an s/m lifestyle, *The Leatherman's Handbook*. Meanwhile, s/m clubs became a fixture of urban nightlife. In New York, the Anvil, the Sewer, and the Cock Ring drew large crowds who came to lose themselves each night in drugs, dark dungeons, and ritualized, anonymous sex. Some clubs offered bondage tables, prison cells for willing victims, or rows of slings and buckets of Crisco to facilitate "fisting." S/m social clubs were founded on both coasts. One of them, the Leather Fraternity in San Francisco, led to the creation of *Drummer* magazine in 1975, early issues of which showed scenes of fisting, urination, bondage, and other forms of consensual sexual torture at the city's sex clubs.[32]

Radicals were torn about the implications of commercialized sexual freedom.* To feminist poet Adrienne Rich, the so-called sexual revolution available in movie theaters and bathhouses was nothing more than "a totally middle-class and narcissistic phenomenon . . . exploiting the myth of sexual 'liberation' for its own ends."[33] But many saw true potential for sexual freedom in commercial sex. After visiting the Club Baths in 1975, lesbian novelist Rita Mae Brown said she believed that such sanctuaries might make sense for women as well as for men. Brown expressed reservations about the world of "one-dimensional sexual activity" and wondered whether a "fuck palace" like the Club Baths represented "the ultimate conclusion of sexist logic" or the pinnacle of "erotic freedom." But in the final analysis, she decided women needed bathhouses too:

* Many were also upset about the rise of organized s/m, a subject covered in chapter 21.

I want the option of random sex with no emotional commitment when I need sheer physical relief. . . . Our Xanadu would be less competitive than the gay man's baths, our laughter would ring in the sauna and you'd touch not only to fuck but just to touch. It is in our interest to build places where we have relief, refuge, release. Xanadu is not a lurid dream, it's the desire of a woman to have options. Like men we should have choices: deep long-term relationships, the baths, short-term affairs. And those choices are not mutually exclusive.[34]

Commercial sex was not ideal, but it would do until the revolution had run its full course.

In San Francisco, this pragmatic view of sexual liberation was endorsed wholeheartedly by Margo St. James, a woman once arrested for prostitution, who became a full-fledged champion for prostitutes' rights. While other feminists were declaring that traditional marriage turned all women into prostitutes by forcing them to trade their bodies for a lifetime of financial support, and were busy trying to free women from this form of "prostitution," St. James wanted to free women to engage in prostitution.

Margo St. James was born in 1937 and raised in Bellinghan, Washington, the child of divorced parents. Pregnant and married at seventeen, she was herself divorced by twenty. As a young adult she read in *Life* magazine about the beatniks, and in 1959 went to San Francisco to join the beatnik community. There she was arrested and convicted of soliciting in 1962, but her conviction was overturned on appeal.[35] Whether or not she was a prostitute at the time of her arrest remains unclear, but by her own testimony, she started working as one after her release.

She then discovered politics and radical feminism through Florynce Kennedy, an outspoken African-American activist who was famous for peppering her public statements with profanity.[36] In 1971, St. James founded WHOM (Whores, Housewives and Other Mothers). Her motive was "sexual freedom, freedom of the body, the recognition of the right to engage in consensual sex with whomever we please for whatever motive; the end to the myth that women who are seductive are evil."[37] WHOM soon evolved into COYOTE (Call Off Your Old Tired Ethics), whose goal was to decriminalize prostitution, provide legal and medical assistance to prostitutes, and "raise the working standards of loose women everywhere." The group was also the first well-organized American effort to promote prostitution as a form of sexual freedom. Decriminalization was not a new concept; it had been tried in Europe in the late nineteenth century, but was fiercely opposed in America. In 1949, forty-eight nations had ratified a United Nations Convention calling for decriminalization; the United States, however, had voted against it.

Margo St. James received extensive publicity on the West Coast and was a regular guest on radio and television talk shows. In 1974, COYOTE sponsored the first National Hookers Convention at Glide Memorial Church and a Hookers' Halloween Ball, billed as "the social event of the year for heterosexuals, bisexuals, trisexuals, nonsexuals, homosexuals, and other minorities who feel discriminated against." The ball made St. James popular with San Francisco's political activists and sexual minorities, though the event was marked by tensions. Some feminists were angered that male transvestites stole the show, and a fight broke out between a transvestite and a member of the renegade Hell's Angels motorcycle gang. Still, St. James considered the event a success, a tribute to her own sexual wit.

At times, however, her humor turned to rage. "Who are the fucking cops to tell me what to do?" she demanded to know. "The illegality of prostitution creates crime. How dare those fuckers point the finger at women? A woman on the street is made to feel that she needs a man. In this society a man is status."[38] Both her humor and her anger fit with New Left and countercultural attitudes; members of the COYOTE board included Kate Millett, Herb Gold, Florynce Kennedy, Ken Kesey, and Paul Krassner.

Though COYOTE was primarily a California-based effort, the notion of legalizing or decriminalizing prostitution found support throughout the nation. In 1972, Boston's public television station WGBH aired a show about legalization and encouraged viewers to respond by mail; 7,460 viewers wrote to register their support for legalization, while only 4,784 wrote in opposition.[39] Many organizations came out in favor of decriminalization in 1974, including the American Bar Association, the National Commission on the Causes and Prevention of Violence, the League of Women Voters, the National Association of Women, and the National Advisory Commission on Criminal Justice Standards and Goals. Conservative pundit George Will went on record favoring decriminalization as well. In 1971 Nevada formally legalized prostitution.[40]

The movement to legalize prostitution came at the same time as social reform efforts became more commercial. As we have seen, Sandstone, that idyll of personal growth and sexual freedom, turned into a profit-making venture in the early seventies. The same transformation marked the decline of Jefferson Poland's Sexual Freedom League. In the late sixties, the Berkeley chapter had begun sponsoring naked parties, which attracted hippies and countercultural types. But before long, ticket prices were introduced. The average age of League members went up, diversity declined, and long-haired hippies all but disappeared from League functions. The new directors of the Berkeley chapter, Tom Palmer and Virginia Miller, actively distanced the organization from radical causes. "We've been accused of being in the forefront of the sexual revolution and that's simply not true," Palmer declared. "We're just a group that publicly admits to what everyone else is doing . . . and we're trying to get it accepted and respectable."[41] League fliers ceased to mention matters like homosexuality, prostitution, nudism, miscegenation, and transvestism. Jefferson Poland's original vision of a pansexual society free of all legal regulations on sexual behavior was quietly abandoned. Poland himself was locked out of the League offices. Capitalism had won and radicalism had most surely lost.

The fact that the sexual revolution became so saturated with commercialism caused some in the movement great concern. Herbert Marcuse pleaded with his followers not to confuse true liberation with the "repressive desublimation" offered by commercialized sex. (Unfortunately, Marcuse failed to further elaborate on this distinction.) Theodore Roszak, in *The Making of a Counter Culture*, urged Americans to see through the false promises of *Playboy* and its ilk:

> In the affluent society, we have sex and sex galore — or so we are led to believe. But when we look more closely we see that this sybaritic promiscuity wears a special social clothing. It has been assimilated to an income level and social status available only to our well-heeled junior executives and the jet set. After all, what does it cost to rent these yachts full of nymphomaniacal young things in which our Playboys sail off for orgiastic swimming parties in the Bahamas?[42]

Roszak believed the hippie generation would crush the commercialization of sex once and for all. Others did too. As psychoanalyst Rollo May wrote of *Playboy* in 1970,

> You discover the naked girls with silicated breasts side by side with articles by reputable authors, and you conclude on first blush that the magazine is certainly on the side of the new enlightenment. But as you look more closely you see a strange expression in these photographed girls: detached, mechanical, uninviting, vacuous — the typical schizophrenic personality in the negative sense of the term. You discover that they are not "sexy" at all but that *Playboy* has only shifted the fig leaf from the genitals to the face.[43]

And in January 1970, Jefferson Poland, literally thrown out of the Sexual Freedom League for being a "troublemaker," organized the Psychedelic Venus Church in San Francisco.* The church's rituals included massage, marijuana, and group sex and were intended to provide an

* Writing about the church, one underground newspaper said: "It's hard to determine the role of orgies in our alternative lifestyle . . . Too many orgies and we'll become jaded, perhaps decadent. But there's still a place for sex in the revolution and spontaneity won't always arise between friends. Periodic celebration for the sisters and brothers — black, female, white, male, brown, gay, yellow, and red — may help to squash the growing trend towards polarization."

alternative to the private SFL parties that charged admission.[44] In New York, the members of the Marxist-oriented Gay Liberation Front denounced gay bars as capitalist institutions bound up with the larger social logic of economic exploitation. Attempting to create alternative environments for gay socializing, students sponsored free dances.[45] Another gay liberation organization, the Red Butterfly, put it in simple, if didactic, terms: "We believe that economic and social democracy are the necessary conditions for [gay] liberation. In Marxist language, we assert that a democratic socialism is the necessary basis for building a classless society, i.e. communism."[46]

Did the free market sap the sexual revolution of its radical potential for restructuring social relations, or did it increase opportunities for erotic expression? This is a question that has been asked and answered many different times, many different ways, but it remains important for anyone who believes that society's sexual attitudes ought to be improved. Several things are clear. First, it would be a mistake to blame the failings of the sexual revolution solely on those who saw opportunities for financial gain. Self-righteous radicals tended to be as solipsistic and insensible as the worst profiteers. The leaders of the Weatherman, for example, who had crusaded to "smash monogamy," ended up bombing federal buildings and applauding the vicious and deranged Manson murders. Second, the sexual revolution would never have gotten off the ground without the free market. Pharmaceutical companies invested in the pill because they saw potential profits; the Supreme Court abolished censorship in no small part because market demand for sexually explicit materials was so high.

Yet when all is said and done, the free market does not guarantee the quality of its merchandise. The problem with allowing the literary marketplace to determine the content of the sexual revolution was vividly demonstrated by the case of Xaviera Hollander, a self-appointed sex expert who published her autobiographical account *The Happy Hooker* in February 1972. The daughter of a Dutch psychiatrist, Hollander made her mark as a Manhattan madame. She was arrested in 1971 in connection with bribing New York City police officers, so the twenty-eight-year-old Hollander was already a well-known figure before she even began to write. Her book allowed her to deny the charges against her and to take advantage of the growing belief that commercial sex was just as "liberated" as other kinds of sex, if not more so. Sexually active from the age of fifteen, Hollander acquired an extensive knowledge of men and women, which she readily shared with her readers. In one chapter she provided sketches of the sexual proclivities of men from around the world. Her recycling of popular stereotypes gave the egos of her white, middle-class readers a boost. Her description of "Orientals" suggests the type of information she offered:

We have a saying that going to bed with an Oriental is like washing your hands — clean and simple. These men are the quickest lovers and the smallest in dimensions. They are so quick and easy to take care of that when the new Chinese restaurant opened recently in my building I arranged to have regular meals sent up to my house in exchange for a monthly screw for every man on the staff, even the cook. Noodles for doodles, you might call it.

Hollander then described an experience with a Japanese client who was so embarrassed by the size of his penis that he used an artificial phallus when having intercourse.

Similar insights about human sexuality were scattered throughout the book. Explaining why one of her "girls" regularly resorted to faking orgasm with clients, Hollander wrote: "Her trouble is, she has been using a vibrator since she was about seventeen, and she is now nineteen and cannot have an orgasm without it, because nothing can match up to the action of one of those machines."[47] The best-selling author was hired by *Penthouse* to write a sexual advice column for the magazine in 1972. Her financial success turned her into an unofficial authority on sexual liberation. Hollander's ability to parlay her iconoclasm into profits, her profits into greater publicity, and her publicity into greater stature as an iconoclast illustrates the fact that a revolution shaped by the marketplace is bound to be built on popular whim rather than carefully considered ideas or deep-seated convictions.

Hollander's brand of sexual expertise was just the sort of commercialized libertarianism that infuriated left-wing social reformers, who were also distraught about the spread of seedy strip clubs, adult theaters, and pornographic bookstores. They continued to yearn for a more innocent kind of sexual paradise, free from the cynicism of the marketplace, but also free from the vision of technocracy that worried people like Theodore Roszak: "the relentless quest for efficiency, for order, for ever more extensive rational control." Roszak claimed that "to liberate sexuality would be to create a society in which technocratic discipline would be impossible."[48] He placed his faith in the counterculture, which, he hoped, would lead to a new race of human beings, committed to the continuous evolution of society. In a similar vein, German radical Rudi Dutschke declared,

> The Revolution is not an event that takes two or three days, in which there is shooting and hanging. It is a long drawn out process in which new people are created, capable of renovating society so that the revolution does not replace one elite with another, but so that the revolution creates a new anti-authoritarian structure with anti-authoritarian people who in their

turn re-organize the society so that it becomes a non-alienated human society, free from war, hunger and exploitation.[49]

Few hippies outside of Berkeley and Amsterdam had the kind of ideological purity to sustain Dutschke's vision, but if there was one group of self-styled sex radicals who truly believed they could defeat sexual commerce, technocracy, and exploitation once and for all, it was lesbian feminists. In fact, lesbian feminists hoped to start the sexual revolution over from scratch. The entire "revolution," they asserted, had been nothing but a male conspiracy to make women more sexually available. The pill had deprived women of the right to say no. Pornography had taught men how to subjugate women for their own sexual pleasure and taught women to submit. If anything, the sexual revolution had only made human beings feel more alienated from themselves than they had before. Lesbian feminists promised to restore the sexual revolution to what they believed was its rightful course.

CHAPTER 19

LESBIAN LIBERATION: EQUAL BUT SEPARATE

I N SEPTEMBER 1973, some 40 million Americans watched as tennis pro Billie Jean King played Bobby Riggs, the one-time top tennis player in the nation, for $100,000. Riggs had claimed that any man could beat any woman, so the match, held in the Houston Astrodome, was hyped as a "battle of the sexes." It was not quite an even match. King beat Riggs 6–4, 6–3, 6–3. Though Riggs at fifty five was twenty-five years older than his female opponent, the crushing defeat was seen as a major victory for women's equality.

Billie Jean King was married, and it did not occur to her millions of fans that she might be sexually attracted to women. But while King struggled to keep her sexual orientation a secret, lesbians across the country were demanding recognition. Moreover, they were calling into question many of the basic tenets of the sexual revolution. Sexual liberation, they declared, would be possible only when gender roles were so thoroughly obliterated that every woman could feel free to call herself a lesbian.

Lesbianism plays a dual role in Western culture. Many men fantasize about watching women have sex with each other, and tolerance for the idea of bisexuality among women is much greater than for the idea of bisexuality among men. But at the same time, the West has often denied the existence of lesbians, or vilified all lesbians as "man-haters," or simply ignored the entire question of female homosexuality. In the 1940s, lesbian characters appeared in films only as jaded, violent criminals, always ready to prey upon younger, prettier women. Lesbianism is both less and more threatening to Western civilization than male homosexuality because lesbianism can be read as either the ultimate expression of femininity or the very denial of femininity itself.

The first lesbian rights organization in the United States was founded during the heyday of the McCarthy era, a time when it was especially dangerous to identify oneself as a sexual outsider. Because lesbians were willing to eschew the roles of wife and mother, they were perceived as threatening America's domestic tranquillity and seemed to endanger the very survival of capitalist democracy. Given the cultural milieu, lesbians were understandably reluctant to identify themselves publicly. Economic considerations encouraged further secrecy. An open lesbian faced nearly impossible odds against pursuing a career. (Even unmarried heterosexual women had to contend with job discrimination.) But Phyllis Lyon and Del Martin, a lesbian couple who lived in San Francisco, decided in 1955 to create a semi-secret social club, which they named the Daughters of Bilitis (after a poem by Pierre Louÿs). It was not long before the DOB established links with the two existing homophile organizations, the Mattachine Society and ONE Inc. In 1965, it started a lesbian periodical, the *Ladder*.

Lesbians kept a low profile throughout the fifties. Even the editors of the *Ladder* never printed the word *lesbian* on the cover. But as the economy grew by leaps and bounds, allowing unmarried women the possibility of financial independence, lesbians slowly became more vocal. In 1963, Barbara Gittings took over the leadership of the *Ladder,* put the "L" word on the cover (with the warning "for sale to adults only"), and declared a new era in lesbian activism.

Though her teachers had long suspected it, Gittings herself did not realize she had sexual feelings for women until after she graduated from high school. Her first glimmers of awareness came when her mother took her to Northwestern University for her freshman year of college. "She sat me down the night before school was supposed to begin and asked me if there was anything I wanted to know about sex. I was already eighteen, so I was very dismissive. But I remember that she said something to warn me about certain women in my freshman dorm. Again, I brushed her off. But I had the sense I was the person she was warning me about."

In her first year of college, Gittings went to the library to learn about homosexuality. "I devoured everything! I looked myself up in legal books. I tried to find myself in encyclopedias. I found everything I possibly could." But what she found frightened her. Lesbianism "was some kind of condition, an alien condition that was a departure from the norm. It was possibly treatable, but possibly not. There was something wrong with people like [me] — everything I read said that we were deviants. So that's what I thought about myself." But something about the information in the books made her question their authority. "For example, I read that homosexuals could not whistle. I could whistle, so I didn't know what to make of that. I learned that the favorite color of homosexuals was green, and my favorite color was not green. I didn't know what to make of that either."

Gittings failed all of her classes freshman year and returned home to Delaware in disgrace. Back at home, she started taking a night school class in abnormal psychology — to learn more about herself — and there met a woman with whom she would have her first sexual relationship. "We passed each other notes, then she drove me home in her car." The experience galvanized Gittings to leave home and move to Philadelphia. Once, she dressed as a boy and went with a male friend to a gay bar. The two were attacked by a group of Marines. With brass knuckles the Marines punched and ripped up her friend's face. It was not long before Gittings joined the homophile movement. At that point, homophile groups were not willing to demand gay rights or even promote gay self-acceptance. Their only goal was to increase public discussion about homosexuality. Most of this discussion consisted of psychiatrists and psychologists offering cures for homosexuality. When she became editor of the *Ladder,* Gittings gave the movement a new aim: social equality for lesbians.[1] It would be some years before the public would pay attention to Gittings's goal, but the process of encouraging women to accept their own lesbian desires had begun.

Few gay women joined Gittings in the fledging homophile movement in the fifties. (Few gay men joined either.) Large numbers of gay women did risk arrest and public humiliation to meet other women at lesbian bars, however. In Buffalo, New York, for example, working-class lesbians socialized at places like Bingo's and the Mardi Gras.[2] There was a thriving lesbian community in Cherry Grove on Fire Island, in the Hamptons of Long Island, organized around bar life. By 1966, there were some thirteen bars in Manhattan where lesbians could meet one another.[3] In the bars of the fifties and early sixties, standard social codes developed. Butch women — those with short hair and masculine clothes — paid for drinks and expected sexual favors in return. Fems, or femmes, who had long hair and a softer appearance, flirted and waited to be asked to dance.

Even in the early seventies, to be a lesbian was to be part of a virtually invisible community. But plenty of women were able to meet each other and form intimate, sexual relationships. One young woman who was living in New York, Sarah Holland, had her first lesbian relationship with the daughter of a wealthy industrialist in 1972. The affair was shrouded in secrecy because both women were worried about their reputation. Holland, for her part, maintained a heterosexual facade by going everywhere on the arm of a young, gay, male doctor. "I was the belle of New York," she says. "I made no demands. I loved to dance so I was ideal. I impressed all of his bosses."[4]

Another woman describes what it was like for her to be a lesbian in college in the early seventies:

> When I was a senior in college, I had one very close friend. And it became clearer and clearer to me that she truly loved me and I loved her, and what love meant, and it really became very evident what was missing in my other relationships. . . . Our relationship grew more and more intense during our senior year. . . . And after I graduated we went on a trip together . . . and we finally made love. . . . The first night that we made love, I felt terrific. It was very, very ecstatic . . . And I just remember going through the day feeling like . . . wait a minute — I thought God would strike me dead?! I thought that I was supposed to feel very remorseful and I was supposed to feel like I had done something very evil?! And that wasn't the case at all. I was very elated and it felt very beautiful . . . after she left I lost twenty pounds. . . . I became very depressed. . . . I didn't know anybody else to talk about it with.[5]

As a group, lesbians felt alienated from the world of gay men. Gay male culture, which tended to emphasize cruising and casual sex, seemed alien to those lesbians who were more relationship-oriented. At first, the rise of gay liberation promised to change the situation between the sexes. Those at the far left of the political spectrum saw connections between homophobia and sexism, so they began to critique all gender roles. Carl Whitman, in his 1969 "Gay Manifesto," warned: "Gay liberation people must understand that women have been treated exclusively and dishonestly as sexual objects. A major part of their liberation is to play down sexual objectification and to develop other aspects of themselves which have been smothered for so long. We respect this."[6] Radicals insisted that anonymous sex in bathrooms and the back rooms of gay bars and the general attitude toward sex in gay culture were the result of gay male self-loathing, in turn a byproduct of the pervasive heterosexism in society. "We must begin to make demands on each [Gay Liberation Front] member," said one radical. "GLF must demand the complete negation of the use of gay bars, tearooms, trucks, baths, streets and other traditional cruising institutions. These are exploitative institutions designed to keep gay men in the roles given to them by the male heterosexual system."[7] Likewise, members of the Come Out Cell, a gay publishing collective, fervently attacked anonymous sex and one-night stands as "unhealthy." A tiny group founded in the early '70s called the Effeminists believed that gay male sexual practices were the direct product of centuries of sexism and urged men to renounce all aspects of conventional masculinity. Not surprisingly, lesbians tended to agree wholeheartedly with these views. But as a rule, gay men were not particularly interested in the analysis of gender roles; they had more immediate concerns on their minds. For them, gay liberation generally meant more sex with more men in more places more of the time. Meanwhile, many gay men viewed lesbians as untrustworthy allies. Even Carl Whitman, who considered himself strongly supportive of feminism, drew a line in the sand. "We . . . understand that a few liberated women will be appalled or disgusted at the open and prominent place that we put sex in our lives; and while this is a natural response from their experience, they must learn what it means for us."[8]

But many lesbians were just as alienated from the women's movement as they were from gay liberation. The feminist movement was filled with women who bristled at the thought of being branded a lesbian. Sarah Holland, who was a member of the New York Radical Feminists when she had her first relationship with a woman, recalls, "We kept our relationship a total secret. We didn't dare tell the other women in New York Radical Feminists. It was a very heterosexually identified group. We would only whisper the word *lesbian*." Reflecting on her early experiences in the women's movement, Robin Morgan wrote: "The very first consciousness-raising session I ever went to gave me the warning. We were talking about sexuality, and I described myself as a bisexual. . . . Every woman in the room moved, almost imperceptibly, an inch or so away from me."[9] Some straight feminists, fearful that just by being associated with women's liberation they would be branded man-hating lesbians, hoped that lesbians would stay far away from the movement. Hostility to lesbians coursed through the veins of the New Left. "If a lesbian is anything," wrote Eldridge Cleaver in *Soul on Ice*, "she is a frigid woman, a frozen cunt, with a warp and a crack in the wall of her ice."[10]

Nobody wanted lesbians out of feminism more than Betty Friedan, who cofounded the National Organization for Women in 1966 and who knew how hard it could be to call oneself a feminist. Friedan was certain that lesbians would undermine the credibility of the movement. But lesbians were a natural constituency for feminism and refused to be silenced. Terrified of the bad publicity that lesbians in the women's movement might cause, Friedan launched a campaign in 1969 to purge NOW of what she called the "lavender menace." Known lesbians were ostracized from NOW circles, and Friedan raised the possibility that all lesbians in NOW were really undercover CIA agents working to destroy feminism from within.

Rita Mae Brown was one of the women unceremoniously forced out of NOW. Born in rural Pennsylvania in 1944 to working-class parents, Brown never saw sexual issues from the same perspective as the urban middle-class, middle-aged women in the feminist movement of the midsixties. "I grew up on a farm; I saw the animals doing it. Sex was no big deal."[11] Brown's mother, who worked in a bakery, was "extravagantly emotional" and open about issues like masturbation. "My mother always said [masturbation] was what you had to do when you couldn't get a hot date." When Brown was in her teens, her family and friends began to suspect that she might be a lesbian. "I wasn't butch, but I played sports and wasn't like the other little girls."

At New York University, Brown got involved in the women's movement. After she was kicked out of NOW for being part of the "lavender menace," she drifted toward gay liberation. But she found neither movement congenial. Feminists tended to be married and heterosexual; gay activists were virtually all men. "I remember going to my third or fourth GLF [Gay Liberation Front] meeting and there were hundreds of men and only two or three women." Furthermore, she said, these men "were only interested in getting laid; they had no political analysis whatsoever." Brown felt little connection to the gay male world. "Gay guys thought life was a fuckathon . . . [that] you could just have sex with as many people as you wanted with no emotional or physical consequences . . . Which was fine, but it wasn't for me."

In 1969, Brown put up a sign at the GLF headquarters in New York inviting women to join a lesbian liberation group. She was going to start her own movement. She knew women who had been involved in the homophile movement of the fifties and early sixties, the women of Daughters of Bilitis, but she felt she had little in common with them. "DOB members, in our minds, were really old, they were in their forties and fifties, and they didn't appear to be political. We were in the self-righteous stage of political organizing. I think they were horrified by us. We were young and brash. They were like, 'Don't ask, don't tell.' We were willing to say who we were. They lived lives of tremendous economic fear."

Later she organized a group of Vassar students, who at feminist gatherings began to raise the issue of same-sex desire. On May 1, 1970, demonstrators wearing T-shirts proclaiming "LAVENDER MENACE" disrupted a Vassar meeting of the Second Congress to Unite Women. The demonstrators, who formed the group Radicalesbians, wrote one of the earliest and most influential statements on the relationship between lesbianism and feminism, "The Woman-Identified Woman," which declared:

In a society in which men do not oppress women and sexual expression is allowed to follow feelings, the categories of homosexuality and heterosexuality would disappear. But lesbianism is also different from male homosexuality and serves a different function in the society. "Dyke" is a different kind of put-down from "faggot," although both imply you are not playing your socially assigned sex role — are not therefore a "real woman" or a "real man." The grudging admiration felt for the tomboy and the queasiness felt around a sissy boy point to the same thing: the contempt in which women — or those who play a female role — are held. And the investment in keeping women in that contemptuous role is very great. Lesbian is the word, the label, the condition that holds women in line. When a woman hears this word tossed her way, she knows she is stepping out of line. She knows that she has crossed the terrible boundary of her sex role. She recoils, she protests, she reshapes her actions to gain approval.[12]

With "The Woman-Identified Woman" as a working manifesto, lesbian feminist groups and separatist communes soon sprang up in several cities, distinguishing themselves from both women's liberation and gay liberation groups.

In 1970, an article in *Time* magazine revealed that Kate Millett, the author of the best-selling book *Sexual Politics,* was bisexual. Millett was an icon of the radical women's movement and *Time* predicted that the revelation would lead to the movement's demise. Instead, a coalition of leading New York radical feminists held a press conference to show their support for Millett. The speakers made it clear that feminism and sexual freedom were linked. Betty Friedan's worst fears were realized. Soon women in radical feminist groups across the country were identifying themselves as bisexual or lesbian. Lesbian liberation was at its height.

The rise of lesbian activism did not end the tensions between gay women and men. Indeed, as lesbian activism grew in strength, the meaning of sexual liberation became ever more a matter of contention. Lesbian feminist Robin Morgan led the battle to redefine sexual freedom in lesbian terms. A former child star, Morgan was familiar with the main tenets of sexual liberalism because, in her twenties, she'd worked for Barney Rosset's Grove Press, where she became disgusted with Rosset's brand of uncritical erotic enthusiasm. But it was the lighthearted lustfulness of gay lib that most troubled Morgan. When the New York chapter of the Gay Activists Alliance showed straight stag films at a gay dance, Morgan was outraged. There was no room for heterosexual pornography in Morgan's revolution. She was even more upset by the presence of transvestites at gay liberation events. The acceptance of cross-dressing was indicative of the movement's acquiescence to conventional gender roles. "We know what's at work when whites wear blackface; the same thing is at work when men wear drag." Lesbian-feminists resented the gay male definition of sexual liberation. As Morgan told 1,500 women at the West Coast Lesbian Feminist Conference in Los Angeles in 1973:

> Every woman here knows in her gut the vast differences between her sexuality and that of any patriarchically trained male's — gay or straight. That has, in fact, always been a source of pride to the Lesbian community, even in its greatest suffering. That the emphasis on genital sexuality, objectification, promiscuity, non-emotional involvement, and tough invulnerability, [was] the male style, and that we, as women, placed greater trust in love, sensuality, humor, tenderness, strength, commitment.[13]

It was not so much that lesbians were "anti-sexual," they insisted, as that they had their own definitions of erotic liberation. Liberated sex meant sex that was not dominated by penetration. Lesbian feminist Sue Katz in a 1971 article described healthy sexuality as "touching and rubbing and cuddling and fondness. . . . Its only goal is closeness and pleasure. It does not exist for the Big Orgasm. It exists for feeling nice."[14] (Of course, such images of healthy feminist sex were strikingly similar to the stereotypical descriptions of "diffuse" feminine eroticism that had pervaded Western culture for centuries.) Many lesbian feminists denounced dildos because they were phallic substitutes. The title of the lesbian feminist magazine *Off Our Backs* expressed the general feeling toward conventional sexuality in the movement.*

Lesbian activists not only rejected alliances with gay men, they actively distanced themselves from straight women. As the Gutter Dyke Collective put it, "Straight/Heterosexual women can't be trusted in any real situation because they will sell you out if it gets too heavy for them — men are the focal point of their lives." The members of the collective maintained that "lesbianism is the only natural way for women to interrelate since we are physical as well as emotional human beings" but recognized that most women living in America (a "male supremacist shit-pile" of a country) might not be able to form homosexual relationships.

---

* The lesbian-feminist critique of "phallic imperialism" could take on comic dimensions. One sex guide for lesbian couples defined the word *penis* as "a dildo substitute" (Anon., *Loving Women* [Nomadic Women, 1975], viii–ix). Lesbians who did not subscribe to such views tended to feel oppressed by the ideological rigidity of their own movement. In the 1980s, one group of lesbian feminists would start a magazine titled *On Our Backs* to show their belief in a broad spectrum of sexual practices, including sadomasochism.

As long as such women vowed not to have sex with men, the Gutter Dykes would accept them as allies. Another group of lesbians made the same point in more theoretical terms. "We consider lesbianism to be inherent in feminist analysis. Further, we see 'straight' feminists, or non-lesbian feminists, to therefore be a contradiction in terms. You cannot be dedicated to eliminating male supremacy (sexism) and, at the same time, be relating to men, who are the enemy."[15]

All the while lesbians were trying to situate their own movement in relation to the gay liberation and women's liberation movements, they were also living in a world shaped by the larger straight sexual revolution, which was transforming the context of lesbian life. For instance, gay women often found it easiest to meet other women at straight strip clubs, where many of the dancers were lesbian. At straight swingers' clubs like Sandstone and Plato's Retreat, women were encouraged to have sex with one another (unwritten rules, however, forbade men to touch other men). Militant lesbian activists derided such bisexual experimentation as a form of living pornography produced purely for male pleasure, but for married women who thought of themselves as straight yet yearned for physical relationships with women, the swinging world expanded the boundaries of the "normal." One married woman, Barbara, appreciated the fact that she and her husband had an open marriage, precisely because she was in love with a woman.[16] For women like Barbara, the sexual revolution made being a lesbian that much easier.

In 1973, the National Organization for Women established a task force on Lesbianism and Sexuality. This seemingly minor act marked a major turning point in the history of lesbianism in the United States. For years, lesbians had been ostracized from mainstream women's groups, including NOW, and had felt all but excluded from the gay liberation movement, with its implicit assumption that sexuality meant *male* sexuality. The NOW task force, the result of years of lesbian organizing, finally gave lesbians a voice within the mainstream women's movement and offered assurance that their own sexual identity mattered. NOW committed itself to working for legislation to prohibit discrimination on the basis of "sexual or affectional preference."

In some sense, it was too little, too late. "We used to say that NOW should change its name to THEN," says Sarah Holland. Most lesbian feminists were already disillusioned with what they called "liberal feminism." As Martha Shelley wrote in an essay titled "Gay Is Good" in 1970, "Liberalism isn't good enough for us. And we are just beginning to discover it. Your friendly smile of acceptance — from the safe position of heterosexuality — isn't enough." Throughout the country, women who shared Shelley's feelings had started their own radical groups. Some had become separatists, believing that all contact with men was undesirable. Some went so far as to tell women not to raise their male children.[17] Others had taken to critiquing labels like "gay," "straight," and "lesbian" in an effort to free human beings from all gender roles. NOW, representing hundreds of thousands of white, middle-class women, was hardly about to endorse such controversial positions. But the very fact that NOW was willing to acknowledge the existence and legitimacy of lesbians in the women's movement suggested that liberals and radicals might be able to find some sort of common ground.

The creation of the NOW Task Force on Lesbianism and Sexuality in 1973 guaranteed lesbians, once and for all, a place in the women's movement. (How many actually wanted it was another question.) It took several years of struggle for the task force to be established, and almost every step along the way was hotly contested. Some wanted a lesbian director, others wanted a straight director. Some wanted it to be named the Task Force on Sexuality, others wanted the word *lesbianism* explicitly mentioned. ("Need I tell you," one NOW officer wrote in frustration to another, "how frankly politically sensitive is the whole subject of sexuality after centuries of taboo, especially about any form of homosexuality?")[18] But slowly conflicts were resolved and NOW made sexual liberation a central concern of the organization. "For many women," wrote the authors of the task force statement of purpose,

> the different values surrounding sex today are confusing. Women of all sexual preferences are affected: asexual, bisexual, heterosexual, homosexual, as are women of all lifestyles: single, married, divorced, widowed or engaged in communal living experiences . . . As a result, the problems of sexual liberation for women are increasingly pressing.

This was a fact few women needed to be told.

CHAPTER 20

SEXUAL FREEDOM ON DEMAND

T HREE EVENTS MARKED 1973 as the watershed of the sexual revolution. First, the television documentary *An American Family*
allowed the nation to witness the implosion of the postwar domestic ideal. Second, the publication of two erotic books by women claimed
to repeal the last taboos on female sexual self-expression. Finally, the
Supreme Court decision in *Roe v. Wade* decriminalized abortion. Together these three events fundamentally altered the national conversation about sexuality and led to new possibilities in personal autonomy.
They also marked a critical convergence of American values: the fierce
belief in independence and personal happiness, the commitment to
equality and opportunity for all (at least in theory), and the nearly
unshakable trust in science and technology. But these three events
would also help reignite long-standing American fears: the fear of anarchy and disunion, the fear of manly women and effeminate men, and
the fear of an amoral world governed by the whimsical laws of supply
and demand in which a human life becomes only as valuable as the
profit it will bring to others.

In the first three months of 1973, millions of Americans sat glued to their
television sets, watching the dissolution of the two-parent, suburban
dream. *An American Family,* a series on PBS by documentary filmmaker
Craig Gilbert, followed the lives of the Louds, a California family accus-

tomed to basking in the sunshine of the era of affluence, with five children, four cars, three dogs, and a swimming pool. Gilbert filmed the family for three hundred hours over the course of seven months, then edited the footage down to twelve one-hour episodes. Pat and Bill Loud's marriage dissolved on camera. The Louds' eldest son, twenty-year-old Lance, revealed his homosexuality to them during the course of the series, and viewers were invited to watch as Pat and Bill struggled with their feelings about it. In one episode, Lance took his mother to a transvestite show in Greenwich Village. But it was perhaps Bill and Pat's marital breakup that had the greatest psychological impact on the nation. "Bill and I have never been able to have a relationship where we could honest-to-God talk to one another," Pat Loud explained on camera. "If we had any sex life, that would be nice. But it's kind of like a courtesy 'Thank you, Ma'am.'" Divorce, *An American Family* suggested, was a plausible option for the sexually dissatisfied.[1]

Before the 1970s, divorce was considered a criminal rather than a civil matter. A man could leave his wife, or a woman her husband, only if the other party could be shown to be guilty of a particular offense, such as adultery, in a court of law. Until the end of the nineteenth century, it had been relatively easy to get a divorce in America. Most states allowed divorce for any one of several hundred reasons. But as the divorce rate soared after the Civil War, state legislatures began to tighten divorce laws, reducing the number of legal grounds for separation. South Carolina, for example, banned divorce outright. As a result, couples seeking separation for reasons not recognized by statute began having to lie in court, claiming adultery or other falsified injuries. In 1949 The New York State Council of Churches blasted New York's divorce law as "an occasion for evasion and hypocrisy." Legal reformers saw that restrictive divorce laws seriously undermined the credibility of the judicial system, especially because it was always easier for the rich to obtain a divorce than for the poor.[2] In most families, divorce remained shameful well into the 1960s. Nonetheless, the divorce rate continued to climb in the twentieth century, with periodic surges and plateaus. Although the divorce rate leveled off in the 1950s, it began to rise once again in 1965. Those who lived in states with restrictive laws, such as New York, and who had the money simply went to places with more liberal laws, like Nevada and Puerto Rico, for a weekend divorce.

For millions of adults who married in the fifties and early sixties, divorce was a welcome alternative to daily disputes and bitter resentment. Most of the adults who married in the fifties did so at a very young age — the average age of marriage in 1959 was nineteen. The low marriage age probably contributed to an especially high number of unhappy unions. In some cases, men and women married without knowing whether they were even sexually compatible. In other cases, men and women married because of the tremendous pressure to hide one's homosexuality. From 1963 to 1969, divorces for couples married less than five years rose 62 percent, and divorces for those married more than five years rose 37 percent. In 1969, the state of California, trying to reduce the number of criminal proceedings, liberalized its divorce laws by introducing the notion of "no-fault" divorce. Divorce was suddenly transformed from a criminal matter to a civil one. A couple could now obtain a divorce on the grounds of "irreconcilable differences." The following year, the National Conference of Commissioners of Uniform State Laws recommended that all states adopt similar no-fault provisions. Many did.

The steady rise in divorce from the midnineteenth century to the midtwentieth was primarily a result of the increasing pressures put on marriage by social changes. Greco-Roman marriage was originally a form of slavery, but by the modern era marriage had come to serve an enormous number of functions in society, from providing the sole acceptable outlet for sexual desires to offering men comfort and shelter from the hostile world of commerce. But in 1966 sociologist Mervyn Cadwallader wrote:

> Marriage was not designed as a mechanism for providing friendship, erotic experience, romantic love, personal fulfillment, continuous lay psychotherapy, or recreation. The Western European family was not designed to carry a lifelong load of highly emotional romantic freight. Given its present structure, it simply has to fail when asked to do so. The very idea of an irrevocable contract obligating the parties concerned to a lifetime of romantic effort is utterly absurd.[3]

By the early seventies, many men and women were fighting to abolish restrictive divorce laws wherever they remained in effect. In New York, for example, activists formed the Committee for Fair Divorce and Alimony Laws, one-third of whose members were women.

Divorce represented different things to different people. Some middle-aged men saw divorce as an opportunity to take advantage of all the sexual revolution had to offer. For feminists, divorce symbolized one form of freedom from the domestic ideology of the 1950s. It was also a way for women to escape from abusive and alcoholic husbands. In February 1969, members of the feminist group Women's International Terrorist Conspiracy from Hell (WITCH) targeted a bridal fair at New York's Madison Square Garden. Wearing black veils, they chanted, "Here come the slaves, off to their graves." They passed out leaflets condemning marriage as a patriarchal institution linked to imperialism, consumerism, and corporate capitalism. At the end of the demonstration, they released 150 live white mice into the auditorium.[4]

At the same time, experts began touting divorce as a "healthy" alternative to the unhappy marriage. These experts suggested that divorce would not only do little psychological damage to children, it would save children from the misery of family tension. A few postulated that divorce had psychological *benefits* for children in that it might give them a more mature, more realistic sense of the world. Unfortunately, these feminist theorists and psychologists failed to recognize that many fathers would resist paying alimony and child support, and that for many mothers, divorce would bring financial instability.[5]

By 1973, secular humanists were unwilling to accept any of the traditional platitudes about marriage. At the prestigious Groves Conference on Marriage and the Family in 1973, the study group on adult single living declared:

> [We see marriage] as an imperialistic norm creating two populations: the married and the unmarried. The latter as a residual category are stigmatized as outcasts. We, on the contrary, affirm singlehood as an achieved status, rather than an involuntary or ascribed one, and a situation which might hold greater potential for autonomy than marriage, which could be viewed with some plausibility as an intrinsically unsatisfactory relationship.[6]

The claim that marriage might be an "intrinsically unsatisfactory relationship" was a bold attack on nineteenth-century notions of romantic love and family life.

The evolution of divorce in America did not begin with the sexual revolution. As noted earlier, divorce rates started to rise in the mid-1800s. But the sexual revolution of the 1960s and '70s created a new context for the national debate on divorce. Divorce went from a necessary evil to a positive good almost overnight. *An American Family* made it clear that Pat and Bill Loud were not meant for each other. In one episode, Bill arrives home from a trip and Pat tells him, "I've seen a lawyer. I want you to move out." Bill does not protest. He and his wife were resigned to their fate. *An American Family* pointed to the profound alienation of the modern couple, but in the end it may have created a new sense of community. Paradoxically, it was television — an instrument that fostered the extraordinary isolation of the nuclear family in the 1950s — that brought Americans together in the 1970s, as they saw with horror and delight that their problems were similar to others'.

❧

Roe v. Wade, probably the most famous Supreme Court decision of the twentieth century, in a single blow struck down anti-abortion laws on the books of almost every state in the union. Actually, it struck down two kinds of laws: strict ones that banned all abortions, and more "liberal" statutes that allowed abortions to be performed in hospitals so long as they were approved by a hospital committee. Justice Harry Blackmun's opinion combined traditional legal theory with a more pragmatic approach to social reform. After studying the law of privacy and the medical literature on abortion, Blackmun decided that during the first three months of pregnancy, a woman had an unlimited right to procure an abortion. During the second three months, a woman could be required, if legislators so wished, to obtain hospital certification. During the final three months, a woman could be denied access to abortion, so long as her own life was not in jeopardy.

The logic of the opinion was controversial, but the immediate effects of the court's decision were clear. Announced on a cold Monday morning in January 1973, it warmed the hearts of millions of women and men who believed in the right to abortion. For years, a large number of lawyers, legislators, and activists had been fighting for repeal — or, at the very least, reform — of restrictive abortion laws. Now it looked like the entire issue was settled once and for all. Every major newspaper in the country applauded the decision. Only the Catholic Church raised a loud protest against the ruling.

Roe v. Wade represented a triumphant victory for the forces of liberalism. It expanded the right to privacy, gave women control over their own bodies, and appeared to remove the last form of punishment for sexually active women. The story of how *Roe v. Wade* came to be illustrates the complexity of the sexual revolution — the strained alliances, the tensions between liberals and radicals, the difficulty in reaching agreement on the meaning of sexual freedom.

Abortion was not a significant issue in American life until the middle of the nineteenth century. Terminating a pregnancy prior to the "quickening" of the fetus was a common practice with no specific moral or political overtones. Abortion was considered just another form of birth control. In the 1850s and '60s, however, some doctors began to fight for laws regulating abortion. These doctors had several motives: They wanted to eliminate unskilled quacks from the medical field; they were worried about the low birthrate of native-born, white women; they disliked the fact that many abortion providers were women; and they wanted to shore up their own professional authority in a time of intense marketplace competition. To accomplish these aims, they launched a veritable crusade against abortion providers.

In the 1890s, physicians won their legal crusade, which gave them almost unlimited control over access to abortion in America. Most states banned abortions, unless they were administered by physicians and were necessary to save the life of the mother.[7] Still, abortion laws were rarely enforced. Some experts in the late nineteenth century estimated that there were 2 million abortions in the United States a year. A 1931 survey of Catholic, Protestant, and Jewish women in the Bronx found that 35 percent had had at least one abortion. It was not until the forties and fifties that government authorities began cracking down on abortion providers, making abortion an especially risky and dangerous proposition for women. Those who were wealthy enough to have private physicians continued to enjoy access to quasi-legal abortions, but poor women were forced to seek out illegal abortions, which were nearly always dangerous. At the same time, hospitals began creating therapeutic abortion boards to determine whether or not a given abortion should be performed. The new boards often limited the number of abortions a doctor might perform in a single year.[8] These boards were supposed to guarantee access to abortion in cases where the life of the mother was threatened, but they ended up merely making it *more* difficult for women to obtain legal abortions.

Although a hospital abortion was usually available to women who had the financial means, pregnancy out of wedlock was surrounded by shame because it was proof of premarital sex, so young women were often too terrified to tell their parents that they needed one. When Helen Gurley Brown was in college, one of her roommates became pregnant. Too scared to go to her parents or a doctor, the girl tried to induce a miscarriage by standing on her head. Brown and her friends tried in vain to help by throwing suitcases on top of the girl.[9]

In the 1960s, liberal-minded lawyers, politicians, and clergymen began to call for the reform of existing laws. They were deeply worried by press reports of deadly illegal abortions and did not realize that most hospitals allowed abortion with the approval of the therapeutic board. In reality, the reforms they sought were only going to make state laws conform to then current practices. (Reform bills usually called for therapeutic abortion boards, even though those boards were already in existence in most hospitals, and offered little hope for poor women, the women who usually sought out the services of illegal abortionists.) Still, the possibility of statutory change galvanized those who were opposed to abortion in all circumstances. The net result of the "reform" movement was the promise of a very long and very fierce battle.

There were two types of underground abortionists in the fifties and sixties: those motivated by concern for the welfare of desperate women and those motivated purely by profit. Because abortion was surrounded with shame and because some cities had special detective squads solely for the purpose of hunting down illegal abortionists, few doctors were willing to take the risks of terminating pregnancies. Those who did became legendary. Robert Spencer, a physician in the coal-mining town of Ashland, Pennsylvania, performed some thirty thousand abortions before he died at the age of seventy-nine in 1969.[10]

Several events transformed abortion into a hot political issue. In 1962, the plight of Sherri Finkbine made headlines across the country. Finkbine, a married mother of four and the star of a local edition of the children's television show *Romper Room* in Phoenix, decided to terminate her fifth pregnancy when she learned that the sleeping pills she had been using were likely to cause major birth defects. It was her doctor who initially recommended that she have a therapeutic abortion — that is, an abortion legally permitted in order to protect the health of the mother. When the thirty-year-old Finkbine tried to warn others about the dangers of thalidomide, the highly toxic ingredient in her pills, by going to the press, the hospital canceled her abortion.* Hospital officials did not want public attention being focused on the fact that they were performing therapeutic abortions in cases where the mother's life, per se, was not in jeopardy. Fearing that she would "be giving birth to a living death," Finkbine went to Sweden for an abortion. In the meantime, Finkbine became a media sensation. As a result, she was denounced by the Vatican, deluged with hostile mail, and fired from her job. A Gallup Poll showed that 52 percent of Americans, however, approved of Finkbine's actions.[11]

In the spring of 1965, an outbreak of German measles (rubella), a disease that causes serious birth defects when pregnant women are exposed to it, further illustrated to many the importance of liberal abortion laws. Some began to realize that the plodding course of legal reform was not enough — only immediate action would help the women most in need. In San Francisco, Pat Maginnis, a woman who had had three illegal abortions (one by an abortionist in Tijuana, Mexico, and two that were self-induced) formed her own organization, the Society for Humane Abortion. Standing on the streets of San Francisco, Maginnis began handing out fliers with information about how to contact south-of-the-border abortionists. Before long, she began traveling the country, giving talks in which she taught women how to induce an abortion. (In 1967, the *New York Times* derided Maginnis, then thirty-eight, as a "zealot" and a "spinster.")[12]

On the East Coast, the Reverend Howard Moody established the Clergy Consultation Service on Abortion. Born in 1912 in Dallas, Texas,

---

*Thalidomide was never approved in the United States; Finkbine's husband had picked up the pills on a trip to England.

Moody was raised by Southern Baptist parents and he married his first love at twenty-two. But Moody eventually decided that moral codes against premarital sex were irrational and harmful. After graduating from Harvard, Moody began pastoral counseling in New York City. Women often came to his Baptist church in Greenwich Village seeking help in coping with unwanted pregnancies. Before long, he realized there was a need for an underground service to help women obtain illegal abortions with qualified, capable doctors. He set up a phone number that women could call to get information about how to contact such doctors.[13]

It was difficult to fight for the liberalization of abortion when certain states still made it a crime to distribute contraceptives to unmarried adults. Such laws were not regularly enforced, but they were a potent reminder of the government's extensive police power. Students at Boston University were especially angry about the law in Massachusetts, because it effectively prevented colleges and universities from distributing any birth control. In 1967 they invited Bill Baird, the champion of birth control for the poor, to come to Boston in order to challenge the state's anti-contraception statutes. After some hesitation, Baird agreed to set up his services in Roxbury, the city's black neighborhood. But he was personally threatened by members of the Black Panthers, who believed he was promoting racial genocide. ("It didn't matter that I was a member of CORE [the Congress of Racial Equality]," Baird says.) In April, Baird addressed an audience of students at Boston University with the intention of getting arrested and challenging the Massachusetts law all the way to the Supreme Court.

When Baird arrived for his scheduled address, a crowd of almost two thousand students had assembled in the auditorium. Reporters and police swarmed the room. "I had to push my way to the podium," Baird recalls. As police waited behind the stage, Baird talked for an hour about the cruelty of laws against birth control. He taunted the police, inviting them to arrest him as well as Catholic leaders who published technically illegal pamphlets describing the rhythm method. He also read the story of Onan in the Bible and encouraged the police to arrest every minister in the state for having read in public about the withdrawal method. When police refused to make a move, Baird offered women in the audience samples of over-the-counter contraceptives. One nineteen-year-old woman (chosen in advance) came to the stage and took a condom and a packet of contraceptive foam. Police immediately descended on Baird.[14]

He was sentenced to three months in prison. In the Charles Street Jail (later closed because guards routinely abused prisoners), Baird was strip-searched, harassed by guards, and subjected to full body-cavity inspections. Prosecutors offered to drop the charges if he would leave the state, but Baird was determined to have his day in court. He had few supporters, however. Betty Friedan dismissed him as a "nut." According to Planned Parenthood, there was "nothing to be gained by action of this kind."[15]

In Chicago, Lonny Myers, an anesthesiologist, mother of five girls, and wife of a prominent oral surgeon, desperately wanted abortion law repeal. Like Baird, Myers had worked for years promoting birth control. Though she was a prominent member of Chicago society, she was also a sex radical, who believed that prohibitions on extramarital sex, pornography, and homosexuality were intolerable. Her fight against abortion laws grew out of her larger concerns about reforming sexual morality. With two associates, she founded the National Association for Repeal of Abortion Laws, or NARAL. At a three-day conference in Chicago in February 1969, Myers announced the beginning of a full-fledged crusade to legalize abortion. Both Bill Baird and Patricia Maginnis addressed the audience, as did Nathan Rappaport, a sixty-nine-year-old physician who told the crowd he had performed some thirty thousand illegal abortions in his thirty-six years as a doctor and had spent nine years in jail for it.[16]

Abortion laws did not become a *feminist* issue until 1968, when radical feminist groups began calling for repeal, pointing out that the restriction of access to abortion represented one of the last barriers to women's sexual liberation. Since no form of birth control was 100 percent reliable, abortion laws penalized women for having sex by keeping the threat of unwanted pregnancy constantly present. At rallies and marches, radical feminists chanted "Free abortion on demand!" On March 24, 1968, New York City feminists organized a rally in support of Bill Baird. "We refuse to be [society's] passive vessels becoming impregnated for the greater good of society," declared one woman at the rally. "We want a society that exists for our good as well as yours!"[17] In Boston, where Baird had been arrested, feminists marched through the streets in October, breaking the law by carrying cans of spermicidal foam. The underground news wire, Liberation News Service, carried articles on safe and unsafe abortion procedures.[18] In Chicago, members of the feminist collective "Jane" performed underground illegal abortions.

Radical feminists and activists like Moody, Baird, Maginnis, and Myers garnered enough press to turn abortion into a major political issue. In state after state, legislators introduced reform bills. In several states, they passed. By 1970, 43 percent of American women over sixteen were in the paid workforce; their financial independence translated into political influence. In the meantime, liberal clergy, guided by the tenets of the new morality, came out in full favor of liberalized abortion laws.

In New York, the state senate's majority leader, a Roman Catholic who was determined to stop the reform movement, introduced a bill that would not just reform the state's abortion laws but repeal them entirely. (It is an old, if cynical, legislative strategy: The goal is to make a bill so extreme, even its original supporters vote against it.) After five hours of debate, the bill, to its author's dismay, was approved by the state senate. It then passed in the assembly and was signed into law on April 11, 1970. New York had become the first state to make it legal for any woman to obtain an abortion from any licensed provider for any reason.

Norma McCorvey, twenty-two years old in 1970, had left her violent, abusive husband soon after she'd married him at age sixteen. She was a drug user, and for a while had been a dealer. Penniless when she got pregnant with her third child (she had given the first two up for adoption), McCorvey wanted an abortion, but they were illegal in Texas, where she lived. In fact, even therapeutic abortions were forbidden. McCorvey went to a lawyer for help, and though he refused to put her in touch with an underground abortionist, he did refer her to Linda Coffee, a young lawyer who was seeking a test case to overturn Texas's abortion law. At first McCorvey was reluctant. But then she managed to get the name of an illegal clinic. The simple sight of the clinic terrified her. In her memoir *I Am Roe,* she wrote:

> What I saw was an old, old, wooden doctor's examining table sitting abandoned in the middle of a big room. The table was dirty. Filthy. So was the whole office. There was dried blood on the floor. And on the examining table. . . . The place smelled horrible. The odor was overpowering. It was ten times worse than anything I had ever smelled before. I'd never smelled anything like it, but somehow I knew what it was. I got sick to my stomach. I ran outside and threw up in the alley.[19]

When she learned that the clinic had been busted by police the week before, she made up her mind to call Linda Coffee, the lawyer looking for a test case.

McCorvey met Coffee and her associate, Sarah Weddington, at a restaurant in downtown Dallas. It was Weddington who did most of the talking. Unbeknownst to McCorvey, Weddington had had an abortion herself in a Mexican clinic when she was twenty-two. She had been asked to pursue a test case by a radical feminist group at the University of Texas. Weddington had then gone to Linda Coffee for assistance. Now Weddington passionately warned McCorvey of all the potential dangers of an illegal abortion, showed her pictures of women who had died trying to use coat hangers and other sharp instruments to abort their own pregnancies, and urged her to accept a role as a plaintiff in a test case that might benefit all women. Though McCorvey was worried the two young women might be trying to rip her off, she agreed to their plan. Afraid of the possible negative publicity, McCorvey became Jane Roe.

As the child inside McCorvey grew, McCorvey continued taking marijuana and drinking wine. (Uneducated and unworldly, she believed that she could wait until the very last moment of her pregnancy to obtain an abortion.)[20] Coffee and Weddington won the Texas trial case, technically making abortion legal in the state. But the prosecutor filed an appeal and vowed to prosecute any doctor who terminated a single pregnancy.

McCorvey gave birth, the baby was adopted, but the appeals case dragged on. Coffee and Weddington won in the state supreme court. The prosecutor again appealed, and the case made its way to Washington. On December 13, 1971, Weddington, at twenty-seven not much older than the average legal clerk, delivered her oral argument before the justices of the U.S. Supreme Court. During the year the nation awaited the outcome in *Roe v. Wade,* Bill Baird's conviction for having publicly displayed and disseminated contraceptive foam at Boston University was finally overturned. In *Eisenstadt v. Baird* the Supreme Court ruled that everyone, including unmarried minors, had a right to use contraception. "If the right of privacy means anything," the court declared, "it is the right of the individual to be free . . . to decide whether to bear or beget a child[.]"[21]

The *Eisenstadt* decision gave Weddington and Coffee hope, but the court then announced that *Roe v. Wade* would have to be reargued. Once again Weddington made her case before the bench. This time the court reached a verdict. By a vote of 7–2, the justices declared that all existing abortion laws in the country were unconstitutionally vague. Justice Harry Blackmun's fifty-one-page opinion stressed that the right to an abortion in the first trimester of pregnancy was protected by the Constitution's implicit guarantee of a right to privacy. It was too late for Norma McCorvey, but it was the beginning of a new era for American women.

Roe v. Wade was the crowning achievement of the sexual revolution. A hundred years of legal prohibition, black-market appointments, and back-alley deaths were ended in a single stroke. Though women would still need the money to pay for abortions, and medical schools were still reluctant to teach their students how to perform them, the threat of pregnancy as a punishment for women's sexual activity was no longer enshrined in the law.

❧

In 1948, Normal Mailer had to coin the word *fug* in *The Naked and the Dead* to avoid obscenity charges. By 1968 there was no word that was considered unprintable. But it was not until 1973, shortly after the *Roe v. Wade* decision, that the literary revolution reached its zenith. That year saw the publication of the first mainstream novel dedicated to female sexual self-expression, Erica Jong's *Fear of Flying*, and the first comprehensive account of female sexual fantasies, Nancy Friday's *My Secret Garden*. These two books were products of the same cultural moment. In 1973, the double standard was on the verge of total disintegration. When Erica Jong proclaimed the virtues of "the zipless fuck," she was addressing a world in which women, after thousands of years of fear and punishment, finally felt entitled to sexual pleasure on demand.

Jong, who was a Barnard College graduate with an MA in fine arts from Columbia, made her literary debut as a poet, but it was *Fear of Flying* that won her an international reputation. The novel's protagonist, Isadora Wing (like her creator, a poet married to a Chinese-American psychoanalyst), leaves her husband to search for the ultimate sexual experience, the perfect orgasm. Jong's goal was to contribute a new type of heroine to American fiction, "a thinking woman who also had a sexual life."[22]

Simultaneously criticizing patriarchal views of female sexuality and offering a woman's notion of sexual liberation, *Fear of Flying* combined full-fledged candor with sharp social criticism. The novel stated the basic premises of sixties secular humanism but did so in explicit terms:

> How hypocritical to go upstairs with a man you don't want to fuck, leave the one you do sitting there alone, and then, in a state of great excitement, fuck the one you don't want to fuck while pretending he's the one you do. That's called fidelity. That's called civilization and its discontents.[23]

Fear of Flying challenged the common wisdom that only men saw the world in sexual terms. As book critic Walter Clemons wrote in *Newsweek*, the novel would "scare any male who believes women 'don't think like that.'"[24] In fact, the first typesetter hired by Jong's publisher refused the job. One reviewer revealed his own anxieties when he described Jong's protagonist as a walking "mammoth pudenda."[25] Another critic said that reading the novel was similar to being locked in an elevator "with a woman who tells you her life story twice over, rapes you and stops you reaching for the Emergency button." Such sexist responses aside, *Fear of Flying* was hugely popular: it sold some 6 million paperback copies in the United States alone. "It made me a household name in much of the world," Jong recalled in an interview, "including China and Russia, where the books aren't published!"[26]

For anyone who still doubted after reading *Fear of Flying* that a woman could have strong sexual desires, Nancy Friday's *My Secret*

Garden surely put the matter to rest. The collection of women's sexual fantasies, solicited by the author through newspaper advertisements, demonstrated once and for all that women were as lustful as men. Friday's book served as both a window on female psychology and a new twist on traditional pornography. *My Secret Garden* made Helen Gurley Brown's *Sex and the Single Girl* seem like a Victorian primer.

The daughter of a financier, Friday attended Wellesley College. In appearance, she had the wholesome innocence and bright-eyed enthusiasm of a small-town girl. She, like Jong, wanted to write a novel about a woman who fantasized about sex with a man other than her husband, but when her editor dismissed the idea as unrealistic, she set out to document the reality of women's sexual desires. Critic Caroline Seebohm, writing in the *New York Times,* proclaimed the result "unquestionably erotic."[27] Some women, it turned out, yearned to be spanked and whipped, others wanted to spank and whip their male partners. Many fantasized about sex with women, and not a few were aroused at the thought of being raped. Others admitted to sexual desires that defied all codes of femininity: "Looking at men, front and back, is a favorite pastime," wrote one woman. "I like to study the shapes of their asses and wonder how they use them when thrusting into a woman, or I wonder what it would be like to penetrate their anuses with a dildo." A fifteen-year-old girl confessed to fantasies of domination.

> I guess that the most common thing in all of my fantasies is to think about having the boy under my control and being able to make him do whatever I want him to do to please me. I think about myself sitting on a big chair like a throne with my skirt pulled up and my panties off and the boy is kneeling between my legs doing cunnilingus to me. Sometimes if I feel really devilish I imagine that I pee in his mouth and he has to swallow it. In the fantasies like this the boy's hands are tied so that he cannot touch me except with his mouth. Usually he is naked and sometimes I imagine that I am whipping him when he is kneeling in front of me like that.[28]

Writer Joan Garrity, who wrote the book's prologue, said that when she showed the book to some men, they "felt their masculinity was threatened." The male readers "were especially furious at the fantasies where women imagined that their husbands were movie or sports stars during their lovemaking."*

Friday was tired of the double standard.

> For men, talking about sex, writing and speculating about it, exchanging confidences and asking each other for advice and encouragement about

---

*Garrity was the anonymous author of the best-selling sex book *The Sensuous Woman.*

it, had always been socially accepted, and in fact a certain amount of boasting about it in the locker room is usually thought to be very much the mark of a man's man, a fine devil of a fellow. But the same culture that gave men this freedom sternly barred it to women, leaving us sexually mistrustful of each other, forcing us into patterns of deception, shame, and above all silence.

Friday continued and expanded the fight for sexual liberation: "If a woman does fantasize, or wants to, then she should accept it without shame or thinking herself freaky — and so should the man. Fantasy should be thought of as an extension of one's sexuality." Friday warned that "no man can be really free in bed with a woman who is not." She wanted to give her female reader a sense of being statistically normal, so that she would "no longer have that vertiginous fright that she alone has these random, often hidden thoughts and ideas."[29]

Together, *Fear of Flying* and *My Secret Garden* took the war against literary taboos to a whole new level. Their contemporaneous publication gave proponents of secular humanism hope that the battle against shame might soon be won. Johns Hopkins biologist John Money declared, "Sexual liberation now can follow the other great liberations — from serfdom, from slavery, from poverty, and from male domination."

The events of 1973 paved the way for a new era of personal autonomy, sexual self-expression, and freedom from fear. At long last, a woman could, like a man, maximize her opportunities for sexual satisfaction.

But Americans were still ambivalent about female sexual equality, just as they were ambivalent about unrestricted liberty for men. An ominous portrait of the sexually liberated couple emerged in the 1972 film *Last Tango in Paris*. Hailed at the time by many as another breakthrough in freedom of expression, *Last Tango* could also be read as a commentary on the logical outcome of sexual self-centeredness. In the film, a man and woman meet regularly in an unfurnished Paris apartment for anonymous sexual encounters. As they explore their fantasies, they become increasingly callous. In one scene, the man rapes and sodomizes the woman. In another, he commands her to penetrate him with her fingers as he describes the many ways in which he would like to desecrate her body. Eventually the two murder each other. *Last Tango* showed only one possible result of the sexual revolution, but its popularity reflected deep-seated cultural anxieties that were ready to swallow the sexual revolution whole. All it would take was a crisis of confidence in American liberalism.

CHAPTER 21

COUNTERREVOLUTION
AND CRISIS

THE SEXUAL REVOLUTION was so sweeping, and it touched the lives of so many in countless ways, it seemed as if the clock could never be turned back on the social and cultural changes of the era. But for various reasons — many of which had nothing to do with the sexual revolution itself — the mood of the nation was slowly changing. The "live-and-let live" attitude of the late sixties and early seventies was about to disappear.

Several developments inspired anxiety about "permissiveness" and "excessive liberalism." First, the student movement was becoming increasingly violent. The bombing of a laboratory at the University of Wisconsin, the terrorist attacks of the Weatherman, the Charles Manson murders: all of these events called into question the virtue of laissez-faire social policies. When radicals announced that they were going to "bring the war home," many Americans became scared. Politicians and judges began to reconsider the merits of liberalism and began instead to support the principle of strong government.

If left-wing violence was not enough to scare policy-makers, drug abuse was becoming epidemic and crime was starting to plague the nation's inner cities. Gender roles were changing faster than ever before. Racial tensions were high. Reports of environmental degradation cast doubt on the virtues of scientific and technological "progress." Revelations of corruption in the Nixon administration, followed by Nixon's own resignation, led to cynicism and frustration. Then — the very same year as *Roe v. Wade* — an economic slump triggered a profound crisis of faith in the ability of modern institutions and secular values to continue to improve the quality of human life.

❦

By the midseventies, the sexual revolution was at its peak. Every month brought a host of new Off Broadway plays with full-frontal nudity, magazines catering to every sexual desire, hard-core sex films in first run theaters, provocative books with sexual themes, new sex education texts and marriage manuals with photographs of the male and female sex organs. Birth control and abortion were more easily accessible than ever before in history. The singles scene was booming, with pick-up bars and discotheques packed from coast to coast. The fashions of the era — including tight jeans and skimpy shorts — fostered a continuously flirtatious environment. Swing clubs were busy on both coasts. Sexually transmitted diseases, though common, were nothing more than a nuisance. As Bob Greene described the situation in *Newsweek:*

> Male prostitutes are now convivial guests on the daytime talk shows. Paperback copies of the *Joy of Sex* are tossed into the grocery shopping bag with the asparagus. Wife-swapping and group sex are such old topics of suburban patio conversation that they are now considered somewhat dreary.[1]

The revolt against the stifling world of the fifties was complete.

The world of continuous consumerism and twenty-four-hour-a-day adult amusement was symbolized by the rise to international prominence of Hugh Hefner, the ruler of a sprawling empire of hotels, clubs, and casinos, who traveled everywhere in his famous Playboy jet, a black DC-9 with the bunny logo emblazoned on the side, which cost $16,000 a day to operate. He was living proof that a man, at least, could avoid domestic responsibilities forever.

In every corner of American society, sexual desire was being discussed, portrayed, and celebrated. For gays in particular, it was a heady time. With the proliferation of bars, discos, and sex clubs, gay life became increasingly open and visible in the nation's major cities. As journalist Andrew Kopkind wrote in 1979:

> In New York now, gays may live in [supportive environments], in heavily gay districts, within a social and economic infrastructure shot through with aspects of gay culture. Gays may work in gay run businesses catering to a gay clientele, or they can get jobs through the gay network in larger establishments, such as department stores, where gays occupy top managerial positions. They eat in gay restaurants, shop on gay avenues in gay boutiques, listen to gay-oriented music, share gay living quarters, dance

in gay discos, vacation in gay garden spots, worship in gay churches, read gay magazines and gay novels, snack on gay pizza and gay hamburgers, see movies by gay directors featuring gay actors and actresses, play softball in gay leagues and hope for victory in the Gay World Series, sail on gay cruises, get high on gay drugs pushed by gay dealers, and spend all their social hours with gay friends.[2]

According to Kopkind, the immense opportunities for gay sex created a new "cock culture." The streets of Greenwich Village, the Castro, West Hollywood, Provincetown, Fire Island, Key West, and other gay enclaves were crowded with throngs of men "cruising" for sex.

Just as gay bars and bathhouses were filled to capacity, lesbian collectives were thriving. It was a time of enormous interest in both sexual liberty and sexual equality. New attention was being paid to the sexual needs of the elderly, as well as those of the mentally and physically disabled. For decades, the sexual needs of these three groups had been all but ignored. When confined in nursing homes or hospitals, the aged and the disabled were almost always denied opportunities for sexual relationships. Social reformers were beginning to realize the peculiar disadvantages of the elderly and the infirm.

The economic downturn that began in 1973 came as a terrible shock to the nation and would have significant consequences for the sexual revolution. Inflation had already begun to rise in 1971, and productivity rates had started to fall, but it was not until the oil crisis of '73 that inflation soared and Americans began to lose confidence in the nation's financial stability. Corporate profits plummeted, declining from 13.7 percent in 1965 to 8 percent in the early seventies. Competition from Japanese car manufacturers did not help. Domestic productivity rates dropped precipitously from an average annual rate of 3.2 percent in the midsixties to a mere 1 percent in the midseventies. To top it off, unemployment began to rise. By 1975, 9 percent of the population was out of work. With OPEC controlling the price of oil exports, America was thrown into an unprecedented period of "stagflation." It was the worst recession since the Great Depression of the thirties. From 1973 on, the mood of the nation was understandably grim.[3]

The fall of the financial markets did not stop Americans from enjoying themselves at discos or from consuming high-priced drugs. But the nation's economic malaise did have an impact on erotic consumerism and the interest in the new sexual utopia. "These are depressed and unsettled times," the author of a book on group sex told *Time* magazine in 1974. "There's a more somber feeling among people, a retreat from sexual frivolity." *Time* reported that sales of sexually explicit materials were down. (Reflecting the sudden turn from sexual liberalism, *Time* now referred to adult bookstores as "dirty-book shops.")[4] The new mood was symbolized by the virtual collapse of Hugh Hefner's publishing empire. In November 1974, Bobbie Arnstein, one of Hefner's most trusted employees, was convicted of selling cocaine and sentenced to fifteen years in prison. In January 1975, she committed suicide. *Playboy* was already feeling the effects of competition from *Penthouse.* Playboy stock plummeted from a 1971 high of $23.50 a share to a mere $2.25. Hefner was forced to sell most of the hotels and clubs he owned, in addition to his famous black jet. Once internationally known for his wealth and lavish lifestyle, Hefner was now famous for his financial calamities.[5]

Sideswiped by the 1973 economic crisis, Americans could no longer devote significant energy or time to sexual liberation. Meeting rent or mortgage payments, holding on to a good job or simply finding a decent one took obvious priority. More and more people were forced to work in the low-paying service sector as major industries practically disappeared overnight. The combination of a depressed economy and desiccated dreams lent a melancholy mood to the midseventies. This despondency could be seen in the cultural products of the period, like the 1974 film *Alice Doesn't Live Here Anymore* and the hit song "Rhinestone Cowboy" from the same year. Movies, music, and television of the seventies emphasized the gritty reality of everyday life. *Taxi Driver, The Taking of Pelham One Two Three,* and *Dog Day Afternoon* portrayed the bleak underside of urban existence. The new attitude was summed up by the title of the popular 1970s television show about a single mother and her two daughters, *One Day at a Time.*

The nation's economic and spiritual woes were complex and difficult to resolve. Neither the left nor the right knew quite how to handle the energy crisis or the decline in the value of the dollar. It was far easier to blame movies, television, pornography, homosexuals, and feminists for America's problems than it was to restore the nation's economic vitality. As a result, the midseventies witnessed a massive assault on secular humanism and, by association, the sexual revolution.

In the new economic climate, many Americans returned to organized religion and biblical revelation for meaning, comfort, and assurance. Evangelicalism boomed. Liberal experts and academics were taken by surprise by the religious resurgence. Believing the common wisdom of the sixties that modernization inevitably fostered secularization, liberal intellectuals had never suspected that fundamentalism would once again sweep the country.[6] But sweep the country it did. Each of the evangelical sects grew in size over the course of the seventies, while the mainline Protestant denominations rapidly shrank. Jehovah's Witnesses increased by 36 percent between 1970 and 1980, the Pentecostal Church of God by 32 percent. Evangelical Christianity was so strong that *Time* labeled 1976 "The Year of the Evangelical."[7] That, of course, was the year the first evangelical Protestant was elected president of the United States. Although Jimmy Carter turned out to be tolerant of gay rights and a supporter of abortion rights, his election gave a new sense of political strength to the evangelical community.

Evangelicalism had a major impact on American life because evangelicals shrewdly consolidated political power. In the sixties, evangelical clergy had been much less outspoken on public policy matters than their liberal brethren. But in the seventies, evangelicals exploited the bully pulpit. Traditionally, evangelicals had been poorer than other Americans, but by the seventies, they had achieved significant levels of affluence. This meant funds were available for political campaigns and contributions, and for starting evangelical radio and television stations.[8] Seeing the possibility of a new political base, leaders of the national Republican Party began targeting Southern evangelicals for support.

The rise of evangelicalism undercut support for a movement to add the Equal Rights Amendment to the Constitution. The ERA, designed to prevent discrimination on the basis of sex, had been passed by Congress in 1972 and then ratified by twenty-two state legislatures. Since only sixteen more states were needed to pass the amendment, its success had been almost guaranteed. But in the midseventies, the conservative evangelical activist Phyllis Schlafly organized a national effort to stop the ERA, claiming that it would destroy the family, foster homosexuality, and hurt women. Almost single-handedly, Schlafly galvanized enough support to defeat the amendment when it was only three states shy of victory.

With the ERA out of the way, evangelicals could focus on the sexual revolution. Numerous social problems looked like solid evidence that the sexual revolution was a destructive force. Gonorrhea, syphilis, and nonspecific urethritis had reached epidemic proportions by the midseventies. The number of reported rapes jumped higher and higher each year: in 1958, there were 3,680 arrests for forcible rape; by 1968, there were 12,659 arrests; by 1975, this figure had reached 17,524.[9] All the while, news reports highlighted the persistent problem of teenage pregnancy. Disease, rape, and teen pregnancy were proof enough to many that the sexual revolution was causing the downfall of Western civilization.

Social scientists knew that the matter was more complicated. There was, for instance, no way to pinpoint the real reason for the rise in rates of sexually transmitted disease in the heterosexual community. While moralists assumed that increased promiscuity was to blame, the decreased use of condoms and spermicides as women began taking the pill might have been the cause. As far as rape is concerned, no one knows for sure if rape itself was on the rise or if more victims were simply reporting the crime. Finally, much confusion surrounded the issue of teenage pregnancy. In fact, teenage pregnancy rates had actually peaked in 1957, when almost 10 percent of all girls ages fifteen to nineteen became pregnant. But most of these girls were married.[10] By the 1970s, the teen pregnancy rate was down, but so was the teen marriage rate, meaning that more teen mothers were unmarried than before.

But with evangelicals taking center stage and blaming secular humanism (the view that religious considerations should be excluded from civil affairs) for society's woes, the public discourse about sexuality was certain to change. In 1973, in response to *Roe v. Wade*, Catholics and evangelical Protestants launched a massive anti-abortion crusade. Activists began demonstrating in front of clinics, "right to life" organizations were formed, and bills were introduced in state legislatures to curb *Roe*'s effects and recriminalize abortion. Fundamentalists also squared off against sex education. Although an overwhelming majority of Americans supported sex education, believing that informative courses would prevent unwanted pregnancy and reduce the transmission of venereal disease, evangelicals and Catholics saw sex education as a threat to their way of life.[11] Accordingly, they flexed their political muscle to keep sex education out of public schools. In one case, the wife of a fundamentalist minister in a Virginia coal-mining town attacked textbooks used in her child's public school on the grounds they were pornographic. The controversy resulted in the resignation of the school superintendent, and a new policy was adopted by the school system making it easier for parents to ban books. The case led to other textbook challenges throughout the nation.[12] In Texas, evangelical Christians Mel and Norma Gabler, with funding from Joseph Coors of the Coors Brewing Company, created the Educational Research Analysis organization to ferret out textbooks with "anti-Christian" and "anti-family" themes. In Philadelphia, the Roman Catholic Church withdrew its financial support for the city's eight thousand Girl Scouts because Scout leaders had planned sex education workshops intended to teach Scouts about birth control and abortion.[13] In the meantime, evangelicals began a crusade against homosexuality, drawing on frightening stereotypes and spurious psychiatric theories. An early-seventies Christian cartoon booklet, "The Gay Blade," showed the marriage ceremony of two wrinkled, sad-looking men accompanied by the caption,

Out of Satan's shadowy world of homosexuality, in a display of defiance against society, they come forth — those who suffer the agony of rejection, the despair of unsatisfied longing — desiring — endless lusting and remorse crying that gay is good — their tragic lives prove that there isn't anything gay about being gay.[14]

What, exactly, evangelicals hoped to accomplish with this sort of derision is unclear, but they probably did manage to make many gays (especially youngsters) afraid of coming out.

The evangelical assault on secular humanism and the sexual revolution coincided with a surge of popular sentiment against commercial sex. Across the country, groups like the Concerned Community Citizens of Mason City, Iowa, mobilized to pass zoning regulations and state laws that would once again limit the availability of sexual material.[15] President Nixon's appointment of the conservative Warren Burger to the Supreme Court in 1969 created the conditions for a new era in censorship. Burger's 1973 decision in *Miller v. California,* a case involving a California man convicted of mailing obscene materials, paved the way for the prosecution of the nation's most famous producers of sexual material. Burger inserted into the law the notion that obscenity could be defined by "local community standards." Such a provision meant that federal authorities could take advantage of small-town juries to bust big-city publishers. *Miller v. California* promised to revive the censorship tactics of the 1950s.*

Exploiting the community standards provision of the Miller case, postal inspectors (using assumed names) in small Kansas towns ordered copies of Al Goldstein's weekly tabloid *Screw.* Federal authorities then indicted Goldstein in Wichita, where he faced a possible sixty-year prison sentence. After a dramatic four-week trial and four hours of jury deliberations, Goldstein was convicted. But he was acquitted at a new trial that was granted because the original prosecutor's final summation was deemed inflammatory.[16] Federal prosecutors also pursued Larry Flynt, publisher of *Hustler* magazine. In a widely publicized obscenity trial in Cincinnati in 1977, Flynt was found guilty of "pandering obscenity" and sentenced to seven to twenty-five years in jail. A few celebrities came to Flynt's defense, as they had in other censorship cases, though this time there was greater reluctance. When Gay Talese took out an advertisement in the *New York Times* describing Flynt as an "American Dissident," many writers and editors refused to sign their names.[17] Says Talese, "Suddenly I was a pariah. The literary elite thought Flynt's constitutional rights weren't worth defending."[18] In 1978, Flynt was shot

* The *Miller* ruling might have ushered in an even more dramatic era of legal repression, but in 1974, in *Jenkins v. Georgia,* a case involving censorship of the Hollywood film *Carnal Knowledge,* the Burger court decided to take a more moderate approach to restricting speech and thus asserted that only "hard-core" material could be declared illegal (Edward De Grazia, *Girls Lean Back Everywhere,* 571).

during the course of another obscenity trial. The bullet cut his spinal cord and left him paralyzed from the waist down.

In the crusade to ban pornography, government agents used ever more militant tactics. In July 1974, federal prosecutor and Bible school teacher Larry Parish ordered the arrest of actor Harry Reems, costar of *Deep Throat,* on obscenity charges. Federal agents awakened Reems in his New York City apartment in the middle of the night, arrested him, and extradited him to Tennessee, on the grounds that *Deep Throat* was obscene by Tennessee standards. It was the first time in American history that an actor had ever been charged under the hundred-year-old federal obscenity statute. Many other actors and filmmakers rushed to Reems's defense, establishing a fund to pay his legal expenses, but on April 30, 1976, a Memphis jury found Reems and eleven other defendants guilty.[19] During the trial, Parish described the film in detail and read from published reviews. As the *New York Times Magazine* noted, Parish's language was so saturated with vulgarity that "the trial could have been said to appeal to the prurient interests of the jurors, and to fall under the very definition of obscenity which was being used to condemn Harry Reems."[20]

In 1974, the same year the Reems case began, the Supreme Court upheld the conviction and prison sentence of San Diego publisher William Hamling for his illustrated version of the report of the Presidential Commission on Obscenity and Pornography. Hamling's edition, issued in November 1970, included hard-core photographs, exactly the kind of photographs the text of the report said were harmless and ought to be decriminalized. Hamling's major mistake may have been his advertising brochure criticizing President Nixon for rejecting the report's conclusions. In any event, the FBI arrested him and in 1972 a federal court sentenced him to four years in jail. He appealed, but the Burger court upheld Hamling's conviction, underlining the authority of the judiciary to ban books.

Pornography had become a symbol for everything that was wrong with America. This view gripped the left as well as the right. Liberals, despite their traditional opposition to censorship, had always flinched from anything that might be deemed "pornography."* As liberals struggled to cope with the collapsing economy and the failures of Lyndon Johnson's Great Society, they too attacked the sexual revolution. "The 'sexual revolution' seems to bring few of the boons promised by the early pioneers who fought for progress in the darkest fifties by adopting gutter

---

*I would argue that liberals dislike pornography because it undercuts the Enlightenment notion of the tabula rasa by emphasizing the extent to which human beings are controlled by their sexual impulses.

language in their classrooms," one liberal critic wrote. "Dedicated pioneers at Berkeley or at Grove Press may assume that more of the same will produce something different, but their assurances grow daily less convincing."[21] Retiring Chief Justice Earl Warren declared in 1969 that he had never meant to decriminalize hard-core pornography, and that the Post Office had both a duty and a right to stop much of the sexually oriented material sent through the mail.[22] Even ACLU attorney Morris Ernst joined the growing chorus of disenchanted liberals. Ernst, who had defended *Ulysses,* the lesbian novel *The Well of Loneliness,* and Marie Stopes's *Married Love* in major obscenity trials in the 1920s and '30s, surprised liberals and conservatives alike in 1970 by publicly denouncing the "display of sex and sadism" that he felt was on the rise.

This display was perhaps most prominent in the nation's newspapers. From 1969 on, the entertainment section of the typical urban newspaper was packed with advertisements for hard-core sex films. In the early seventies, newspapers began restricting and regulating the use of suggestive illustrations in ads for films. By the end of 1973, thirty-five daily newspapers had instituted some policy regulating movie ads.[23] Often newspapers took advantage of the ratings system, introduced in 1968, which classified movies as either G (general audiences), M (mature young people), R (restricted to those accompanied by an adult over sixteen), and X (no one under sixteen admitted). At first, the X rating was given to any film with "adult" content (*A Clockwork Orange, Midnight Cowboy,* and Pier Paolo Pasolini's *Decameron* all received X ratings), so it did not necessarily indicate a hard-core pornographic film, but newspapers nonetheless began banning ads for all X-rated pictures.[24] (Such actions were not always popular with readers. Jim Copley, the publisher of the *San Diego Union and Tribune,* banned all X-rated film advertisements in August 1969; a poll taken in 1975 found that 68 percent of San Diego residents thought the ban was a form of improper censorship.)[25] Over time, as theaters specializing in sex films continued to proliferate, more and more newspapers implemented regulatory policies.

Segregating ads for sex films presented practical and theoretical difficulties. At first, the *New York Times* was reluctant to restrict advertising and chastised other newspapers for doing so. The publisher of the *Times* felt banning ads for all X-rated movies was a blunt method of censorship: Some X-rated films were rated X for heavy violent content rather than sexual content (interestingly enough, the *Times* saw no reason to ban ads for violent films), while some films with sex were worthy of patronage by *Times* readers because they were works of art.[26] To avoid these dilemmas, the *Times* decided to distinguish "true" pornographic films from other X-rated and nonrated films. Advertisements for films deemed pornographic would be restricted to a one-inch box and would not be allowed to contain any information other than the name of the film, the address of the theater, and the hours of performance. The policy banned all illustrations.

The newspaper's assistant general attorney, Katherine Darrow, opposed the new policy because it treated advertisements for films differently from advertisements for either books or plays. Darrow was concerned that the policy would establish a "flagrant double-standard." The policy was also opposed by John D. Pomfret, senior vice president of the newspaper, who argued it would so restrict information that it would do the reader a disservice. Gays might end up going to movies for straights and straights going to movies for gays. Pomfret believed that censorship ought to be "repugnant" to everyone at the *Times* and warned the adoption of the new policy would damage the paper's reputation.[27]

Senior executives at the *Times* were unmoved; they decided to go ahead with the new policy, which was announced on June 21, 1977. (Enraged, pornographic theater owners retaliated by boycotting the paper entirely and running their ads in the *New York Post* and the *New York Daily News.* But eventually these newspapers established their own censorship policies.) Broadway theater owners supported the *Times* because they too resented the presence of X-rated theaters in Times Square.[28] In fact, the 42nd Street Theater Row, which included the Black Theater Alliance, Actors and Directors Lab, Playwrights Horizons, Harlem Children's Theater, Lion Theater Company, and the South Street Theater Company, organized their own campaign to fight porn and prostitution in the neighborhood.[29] Meanwhile, the Motion Picture Association of America narrowed the scope of its X rating. Originally meant to include any film containing significant discussion of sexual topics, eroticism, or violence, the X was redefined to designate only those films with hard-core sex. The new, sex-specific category made it easier for police, local zoning boards, and movie theater owners to segregate sexuality.

The new sense of panic surrounding sexuality affected the music industry as well. In 1975 controversy erupted over country singer Loretta Lynn's song "The Pill," an ode to the oral contraceptive's liberating qualities. Though the song was certainly tame by the standards of the day, and the pill had been celebrated in the media for over a decade, Lynn's song came at the wrong time: women's sexual freedom was now seen as threatening to the social order. Conservatives denounced "The Pill" and radio stations refused to play it.

❧

On the far left of the political spectrum, feminists were beginning to attack the iconography of sex in mass culture. In March 1971, two female students at Princeton University entered a male undergraduate's room and slashed his nude pinups.[30] The two women, Chris Stansell and Susan Petty, both lived in the dorm, which was predominantly male. Stansel recalls, "The guy upstairs in a single was known for papering his room wall to wall with *Playboy* pinup foldouts. It was spring, we were full of piss and vinegar and energy and ire . . . [there was a] lack of space — physical, mental, emotional — for women (this was the second year of coeducation). The idea that everywhere on the campus women were objectified as sex objects, rather than taken as people, was very much in the air and this guy's room seemed to embody that problem." Stansell and Petty took some sculpting tools and "headed up the stairs to do in his pinups."[31] The two were eventually brought before the university disciplinary committee and were given minor reprimands.

Feminists' reaction in the early seventies against the machismo of male sexuality went beyond college vandalism. Two members of NOW declared in 1973, "Feminism is humanism and sex today can be de-humanizing: feminists disagree with competition between women for men, and with treating sex as an indoor sport, with scores tallied in numbers and types of orgasms."[32] With men using sex and sexual vulgarity to remind women of their second-class status in society, it was easy to become disgusted with male behavior. Men in the sex industry were especially notorious for being hostile to women. "When I worked for [publisher] Ed Mishkin writing [sex] novels, there was a rule in the company," says Jason Glick (a pseudonym), now a graduate student in history. "The woman was always supposed to get punished in the end. The more she was humiliated the better."[33] Seeing the entire sex industry as a bastion of misogyny, feminists began fighting commercial pornography in the 1970s. Some photographed men as they entered porn theaters and then posted the photographs throughout the community. In Seattle, feminists attacked adult bookstores with stink bombs. In New York, three pornographic theaters were firebombed.[34]

Feminists were particularly concerned about the popularization of sadomasochistic imagery. Anal rape was an increasingly familiar theme in literature and film, with the scene of forced sodomy and humiliation in 1973's *Last Tango in Paris* one of the most celebrated cinematic moments of the era. In 1974, the fashion industry introduced "s/m chic." In the window displays of Madison Avenue, mannequins were posed in brutal scenes suggesting sexual assault. Women knelt at the feet of their abusers. Men held their fists clenched. Similarly ugly scenarios decorated department store catalogs. A particularly notorious billboard for a record album pictured a bruised woman declaring, "I'm black and blue from the Rolling Stones."[35]

In response, a group of feminists created the Women's Anti-Defamation League.

For the vast majority of men and women who engaged in s/m, it was simply a form of pleasure, indeed of "sexual play," having nothing to do with domestic abuse. The explicit theatricality, costumes, and role-playing of s/m offered the spice of variety. But feminists were appalled and outraged by the rise of s/m, believing it to be the reflex of a repressed culture. At its best, they reasoned s/m was merely a symptom of self-hatred, at its worst, it was the first step toward sexual fascism.

The triumph of sexual liberalism raised new, difficult questions. What sort of community would be built by men and women for whom sexual pleasure was their first priority? Would they remember to value the beautiful, the just, and the common good? Or would they sink into solipsism and selfishness? Could education truly conquer irrational impulses and sexual exploitation? Or would the darker, violent side of human sexuality eventually triumph over reason and rationality?

In October 1975, the *New York Post* carried an article about the alleged production of pornographic movies in South America in which actresses were actually murdered during filming. These so-called snuff films were supposedly being shipped to the United States to be viewed by men sexually aroused by the thought of rape and murder. Whether or not such films were actually made remains uncertain, but rumors about snuff films spread like wildfire.[36] Four months after the *Post* article, *Snuff*, a fiction film about pornographic murder, opened in New York.[37] Soon thereafter, feminism became almost exclusively focused on stopping the sale of pornography.*

If snuff films were not enough to worry about, Hugh Hefner, one of the self-proclaimed leaders of the sexual revolution, was out to destroy feminism himself. A memo he wrote that was leaked to the press by a *Playboy* secretary revealed his antipathy toward the women's movement. Hefner had been planning to run a piece on the women's movement by feminist writer Susan Braudy, but then changed his mind. "What I want," he wrote in the now infamous memo,

> is a devastating piece that takes militants apart. . . . What I'm interested in is the highly irrational, emotional, kookie trend that feminism has taken. These chicks are our natural enemy. It is time to do battle with

---

*A movement to fight images of violence against women was spearheaded in California, where feminists organized Women Against Violence Against Women, but the group did not last long, falling apart in 1978. The San Francisco group Women Against Violence in Pornography and Media was more successful. This second group organized the first "Take Back the Night" march in 1979 (Susan Brownmiller to Barbara Demming, 4 March 1979, WAP Collection, Schlesinger Library, Harvard University). Speculation about the possible existence of snuff films was revived by the 1999 film *8mm*.

them and I think we can do it in a devastating way. . . . The only subject related to feminism that is worth doing is on this new militant phenomena [sic] and the only proper *Playboy* approach to it is one that devastates it. If you analyze all of the most basic premises of the extreme form of new feminism, you will find them unalterably opposed to the romantic boy-girl society that *Playboy* promotes. It is up to us to do a really expert, personal demolition job on the subject.[38]

After the memo was made public, Hefner appeared on *The Dick Cavett Show* in an attempt to repair the damage. But his opponent, Susan Brownmiller, author of *Against Our Will: Men, Women, and Rape*, won the day. Asked to define the meaning of sexual equality, Brownmiller responded, "When Hugh Hefner comes out here with a cotton tail attached to his rear end, then we'll have equality."

The memo incident gave feminists a new opportunity to critique the images of women in conventional pornography. Susan Braudy published her original article in *Glamour* magazine under the title "The Article I Wrote on Women That Playboy Would Not Publish." In it she asked,

> Why can't a magazine written to titillate men present a full picture of the real woman to those big, brave men? Why must she be a fantasy figure so de-humanized as to be really de-sexed — hairs plucked, smells replaced, pores filled with make-up, smoothed to unthreatening blandness? Is the *Playboy* male so weak, so ultimately unable to cope with reality and real women that the fantasy creature of his glossy *Playboy*-inspired reveries must be mechanized, passive, manipulable and controllable?[39]

In the meantime, many feminists had begun to take sexual freedom for granted. Susan Brownmiller, for instance, had joined the feminist movement already confident that she was sexually liberated. Born in 1935, sexually active from the time she was nineteen, and, by her own testimony, "multiply orgasmic," she did not see eroticism as an important political aim.[40] Increasingly, she and other feminists saw sexual danger as the most pressing issue of the day. They weren't neo-puritans, espousing "sexual repression"; rather, they felt that the battle for female sexual pleasure had largely been won, while the war against sexual violence had yet to begin.*

---

*The adversarial legal system made prosecuting rapists difficult if not impossible. Rapists left little evidence of their crimes (before DNA testing made it possible to identify a rapist by his semen) and juries, reverting to the double standard, were inclined to discount the testimony of women who were sexually active before an alleged rape. From the start, sexual coercion was a feminist issue, but early feminists, coming out of the civil rights movement, were wary of discussing rape because Southern whites had a long history of lynching any black man so much as accused of rape. In 1975, Susan Brownmiller addressed the issue directly in *Against*

Increasingly concerned about regulating sexual expression rather than liberating it, radical feminists organized to combat pornography, operating on the premise that pornography demeaned women and inspired men to rape. Most feminists still believed in the distinction between "healthy" and "unhealthy" representations of sexuality. Gloria Steinem claimed that one could distinguish between "pornography" and "erotica," much as the Kronhausens had in the late fifties and early sixties suggested that the law could distinguish between "pornography" and "erotic realism." The problem with Steinem's logic was that she seemed to think that only a woman could properly be trusted to make the distinction.

It was not long before some feminists hit upon the idea of working with the religious right to form a coalition against pornographers. In 1977, Lois Gould, a member of the fledgling Women's Anti-Defamation League, wrote about her epiphany in the "Hers" column of the *New York Times*. She described how after watching one of the *Godfather* films, she realized that men get "where they want to go by doing business with their sworn enemies." It might be necessary, she argued, to align with the religious right in the fight over pornography, even with conservatives who used the label "feminist" as a curse word. "Feminists are hardly godfathers (or mothers) in training; nor do we want to be. But we do want power, and we do want to win. And we do need to be aware of what it takes."[41] In other words, Gould argued, feminists would have to join forces with traditional anti-pornography crusaders in order to put pornographers out of business.

At first, many radical feminists expressed horror at Gould's realpolitik. Andrea Dworkin wrote in a letter to the editor:

> To me, the values in Lois Gould's article on . . . pornography/feminism are repugnant . . . The fight against those who deny others freedom and dignity is not divisible. Compromise with totalitarian ideology does not facilitate communication. It only encourages the atrophy of a vision of authentic justice which is the feminist contribution to history.

Dworkin said she found the idea of forging a coalition with the religious right "pernicious." Noting that all the radical feminists at the initial meeting of the Women's Anti-Defamation League supported gay and lesbian rights, Leah Fritz wrote: "It is inconceivable that we could in any way join our cause with those who would deny us, our sisters, or our brothers, our human rights."[42]

Our Will: Men, Women, and Rape, a book inspired by a consciousness-raising session dealing with sexuality during which Brownmiller listened to women discuss how they had been raped. Brownmiller herself had never been raped, but she was moved to begin writing about sexual violence from a feminist perspective.

Gould's public suggestion to align with the religious right was so startling and contrary to feminist principles that the Women's Anti-Defamation League quickly collapsed. In the meantime, evangelicals were increasing in strength. With liberals and leftists helping out with the campaign against pornography, evangelicals began targeting another aspect of the sexual revolution: gay rights.

In 1977, the singer and actress Anita Bryant initiated a campaign to repeal legislation that banned discrimination against homosexuals in Dade Country, Florida. Accusing homosexuals of abusing and recruiting children, Bryant developed rhetorical strategies designed to incite fear and hatred. The Reverend Jerry Falwell (who claimed that "so-called gay folks would just as soon kill you as look at you") and other evangelical leaders came to her aid. Within six months, Bryant was victorious: The law was overturned. Support for gay rights came from unlikely sources, such as *Hustler,* which printed an editorial in defense of gay rights in July 1977, but it was too little, too late. The success of Bryant's Save Our Children campaign, as she ingeniously called it, inspired similar legislative battles throughout the country, and anti-discrimination bills were repealed or blocked in every case. That same year, a Tacoma, Washington, school district fired an openly gay school-teacher; the move was approved by the state supreme court.[43] In California, state senator John Briggs attempted to prohibit homosexuals from working as public-school teachers. This time, gays found enough support, from both Democrats and Republicans, to block the effort. But social conservatives responded quickly by forming a new political organization, Christian Voice. In 1977, the 12.7-million-member Southern Baptist Convention declared at their annual meeting that "homosexuality is a sin" and vowed to keep homosexuals out of the clergy and other church staff positions.[44] In Boise, Idaho, the police department fired six women for alleged lesbian activity, and in Tucson, four teenagers who selected a man outside a gay bar and beat him to death were granted probation.[45] It was clear that evangelicals could rely on popular homophobia to support their cause.

In the late seventies, gay men and women had few straight allies they could turn to for support. Though many expressed a benevolent tolerance for those burdened with homosexual desires, the notion always hovered in the background of the straight sexual revolution that true emancipation would mean freedom *from* homosexuality, not freedom to be homosexual; at the very least, homosexuals would discover their capacity for heterosexual feelings. Discussions about homosexuality often took an ugly tone. The neoconservative intellectual Normal Podhoretz, for instance, accused homosexuals in 1977 of weakening the nation.[46] Such remarks fueled anti-gay violence. In San Francisco in

1978, openly gay official Harvey Milk was gunned down by a conservative politician.

Gay liberation itself was running out of steam. Like many feminists, gay men now tended to take sexual freedom for granted. With new gay clubs and bookstores springing up every day, the sexual revolution seemed like a fait accompli. Interest in the politics of sexual freedom dwindled. By the late seventies, gay liberation leaders were doubtful about the prospects of organized social change. Activist Dennis Altman wrote in 1977, "Now for the first time, I find myself totally pessimistic about the American future." To Altman, gay America had become "decadent," suffering "a decline in moral and spiritual vigor." Altman saw the rise of an openly gay culture as the paradoxical cause of the movement's decline:

> Comparative relaxation of the taboos against homosexuality has led to a blossoming of bars, saunas, restaurants and theaters which hold out the promise of endless gang-bangs available across the length and breadth of the country...what [this] represents however is the emergence of a luxury-oriented, commercial gay world where instant sex is provided in surroundings of some opulence.... [This] has had the effect of giving many male homosexuals the illusion that oppression is a thing of the past.[47]

With Fire Island, Key West, and San Francisco thriving as gay meccas and other cities home to dozens of gay bars, the whole point of gay liberation seemed moot. The gay liberation movement revived briefly in 1977 when Anita Bryant launched her Dade County crusade (one gay activist threw a pie in Bryant's face at a press conference), but the movement was gasping for breath.

Even if evangelicals had never targeted secular humanism, the persistence of exploitative sexual attitudes, magnified by the mass marketing of sexual stimulation, made many disillusioned about the virtues of sexual liberalism. In the midseventies, *Hustler* magazine ran photos of females without pubic hair under the title "Adolescent Fantasy." The magazine was deluged with enthusiastic responses. Thomas E. Hoeflinger of Dayton, Ohio, wrote to request "more of this age group." W. N. Webb of San Francisco wrote, "Being a dirty old man I definitely appreciated the February pubescent pictorial." One writer wrongly assumed that the illustrations had to be drawings. "Even though they were only drawings, that young supple body was a turn-on for me. As a school teacher there has been more than one young teenager I have wanted to spread buttocks on, and lick clean." To those who doubted whether the models really were prepubescent, the editors insisted they were. "The 'Adolescent Fantasy' was for real!" they wrote. With a regular comic strip titled "Chester the Molester," *Hustler* sneered at those with ethical concerns about the exploitation of children.

Those concerns, however, were well merited. In 1973, in Houston, Texas, Dean Coril, age thirty-three, sexually assaulted and murdered twenty-seven boys before one shot and killed Coril in self-defense. Around this time, the FBI arrested nineteen men, three of them millionaire businessmen, who had established a Boy Scout troop in the South for the express purpose of sexually exploiting young males.

Child pornography was now being mass produced by men like Washington, D.C., pornographer Lynn Womack, who was arrested in 1969 for selling a magazine titled *Phallic Development in the Pre-Adolescent*.[48] Womack's Aquarius Press catalog announced, "Our slidesets cover the age range from six to sixteen . . . and many different racial types, nationalities, body types, builds, ages, hair and eye colors."[49] Several magazines devoted to adult–child sex were started in the seventies.[50] Police discovered that two sex films featuring young children, *Lollitots* and *Lollipops*, were being widely circulated. In March 1973, police raided the Texas home of suspected child-pornographer John D. Norman, who had first been arrested in 1954 on sodomy charges and thirteen times after that, and allegedly found thirty thousand index cards marked with the names of potential customers.* Teenage prostitution was rising so fast, Los Angeles police were forced to organize a Sexually Exploited Child Unit in 1976.[51]

By 1977, authorities suspected that a national child-pornography and pedophile ring was based in Chicago. John Norman, who at the time was serving four years at the Illinois state prison for having had sex with ten-year-old boys, had begun publishing a newsletter from prison to tell others about his "Delta" project. The goal of the project was to create a system of "Delta" houses across the country in which adult male "dons" would preside over young male "cadets." The cadets Norman intended to recruit were prostitutes and foster home runaways. Norman's co-founders of the Delta project were Philip R. Paske, a convicted murderer; David Berta, a child-pornographer; and two other men with arrest records. They sent their newsletter, *Hermes*, to seven thousand

---

*According to press reports, some of the names were those of prominent federal employees. Police said they shipped the cards to the State Department, but that State Department officials destroyed them. The State Department action made many suspicious of a governmental cover-up because the officials could provide no clear justification for it. Apparently, the officials said they checked the names to see if there were any problems with passport authorization and, finding none, destroyed the cards. (See "Chicago Is Center of National Child Porno Ring," *Chicago Tribune*, 16 May 1977, front page.)

men across the country. In May, Chicago police arrested David Welch on the grounds that he had made child pornography featuring his own foster son.[52]

The *Chicago Tribune* featured stories about the child-pornography and pedophilia cases on its front page for several days in a row. "A nationwide homosexual ring with headquarters in Chicago has been trafficking in young boys, sending them across the nation to serve clients willing to pay hundreds of dollars for their services," the *Tribune* declared. Needless to say, panic about child pornography spread quickly.

The following year, anti-pornography feminism exploded onto the national scene when a new East Coast group, Women Against Pornography, was born. WAP members declared that pornography had "nothing to do with sex and everything to do with degradation of women, subjugation of women, and violence against women." East Coast WAP members held a major demonstration in Times Square in New York on Saturday, October 20, 1979.[53] Feminists around the nation organized "Take Back the Night" rallies to protest rape and sexual harassment.

With the sluggish economy, secular humanism under assault, and exploitative attitudes everywhere in evidence, few had the time, the resources, or the motivation to champion the First Amendment. To many, the doctrine of free speech seemed like a failure. From evangelical churches to the Supreme Court, anti-pornography sentiment was growing. Feminists, once attacked for being anti-sex, were now applauded for their anti-pornography views. Suddenly, more and more women were attracted to the anti-pornography position. Even Andrea Dworkin, who had once championed incest and graphic representations of sex, became a fervent anti-porn activist. Then, in 1980, the movement was invigorated by a surprise event. Linda Lovelace, the internationally known star of the film *Deep Throat*, published *Ordeal*, an account of her experiences during the making of the film. Lovelace said she had been forced to perform the sex scenes in *Deep Throat* by her husband, Chuck Traynor, who had beaten her and threatened her with a gun if she refused to comply. People across the nation were horrified. Here was a woman famous as an uninhibited sex artist who was now saying she had been systematically raped and tortured before their very eyes.

The so-called sexual revolution had gone too far, anti-pornography activists asserted. The only problem was that the anti-pornography movement itself was still haunted by the puritanical attitudes of the pre–sexual revolution period. The symbol selected by WAP members was a giant, and realistic, human eye. The eye suggested that feminists were staring back at the men who gazed at women as if they were "sex objects," and that anti-porn feminism would keep male sexual practices under surveillance. WAP members apparently missed the ironic resemblance of the symbol to the infamous posters declaring "Big Brother Is Watching" in George Orwell's novel of totalitarian dystopia, 1984.

In September 1979, WAP held its first East Coast conference on feminism and pornography. Workshops included "Porn and Me," "Porn, Me and Men," and slide shows of pornography. Men were banned from the conference. Organizers stated explicitly that speeches were to be geared toward the theme "Why I'm Against Pornography." A flier for the conference suggests the tension that existed between the desire for serious analysis of the issue of pornography and a more absolutist, activist approach. Inviting potential participants, the flier stated: "We will explore the complexities of the issue, discuss our questions and feelings and develop analysis and strategy." But it also declared: "PORNOGRAPHY IS NOT HARMLESS ENTERTAINMENT. PORNOGRAPHY IS VIOLENCE AGAINST WOMEN."

WAP took liberties with the truth in a way that other groups did not. For example, WAP asserted: "The pornography industry makes $4 billion a year by producing, distributing and selling images of women being bound, raped, tortured, mutilated and murdered for sexual stimulation and pleasure." As s/m images constituted only a fraction of the pornographic market in the late seventies, such a statement was simply untrue. But the anti-pornography movement tapped in to national nostalgia for "the good old days." One woman at a "Take Back the Night" steering committee meeting expressed her longing for the 1940s, when "the streets were safe any time of the day."[54] The pain and difficulty of life under the double standard was already disappearing from memory.

Some of the letters sent to Women Against Pornography confirmed the group's suspicions about male attitudes toward women. One writer who claimed to be a brothel owner wrote, "Dear Girlies, We men make very good money from you little ladies. You can't stop us. Ha Ha Ha Ha Ha. . . . You dumb cunts." Accompanying the letter were hard-core pornographic clippings and two articles on brothels in Las Vegas. On the other hand, Women Against Pornography members had a tendency to classify any and all critical correspondence as "hate mail." One letter filed under the heading "Hate Mail" was from a self-proclaimed male feminist who wrote, "Never did I dream that feminists would embrace censorship! I suggest you direct your efforts toward the real pornography against women: the Bible and religion in general. What are you trying to do anyway? Appeal to the right-wing Christians you've had so much trouble with?" The letter was signed, "With great sadness."[55] By tossing such letters into the "hate mail" pile, WAP members showed themselves to be unable, or unwilling, to distinguish between obvious opponents and concerned allies.

Anti-pornography feminists used a variety of tactics. One of the most successful was to publicize a June 1978 *Hustler* magazine cover showing a nude woman being ground into meat. The illustration bore out all the arguments made by WAP: that pornography treated women like "meat," that pornography was a form of misogyny, that violence and pornography were linked. WAP overlooked the fact that *Hustler* often contained cartoons showing men in similarly degrading and vile situations. One 1977 cartoon, in fact, depicted an imbecilic "organ grinder" grinding his own penis. There were other problems with the WAP tactic. By copying and enlarging the *Hustler* image and displaying it in public places, WAP members were "assaulting" women and children with the very images they claimed were so degrading and harmful.

Most significant was that WAP, led by Andrea Dworkin and legal scholar Catherine MacKinnon, forged a close alliance with the religious right. Dworkin, who had once spoken out against such a hypothetical alliance as a "compromise with totalitarian ideology," now adopted a more pragmatic political style. WAP members borrowed many tactics from the right, including the use of a slide show (a favorite technique of anti-abortion activists) to demonstrate that pornography was degrading to women. Sexual liberals were now truly on the defensive.

Despite the growing shadow of sexual exploitation, a significant number of Americans continued to support the essential elements of the sexual revolution. By 1977, polls found that 50 percent of Americans surveyed opposed laws preventing theaters from showing X-rated films. Seventy-seven percent said they believed public schools should provide sex education. Even more significant was the fact that almost 70 percent said they would approve schools teaching methods of birth control. Over 90 percent of Americans surveyed said they believed birth control information should be freely available. Over 80 percent said birth control information should be available to teenagers. Almost half of all college students said they believed a man and woman should live together before deciding whether or not to marry.[56] Several polls found that a majority of Americans supported legislation that would protect gays and lesbians from employment discrimination.[57]

But beneath the surface of American optimism, confusion and frustration still existed. One night in February 1975 in Peru, Indiana, after Eunice Lake's husband had had sex with another woman as part of their open arrangement, Eunice was overcome with anger and frustration. Lying beside her husband Trevor, she began to masturbate, knowing that the sight of a woman masturbating revolted him. As Trevor "turned his head with a look of disgust," Eunice had "a momentary urge to smash him over the head with the vibrator." Instead, she hurled it against the wall. It cracked into pieces.[58]

By the midseventies, faith in sexual liberation was cracking. Early proponents of the sexual revolution had believed that by treating sex as a "private" matter instead of one subject to government regulations, society would benefit. Now, however, sex was spilling into the public sphere in ever new and more complicated ways. In Virginia Beach, Virginia, two girls, ages eleven and thirteen, brought photographs of their mother naked with another man (who was not their father and who happened to be black) to school and showed them to friends. When school authorities learned of the photographs, they contacted the police. Police officers then raided the girls' home and found numerous pornographic magazines and multiple photographs of the girls' parents, Aldo and Margaret Lovisi, having sex with Earl Romeo Dunn, whom the Lovisis had met through an ad in the magazine *Swinger's Life*. Pictures showed Margaret Lovisi performing fellatio on her husband and on Dunn. The police arrested the Lovisis and charged them with committing sodomy and crimes against nature.[59] The couple were convicted in a Virginia Beach court (Aldo was sentenced to two years in prison, Margaret got five years); the convictions were upheld in a 1976 federal appeals decision and then reaffirmed by the Supreme Court. If sexual impulses could not be kept in check by citizens themselves, those impulses would be contained by the steel bars of a jail cell.

While both the right and the left poured fire on the sexual revolution, there was not, as this book has tried to make clear, any united coalition of "sexual revolutionaries" to fight back. Faint praise for First Amendment rights and sex education were no match for the systematic efforts of passionate social conservatives and anti-pornography feminists indifferent to rational argument. Part of the problem was that many different definitions of "sexual liberation" were being propounded. Sexual revolutionaries, if we may call them that, shared only a few vague principles in common. They agreed on the evils of hypocrisy, ignorance, superstition, shame, and fear. They opposed sexual "repression" and "exploitation." But what constituted repression and exploitation remained open to debate. Was anonymous sex liberated or repressed?

Was sadomasochism playful or exploitative? Was monogamy the answer or the problem?*

With many social and economic problems plaguing the nation but no one clearly at fault, sexual liberalism served as a practical scapegoat for society's ills. The 1975 film *Shampoo* emphasized the pathos of casual sex. In the 1977 movie *Looking for Mr. Goodbar,* Diane Keaton's patronage of a singles bar ends in her brutal murder by a pickup. The movie's message was clear: Promiscuity was inherently dangerous. A year later, the feature film *Hardcore* warned parents that their daughters might run away to act in porn films and never be heard from again. Some films of the early eighties, such as *American Gigolo* and *Cruising,* were virulently homophobic.[60]

By the early eighties, social conservatives were on the warpath, intent on destroying the last vestiges of secular humanism. The sudden rise of evangelical activism caught the attention of Howard Phillips of the Conservative Caucus, John Dolan of the National Conservative Political Action Committee, Paul Weyrich of the National Committee for the Survival of a Free Congress, and the conservative political fund-raiser Richard Viguerie, who decided to harness evangelical enthusiasm for the Republican Party. They helped organize a group called the Moral Majority in 1979 and chose Jerry Falwell, the minister of the independent Thomas Road Baptist Church in Lynchburg, Virginia, to be its figurehead. The Moral Majority — though it did not in fact represent majority opinion in the United States — pushed for government by theocracy. The organization blasted secular humanism as the work of the devil and denounced all forms of knowledge that contradicted fundamentalist readings of the Bible.

Despite rapidly escalating rates of sexually transmitted disease, Republicans in Congress killed what was to be the first national study of sexual practices. In April 1981, a Republican senator introduced a "chastity bill," intended "to promote self-discipline and chastity, and

---

*One might argue that sexual utopianism died simply because it produced the very forms of sexual expression its proponents said it would stamp out. Didn't the sexual revolution lead to more rape, more child abuse, more jealousy, more unhappiness, more divorce? The truth is, we will never know. There is no way to test whether the sexual revolution was responsible for such social problems. It is possible, after all, that if the major events of the sexual revolution had not occurred — that is to say, if censorship laws had never been overturned, if the double standard had never been challenged, if gay liberation had never begun — there might be *more* rape, *more* child abuse, *more* jealousy, *more* unhappiness, *more* divorce than there is today. As dissatisfying as it may be, we simply have no way of knowing how history would have turned out had it followed a different course. All efforts purporting to demonstrate which social problems the sexual revolution caused and which it solved must be regarded with suspicion.

other positive family centered approaches to the problems of adolescent promiscuity and adolescent pregnancy."[61] Though the bill failed in Congress, liberals and radicals issued only quiet protests and also abandoned efforts to pass federal gay rights legislation.

Social conservatives may have regarded themselves as morally superior, but the evidence suggests otherwise. Many of those who led the war against the sexual revolution in the late seventies and eighties were later accused of unethical or criminal acts themselves. In 1987, televangelist Jim Bakker was forced to admit to an extramarital affair with his secretary Jessica Hahn. Bakker had tried to keep Hahn silent with hush money, but she talked anyway. There were also claims that Bakker had experimented with bisexuality. Meanwhile, Bakker, who lived in extravagant luxury, was convicted of fraud and sentenced to eight years in prison. The following year, fellow televangelist Jimmy Swaggart publicly confessed to paying prostitutes for sex. Robert Tilton, a Texas televangelist, was barraged with lawsuits for fraud and tax evasion. It is possible that the sexual revolution was a convenient target for those who wanted to deflect investigations into white-collar crime and corruption.

About to give a speech in Texas, Gloria Steinem was delighted to see dozens of people carrying signs saying "GLORIA STEINEM IS A HUMANIST." She assumed they were supporters, sympathetic to the goals of the women's movement. "But as I got closer and saw the hatred in their faces," she recalls, "I realized they were right-wing pickets to whom *humanist* — or any other word that means a belief in people instead of an authoritarian god — is the worst thing you can be."[62]

Under attack from all sides and forced to retreat, sexual liberals were utterly unprepared to deal with the discovery of a new, incurable, sexually transmitted disease in 1979. Herpes Simplex II, or genital herpes, was viral rather than bacterial, so it could not be stopped with penicillin or other antibiotics. Its symptoms included painful, itchy blisters, and the disease could be dormant for long periods of time and then suddenly flare up. The media, hungry for the kind of attention-grabbing stories about sex that had become so hard to find as liberation made sex ho-hum, turned herpes into a national crisis. In one article, *Time* magazine called herpes "the new sexual leprosy"; in another, "today's scarlet letter." Herpes was touted as evidence that promiscuity was a violation of the "natural order." Those with herpes were treated — and they treated themselves — as social outcasts, punished by God for having illicit sex. The cover of a popular book on the disease featured the word *herpes* emblazoned in red capital letters. An article in the *Soho Weekly News* in 1981 typified the media's response to the virus. "Like many women who grew up during the sexual revolution, Susan was determined to take control over her life — to be free, whatever that meant. But now she is out of control in the worst way possible — out of control of her own body." As historian Allan Brandt noted in 1985,

> From a strictly scientific standpoint genital herpes is more of an annoyance than a danger; but for many who become infected it is a serious problem . . . Guilt, anger and remorse are all widely reported among herpes sufferers . . . Stress builds for herpes victims with the possibility of each new relationship or potential sexual encounter . . . Clearly, for many individuals who become infected, herpes is a tragedy. It is a tragedy, however, not because of its physiological implications, but because of the stigma and psychological ramifications the disease carries with it.

Not only did journalists stigmatize those with herpes (often referring to them condescendingly as "herpetics"), they exploited the disease in the search for bold headlines about the end of the sexual revolution. *Time* magazine enthusiastically declared, "Perhaps not so unhappily, [herpes] may be a prime mover in helping to bring to a close an era of mindless promiscuity."[63] *Time*, apparently, was more interested in ending the sexual revolution than in finding a cure for herpes.

The manner in which the media responded to herpes foreshadowed the way the nation would respond to AIDS. Identified in the mid-1980s, acquired immune deficiency syndrome was a fatal disease, not a minor annoyance like herpes, but its link to gay male sex practices, not its gravity alone, shaped public discourse about it. Had the sexual revolution continued to run its course, the nation's response to the AIDS epidemic might have been entirely different. The federal government might have taken immediate steps to promote the use of condoms, extensive funds might have been allocated for AIDS research, and schools might have actively encouraged masturbation, sensual massage, and other safe-sex practices. Instead, of course, the nation was alternately swept up in panic and denial. Masters and Johnson put their imprimatur on the myth that one could get AIDS from a toilet seat.[64] Then-President Ronald Reagan did not mention the word *AIDS* in a speech until seven years into the epidemic, when 25,000 lives had already been lost. Conservatives fought efforts to distribute condoms in schools. Reason gave way to emotion, empathy to fear.

By the early eighties, the sexual revolution was out of steam. People did not suddenly stop having sex outside of marriage, or having same-sex relationships, or consuming pornography. But Americans became more pessimistic about human sexuality. The quest to abolish hypocrisy, ignorance, shame, self-loathing, and the fear of sexual expression had run its course. Americans had become resigned to their own moral contradictions and intellectual inconsistencies. Many had accepted the power of the state and the authority of religious spokesmen to dictate sexual morality. Intellectuals who had once looked to Marcuse and Brown as prophets of sexual freedom now turned to French philosopher Michel Foucault, who insisted that sexual liberation was all but impossible. The more people tried to free themselves from sexual repression, Foucault argued, the more entangled in prescriptive norms they would end up.

For all its faults and limitations, the sexual revolution had contributed to an era of openness, self-examination, and questioning of the status quo. It was a time of popular inquiry into important philosophical questions. For twenty-some years, a significant segment of the population had publicly explored the possibility of a rational approach to personal behavior and social organization. That exploration had led to many ideas and recommendations that were less than logically sound themselves. But it had been an era of commitment to the principle of consistent thought and action. It had been an era of devotion to the idea of freedom in all its forms. It had been an era of erotic possibility. Now that era was over.

EPILOGUE

IN 1994, SURGEON GENERAL JOYCELYN ELDERS, RESPONDING TO
the AIDS crisis, recommended that schools discuss the safety benefits of masturbation over intercourse. She was summarily fired. Virtually
no one in the nation rallied to her side.

There are several ironies to the Elders incident. Two decades earlier,
Elders would have had numerous defenders. Her suggestion would have
been interpreted in light of the ongoing sexual revolution. Her ideas might
still have seemed provocative to some, but many educated adults would
have recognized the obvious importance of teaching children a pragmatic
approach to avoiding an incurable, life-threatening disease over maintain-
ing reticence about a practice as timeless and widespread as masturbation.

The man who fired Elders was none other than President Clinton. As
the Monica Lewinsky affair later revealed, Clinton is no exemplar of traditional morality. Or, rather, Clinton is just that: a man who practices
the traditional rites of hypocrisy. When it came to the health of the
nation's children, Clinton was unwilling to speak up for a secular, rational approach to sexuality because it might cost him public approval.
When it came to his own personal pleasure, Clinton was quick to act on
his desires and lie as necessary.

The point is not to blame the president for his all too human failings.
The real point is to recognize how deeply ambivalent most of us remain
about human sexuality. We remain ashamed of our own desires, alienated from our own bodies, fearful of the judgment of our neighbors,
calmly hypocritical and deceitful.

Fortunately, the sexual revolution did accomplish many positive things. Even though various religions still disapprove of contraception, there is no longer any real social stigma attached to using birth control. The double standard is less pervasive than it once was. Premarital sex is acknowledged as a reality by the mass media. Abortion is still legally available. Censorship is much rarer than it used to be. There are nude beaches in a number of states. Gays and lesbians enjoy unprecedented visibility and freedom. Interracial marriages are legal and interracial romances are represented in film and on television. College parietal rules are, for all intents and purposes, but a distant memory. Sexually explicit films are readily available at video stores throughout the nation.

But overall, the sexual revolutionaries of the sixties and seventies did not accomplish nearly as much as they had hoped they would. First, as the Elders incident reveals, many of the backward attitudes that existed prior to the sexual revolution have persisted despite the best efforts of sexual liberals to stamp them out. Adolescents of both sexes still look down on girls who are too "easy." Birth control remains expensive, and it is often not covered by medical insurance. Abortion providers must fear for their own lives. Politicians still say one thing about sex and do another. The religious right still tries to appeal to "decency" in order to censor provocative art. Gay unions are not legally recognized, while homophobia and gay bashing are still rampant in some areas and may even be on the rise. Gang bangs still occur at college fraternities. Many young men still possess callous attitudes toward women. Nonsexual nakedness remains almost entirely taboo in family films and television and even in news magazines. Depictions of violence and simulated violence remain staples of popular entertainment while the portrayal of sex and simulated sex continue to provoke controversy. The result is a world in which professional wrestling, designed to trick the naive into believing that grown men in tight underwear are really trying to hurt one another, is good clean fun, but television shows that deal sensitively with homosexuality are denounced from the pulpits of the nation.

At the same time, it is necessary to acknowledge that the sexual revolution has had some untoward results of its own. Many of the rights and privileges won by the sexual revolutionaries of yesterday are now frequently abused. There are mobsters who use the First Amendment to fight the closing of their strip clubs, phone-sex companies that litter the streets with their advertisements, parents who exploit their own children for sex. And sometimes our consumer culture seems caught in a spiral of ever-increasing vulgarity.[1]

❧

For those of us who were children during the late sixties and early seventies, the sexual revolution was a mixed blessing. Looking back, it is hard not to wonder what role children were supposed to play in the sexually liberated utopia that many hoped was on the horizon. While the sexual revolution was in full swing, America was a paradise for adults but something of a purgatory for children. The entire culture catered to adult needs, providing endless entertainment and opportunities for self-expression. There were pickup bars, swing clubs, and vacation resorts designed to facilitate sexual encounters. There were group sex retreats and plenty of private orgies to attend. There were porn theaters, sex shops, and strip clubs galore. It was a world in which children did not quite belong, in which it was easy for them to feel "in the way."

When parents were devoted to their own sexual pleasure, children could become a mere distraction. On one occasion, Eunice Lake was forced to miss her daughter's school program because she had an appointment with her sex therapist.[2] Glen Murphy (a pseudonym), another swinger, recalls that he once left their young son, Tom, at home with his wife, Susan, while he was out of town. Tom caught his mother in the shower with another man. "When I arrived at the airport, Susan and Tom were there to greet me. Tom was about eight years old. In a really loud voice he yells, 'Daddy! Daddy! Mommy took a shower with Mr. Gage.' The airport was one of those domed kinds, so his voice echoed throughout the entire place. I was mortified and I had to explain to him why it was okay for Mommy to be in the shower with another man but not okay to talk about it in the airport."[3]

I don't want to suggest that children were necessarily "damaged" by their parents' sexual lifestyles. Contrary to popular wisdom, there is no scientific evidence to support the premise that children can only thrive in heterosexual, monogamous unions. Tom Murphy, for one, believes his parents' open marriage provided him with valuable male role models. "I actually considered [my mother's lover] a kind of uncle, he was kind of a surrogate father at times. . . . If my father was unable to deal with a situation — for example, teaching me to drive made him really uptight — this guy was able to help. He was a bus driver, so he was cool with it."[4]

The problem with the sexual liberalism of the early seventies was not that adult behavior had a direct, negative impact on children (though sometimes it did, as in all historical eras and human societies). The real problem was that children's emotional needs were often overlooked because the focus of the culture was so geared to adults and their desires. On stage and screen young children were virtually absent, or else they appeared as preadolescent prostitutes or sexually curious saplings.[5]

Indeed, when the culture's focus was on children, it often put them in a sexual light. There was, for instance, a small movement to promote pedophilia, a practice that was glamorized in the 1962 Hollywood version of *Lolita*. In Los Angeles in the early seventies, members of the Guyon Society proclaimed, "Sex before eight, or else it's too late." Farther north along the coast, several members of the Sexual Freedom League formed a "Childhood Sensuality Circle" in January 1971. Though the circle members disavowed the "exploitation of children for any purpose," they denied the notion that sex between an adult and a child was automatically exploitative.[6] In the late seventies, the National Association for Man Boy Love began insisting that children could benefit from sexual relationships with adults.

Although pro-pedophilia organizations had few members, the adult-centered attitudes were widespread. The children of mate-swapping swingers and sexually liberated couples often felt alienated and out of place in the world of erotic exuberance. Wisconsin businesswoman Valerie Goldberg, who grew up in a Manhattan apartment where the walls were covered with photographs of nude women, including some of her mother, felt uncomfortable in her own home. "The tenor of the house was extremely sexualized. My father had all of his pictures of his girlfriends, but my mother liked a very sexualized environment as well. . . . She was having an affair with the husband of one of her best friends. My mother was always looking in my drawers and invading my privacy. . . . She used to have naked photographs of herself hanging in the apartment, and I thought, 'What kind of a woman would do that for the delivery men to see?' It was like growing up in the *Playboy* mansion."[7]

It is understandable that men and women who were raised in the repressive forties and fifties would want to provide a more open, more honest world for their own children. Sometimes, however, the good intentions of sexually liberated parents had the opposite effect of what was intended. Jody West (a pseudonym), who works in Washington, D.C., for a nonprofit firm, often wished her parents would talk to her about sex *less,* rather than more. They not only discussed in great detail their own bedroom experiences with Jody, but often expressed astonishment that she wasn't yet sexually active herself. "I really appreciated that my parents were so open about sex, but, at the same time, I felt more pressure to lose my virginity from my father and stepmother than from anyone else. When I had my very first date with a boy — I'd never even been kissed — I brought him over for a soda or something. My father found out he was coming and put condoms on every bed in the house. I was so embarrassed I wanted to cry." When Jody was eleven, her father and stepmother invited her to watch them have sex — not once, but twice. "I said no, of course, but that only reinforced my image as the family prude. What can I say? Most of my childhood, I was angry and depressed."[8]

As these examples illustrate, the noble effort to eliminate sexual guilt and shame sometimes resulted in adults having little respect for the privacy of children. Most parental attempts to educate children, and be honest with them, were certainly well meaning, but they sometimes failed to take into account the complex relationship between parent and child. I won't ever forget the time my own father and stepmother recommended that I lose my virginity with a prostitute rather than a girl-friend. "It's very dangerous to confuse sex and love," my stepmother told me when I was twelve. "That's why it's much better for a man to do it the first time with a hooker."[9] I certainly wasn't "harmed" by her words, but I was confused by them. And I was left with the feeling that we would never be able to understand one another; that if I were going to talk to someone about my sexual feelings and experiences, it would never be with her.

Those of us who were born in the late sixties and early seventies tend to have a certain ambivalence about the sexual revolution. In part, it is hard for us to appreciate how stifling life was before the social and cultural changes of the era. But we also know that "more talk" about sex does not necessarily mean more understanding. Listening is just as important for a relationship as talking — perhaps even more important. Missing from the sexual revolution was an appreciation of the value of listening.

In the aftermath of the sexual revolution, we are confronted with new, ever more complicated dilemmas: How do we acknowledge the sexual desires of children and teach them about their choices without invading their privacy or making them feel pressured to have sex? How do we craft laws and workplace policies that prevent sexual harassment but do not encourage witch hunts or further alienate us from our own bodies? How do we weigh the benefits of easy access to abortion against the need for limits on fetal experimentation and genetic engineering? How do we protect free speech but maintain aesthetic standards for our communities, our literature, our art?

The sexual revolution was neither all good nor all bad, neither all successful nor all for naught. We should be wary of those who blame the sexual revolution for all of society's ills and equally wary of those who refuse to recognize the value of some regulation of public sexual expression. Now that the sexual revolution is long over, the New Right has begun to lose its sway over the public, and new medicines mean AIDS is no longer a death sentence, we can perhaps begin to reflect critically on our own beliefs and behavior.

Our attitudes about sex are important because they shape both our private and public lives. They tell us about our assumptions and our priorities. The ways we reconcile in the sexual arena our wants and our responsibilities, our personal beliefs and our commitment to liberty, equality and justice for all, reflect on the ways we reconcile such tensions in other arenas as well. Sexual desire is part of the human condition. Our willingness to examine our sexual attitudes — or our determined refusal to do so — will always remain a useful measure of our commitment to a truly enlightened society.

Much, if not most, of the pleasure associated with sex comes not from *having* sex but from talking about having it. Stimulation and orgasm are certainly enjoyable, but it is the meaning we attach to sex through conversation that gives such physical sensations their true potency. Whether it be in the locker room, the bedroom, or the boardroom — before, during, or after — our conversations about sex (even our inner conversations with ourselves) shape our experience of it. For all its faults, the sexual revolution taught us how to speak about sex more directly, more clearly, and, most important, more authentically than we ever knew how to before. We may not always take advantage of all the sexual revolution has made available to us in this regard, but the possibility of doing so is now ours so long as we hold on to it.

There are many gaps left to fill in the historical picture of the sexual revolution. There are countless stories to tell. In years to come, new collections of manuscripts and personal papers will become available, yet people who lived through the period will pass away. These developments will make research on the period both more and less challenging. For now, the sexual revolution is part of our national mythology, secured there by both the left and the right. If a new sexual revolution should once again shake up our values and beliefs, as one no doubt will, then the meaning and mythology of the sexual revolution of the sixties and seventies will change once again. At the moment we can only wait and see what moral questions, erotic preferences, and public pleasures the next century will bring.

NOTES

INTRODUCTION

[1] In addition to promoting birth control and abortion, Reich had a very specific definition of sexual liberation, which he equated with perfection of the orgasm. Interestingly, Reich believed that heterosexual intercourse was the only form of sexual contact that would allow one to experience maximum pleasure and, thereby, liberation. Reich first used the phrase "sexual revolution" to refer to the developments then taking place in the Soviet Union, where birth control and abortion were briefly championed by the state. Such liberal policies were quickly reversed by Stalin. See Wilhelm Reich, *Der Sexuelle Kampf der Jugend* (reprint ed., Graz: Verag O, n.d., [1932]); Reich, *The Sexual Revolution,* trans. Thomas P. Wolfe (Orgone, Maine: The Orgone Institute Press, 1945; reprint ed., New York: Farrar, Strauss and Giroux, 1960). For the most recent scholarly account of Reich's role in the German sex movement, see Atina Grossman, *Reforming Sex: The German Movement for Birth Control and Abortion Reform* (New York: Oxford, 1995), 124–27. Grossman argues that Reich's role in the movement has been overstated.

[2] Pitirim Sorokin, *The American Sex Revolution* (Boston: F. Porter Sargent, 1956), 54; originally published as a magazine article and reproduced as a pamphlet.

CHAPTER 1

[1] Helen Gurley Brown, *Sex and the Single Girl* (New York: B. Geis, 1962), 257.

[2] Quoted in Shana Alexander, "Singular Girl's Success," *Life,* 1 March 1963, 60–62.

[3] Brown, *Sex and the Single Girl,* 35; 15.

[4] Information for this chapter based on interview with Helen Gurley Brown by the author, New York, 29 January 1996.

[5] Brown, *Sex and the Single Girl*, 7.

[6] Christine Stansel, *City of Women: Sex and Class in New York, 1798–1860* (New York: Knopf, 1986); Timothy J. Gilfoyle, *City of Eros: New York City, Prostitution, and the Commercialization of Sex, 1790–1920* (New York: Norton, 1992); Ruth Rosen, *The Lost Sisterhood: Prostitution in America, 1900–1918* (Baltimore: Johns Hopkins University Press, 1982).

[7] See, for instance J. P. Edwards, "Do Women Provoke Sex Attack?" *Cosmopolitan*, March 1960, 38. Edwards alleged that rape was largely the result of "an unconscious predisposition on the part of the victim." To this day, women in Arab nations who are raped may be forced to marry their attackers, or may even be murdered by their own male family members for being "wanton."

[8] On free-love advocates in the nineteenth century, see Taylor Stoehr, ed., *Free Love in America: A Documentary History* (New York: AMS Press, 1979); John C. Spurlock, *Free Love: Marriage and Middle-Class Radicalism in America, 1825–1860* (New York: New York University Press, 1988). On Margaret Mead and the anthropological revolution, see Phyllis Grosskurth, *Margaret Mead* (New York: Penguin, 1988). On early-twentieth-century marriage manuals, see Michael Gordon, "From an Unfortunate Necessity to a Cult of Mutual Orgasm: Sex in American Marital Education Literature, 1830–1940," in *Studies in the Sociology of Sex*, ed. James M. Henslin (New York: Appleton-Century-Crofts, 1971), 53–77. On working-class women in the pre–World War I era, see Kathy Peiss, *Cheap Amusements: Working Women and Leisure in Turn-of-the-Century New York* (Philadelphia: Temple University Press, 1986).

[9] Lea Jacobs, *The Wages of Sin: Censorship and the Fallen Woman Film 1928–42* (Madison, WI: University of Wisconsin Press, 1991), 10–12; Marybeth Hamilton, *"When I'm Bad, I'm Better": Mae West, Sex, and American Entertainment* (New York: HarperCollins, 1995), 228; interview with Sylvia Weil by the author, telephone, 7 August 1998.

[10] Karl Fleming and Anne Taylor Fleming, *The First Time* (New York: Simon & Schuster, 1975), 26.

[11] Elaine Tyler May, *Homeward Bound: American Families in the Cold War Era* (New York: Basic, 1988).

[12] Interview with Gloria Steinem by the author, Princeton, 5 December 1997; Albert Ellis, *The American Sexual Tragedy*, 2nd ed. (New York: Lyle Stuart, 1962), 70.

[13] Paula J. Caplan, *The Myth of Women's Masochism* (New York: Dutton, 1985), 17–41; Barbara Ehrenreich and Deirdre English, *For Her Own Good: 150 Years of the Experts' Advice to Women* (Garden City, N.Y.: Anchor, 1978).

[14] Quoted in Brett Harvey, *The Fifties: A Women's Oral History* (New York: HarperCollins, 1993), 12.

[15] Guccione quoted in Fleming and Fleming, *First Time*, 78; interview with Ronald Jones by the author, telephone, 27 August 1997. In many ways, a "gang bang" was the archetypal activity for the midcentury young male. It allowed a boy to express his interest in women without seeming overly preoccupied with the other sex; it allowed him to engage in activity with his male peers; it allowed him

to be aggressive yet social, selfish yet sharing. Hence young white men who participated in gang bangs were rarely prosecuted for rape; rather, they tended to receive encouragement from their fathers and other older males.

[16] Rickie Solinger, *Wake Up Little Susie: Single Pregnancy and Race Before Roe v. Wade* (New York: Routledge, 1992), 13. Alfred Kinsey, *Sexual Behavior in the Human Female* (Philadelphia: Saunders, 1953), passim. On Kinsey, see Paul A. Robinson, *The Modernization of Sex: Havelock Ellis, Alfred Kinsey, William Masters, and Virginia Johnson* (New York: Harper & Row, 1976), 42–119; Janice M. Irvine, *Disorders of Desire: Sex and Gender in Modern American Sexology* (Philadelphia: Temple University Press, 1990), 31–66; Wardell Pomeroy, *Dr. Kinsey and the Institute for Sex Research* (1972; reprint, New Haven, Conn.: Yale University Press, 1982); Regina Markett Morantz, "The Scientist as Sex Crusader: Alfred C. Kinsey and American Culture," *American Quarterly* 29 (1977): 563–89; James H. Jones, *Alfred C. Kinsey: A Public/Private Life* (New York: Norton, 1997). Rather than attempt to gather a random sample, Kinsey interviewed as many subjects as he could find. His study of midcentury sexual behavior remains the best in existence, though it is seriously flawed and his data must be used with extreme caution.

[17] Diary of Eunice Lake [pseud.], 14 December 1974, Robert Rimmer collection, Mugar Memorial Library, Boston University. "Eunice Lake" was a pseudonym she chose when she considered publishing the diary.

[18] Bertrand Russell, *Marriage and Morals* (New York: Liveright, 1929), 162. According to Russell, "when it became known that [Lindsey] used [his knowledge of juvenile behavior] to promote the happiness of the young rather than to give them a consciousness of sin, the Ku Klux Klan and the Catholics combined to oust him."

[19] Barry Feinberg and Ronald Kasrils, eds., *Bertrand Russell's America*, vol. 1 (1973; reprint, New York: Viking, 1974), 135–67. See also Caroline Moorehead, *Bertrand Russell: A Life* (New York: Viking, 1992), 431–36.

[20] Pomeroy, *Dr. Kinsey*, 380; Irvine, *Disorders of Desire*, 66; 64.

[21] Grace Metalious, *Peyton Place* (New York: Julian Messner, 1956), 8, 203; Emily Toth, *Inside Peyton Place: The Life of Grace Metalious* (Garden City, N.Y.: Doubleday, 1981).

[22] See, for instance, Edmund Bergler, "A Psychoanalyst's Case for Monogamy," *Harper's Bazaar*, May 1957, 120–21, 172–80. In an ad hominem attack, Bergler claimed that those such as Ellis who criticized monogamy were themselves neurotic: "Neurotics have added a new chapter to the oldest story in the world: they have enlarged the meaning of love and sex to include counterfeit-love and counterfeit-sex." Bergler asserted that Freud lent no support to anti-monogamous views, but Freud was actually somewhat ambiguous on the subject. In "'Civilized' Sexual Morality and Modern Nervousness," Freud wrote: "We have found it impossible to give our support to conventional sexual morality or to approve highly of the means by which society attempts to arrange the practical problems of sexuality in life. We can demonstrate with ease that what the world calls its code of morals demands more sacrifices than it is worth." Sigmund Freud, *General Introduction to Psychoanalysis* (1917; reprint, New York: Collier, 1963), 441.

[23] Margaret Culkin Banning, "The Case for Chastity," *Reader's Digest*, July 1961, 46–50; H. Whitman, "How to Tell Your Daughter Why She Must Keep Her Self

Respect," *Better Homes and Gardens,* October 1961, 118; B. M. McKinney, "Is the Double Standard Out of Date?" *Ladies' Home Journal,* May 1961, 10; "Vassar and Virginity," *Newsweek,* 21 May 1962, 86.

24 Brown, *Sex and the Single Girl,* 65; 222–23; 71; 30.

25 "Playboy Interview: Helen Gurley Brown," *Playboy,* April 1963, 54.

26 "The Womanization of America," Playboy Roundtable, *Playboy,* June 1962, 43.

27 Philip Wylie, "The Career Woman," *Playboy,* January 1963.

CHAPTER 2

1 Lewis Lapham, "The Great Idea Boy," *Saturday Evening Post,* 13 February 1965, 74.

2 *San Francisco Chronicle,* 12 June 1964, 1.

3 *New York Times,* 22 June 1964, 30; 23 June 1964, 30; 11 July 1964, 12; 7 August 1964, 55; Gloria Steinem, "Gernreich's Progress; or, Eve Unbound," *New York Times Magazine,* 31 January 1965, 18–24.

4 *New York Times,* 22 June 1964, 30.

5 Lapham, "Great Idea Boy," 74.

6 John D'Emilio, *Sexual Politics, Sexual Communities: The Making of a Homosexual Minority in the United States 1940–1970* (Chicago: University of Chicago Press, 1983), 62, 67. Reporters knew that Gernreich was gay but used coded expressions to tell their readers. Lewis Lapham described Gernreich as "shy and elusive," noted that he disliked discussing "the details of his private life," and remarked that he was "deeply attached" to his mother. It's interesting to note, also, that D'Emilio does not identify Gernreich by name but rather by the initial "R."

7 Adam Clapham and Robin Constable, *As Nature Intended* (London: Heinemann, 1982); Karl Eric Toepfer, *Empire of Ecstasy: Nudity and Movement in German Body Culture, 1910–1935* (Berkeley: University of California Press, 1997).

8 *Sunshine Book Co. v. Summerfield,* 355 U.S. 372 (1958). Needless to say, any image that portrayed sexual acts was not granted protection. There is almost nothing of a scholarly nature on the history of American nudism, but see Read Schuster, "Nudist Beginnings," *Clothed with the Sun* 6 (Spring 1986), 21–29; William E. Hartman, Marilyn Fithian, and Donald Johnson, *Nudist Society: The Controversial Study of the Clothes-Free Naturist Movement in America* (1970; reprint, Los Angeles: Elysium Growth Press, 1991).

9 John Hubner, *Bottom Feeders: From Free Love to Hard Core — The Rise and Fall of Counter-Culture Heroes Jim and Artie Mitchell* (New York: Doubleday, 1993), 58. On the history of breast implants, see Elizabeth Haiken, *Venus Envy: A History of Cosmetic Surgery* (Baltimore: Johns Hopkins University Press, 1997).

10 See Charles Lockwood, *Suddenly San Francisco: The Early Years of an Instant City* (San Francisco Examiner Special Projects, 1978), 93–99; Raymond Mungo, *San Francisco Confidential: Tales of Scandal and Excess from the Town That's Seen Everything* (Secaucus, N.J.: Carol, 1995), 22–23; Gladys C. Hansen, *San Francisco Almanac: Everything You Want to Know About the City* (San Francisco: Chronicle Books, 1975); Doris Muscatine, *Old San Francisco: The Biography of a City, from Early Days to Earthquake* (New York: Putnam, 1975); Curt Gentry, *The Madams of San Francisco* (1964; reprint, New York: Ballantine, 1971); Jacqueline Baker

Barnhart, *The Fair but Frail: Prostitution in San Francisco, 1849–1900* (Reno: University of Nevada Press, 1986); Allan Bérubé, *Coming Out Under Fire: The History of Gay Men and Women in World War Two* (New York: Free Press, 1990), 273.

[11] On the Beats, see Bruce Cook, *The Beat Generation* (New York: Scribner, 1971); Steven Watson, *The Birth of the Beat Generation: Visionaries, Rebels, and Hipsters, 1944–1960* (New York: Pantheon, 1995).

[12] On Hefner's rise to fame, see Russell Miller, *Bunny: The Real Story of Playboy* (London: M. Joseph, 1984).

[13] Chronology of Playboy Enterprises history, unpublished, Playboy Enterprises, Chicago, 16. On the history of *Playboy* and the clubs, see Gretchen Edgren, *The Playboy Book: Forty Years* (Santa Monica, Calif.: General Publishing Group, 1994); Ellen Lupton, "Playboy's Penthouse Apartment," in *Stud: Architectures of Masculinity,* ed. Joel Sanders (New York: Princeton Architectural Press, 1996) 28–41; Gay Talese, *Thy Neighbor's Wife* (Garden City, N.Y.: Doubleday, 1980); Frank Brady, *Hefner* (New York: Macmillan, 1974); Victor Lownes, *The Day the Bunny Died* (Secaucus, N.J.: Lyle Stuart, 1983); Oriana Fallaci, "Hugh Hefner: 'I Am in the Center of the World,'" *Look,* 10 January 1967, 54–57; *New York Times,* 26 June 1963, 26; Simon Nathan, "About the Nudes in Playboy," *U.S. Camera,* April 1962, 45–47, 68–80; Calvin Tomkins, "Playboy of the Western World," *Saturday Evening Post,* 23 April 1966, 96–101; "Think Clean," *Time,* 3 March 1967, 76–82. The best critical study of *Playboy*'s role in American history is to be found in Barbara Ehrenreich, *The Hearts of Men: American Dreams and the Flight from Commitment* (Garden City, N.Y.: Doubleday, 1983).

[14] "Disneyland for Adults," *Playboy,* October 1963, 166.

[15] William L. O'Neill, *American High: The Years of Confidence, 1945–1960* (New York: Free Press, 1986).

[16] Quoted in Arthur Berger, "Varieties of Topless Experience," *Journal of Popular Culture,* vol. 4, no. 2 (1970): 419–24. See also "Topless," *Playboy,* September 1966, 160–67.

CHAPTER 3

[1] Lyndon Johnson, "State of the Union," reprinted in *New York Times,* 5 January 1965.

[2] John M. Riddle, *Contraception and Abortion from the Ancient World to the Renaissance* (Cambridge, Mass.: Harvard University Press, 1992), 57–73; John T. Noonan, Jr., *Contraception: A History of Its Treatment by Catholic Theologians and Canonists* (Cambridge, Mass.: Belknap, 1965), 9–29.

[3] See Noonan, *Contraception,* 171–99.

[4] Ibid., 387–437.

[5] Nicola Kay Beisel, *Imperiled Innocents : Anthony Comstock and Family Reproduction in Victorian America* (Princeton, N.J.: Princeton University Press, 1997); Heywood Broun and Margaret Leech, *Anthony Comstock: Roundsman of the Lord* (New York: Boni, 1927).

[6] The history of the birth control movement is now extensively documented. See Carole R. McCann, *Birth Control Politics in the United States, 1916–1945* (Ithaca, N.Y.: Cornell University Press, 1994); Ellen Chesler, *Woman of Valor: Margaret*

Sanger and the Birth Control Movement in America (New York: Simon & Schuster, 1992); Linda Gordon, *Woman's Body, Woman's Right: Birth Control in America*, rev. ed. (New York: Penguin, 1990); James Reed, *The Birth Control Movement and American Society: From Private Vice to Public Virtue* (1978; reprint, Princeton, N.J.: Princeton University Press, 1983); David M. Kennedy, *Birth Control in America: The Career of Margaret Sanger* (New Haven, Conn.: Yale University Press, 1970); J. M. Ray and F. G. Gosling, "American Physicians and Birth Control, 1936–1947," *Journal of Social History* 18 (1985): 399–411; Cynthia Goldstein, "The Press and the Beginnings of the Birth Control Movement in the United States," Ph.D. diss., Pennsylvania State University, 1985; David J. Garrow, *Liberty and Sexuality: The Right to Privacy and the Making of Roe v. Wade* (New York: Macmillan, 1994). A useful bibliographic source is Gloria Moore and Ronald Moore, *Margaret Sanger and the Birth Control Movement: A Bibliography, 1911–1984* (Metuchen, N.J.: Scarecrow Press, 1986).

[7] Ashley Montagu, "The Pill," *Phi Delta Kappan*, May 1968, 480–84.

[8] Quoted in Elizabeth Siegel Watkins, *On the Pill: A Social History of Oral Contraceptives, 1950–1970* (Baltimore: Johns Hopkins University Press, 1998), 36.

[9] Bernard Asbell, *The Pill: A Biography of the Drug That Changed the World* (New York: Random House, 1995).

[10] Sam Blum, "The Pill," *Redbook*, January 1966, 76; "Freedom From Fear," *Time*, 7 April 1967, 78; Gloria Steinem, "The Moral Disarmament of Betty Coed," *Esquire*, September 1962, 98.

[11] Quoted in "The Pill," *Redbook*, 74.

[12] Stephen Bloom, " 'The Pill': Hard to Swallow," review of Asbell, *The Pill, Washington Post*, 26 July 1995. Asbell does not give any indication of the origin of the pill's generic name in his account, but Bloom claims the first use of the term "the pill" can be found in Huxley's *Brave New World Revisited*: "Many of us choose birth control — and immediately find ourselves confronted by a problem that is simultaneously a puzzle in physiology, pharmacology, sociology and even theology. 'The Pill' has not yet been invented."

[13] "The Pill," 76.

[14] Madeline Gray, *Margaret Sanger: A Biography of the Champion of Birth Control* (New York: R. Marek, 1979), 435.

[15] Two recent articles discuss family planning policy in the 1960s but do not explore the religious controversies over those policies. See Donald Critchlow, "Birth Control, Population Control, and Family Planning: An Overview," *Journal of Policy History* 7 (1995): 1–21; John Sharpless, "World Population Growth, Family Planning and American Foreign Policy," *Journal of Policy History* 7 (1995): 72–102.

[16] Elly Foote to ACLU, 30 July 1963, ACLU papers, Mudd Library, Princeton University.

[17] Information in this chapter based on interview with Bill Baird by the author, telephone, 12 December 1997; see also Garrow, *Liberty and Sexuality*, 314–17.

[18] Connecticut General Statute, Revised 43-32, 54-196 (1958).

[19] Quoted in *PPLC* [Planned Parenthood League of Connecticut] *News*, May 1975, in the FPOHP-Griswold collection, Schlesinger Library, Harvard University.

[20] Garrow, *Liberty and Sexuality*, 131–54. Estelle Griswold Oral History, FPOHP-Griswold collection.

[21] See Susan Friedland, "The Bitter Pill: A Study of Pembroke University's [sic] Birth Control Policies During the 1960's," unpublished senior thesis, Brown University, 1988.

[22] Danny Noble, "Freud Wouldn't Approve," American University *Eagle*, 11 January 1966.

[23] Letters to the editor, American University *Eagle*, 11 February 1966; the original copy of the letter is in the university archives, Gellman Library.

[24] Beth Bailey, "Prescribing the Pill: Politics, Culture and Sexual Revolution in America's Heartland," *Journal of Social History* 30, no. 4 (1997).

[25] *Philadelphia Inquirer*, 29 September 1965. At the time, North Philadelphia was composed of 29 percent whites and 71 percent nonwhites, 15 to 20 percent of whom were Puerto Rican. The Philadelphia NAACP eventually endorsed the state's proposed birth control program; but debate in Pennsylvania over the racial dynamics of contraception continued throughout the sixties.

[26] *New York Times*, 11 August 1968, 44.

[27] "The Black Woman and Birth Control," *Ebony*, March 1968, 29–32.

CHAPTER 4

[1] Jefferson Poland and Sam Sloan, eds., *The Sex Marchers* (Los Angeles: Elysium Press, 1968); "Sexual Freedom?" *Newsweek*, 6 September 1965, 20; "The Free Sex Movement," *Time*, 11 March 1966, 66; Arthur Hoppe, "The Defenders of Skinny-Dipping," *San Francisco Chronicle*, 25 August 1965, 41. See also Linda Grant, *Sexing the Millennium* (New York: Grove, 1994), 135–46. This being 1965, the four protesters did not even take off their suits until they were well under water.

[2] Poland and Sloan, *Sex Marchers*, 43. Information for this chapter came from correspondence between the author and Poland.

[3] Jefferson Poland to Dr. William Erwin, Free University of New York, 22 September 1965, Sexual Freedom League (SFL) collection, Bancroft Library, University of California at Berkeley.

[4] Candace Falk, *Love, Anarchy, and Emma Goldman*, rev. ed. (New Brunswick, N.J.: Rutgers University Press, 1990); Alice Wexler, *Emma Goldman: An Intimate Life* (New York: Pantheon, 1984); Stoehr, *Free Love in America*; Roger A. Bruns, *The Damndest Radical: The Life and World of Ben Reitman, Chicago's Celebrated Social Reformer, Hobo King, and Whorehouse Physician* (Urbana: University of Illinois Press, 1987); Emma Goldman, *Marriage and Love* (New York: Mother Earth, 1916), microfilm, Schlesinger Library; Mary Gabriel, *Notorious Victoria: The Life of Victoria Woodhull, Uncensored* (Chapel Hill, N.C.: Algonquin Books of Chapel Hill, 1998); Barbara Goldsmith, *Other Powers: The Age of Suffrage, Spiritualism, and the Scandalous Victoria Woodhull* (New York: Knopf, 1998); Lois Beachy Underhill, *The Woman Who Ran for President: The Many Lives of Victoria Woodhull* (Bridgehampton, N.Y.: Bridge Works, 1995). Other free-love advocates are described in Spurlock, *Free Love*.

[5] Poland and Sloan, *Sex Marchers*, passim.

6 Leo Koch, mimeograph, SFL collection.

7 Interview with Tuli Kupferberg by the author, New York, 30 December 1995.

8 Reich was in trouble with the FDA for transporting "orgone" boxes across state lines; the boxes were meant to be therapeutic devices designed to trap "orgone" energy. It is not known why the FDA destroyed Reich's personal library. Norman Mailer, Saul Bellow, Paul Goodman, and William Burroughs were all in Reichian therapy at some point and kept his ideas alive in bohemian circles. Reich died in federal prison. Myron Sharaf, *Fury on Earth: A Biography of Wilhelm Reich* (New York: St. Martin's, 1983), 335–57; interview with Myron Sharaf by the author, Boston, 3 October 1994; interview with Marvin and Betty Mandel by the author, Boston, 2 October 1994. Sympathetic biographical and intellectual sketches of Reich include Charles Rycroft, *Reich* (London: Fontana, 1971), and James Wyckoff, *Wilhelm Reich: Life Force Explorer* (Greenwich, Conn.: Fawcett, 1973).

9 Interview with Randy Wicker by the author, New York, 29 December 1995. Wicker's homophile activities are discussed in D'Emilio, *Sexual Politics, Sexual Communities*, 125, 158–61. See also "The Hippie Business," *New Republic*, 10 June 1967, and Daniel Hurewitz, *Stepping Out: Nine Tours Through New York City's Gay and Lesbian Past* (New York: Holt, 1997), 295. Hurewitz interviewed Wicker for his book.

10 Wicker interview; Kupferberg interview.

11 Bob Holmes to Jefferson Poland, 17 June 1964, SFL collection.

12 Poland and Sloan, *Sex Marchers*, 14. Susan Sontag wrote a glowing review of *Flaming Creatures* in 1964 in the *Nation*, reprinted in *Against Interpretation* (1966; reprint, New York: Anchor, 1990), 226–31. In addition, the film won *Film Culture* magazine's Fifth Independent Film Award. See also Richard H. Kuh, *Foolish Figleaves? Pornography in — and out of — Court* (New York: Macmillan, 1967), 40, 96.

13 Jefferson Poland to Tuli Kupferberg, 16 August 1964; Poland to *Esquire*, 7 October 1964; Deputy Director, New York Public Library, to Poland, 20 October 1964; Poland to Deputy Director, NYPL, 16 November 1964, SFL collection. It is unclear to what extent the protest actually caused a change in the library's policies.

14 "March to Legalize Prostitution Out of Step with Law," *New York Daily News*, 24 August 1964. In his novel *The Harrad Experiment* (see chapter 6, below), Robert Rimmer mocked the New York League for Sexual Freedom's protests as "pitiful and foolish."

15 A Homosexual League of New York had been founded in 1962 but was short-lived. Donn Teal, *The Gay Militants* (1971; reprint, New York: St. Martin's, 1995), 28. Randy Wicker essentially led a one-man campaign to increase homosexual visibility from 1962 to 1965. The campaign, which directly resulted in articles on gay rights in the *Village Voice, Harper's,* and the *New York Post*, was surprisingly successful. See D'Emilio, *Sexual Politics, Sexual Communities*, 158–62.

16 Randolfe Wicker to Robert McNamara, 20 September 1964, SFL collection; Poland and Sloan, *Sex Marchers*, 51–52. For a provocative analysis of the Walter Jenkins affair, see Lee Edelman, "Tearooms and Sympathy, or, The Epistemology of the Water Closet," in *The Lesbian and Gay Studies Reader*, ed. Henry Abelove et al. (New York: Routledge, 1993), 553–74.

[17] Randy Wicker to Jefferson Poland, March 1965, SFL collection.

[18] University of California at Berkeley Police Department Report 27222; "Report and Recommendations of the Ad Hoc Committee on Student Conduct," n.d., Social Protest collection, Bancroft Library, UC Berkeley.

[19] Alpha Epsilon Pi to Chancellor Myerson, 25 March 1965, Social Protest collection.

[20] Correspondence dated 8 July 1965, Social Protest collection.

[21] Milton Viorst, *Fire in the Streets: America in the 1960s* (New York: Simon & Schuster, 1979), 301.

[22] *Daily Californian*, 12 March 1965, 19 May 1965, Social Protest collection; Poland and Sloan, *Sex Marchers*, 17.

[23] Professor Thomas Parkinson to Professor Whinnery, 16 March 1965, Social Protest collection.

[24] See, for instance "Sexual Freedom?" *Newsweek*, 6 September 1965, 20.

[25] Lester Kirkendall, "Sex Education: A Reappraisal," *The Humanist*, Spring 1965, 75–85.

[26] "Sex Comes to Stanford," *San Francisco Chronicle*, 4 January 1966, 66.

[27] Sexual Freedom League brochure, c.1966, Peter Stafford collection, Columbia University.

[28] Quoted in "The Free Sex Movement," *Time*, 11 March 1966, 66.

[29] Sexual Freedom League brochure, c.1966. "Make Love, Not War" — unlike other slogans of the day, such as "Fuck for Peace" — could be printed in any newspaper. Dana Lancaster, age twenty-three, was arrested in Berkeley in 1965 for wearing a button reading "Fuck for Peace." Poland and Sloan, *Sex Marchers*, 8.

[30] "Free Sex Movement," 66; Sexual Freedom League brochure, c.1966.

[31] "Resolution on Race and Gender as Sexual Restrictions" proposed to Thanksgiving Sexual Rights Conference Meeting, 25–26 November 1966, CSFF, SFL collection.

[32] *New York Times*, 25 April 1966, front page.

[33] Group for the Advancement of Psychiatry, Committee on the College Student, *Sex and the College Student* (New York: Atheneum, 1966), 98. The GAP authors, citing the Kinsey Reports and developments in the field of psychology, even recognized homosexuality as a normal part of college life. In the report's most controversial statement, the authors recommended that administrators ignore private homosexual activity among students. These recommendations were publicized in mainstream newspapers; see "Psychiatrists Offer Colleges Sex Advice," *New York Times*, 12 December 1965, front page.

CHAPTER 5

[1] See, for example, Laurel Thatcher Ulrich, *Good Wives: Image and Reality in the Lives of Women in Northern New England, 1650–1750* (New York: Vintage, 1982), 89–105. A good summary of recent work on Puritan sexuality and American sexuality in general can be found in John D'Emilio and Estelle B. Freedman, *Intimate Matters: A History of Sexuality in America* (New York: Harper & Row, 1988).

² John Willett, "Ugh . . . ," *Times Literary Supplement,* 14 November 1963, reprinted in *William S. Burroughs at the Front: Critical Reception, 1959–1989,* ed. Jennie Skerl and Robin Lydenberg (Carbondale: Southern Illinois University Press, 1991). Ihab Hassan, "The Subtracting Machine: The Work of William Burroughs," *Critique* 6 (1963), reprinted in *William S. Burroughs at the Front,* 55. *Playboy,* January 1963, 34.

³ General works on the history of censorship include Charles Rembar, *The End of Obscenity: The Trials of Lady Chatterley, Tropic of Cancer, and Fanny Hill* (New York: Random House, 1968) and Edward de Grazia, *Girls Lean Back Everywhere: The Law of Obscenity and the Assault on Genius* (New York: Random House, 1992). An account sympathetic to the cause of censorship is Rochelle Gurstein, *The Repeal of Reticence: A History of America's Cultural and Legal Struggles over Free Speech, Obscenity, Sexual Liberation, and Modern Art* (New York: Hill and Wang, 1996). The most helpful reference work is de Grazia, *Censorship Landmarks* (New York: Bowker, 1969).

⁴ Leslie Fishbein, "Freud and the Radicals: The Sexual Revolution Comes to Greenwich Village," *Canadian Review of American Studies* 12, no. 2 (Fall 1981): 183–84; Fishbein, *Rebels in Bohemia: The Radicals of the Masses, 1911–1917* (Chapel Hill: University of North Carolina Press, 1982).

⁵ Arnold Maddaloni, "Schroeder — The Public Excuser: A Biographical Outline to Which Are Added Some Published Opinions Concerning His Personal Traits" Stamford, Conn., 1936), Ben Reitman Papers, University of Illinois at Chicago Center; Theodore Schroeder, *"Obscene Literature" and Constitutional Law* (privately printed, 1911), Schroeder papers, Columbia University. On the history of the ACLU, see Samuel Walker, *In Defense of American Liberties: A History of the ACLU* (New York: Oxford University Press, 1990). The ACLU shunned obscenity cases for many years.

⁶ On the *Ulysses* case, see Paul Vanderham, *James Joyce and Censorship: The Trials of Ulysses* (New York: New York University Press, 1998); Michael Moscato and Leslie LeBlanc, eds., *The United States of America v. One Book Entitled Ulysses by James Joyce: Documents and Commentary: A 50-Year Retrospective* (Frederick, Md.: University Publications of America, 1984); *The United States of America v. One Book Entitled Ulysses,* 8 F. Supp. 182 (1933).

⁷ D. H. Lawrence, "Pornography and Obscenity" (1929), in *The Portable D. H. Lawrence,* ed. Diana Trilling (New York: Penguin, 1977), 653–57.

⁸ Eberhard Kronhausen and Phyllis Kronhausen, *Pornography and the Law: The Psychology of Erotic Realism and Pornography* (New York: Ballantine, 1959), 23.

⁹ Phyllis and Eberhard Kronhausen, comp., *Erotic Art: A Survey of Erotic Fact and Fancy in the Fine Arts* (New York: Grove, 1968), 22.

¹⁰ George P. Elliot, "Against Pornography," in *Perspectives* 87. Originally published in *Harper's,* 8 March 1965, 51–60.

¹¹ Kronhausen and Kronhausen, *Pornography and the Law,* 23.

¹² Paul Goodman, "Pornography, Art and Censorship," in *Perspectives* 59. Originally published in *Commentary,* March 1961, 203–12.

¹³ See William Karl Thomas, *Lenny Bruce: The Making of a Prophet* (Hamden, Conn.: Archon, 1989).

[14] Kenneth Tynan, Foreword, *How to Talk Dirty and Influence People: An Autobiography* by Lenny Bruce (Chicago: Playboy Press, 1972), 8.

[15] Quoted in *Contemporary Authors* vol. 89–92, 456.

[16] De Grazia, *Girls Lean Back,* 444–49.

[17] Hearings Before the Select Committee on Current Pornographic Materials, House of Representatives, 82nd Congress, 1952, 153.

[18] James Gilbert, *A Cycle of Outrage: America's Reaction to the Juvenile Delinquent in the 1950s* (New York: Oxford University Press, 1986), 80.

[19] Committee on the Bill of Rights, Report on Book Burning, Record of the Bar of the City of New York, vol. 10, no. 3, March 1955.

[20] House Hearings, *Current Pornographic Materials,* 342.

[21] On the Roth and Alberts cases, see Leon Friedman, ed., *Obscenity: The Complete Oral Arguments Before the Supreme Court in the Major Obscenity Cases* (New York: Chelsea House, 1970), 7–65; Kuh, *Foolish Figleaves?,* 27–42; Talese, *Thy Neighbor's Wife,* passim; Brief of Morris Ernst, *Samuel Roth v. United States,* Grove Press papers, Syracuse University Library; *Roth v. United States,* 354 U.S. 476 (1957); interview with Roger Fisher by the author, Cambridge, 5 September 1994. For reasons that are unclear, Violet Alberts was not sent to jail with her husband.

[22] *Sunshine Book Company v. Summerfield,* 355 U.S. 372 (1958).

[23] Quoted in de Grazia, *Girls Lean Back,* 298fn.

[24] On Rosset, see S. E. Gontarski, "Dionysus in Publishing: Barney Rosset, Grove Press, and the Making of a Countercanon," *Review of Contemporary Fiction* 10, no. 3, (Fall 1970): 7–19; John Oakes, "Barney Rosset and the Art of Combat Publishing: An Interview," ibid., 20–57. On the "Howl" case, see Lawrence Ferlinghetti, "Horn on Howl" (1957) in *The Portable Beat Reader,* ed. Ann Charters (New York: Penguin, 1992), 254–63.

[25] Harry T. Moore, review of Grove Press edition, *New York Times Book Review,* 3 May 1959. In 1932, two years after Lawrence's death, Knopf had published an expurgated version of the text. According to a Lawrence biographer, the Knopf edition was a "mutilated," "emasculated" version which "omit[ed] Lawrence's faithful descriptions of the love experience and his use of the four-letter words in a way which [Lawrence] believed was therapeutic." In 1944, Dial Press published an early version of the book which had few of Lawrence's more daring scenes. Nevertheless, the New York Society for the Suppression of Vice seized four hundred copies of Dial's book. There were other attempts to publish portions of *Lady Chatterley's Lover,* but they had all led to prosecutions and arrests.

[26] Donald Lucas, secretary general of the Mattachine Society, to Barney Rosset, 20 January 1960, Grove Press papers, Syracuse University.

[27] Henry Miller, *Tropic of Cancer* (New York: Evergreen, 1980), 5.

[28] John Ciardi, "Manner of Speaking," *Saturday Review,* 30 June 1962, 13. Interview with Andrea Dworkin by the author, New York, 22 February 1995.

[29] Anthony Lewis, "The Most Recent Troubles of 'Tropic,'" *New York Times,* 21 January 1962.

[30] Quoted in Rembar, *End of Obscenity,* 211.

[31] Interview with Barney Rosset by the author, New York, 20 February 1994.

[32] Kuh, *Foolish Figleaves?*, 64.

[33] *Jacobellis v. Ohio,* 84 S. Ct. 1676 (1964).

[34] "Inquiry into Smut Urged by Doctors," *New York Times,* 24 November 1964.

[35] American Library Association, *Newsletter on Intellectual Freedom,* November 1964, 79.

[36] New York League for Sexual Freedom flier, Albert Ellis's personal papers.

[37] *A Book Named "John Cleland's Memoirs of a Woman of Pleasure" v. Attorney General,* 86 S. Ct. 975 (1966).

[38] The idea of using the concept of "pandering" to convict pornographers was originated by Sheldon Glueck in the 1950s. Glueck suggested the pandering theory to Louis B. Schwartz of the American Law Institute in a letter dated 31 January 1956, Sheldon Glueck collection, Harvard Law Library. Nonetheless, the court found Ginzburg guilty of a crime for which he was never charged or indicted. See the dissenting opinions by Justices Harlan and Stewart, *Ginzburg v. United States,* 86 S. Ct. 969 (1966). Because of a bureaucratic error, Ginzburg served only three years of his sentence.

[39] This theory is suggested by Gay Talese in *Thy Neighbor's Wife,* 321. Ginzburg's attorney, Sydney Dickstein, on the other hand, says racial attitudes had nothing to do with the case. Interview with Dickstein by the author, telephone, 25 November 1997.

[40] De Grazia, *Girls Lean Back,* 480.

[41] Ted Morgan, *Literary Outlaw: The Life and Times of William S. Burroughs,* (New York: Holt, 1988), 35.

[42] Quoted in ibid., 296.

[43] *Attorney General v. A Book Named Naked Lunch* 218 N.E. 2d 571 (1966).

[44] Harry Levin, "The Unbanning of Books," in *Perspectives on Pornography,* ed. Douglas A. Hughes (New York: St. Martin's 1970), 20. First published in the *Atlantic Monthly,* 1966.

CHAPTER 6

[1] Robert H. Rimmer, *The Harrad Experiment* (New York: Bantam, 1967), 62.

[2] Ibid., 7.

[3] Ibid., 41, 172.

[4] "Apology from a Man in Search of a Fulcrum," unpublished manuscript (1969), Robert Rimmer collection, Mugar Memorial Library, Boston University, later published in Rimmer, comp., *The Harrad Letters to Robert H. Rimmer* (New York: New American Library, 1969). Betty Friedan to Robert Rimmer 6 January 1968; Mary-Averett Seelye to Rimmer 23 January 1968, Rimmer collection. Friedan wrote: "I have been recommending your book to a good many future-minded people in a number of fields and it may lead to all sorts of interesting things, even to new architectural thinking on dormitory design." Abraham Maslow to Rimmer, 8 November 1967; Tolbert McCarrol to Rimmer, 26 January 1967, Rimmer collection.

5 Letters to Robert Rimmer from Gary Hawkins, 30 July 1969; George Gutierez, 8 June 1968; Lynn Rabinow, August 1967; Mrs. Barry Asch, n.d.; Linda Schummer, 22 July 1967; anonymous fan, 16 March 1967, all in the Rimmer collection.

6 Robert H. Rimmer, Afterword, *The Harrad Experiment, Special Anniversary Edition* (Buffalo: Prometheus Books, 1990), 313.

7 Interview with Robert Rimmer by the author, Boston, 15 April 1994.

8 James R. Smith and Lynn Smith, eds., *Beyond Monogamy: Recent Studies of Sexual Alternatives in Marriage* (Baltimore: Johns Hopkins University Press, 1974), 2–3.

9 Letters to Robert Rimmer from Burleigh Angle, 13 April 1967; John Evans, 11 November 1968; Sharon Meyers, 8 January 1968; "Memorandum: To Members of Mr. Stark's G.S. 100 Preceptorial," January 1968; Walter Hunt to Rimmer, 12 February 1969, all in the Rimmer collection.

10 Interview with Linda Price [pseud.] by the author, telephone, 3 July 1998.

11 Interview with Scott Bloom [pseud.] by the author, telephone, 3 July 1998.

12 Paul E. Johnson and Sean Wilentz, *The Kingdom of Matthias* (New York: Oxford University Press, 1994).

13 Midpeninsula Free University Catalogue (Winter 1968), Rimmer collection. Talese, *Thy Neighbor's Wife*, 330. Reese Danley Kilgo, "Can Group Marriage Work?" in *Sexual Issues in Marriage: A Contemporary Perspective,* ed. Leonard Gross (New York: Spectrum, 1975), 223. Quoted in Grant, *Sexing the Millennium*, 165. Rimmer, *Harrad Letters* and *You and I . . . Searching for Tomorrow* (New York: Signet, 1971). Cited in Morton Hunt, "The Future of Marriage," in *The Sensuous Society* (Chicago: Playboy Press, 1973), 113.

14 Robert Heinlein to Lurton Blassingame, 21 October 1960, in *Grumbles from the Grave: Robert A. Heinlein,* ed. Virginia Heinlein (New York: Del Ray, 1989), 229.

15 Interview with Charlie Dellin [pseud.] by the author, telephone, 22 May 1998.

16 Interview with Oberon Zell by the author, telephone, 9 June 1998.

17 Interview with Morning Glory by the author, telephone, 9 June 1998.

18 Interview with Art Green [pseud.] by the author, telephone, 17 May 1998.

19 Interview with Howard Kolding [pseud.] by the author, telephone, 6 June 1998.

CHAPTER 7

1 *Loving v. Virginia,* 388 U.S. 1 (1967); Robert J. Sickels, *Race, Marriage and the Law* (Albuquerque: University of New Mexico Press, 1972); Peter Irons and Stephanie Guitton, eds., *May It Please the Court: The Most Significant Oral Arguments Made Before the Supreme Court Since 1955* (New York: New Press, 1993), 277–89.

2 On the intersection of racial and sexual attitudes in American history, see Martha Hodes, ed., *Sex, Love, Race: Crossing Boundaries in North American History* (New York: New York University Press, 1999).

3 Eugene D. Genovese, *Roll, Jordan, Roll: The World the Slaves Made* (1965; reprint, New York: Random House, 1975), 458–75.

4 In one instance, spectators cheered as a sixteen-year-old white boy dragged the body of a dead black man through the streets by his genitals. Iver Bernstein, *The*

New York City Draft Riots: Their Significance for American Society and Politics in the Age of the Civil War (New York: Oxford University Press, 1990), 29–31.

[5] Norman Mailer, "The White Negro: Reflections on Hipsterism," reprinted in *Advertisements for Myself* (New York: Putnam, 1959), 374–75. Hilary Mills points out that Mailer's concept of the white Negro derived almost directly from Chandler Brossard's 1952 novel *Who Walk in Darkness* about a black man who passes for white. See Mills, *Mailer: A Biography* (New York: Empire, 1982), 180.

[6] Gene D. Matlock, "Here's Why Whites Persecute Negroes," *Pittsburgh Gazette,* 8 March 1958, 5. See also Robert Staples, "The Mystique of Black Sexuality," *Liberator* 7 (March 1967); Robert Staples, comp., *The Black Family: Essays and Studies,* 2nd ed. (Belmont, Calif.: Wadsworth, 1978); Frantz Fanon, *Black Skin, White Masks,* trans. Charles Lam Markham (New York: Grove, 1967); Alvin Poussaint, "Sex and the Black Male," *Ebony,* August 1972, 114–20; Charles Herbert Stember, *Sexual Racism: The Emotional Barrier to an Integrated Society* (New York: Elsevier, 1976).

[7] *Time,* 1 June 1959, 19. "The Final Question," *Fact,* January-February 1966, 3–13.

[8] Daniel Patrick Moynihan, "The Negro Family: The Case for National Action" (Washington, D.C.: U.S. Government Printing Office, 1965), 8–9. On the Moynihan Report, see Lee Rainwater and William L. Yancey, *The Moynihan Report and the Politics of Controversy* (Cambridge, Mass.: MIT Press, 1967). On the history of American attitudes toward race and illegitimacy, see Solinger, *Wake Up Little Susie.* On the sociology of race and contraception, see Joseph McFalls and George Masnick, "Birth Control and the Fertility of the U.S. Black Population, 1880–1980," *Journal of Family History* 6 (1981): 89–106; Jessie May Rodrique, "The Afro-American Community and the Birth Control Movement, 1918–1942," Ph.D. diss., University of Massachusetts, 1991; Simone Marie, "Race, Class and Reproduction: The Evolution of Reproductive Policy in the United States," Ph.D. diss., Clark University, 1989; McCann, *Birth Control Politics.*

[9] Thomas Edwards Brown, "Sex Education and Life in the Negro Ghetto," *Pastoral Psychology,* May 1968; 45–54.

[10] Interview with Professor Nell Painter by the author, Princeton, 13 November 1997.

[11] Interview with Donna Stanton [pseud.] by the author, telephone, 10 November 1997.

[12] Alvin F. Poussaint, "The Stresses of the White Female Worker in the Civil Rights Movement in the South," *American Journal of Psychiatry,* October 1966, 401–407. See also Sara Evans, *Personal Politics: The Roots of Women's Liberation in the Civil Rights Movement and the New Left* (1979; reprint, New York: Vintage, 1980), 24–101.

[13] Quoted in Mary Aickin Rothschild, *A Case of Black and White: Northern Volunteers and the Southern Freedom Summers, 1964–1965* (Westport, Conn.: Greenwood, 1982), 135. See also Sally Belfrage, *Freedom Summer* (New York: Viking, 1965).

[14] Quoted in Evans, *Personal Politics,* 80.

[15] Rothschild, *Case of Black and White,* 127–44.

[16] Eldridge Cleaver, *Soul on Ice* (New York: McGraw-Hill, 1967). Stanley Pacion responded in *Dissent:* "Rather than breaking through the reader's conditioned

thought patterns and responses, [*Soul on Ice*] plays on them. Its doctrines of racial and biological superiority, though novel because Cleaver reverses them, have a long history of acceptance in the West . . . Cleaver's scorn for the impotent, weak, degenerate intellectual and his praise of black virility have an all too familiar ring." Quoted in Kathleen Rout, *Eldridge Cleaver* (Boston: Twayne, 1991), 39.

[17] Rout, *Eldridge Cleaver*, 85.

[18] Cleaver, *Soul on Ice*, 14.

[19] Cleaver quoted in Andrew Kopkind, "To Off a Panther," in *Decade of Crisis: America in the '60s* (New York: World, 1972), 59–60.

[20] *The Struggle for Equality*, dir. Jeff Dupre, 1996, documentary film.

[21] Frank C. Tribbe to Albert Ellis, 16 August 1965, Albert Ellis papers, personal collection

[22] *Time*, 29 September 1967, 28.

[23] Quoted in Irons and Guitton, *May It Please the Court*, 286.

CHAPTER 8

[1] On the youth culture of the sixties, see Todd Gitlin, *The Sixties: Years of Hope, Days of Rage* (New York: Bantam, 1987); Joan Didion, *Slouching Towards Bethlehem* (New York: Farrar, Straus & Giroux, 1968); David Caute, *The Year of the Barricades: A Journey Through 1968* (New York: Harper & Row, 1988); James Miller, *Democracy Is in the Streets: From Port Huron to the Siege of Chicago* (New York: Simon & Schuster, 1987); Viorst, *Fire in the Streets*; Morris Dickstein, *Gates of Eden: American Culture in the Sixties* (New York: Basic, 1977); Charles R. Morris, *A Time of Passion: America, 1960–1980* (New York: Harper & Row, 1984).

[2] It had been a hard year for Yale. On St. Patrick's Day, over a thousand students had participated in a snowball fight that forced the school to impose a curfew on all four thousand undergraduates; some Irish students later claimed that the snowball fight was a racially motivated, anti-Irish riot. On the Suzie scandal, see "Morals Charges Weighed at Yale," *New York Times*, 17 January 1960, 66; "Twenty at Yale Fined in Morals Case, Eight Still in School to be Expelled," *New York Times*, 28 January 1960; "Three More at Yale Held on Sex Charge," *New York Times*, 20 January 1960; "Eleven More Arrested in Scandal at Yale," *New York Times*, 27 January 1960. Author interview with David P., 10 February 1998.

[3] Eleanor D. Macklin, "Going Very Steady: Cohabitation in College," *Psychology Today*, November 1974, 56.

[4] Group for the Advancement of Psychiatry, *Sex and the College Student*, 9.

[5] G. B. Blaine, *Sex Mores in Transition* (Cambridge, Mass.: Office of the Dean of Harvard College, 1963).

[6] Jennie Loitman Barron, "Too Much Sex on Campus," *Ladies' Home Journal*, February 1964, 48–52. See also Willard Dalrymple, MD, "A Doctor Speaks of College Students and Sex," *Princeton Alumni Weekly*, 15 March 1966, 21–25.

[7] Quoted in James G. Allen et al., "Coeducational Residence Halls," *Journal of College Student Personnel* 6, no. 2 (December 1964): 82–87.

8 See Carl Danziger, *Unmarried Heterosexual Cohabitation* (San Francisco: R & E Research Associates, 1978).

9 Matthew R. Sgan, "Social Area and Room Visiting Privileges in College Housing," *Journal of College Student Personnel* 6, no. 5 (September 1965): 269–71.

10 "Testimony Given by Linda LeClair at Judicial Council Hearing," 16 April 1968, Linda LeClair collection, Barnard College archives. See Beth Bailey, "Sexual Revolution(s)," in *The Sixties*, ed. Farber, 235–62. Bailey argues that for LeClair the real issue was not sexual rights but equal rights; she thus portrays LeClair as a radical feminist. The primary source record contradicts Bailey's claim.

11 Letters to President Peterson; "Barnard College — Not By Itself," WDIX radio station, Orangeburg, South Carolina, Linda LeClair collection.

12 Deirdre Carmody, "Barnard Protest Follows Affair," *New York Times*, 15 March 1968, 42; "Barnard Opens Hearing on Sophomore Who Lied," *New York Times*, 12 April, 1968, 71; Deirdre Carmody, "Barnard Considering Decision on Student Living with Man," *New York Times*, 17 April 1968, 51; Deirdre Carmody, "Barnard Unit Against Expelling Girl Who Lives With Boyfriend," *New York Times*, 18 April 1968, front page; Deirdre Carmody, "Head of Barnard Asks Parents of Defiant Girl for Their Views," *New York Times*, 19 April 1968, front page. John Fenton, "Father Despairs of Barnard Daughter," *New York Times*, 20 April 1968, 27; "Barnard Girl Plans to See Her Parents," *New York Times*, 21 April 1968, 72; "Sex and the Single College Girl," *New York Times*, 21 April 1968, sec.4, 9; Deirdre Carmody, "Barnard President Delays Action on Defiant Girl," *New York Times*, 9 May 1968, 42.

13 United Press International, 28 February 1969.

14 Andrew Hacker, "The Pill and Morality," *New York Times Magazine*, 21 November 1963, 138.

15 Ira L. Reiss, *The Social Context of Premarital Sexual Permissiveness* (New York: Holt, Rinehart and Winston, 1967). "Sexual Freedom," *PTA Magazine*, April 1968, 2–6. Erwin O. Smigel and Rita Seiden, "The Decline and Fall of the Double Standard," *Annals of the American Academy of Political and Social Science*, March 1968, 6–17.

16 "An Intimate Revolution in Campus Life," *Life*, 20 November 1970, 32–41.

17 Interview with Sean Wilentz by the author, Princeton, 17 November 1997.

18 Interview with Valerie Goldberg [pseud.] by the author, telephone, 30 August 1997.

19 Timothy Miller, *The Hippies and American Values* (Knoxville: University of Tennessee Press, 1991), 64.

20 "Lovers of the World, Unite," *Cavalier*, February 1967.

21 Interview with Jack Gelfand by the author, Princeton, 10 August 1997.

22 J. L. Simmons and Barry Winograd, *It's Happening: A Portrait of the Youth Scene Today* (Santa Barbara: Marc-Laird, 1966), 109–10.

23 David E. Smith, "Sexual Practices in the Hippie Subculture," *Medical Aspects of Human Sexuality*, April 1972, 142–51.

24 Interview with Andrew Wallace by the author, New York, 30 April 1997.

25 Evans, *Personal Politics*, passim. On gender roles in the 1960s see Peter G. Filene, *Him/Her/Self: Sex Roles in Modern America*, 2nd ed. (Baltimore: Johns Hopkins University Press, 1986), 177–221.

[26] Alice Echols, *Daring to Be Bad: Radical Feminism in America, 1967–1975* (Minneapolis: University of Minnesota Press, 1989), 120, 123.

[27] Interviews by the author with Anne Koedt, New York, 28 January 1996; Rita Mae Brown, telephone, 22 December 1997; Elizabeth Gipps, telephone, 20 June 1998.

[28] Interview with Stephanie Black [pseud.] by the author, telephone, 20 June 1998.

[29] Interview with Betty Dodson by the author, New York, 12 September 1995.

[30] Abe Peck, *Uncovering the Sixties: The Life and Times of the Underground Press* (New York: Pantheon, 1985), 47; see also Gitlin, *The Sixties*, 219.

[31] Crumb quoted in Peck, *Underground Press*, 51. Shulamith Firestone, *The Dialectic of Sex: The Case for Feminist Revolution* (1970; reprint, New York: Bantam, 1972), 143.

[32] Gloria Steinem, "The Moral Disarmament of Betty Co-ed," *Esquire*, September 1962, 154–55.

[33] Kate Millett, *Sexual Politics* (Garden City, N.Y.: Doubleday, 1970), 62.

[34] Ibid., 23.

[35] Alix Kates Shulman, "Sex and Power: Sexual Bases of Radical Feminism," *Signs* 5 (1980): 593.

[36] Robin Morgan, *Going Too Far: The Personal Chronicle of a Feminist* (New York: Random House, 1977), 165, 166. Atkinson quoted in Dana Densmore, "On Celibacy," in *Voices from Women's Liberation*, ed. Leslie Tanner (New York: New American Library, 1970), 264; also quoted in Alice Echols, "The Taming of the Id: Feminist Sexual Politics 1968–83," in *Pleasure and Danger: Exploring Female Sexuality*, ed. Carole S. Vance (Boston: Routledge & K. Paul, 1984), 57. Interview with Ti-Grace Atkinson by the author, New York, 20 May 1997; see also Atkinson, *Amazon Odyssey* (New York: Links, 1974).

[37] Interview with Ellen Willis by the author, New York, 20 May 1997; Dana Densmore, *No More Fun and Games* 1, no. 1 (October 1968, reprinted December 1969). See also Dana Densmore, "Independence from the Sexual Revolution," in *Notes from the Third Year: Women's Liberation* (New York, 1971).

[38] J. McGough and C. Lindt Gollin, "Coeducational Housing: A Survey of Student Opinion at the American University," December 1969, American University archives, Gellman Library. The survey reflected the responses of 442 students.

CHAPTER 9

[1] In a survey of 500 Catholic couples in northern New Jersey, 422 of the couples said they believed the Church would ultimately allow a woman to take the pill for one reason or another. Rev. James T. McHugh, "Family Life Survey, Preliminary Report," 19 March 1965, National Catholic Welfare Conference (NCWC) Records, Washington, D.C. In 1930, Pope Pius XI issued the encyclical *Casti Connubii* declaring all contraception to be illicit. In 1951, however, Pope Pius XII indicated that married couples might morally avoid intercourse during the fertile period of a woman's menstrual cycle. In 1958, Pius XII stated that there were permissible uses of "artificial contraception" — for example, on the advice of a physician to prevent uterine disease — but that the use of the pill with the intention of preventing conception was expressly prohibited. Three years later, Pope John XXIII

made it plain that population control was not a valid use of the pill. See John R. Cavanagh, *The Popes, the Pill, and the People: A Documentary Study* (Milwaukee: Bruce, 1965), 7. In 1962, John XXIII convened the Second Vatican Council, which led to a new spirit of ecumenism within the Church, causing many to believe that the Church would formally approve "artificial" contraception.

2 See, for example, Charles F. Westoff et al., *Family Growth in Metropolitan America* (Princeton, N.J.: Princeton University Press, 1961), and Ronald Freedman, Pascal K. Whelpton, and Arthur A. Campbell, *Family Planning, Sterility and Population Growth* (New York: McGraw-Hill, 1959). This second study found that 57 percent of married Catholics were engaging in some form of family planning, with 30 percent using unapproved methods. On the history of Catholicism in the United States, see James Hennesey, *American Catholics: A History of the Roman Catholic Community in the United States* (New York: Oxford University Press, 1981), which touches briefly on the 1960s; Jay P. Dolan, *The American Catholic Experience: A History from Colonial Times to the Present* (Garden City, N.Y.: Doubleday, 1985); Patrick Allitt, *Catholic Intellectuals and Conservative Politics in America, 1950–1985* (Ithaca, N.Y.: Cornell University Press, 1993), contains a section on sexual politics and contraception, 163–203. On the pill controversy, see Loretta McLaughlin, *The Pill, John Rock, and the Church: The Biography of a Revolution* (Boston: Little, Brown, 1982), and Asbell, *The Pill.*

3 On this controversy, see McLaughlin, *The Pill, John Rock, and the Church*. On Rock's contribution to the development of the pill, see also Reed, *The Birth Control Movement*, passim. There were efforts to have Rock excommunicated, but these were blocked by his powerful ally, Cardinal Cushing of Boston (McLaughlin, *The Pill*, 156–57). The bishop was Monsignor Francis W. Carney of Cleveland, quoted in McLaughlin, 164.

4 Fan letter to John Rock, 12 January 1964, Countway Medical Library, Harvard University.

5 "Summaries of 'News of Population and Birth Control,' published by the International Planned Parenthood Federation of America, March–Nov. 1962," NCWC Memorandum, NCWC Records.

6 See, for example, Father John J. Lynch, S.J., "Progestational Steroids: Some Moral Problems," *Linacre Quarterly* 25: 93–99. John C. Ford, professor of moral theology at Catholic University, encouraged the director of the NCWC Family Life Bureau to accept Lynch's reasoning: John C. Ford, S.J., to Rt. Rev. Msgr. Irving A. DeBlanc, 18 May 1961, NCWC Records.

7 Memo, n.d., n.a., NCWC Records.

8 *Planned Parenthood News*, Spring 1960.

9 Also see "Book of the Month," *Catholic World,* December 1961, 173–74, NCWC Records. In the Lambeth Conferences of 1930 and 1958, the British Council of Churches accepted birth control. See Francis Canavan, "Reflections on the Revolution in Sex," *America,* 6 March 1965, 312–15.

10 Alastair Heron, ed., *Towards a Quaker View of Sex: An Essay by a Group of Friends* (London: Friends House, 1963), 36.

11 Canavan, "Reflections," 312–15.

12 Heron, *Towards*, 40.

[13] Quoted in Canavan, "Reflections," 314.

[14] David Lawrence Edwards, ed., *The "Honest to God" Debate: Some Reactions to the Book "Honest to God"* (London: SCM Press, 1963), 7–12.

[15] John A. T. Robinson, *Honest to God* (Philadelphia: Westminster Press, 1963), 118–19.

[16] Canavan, "Reflections," 312–15.

[17] "Cleric Asks Aid to Homosexuals; Criticizes Church on Counseling," *New York Times,* 12 August 1963, 43. "The New Protestant Debate Over Sex," *Redbook,* October 1964, 56–57, 104–106.

[18] All quoted in Miller, *Bunny,* 119; 121–22.

[19] See Harvey Cox, ed., *The Situation Ethics Debate* (Philadelphia: Westminster Press, 1968), 9. Esalen catalog, 1966; Janus Society newsletter, January 1966, Albert Ellis's personal papers. *New York Times,* 29 November 1967, 1.

[20] Joseph Walsh, "Sex and the College Campus," *Commonweal,* 24 February 1967, 596. Sidney Callahan, "Human Sexuality in a Time of Change," *Christian Century,* 28 August 1968, 1079–80.

[21] Interview with Ted McIlvenna by the author, San Francisco, 20 March 1995.

[22] D'Emilio, *Sexual Politics, Sexual Communities,* 192–94.

[23] Playboy Panel on Homosexuality, reprinted in *The Sensuous Society,* 83–107.

[24] David Mace, "The Sexual Revolution: Its Impact on Pastoral Care and Counseling," *Journal of Pastoral Care* 25, no. 4 (December 1971): 220–32.

[25] See the Reverend Raymond Lawrence, "Guidelines for a Flexible Monogamy" and "The Affair as a Redemptive Experience," in *Adventures in Loving,* ed. Robert Rimmer (New York: New American Library, 1973), 58–69.

[26] Interview with Jonathan West [pseud.] by the author, telephone, 10 June 1998.

[27] As Barbara Ehrenreich et al. point out in *Re-making Love: The Feminization of Sex* (Garden City, N.Y.: Doubleday, 1986), evangelical Christians actually imbibed some of the basic doctrines of the sexual revolution and began encouraging married couples to add spice to their sexual lives.

CHAPTER 10

[1] Kenneth Tynan, *Curtains* (New York: Atheneum, 1961), 369.

[2] Both quoted in Martin Gottfried, *Opening Nights: Theater Criticism of the Sixties* (New York: Putnam, 1969), 657–68.

[3] Quoted in Kathleen Tynan, *The Life of Kenneth Tynan* (New York: Morrow, 1987), 370.

[4] Jack Kroll, "Eros Goes Public," *Newsweek,* 30 June 1969, 81.

[5] Tynan, *Life of Kenneth Tynan,* 58–59; 32.

[6] Quoted in Jack Kroll, "Waiting for Calcutta," *Newsweek,* 16 June 1969, 107.

[7] Kathleen Tynan, 362.

[8] Interview with Pamela Pilkenton [pseud.], telephone, 8 June 1998.

[9] Interview with Jacques Levy by the author, telephone, 7 June 1998.

[10] "Report of Commissioner Charles H. Keating, Jr.," *The Report of the Commission on Obscenity and Pornography* (1970), 610.

[11] Kroll, "Eros Goes Public."

[12] Bernard Grossman, "Need Theater Breed the Ridiculous?" *Performing Arts Review* 1, no. 2 (1970): 201–206. See also Delores Brudick's response to Grossman's article, "The Moral Function of 'Immoral' Theater," *Performing Arts Review* 1, no. 3 (1970): 445–51.

[13] "Sex and the Arts," *Newsweek,* 14 April 1969.

[14] See Jack W. McCullough, *Living Pictures on the New York Stage,* (Ann Arbor, Mich.: UMI Research Press, 1983), passim.

[15] Dan Sullivan, "Nudity Moves Into Center Stage," *New York Times,* 25 April 1968, 52. "Theater of the Nude," *Playboy,* clipping, 1968, Rochelle Owens collection, Boston University. J. L. Styan, *Modern Drama in Theory and Practice,* vol. 2 (New York: Cambridge University Press, 1981), 169–70.

[16] Vivian Cruise to John Wallach, 7 July 1967.

[17] C. L. Sulzberger, "Foreign Affairs: Sex and Sense," *New York Times,* 5 December 1969.

[18] Martin Esslin, "Nudity: Barely the Beginning," *New York Times,* 15 December 1968.

[19] *New Republic,* 12 April 1969, 29.

[20] Interview with original cast member by the author; Larry Bercowitz, n.t., *East Village Other,* 2 April 1969.

[21] Arthur Knight and Hollis Alpert, "Sex in Cinema, 1969," *Playboy,* November 1969, 264.

[22] See, for example, "'Chelsea Girls' Film Is Seized in Boston by Vice Detectives," *New York Times,* 31 May 1967; Underground Film Is Seized at U. of Michigan Showing," *New York Times,* 29 January 1967, 27.

[23] "The Sixties — Hollywood Unbuttons," *Playboy,* April 1968, 204.

[24] See Vilgot Sjöman, *I Am Curious (Yellow): The Complete Scenario of the Film with Over 250 Illustrations,* trans. Martin Minow and Jenny Bohman (New York: Grove, 1968).

[25] *New York Times,* 11 March 1969, 42; 7 June 1969.

[26] Quoted in James Riordan and Jerry Prochnicky, *Break On Through: The Life and Death of Jim Morrison* (New York: Morrow, 1991), 186.

[27] Ibid., 298.

[28] "Photographer Says Mrs. Onassis Used Judo on Him," *New York Times,* 6 October 1969.

[29] Gottfried, *Opening Nights,* 658.

[30] On the phenomenon of performativity, see Judith Butler, *Excitable Speech: A Politics of the Performative* (New York: Routledge, 1997).

[31] Al Hansen, *A Primer of Happenings and Time/Space Art* (New York: Something Else Press, 1965).

[32] Allan Kaprow, *Assemblage, Environments and Happenings* (New York: Abrams, 1966), 324, 339. These two happenings did not have spectators, per se, but all the participants were amateurs and the happenings were photographed.

[33] Arno Karlen, "The Sexual Revolution Is a Myth," *Saturday Evening Post,* 28 December 1968, 12.

CHAPTER 11

[1] Both quoted in Fleming and Fleming, *First Time,* 136; 254.

[2] Morton Hunt, *Sexual Behavior in the 1970s* (New York: Dell, 1974), 66–67.

[3] Philip Roth, *Portnoy's Complaint* (New York: Random House, 1969), 17; 134.

[4] It is important to note that *Portnoy's Complaint* can be read as a sexist diatribe against women. See Lynne Segal, *Straight Sex: Rethinking the Politics of Pleasure* (Berkeley: University of California Press, 1994), 22.

[5] Alfred C. Kinsey et al., *Sexual Behavior in the Human Male* (Philadelphia: Saunders, 1948), 510.

[6] Quoted in Bennet and Rosario, "Introduction," *Solitary Pleasures,* 1–17.

[7] Bennett and Rosario, "Introduction: The Politics of Solitary Pleasures," in *Solitary Pleasures,* 1–18. On the anti-circumcision movement, see Alex Comfort, *The Anxiety Makers: Some Curious Preoccupations of the Medical Profession* (1967; reprint, New York: Dell, 1969); Vern L. Bullough and Bonnie Bullough, *Sin, Sickness, and Sanity: A History of Sexual Attitudes* (New York: Garland, 1977), 68–70. Consider the following medical advice from 1935:

> I suggest that all male children should be circumcised. This is "against nature," but that is exactly the reason why it should be done. Nature intends that the adolescent male shall copulate as often and as promiscuously as possible, and to that end covers the sensitive glans so that it shall be ever ready to receive stimuli. Civilization, on the contrary, requires chastity, and the glans of the circumcised rapidly assumes a leathery texture less sensitive than skin. Thus the adolescent has his attention drawn to his penis much less often. I am convinced that masturbation is much less common in the circumcised. With these considerations in view it does not seem apt to argue that "God knows best how to make little boys."
> — R. W. Cockshut, "Circumcision," *British Medical Journal,* 2 (1935): 764.

[8] Reay Tannahill, *Sex in History* (New York: Stein and Day, 1980), 343. Bullough, *Sin, Sickness,* 55–73.

[9] C. S. Lewis, *The Scewtape Letters* (Uhrichsville, OH: Barbour Publishing, 1974).

[10] Fleming and Fleming, *First Time,* 40.

[11] Kinsey, *Sexual Behavior in the Human Male,* 513.

[12] "Sex Education of the Physician," Ortho Panel Report, clipping, Mary Steichen Calderone collection, Schlesinger Library, Harvard University. The study found that 20 percent of faculty members believed that masturbation led to insanity.

[13] Lynn and Kellerman both quoted in Fleming and Fleming, *First Time,* 171; 111.

[14] Kinsey, *Sexual Behavior in the Human Female,* 166–71. For a feminist evaluation of psychoanalysis, see Susan Lydon, "The Politics of Orgasm," in *Sisterhood Is Powerful: An Anthology of Writings from the Women's Liberation Movement,* ed. Robin Morgan (New York: Vintage, 1979), 219–28.

[15] Kinsey, op. cit., 135; 142.

[16] Material on Dodson comes from Betty Dodson, *Liberating Masturbation: A Meditation on Self Love* (New York: Bodysex Designs, 1974), and an interview with Dodson by the author, New York, 12 September 1995.

[17] Unidentifiable clipping, Dodson's personal collection.

[18] Steinem interview.

[19] For information on the Atthis Collective, I wish to thank Saralyn Chestnut, who attended its workshops, and mentioned them in a paper on the Charis Bookstore at the American Historical Association Annual Conference, Atlanta, 1995.

[20] Betty Dodson, "Getting to Know Me," *Ms*, August 1974, 106–9. The letters are in Dodson's personal collection.

[21] Hunt, *Sexual Behavior*, 83; 99.

CHAPTER 12

[1] The Stonewall riots are described by Morty Manford in Eric Marcus, ed., *Making History: The Struggle for Gay and Lesbian Equal Rights, 1945–1990: An Oral History* (New York: HarperCollins, 1993), 199–204. There are numerous accounts of what happened that night, each with a slightly different chronology of events. See Martin Duberman, *Stonewall* (New York: Dutton, 1993), 181–212. Brief accounts can also be found in D'Emilio, *Sexual Politics, Sexual Communities*, 231–33; Teal, *Gay Militants*, 1–7; Toby Marotta, *The Politics of Homosexuality* (Boston: Houghton Mifflin, 1981), 71–76.

[2] On life before Stonewall, see D'Emilio, *Sexual Politics*, 40–53.

[3] There is now a rich literature on the history of how modern science came to define and describe homosexuality as both an identity and a pathology. See, for instance, Michel Foucault, *The History of Sexuality*, vol. 1, trans. Robert Hurley (New York: Pantheon, 1978); Randy Trumbach, "Gender and the Homosexual Role in Modern Western Culture: The 18th and 19th Centuries Compared," in *Homosexuality, Which Homosexuality?* ed. Dennis Altman et al. (London: GMP, 1989), 149–69; Jeffrey Weeks, *Coming Out: Homosexual Politics in Britain from the Nineteenth Century to the Present* (London: Quartet, 1977); Weeks, *Sex, Politics, and Society: The Regulation of Sexuality Since 1800* (London: Longman, 1981): David F. Greenberg, *The Construction of Homosexuality* (Chicago: University of Chicago Press, 1988). Historian George Chauncey has given substantial attention to how gay men used language to identify and classify themselves: Chauncey, *Gay New York: Gender, Urban Culture, and the Making of the Gay Male World 1890–1940* (New York: Basic, 1994). Since so many aspects of sexuality are socially constructed — not the least of which is the very notion of sexual identity — the labels "gay," "lesbian," and "straight" are highly problematic and have been all but discarded by queer theorists. Nonetheless, I have found it nearly impossible to write narrative history without falling back on these traditional, identitarian terms. As someone whose own sexuality has never conformed nicely to such simple categorizations, I appreciate the critique of simplistic labels both intellectually and emotionally, but I have found it necessary to sacrifice a certain amount of accuracy for the sake of overall clarity.

[4] Widespread homophobia made it dangerous for gays to identify themselves and thus deprived young gays of information about themselves. But the hunt for homosexuals could also have the opposite effect. In the military, for instance, the

practice of grilling recruits about their sexual histories inadvertently informed thousands of young men about homosexual behavior and customs. Young men came out of the Army and Navy well educated about homosexual life. See Bérubé, *Coming Out Under Fire.*

5 On the impact of Prohibition and its repeal, see George Chauncey, *Gay New York.* On cultural anxieties in the early sixties, see Lee Edelman, "Tearooms and Sympathy, or, The Epistemology of the Water Closet," in *The Lesbian and Gay Studies Reader,* ed. Henry Abelove et al. (New York: Routledge, 1993).

6 See Ehrenreich, *Hearts of Men,* 14–28.

7 See John D'Emilio, "The Homosexual Menace: The Politics of Sexuality in Cold War America," in *Passion and Power: Sexuality in History,* ed. Kathy Peiss and Christina Simmons (Philadelphia: Temple University Press, 1989), 226–40; George Chauncey, "The Postwar Sex Crime Panic," in *True Stories from the American Past,* ed. William Graebner (New York: McGraw-Hill, 1993), 160–78.

8 See Robert J. Corber, *In the Name of National Security: Hitchcock, Homophobia, and the Political Construction of Gender in Postwar America* (Durham, N.C.: Duke University Press, 1993).

9 "Remarks made by Dr. Anne Clark to Framingham women," 13 May 1959, box 7, folder 69, MSSH collection, Schlesinger Library.

10 ACLU papers, Mudd Library, Princeton University.

11 Quoted in Peter Fisher, *The Gay Mystique* (New York: Stein and Day, 1972), 145.

12 "Growth of Overt Homosexuality in City Provokes Wide Concern," *New York Times,* 17 December 1963, 1. "The Homosexual in America," *Time,* 21 January 1966, 41. Andrew Kopkind, *The Thirty Years' Wars: Dispatches and Diversions of a Radical Journalist, 1965–1994* (London: Verso, 1995), xxiii.

13 "Homosexuality in America," *Life,* 26 June 1964, 66–74. Three months after the *Life* article, the *New York Times* noted that raids on gay bars were increasing: Sam Blum, "To Get the Bars Back on Their Feet," *New York Times Magazine,* 27 September 1964, 68. See also Chris Mohr, "World of Affluent Youth Favors 'In' Dancing at City Hideaways," *New York Times,* 30 March 1964, 84.

14 "Growth of Overt Homosexuality"; "Cafe Drive Turns to Homosexuals," *New York Times,* 1 December 1960.

15 Donald Vining, *A Gay Diary* (New York: Pepys, 1979), 30 May 1955, 47; 13 June 1957, 120; 3 November 1955, 74.

16 Interview with George Mansour by the author, Cambridge, 15 October 1994. Interview with Kenneth Pitchford by the author, New York, 22 February 1995. On at least one occasion, Jack Kerouac, William Burroughs, and Allen Ginsberg went together to the Everard, where they had sex and Kerouac was fellated by French sailors. Barry Miles, *Ginsberg: A Biography* (New York: Viking, 1989), 68.

17 The following extract gives a good sense of the Janus Society's position:

> Many of the other homophile organizations have stayed relatively free of trouble because they have confined their interests to what is known abstractly as the "rights of the homosexual." Janus, through *DRUM,* has taken a different view. We center our attention on the homosexual himself. Our objective, in a word, is a gay *Playboy,* with the news coverage of *Time.* In so striving, we are rocking the boat. By putting the "sex" back into homosexuality,

by producing a magazine geared to the homosexual as an individual who is something other than an abused, ever-sinned-against outcast, by approaching our goals with a light and sometimes audacious view, and by being unequivocally pro-homosexual, we will continue to rock the boat.

— "For Members Only," Janus Society newsletter, February 1965, Janus folder, International Gay Information Center, New York Public Library.

[18] F. Valentine Hooven, *Beefcake: The Muscle Magazines of America, 1950–1970* (Koln: Benedikt Taschen, 1995), 122. The move toward ever more explicit imagery continued. By the late sixties, several magazines were available showing fully nude males. In 1967, in Los Angeles, the owners of Directory Services Incorporated were indicted on twenty-seven counts of obscenity after sending photographs of male nudes through the mail, but with help from the Mattachine Society, which supplied expert witnesses for the defense, the owners were acquitted. Interview with Hal Call by the author, San Francisco, 8 July 1996.

[19] Karla Jay and Allen Young, "Out of the Closets into the Streets," in *Out of the Closets: Voices of Gay Liberation,* ed. Karla Jay and Allen Young (New York: Douglas, 1972), 8–10. Thomas Maddux, acting chairman, Texas Student League for Responsible Sexual Freedom, to ACLU, 11 March 1966, ACLU papers.

[20] See D'Emilio, *Sexual Politics,* 108–25.

[21] Stephen Donaldson [pseud.], "The Anguish of the Student Homosexual," *Columbia Spectator,* April 1968. Idem, letter to the editor, *New York Times,* 3 December 1967. Interview with Jim Shenton by the author, telephone, 14 October 1998.

[22] Murray Schumach, "Columbia Charters Homosexual Group," *New York Times,* 3 May 1967 (the article is filled with inaccuracies).

[23] Bertram Selverstone to Grayson Kirk, 7 May 1967. Grayson Kirk to John C. Fowler, 12 June 1967; to *L.A. Daily Journal,* 1 June 1967, Columbia University archives.

[24] Quoted in Teal, *Gay Militants,* 40. The "Statement of Purposes" of the Student Homophile League at Cornell University declared: "SHL is not a social organization, but rather a civil libertarian and educational one." Student Homophile League collection, Cornell University library. D'Emilio, *Sexual Politics,* 210.

[25] On the history of the gay press, see Rodger Streitmatter, *Unspeakable: The Rise of the Gay and Lesbian Press in America* (Boston: Faber and Faber, 1995).

[26] Quoted in Marotta, *Politics of Homosexuality,* 186.

[27] For a discussion of the Janus-faced nature of the play, see Nicholas de Jongh, *Not in Front of the Audience: Homosexuality on Stage* (New York: Routledge, 1992), 133–39.

[28] On the APA and the successful campaign to remove homosexuality from the DSM, see Ronald Bayer, *Homosexuality and American Psychiatry: The Politics of Diagnosis* (New York: Basic, 1981). "Family Life Education: A Community Responsibility (Proceedings of a Symposium on Sex Education for Those Involved in Any Aspect of Education or Counseling)," 8, 23 September 1967, Toronto, Mary Steichen Calderone collection, Schlesinger Library, Harvard University.

[29] Joshua S. Golden, "What Is Sexual Promiscuity?," *Medical Aspects of Human Sexuality,* October 1968, 52.

30 Alfred Chester, "Fruit Salad," *New York Review of Books* clipping, Grove Press papers, Syracuse University Library.

31 Marvin Garson, "Queer Power for Queer People," *San Francisco Express Times,* 21 January 1969, 7, Peter Stafford collection, Columbia University library. (Garson's article was published nearly twenty years before AIDS activists began chanting, "We're here, we're queer, get used to it!") L. Craig Shoomaker to Dick Leitsch, 1 February 1969, International Gay Information Center collection, New York Public Library.

32 Quoted in Marotta, *Politics of Homosexuality,* 144.

33 Quoted in Teal, *Gay Militants,* 38–39.

34 "The Homosexual: Newly Visible, Newly Understood," *Time,* 31 October 1969, 56–67.

35 Joseph Epstein, "The Struggle for Sexual Identity," *Harper's,* September 1970, 51.

36 Quoted in Marotta, *Politics of Homosexuality,* 184.

37 Mark Thompson, ed., *Long Road to Freedom: The Advocate History of the Gay and Lesbian Movement* (New York: St. Martins, 1994), 35–37.

38 Flier, Christopher Street Liberation Day committee, Mickey Zacuto collection, Lesbian History Archives, Brooklyn, New York.

39 Marotta, *Politics of Homosexuality,* 80. It is important to remember that most activists in the 1960s, not just gay ones, saw themselves as participants in a revolution that many believed was on the verge of transforming American society forever.

40 Norman Mailer, *Cannibals and Christians* (New York: Dial, 1966), 200–201.

41 Helen Lawrenson, "Androgyne, You're a Funny Valentine," *Esquire,* March 1965, 80–83.

42 Quoted in Peter Babcock, "Meet the Women of the Revolution," *New York Times Magazine,* 9 February 1969, 34.

43 Charles Winick, "The Beige Epoch: Depolarization of Sex Roles in America," *Annals of the American Academy of Social Science,* March 1968, 18–24.

44 Dan Wakefield, "The War at Home," *Atlantic Monthly,* October 1969, 119. Paradoxically, as Barbara Ehrenreich points out in *The Hearts of Men,* this was the period when self-identified gay men were increasingly wearing hypermasculine hairstyles and uniforms.

45 *HI!: The Newsletter of the Homosexuals Intransigent!,* n.d., Homosexuals Intransigent folder, Mattachine collection, International Gay Information Center, New York Public Library.

46 Fisher, *Gay Mystique,* 227.

47 Jay and Young, "Out of the Closets," 29.

48 Paul Goodman, "Memoirs of an Ancient Activist," *Win* magazine, 1969, reprinted in *The New Gay Liberation Book: Writings and Photographs About Gay (Men's) Liberation,* ed. Len Richmond (Palo Alto, Calif.: Ramparts Press, 1979), 36, 37.

49 Interview with Jim Kepner by the author, Los Angeles, 27 November 1995. To raise money for the League, Poland sold his own sexual services to men and women alike, though he charged a higher rate for men.

50 Marotta, *Politics of Homosexuality,* 80.

51 Jonathan Ned Katz, "Introduction to the 1995 Edition," Teal, *Gay Militants*, xviii–xx.

52 *Screw*, 4 July 1969; reprinted in Teal, *Gay Militants*, 10.

53 Interview with Michael Bronski and Charlie Shively by the author, Cambridge, 28–29 April, 1994.

54 Thompson, *Long Road to Freedom*, 36–37. John R. Burger, *One-Handed Histories: The Eroto-Politics of Gay Male Video Pornography* (New York: Haworth, 1995), 16.

55 Marotta, *Politics of Homosexuality*, 196.

56 "Self-Indulgence as an Act of Revolution," *Fag Rag*, n.d., 1, Michael Bronski's personal papers. The idea was a form of gross Marcusianism; see chapter 16.

CHAPTER 13

1 *Hospital Physician*, June 1970.

2 William H. Masters and Virginia E. Johnson, *Human Sexual Inadequacy* (Boston: Little, Brown, 1970), 193–213, 358–59.

3 Richard Rhodes, "A Short Course in How to Be Happy," *Book World*, 14 June 1970.

4 Harold Lief, "The Therapeutic Adequacy of Masters and Johnson," *Psychiatry and Social Science Review*, October 1970, 4. "Sexual Inadequacy: What Can Be Done," *Life*, 1 May 1970, clipping, Mudd papers.

5 See Vern L. Bullough, *Science in the Bedroom: A History of Sex Research* (New York: Basic, 1994), 196–200.

6 See Irvine, *Disorders of Desire*, 78; 192. The best analysis of Masters and Johnson can still be found in Robinson, *Modernization of Sex*, 120–90, which highlights the many ways Masters and Johnson shielded themselves with the trappings of science. Behind their scientistic facade were a host of ideological assumptions and unscientific techniques. Robinson shows how Masters and Johnson reaffirmed the value of heterosexual union and even marriage, while claiming to be "value-free" in their work.

7 Masters and Johnson, "Sex and Marriage," *Redbook*, September 1970, 83, clipping, Mudd papers. See Ruth and Edward Brecher, ed., *An Analysis of "Human Sexual Response"* (Boston: Little, Brown, 1966).

8 Masters quoted in Irvine, *Disorders of Desire*, 81. Robinson, *Modernization of Sex*, 123.

9 "Roundtable: Frigidity," *Medical Aspects of Human Sexuality* 11, no. 2 (February 1978): 30.

10 Letters to the editor, *Medical World News*, 12 June 1970.

11 "The Womanization of America," Playboy Roundtable, *Playboy*, June 1962.

12 "Craftsmen of Sexuality," *New York Times*, 27 April 1970. "Sexual Double Standard," *Washington Post*, 22 April 1970.

13 Masters and Johnson, "Sex, Guilt and the Double Standard," *Redbook*, October 1970, 117.

14 Lief, "Therapeutic Adequacy."

[15] Theodore Van de Velde's *Ideal Marriage* (1930) is considered the prototype of the modern marriage manual. For a brief analysis of early marriage manuals, see Michael Gordon, "From an Unfortunate Necessity to a Cult of Mutual Orgasm: Sex in American Marital Education Literature 1830–1940," in *The Sociology of Sex*, 53–77.

[16] Raymond Wagoneer, Emily Mudd, and Marshall Shearer, "Training Dual Sex Teams for Rapid Treatment of Sexual Dysfunction," May 1973, box 3, folder 159, Mudd papers.

[17] Diary of Eunice Lake [pseud.], 27 December 1974, Robert Rimmer collection. "Eunice Lake" was a pseudonym chosen by the author when she considered publishing the diary.

[18] Leticia Kent, "Vital Questions that People Don't Ask . . . And Should: An Exclusive Interview with Masters and Johnson," *Vogue*, 15 August 1971, 91.

[19] Patricia E. Raley, *Making Love: How to Be Your Own Sex Therapist* (New York: Dial, 1976), 205.

[20] "All About the New Sex Therapy," *Newsweek*, 27 November 1972, 65.

[21] Masters and Johnson, *The Pleasure Bond: A New Look at Sexuality and Commitment* (Boston: Little, Brown, 1974), 251–68. According to some reports, Masters resisted such forays into unscientific terrain but Johnson was eager to speak on emotional and psychological issues.

[22] Philip Nobile, "What Is the New Impotence and Who's Got It?" *Esquire*, October, 1972, 95–98, 218.

[23] George Ginsberg, William Frosch, and Theodore Shapiro, "The New Impotence," *Mental Health Digest* 4, no. 4: 19–20. In the *Esquire* article, Ginsberg is quoted as saying that he does not *blame* the women's movement for the problem: "This is not a question of women's lib, but rather the way a man perceives it." See M. L. Elliot, "The Use of 'Impotence' and 'Frigidity': Why Has 'Impotence' Survived?" *Journal of Sex and Marital Therapy* 11: 51–56.

CHAPTER 14

[1] Judy Klemsrud, "Plain Brown Wrappers Are Out," *New York Times*, 15 August 1970. By the end of 1971, Reuben had earned over $1 million in royalties. Royalty Statement 1 July 1971–31 December 1971, Harold Matson Co. collection, Columbia University.

[2] Craig Tennis to David Reuben, 8 April 1971, Harold Matson Company collection, Columbia University.

[3] David R. Reuben, *Everything You Always Wanted to Know About Sex* . . . *But Were Afraid to Ask* (New York: David McKay, 1969), 53; 233.

[4] John Money and Robert Athanasiou, unpublished review of *Everything You Always Wanted to Know*, 1971, Institute for Research in Sex, Gender and Reproduction, Indiana University.

[5] Reuben, *Everything*, 149; 147–48.

[6] Ibid., 69; 41.

[7] "More Than You Want to Know About Sex," *Newsweek*, 24 August 1970, 42; Lige Clark and Jack Nichols, "World's Most Freaked Out Shrink," *Screw*, 9 February

1970, 21, Arthur Bell papers, International Gay Information Center, New York Public Library.

[8] Quoted in "Sex: How to Read All About It," *Newsweek,* 24 August 1970, 42.

[9] Bayer, *Homosexuality and American Psychiatry,* 98. The book was eventually removed from the reading list after gay activists protested.

[10] C. Nash Herndon and Ethel M. Nash, *Journal of the American Medical Association* 180 (5 May 1962): 395.

[11] *Journal of the American Medical Association,* 194, no. 4 (25 October 1965): 145.

[12] "Roundtable: Frigidity," *Medical Aspects of Human Sexuality* 11, no. 2 (February 1978): 31.

[13] Judd Marmor to Lonny Myers, 18 November 1971, Lonny Myers collection, University of Illinois at Chicago Center.

[14] *Sexology* was a sex education magazine founded in 1933 and intended to be a "documentation of facts, pure and simple, with that difference, however, that all articles are written so that anyone can understand them." Aimed at men, sixteen years and older, *Sexology,* "devoted to the science of sex hygiene," was sold on newsstands. It was published by Hugo Gernsback, a science-fiction publisher and amateur inventor.

[15] *Medical Aspects of Human Sexuality,* clipping, n.d., Myers collection.

[16] See Gordon V. Drake, *SIECUS: Corrupter of Youth* (Christian Crusade Publications, 1969), Mary Steichen Calderone collection, Schlesinger Library, Harvard University.

[17] Mary Steichen Calderone to Lonny Myers, 23 October 1970, in Lonny Myers Oral History, Family Planning Oral History Project, Schlesinger Library. A copy of the letter is also in the Myers collection.

[18] Playboy Interview: Mary Steichen Calderone, *Playboy,* April 1970, 63–240. See also the Mary Steichen Calderone Oral History, Family Planning Oral History Project, Schlesinger Library.

[19] William Edward Glover, Homosexual Information Center, to Nat Lehrman, senior editor, *Playboy,* 16 March 1970, Calderone collection.

[20] John Leo, "Fight on Sex Education is Widening," *New York Times,* 20 May 1968.

[21] "Examples of Basic Concepts Related to Sex Education Curriculum Construction, Grades K to 12," 1996 mimeograph, Institute for Sex Education collection, University of Illinois at Chicago Center.

[22] Howard S. Hoyman, "Basic Issues in School Sex Education," *Journal of School Health,* January 1953, reprint, Institute for Sex Education. Outside of the medical profession, sex educators were developing more objective and pragmatic approaches to teaching children about the body. Lester Kirkendall, who began his career as a sex educator at the University of Oregon using, by his testimony, "a conventional and traditional repressive framework," eventually realized "that this did not help the counselee; sometimes it even made the problem worse." In the early sixties, Kirkendall began trying to talk to students without being didactic. Lester Kirkendall, "Now Is the Time to Prepare! The Need for Social Hygiene Education in a Long Range Program," *Journal of Social Hygiene,* November 1942, reprint. Lester Kirkendall, "Autobiographical Statement," unpublished, Institute for the Advanced Study of Human Sexuality, San Francisco.

[23] Jerry M. Lama, Office of VD Information and Education, Chicago Board of Health to Institute for Sex Education Conference, 6 November 1970, Institute for Sex Education collection.

[24] Stanley E. Willis III, "Sexual Promiscuity as a Symptom of Personal and Cultural Anxiety," *Medical Aspects of Human Sexuality* 1, no. 2 (October 1967): 22.

[25] Marion O. Lerrigo and Helen Southard, *Approaching Adulthood* (Chicago: American Medical Association, 1970), 15–18.

[26] Charles Silverstein, "Ethics of Behavioral Intervention," *Journal of Homosexuality*, Spring 1977, reprinted in *New Gay Liberation Book*, 132. See also Martin Duberman, *Cures: A Gay Man's Odyssey* (New York: Dutton, 1991), and Bayer, *Homosexuality and American Psychiatry*.

[27] On the hearings, see Barbara Seaman, *The Doctors' Case Against the Pill* (Alameda, Calif.: Hunter House, 1995, rev. ed.), vi–ix, 1–7; Grant, *Sexing the Millennium*, 177–83.

CHAPTER 15

[1] *The Report of the Commission on Obscenity and Pornography* (New York: Bantam, 1970), 59.

[2] Ibid., 121–35; 262.

[3] Ibid., 157–59.

[4] James Jones to Burroughs Mitchell, 29 March 1950, in *To Reach Eternity: The Letters of James Jones,* ed. George Hendrick (New York: Random House, 1989), 160–63.

[5] Hearings Before the Subcommittee to Investigate Juvenile Delinquency, U.S. Senate, 1955, 277; 307; 311.

[6] See, for instance, the testimony of Roy Blick, ibid., 280.

[7] Juvenile Delinquency, 72.

[8] Karen Essex and James L. Swanson, *Bettie Page: The Life of a Pin-Up Legend* (Los Angeles: General, 1995).

[9] Juvenile Delinquency, 236.

[10] FBI Law Enforcement Bulletin, 1 January 1960, Lynn Womack collection, Cornell University library.

[11] "Hoover for Check on All Teachers," *New York Times,* 3 July 1962.

[12] FBI Law Enforcement Bulletin.

[13] *Report,* 413–14; 187–95.

[14] *Report,* 273. NB: "It was found that changes in the incidence of sex offenses could not be attributed to legislative change, alteration of law enforcement practices or modified police reporting and data collection procedures."

[15] Ibid., 279.

[16] Ibid., 240.

[17] Ibid., 445.

[18] Walter Kendrick, *The Secret Museum: Pornography in Modern Culture* (New York: Viking, 1987), 1–15.

[19] See, for instance, Todd Gitlin, "The Left and Porno," in *Men Confront Pornography: Twenty-Five Men Take a Candid Look at How Pornography Affects Their Lives, Politics and Sexuality,* ed. Michael S. Kimmel (New York: Penguin, 1990), 102–104.

[20] Quoted in *New York Times,* 12 August 1970.

[21] "Senate Leaders in Both Parties Denounce Findings of Pornography Panel," *New York Times,* 2 October 1970; *New York Times,* 14 October 1970.

[22] *Report,* 456–59.

[23] Ibid., 582.

[24] *New York Times,* 25 October 1970, 71.

CHAPTER 16

[1] Theodore Roszak, *The Making of a Counter Culture: Reflections on the Technocratic Society and Its Youthful Opposition* (Garden City, N.Y.: Doubleday, 1969), 84.

[2] Herbert Marcuse, *Eros and Civilization: A Philosophical Inquiry into Freud* (1955; reprint, Boston: Beacon, 1966), 92, 93, 199, 201.

[3] Interview with Lee Baxandall by the author, Oshkosh, WI, 21 April 1996.

[4] "Freud's Disciple," *Time,* 15 July 1966, 82.

[5] For the best comparison of Marcuse and Brown, see Roszak, *Making of a Counter Culture,* 82–123; see also Herbert Marcuse, "Love Mystified: A Critique of Norman O. Brown," *Commentary,* February 1967, 71–75.

[6] Norman O. Brown, *Life Against Death: The Psychoanalytical Meaning of History* (Middletown, Conn.: Wesleyan University Press, 1959), 307, 308.

[7] Frederick S. Perls, *Ego, Hunger and Aggression: A Revision of Freud's Theory and Method* (1945; reprint, New York: Random House, 1969).

[8] Martin Shepard, *Fritz: An Intimate Portrait of Fritz Perls and Gestalt Therapy* (New York: Dutton, 1975), 57–63.

[9] Quoted in ibid., 92.

[10] Ibid., 70.

[11] Ibid., 58–59.

[12] Quoted in ibid., 159.

[13] Ibid., 197.

[14] Interview with Osha Neumann by the author, telephone, 12 February 1997.

[15] Interview with Camille Paglia by the author, telephone, 17 February 1997.

[16] Marcuse, *Eros and Civilization,* 202.

[17] Ibid., 227–29. Marcuse scoffed at every sixties attempt to eroticize daily life. He was "horrified" by encounter groups like Esalen and sharply critical of pornography. See "A Conversation with Herbert Marcuse," *Psychology Today,* February 1971, 39.

[18] "Conversation," 39.

[19] Interview with Osha Neumann.

[20] Quoted in Shepard, *Intimate Portrait*, 88; 131.

[21] See Ehrenreich, *Hearts of Men*, 95–97.

CHAPTER 17

[1] Elizabeth Andrus, "Oom the Omnipotent: The Tantrik Order in America," unpublished senior thesis, Princeton University, 1999.

[2] Though the legitimation of group sex reached its apex in the 1960s and '70s, the orgy has a long history. Part of the legitimation of group sex, in fact, was the documentation of this history. A recent and interesting discussion of group sex in eighteenth-century England can be found in Lawrence Stone, "Libertine Sexuality in Post-Restoration England: Group Sex and Flagellation among the Middling Sort in Norwich in 1706–07," *Journal of the History of Sexuality*, April 1992, 511–26.

[3] Singles, inexperienced couples, couples with marital discord, unattractive couples, and "hippie-type couples" were not welcome at Golden Sphinx socials. Golden Sphinx newsletter, December 1971, Institute for Sex Research. A rumor was common that some groups played "the key game" in which all the husbands at a particular party would throw their car keys into a pile on the floor. Each woman would then choose a random set of keys from the pile and go home to have sexual intercourse with the owner of the keys. This rumor was repeated and then dismissed as a myth in an article on "The Philosophy of Wife-Swapping" in a swingers' brochure titled *Kindred Spirits*, vol. 1, no. 2, n.d., Kinsey Institute, but the key game was featured prominently in the 1997 feature film *The Ice Storm*. In 1973, *Time* estimated there were twenty swingers' clubs in Southern California alone. Information on Club Wide World comes from an interview with Bob McGinley by the author, telephone, 23 January 1997; on the swingers convention, see Duane Denfeld, "Swinging: The Search for an Alternative," in *Sexual Issues in Marriage: A Contemporary Perspective*, ed. Leonard Gross (New York: Spectrum, 1975), 217–30.

[4] For examples of sociological work on swinging, see Gilbert Bartell, "Group Sex Among the Mid-Americans," *Journal of Sex Research* 6: 113–30; James and Lynn Smith "Co-Marital Sex and the Sexual Freedom Movement," ibid., 132–42; Carolyn Symonds, "Pilot Study of the Peripheral Behavior of Sexual Mate Swappers," master's thesis, University of California, Riverside, 1968. Brian G. Gilmartin, *The Gilmartin Report* (Secaucus, N.J.: Citadel, 1978), originally written as his doctoral dissertation, "The Social Antecedents and Correlates of Comarital Sexual Behavior," at the University of Iowa, 1976, was supported by funds from the NSF.

[5] For a breezy history of American attitudes toward "hygiene," see Suellen Hoy, *Chasing Dirt: The American Pursuit of Cleanliness* (New York: Oxford University Press, 1995).

[6] Eunice Lake diary, 26 January 1975, Robert Rimmer collection, Boston University.

[7] Ibid., 20 March 1975.

[8] Ibid., 15 January 1974; 27 January 1975.

[9] Burgo Partridge, *A History of Orgies* (1958; reprint, New York: Crown, 1960), 20–22.

[10] Quoted in ibid., 55–57.

[11] Ibid., 123–37.

[12] All quotations from interview with Howard Bellin by the author, New York, 3 February 1998.

[13] Interview with John Lobell and Mimi Lobell by the author, telephone, 2–3 May 1998.

[14] Margo Rila, "Group Sex and the History of the Sexual Freedom League," presentation before the Institute for the Advanced Study of Human Sexuality, San Francisco, February 1977.

[15] Dennis Sanders, *Gay Source: A Catalog for Men* (New York: Coward, McCann & Geoghegan, 1997), 196.

[16] "Since everyone hates going the the doctor, especially since in many cases he's just going to give you a shot or oral penicillin and send you packing, many sexually active men have taken to popping tetracycline or other antibiotics at the first sign of a discharge, or even after a night on the town" (ibid., 196).

[17] For a fascinating (if problematic) account of the rise of an anti-jealousy ethos in American life, see Peter N. Stearns, *American Cool: Constructing a Twentieth-Century Emotional Style* (New York: New York University Press, 1994).

[18] Eunice Lake diary, 29–30 January, 1 February, 4 April 1975.

[19] On the limits of "identity" as a framework for conceptualizing sexual desire, see Greenberg, *Construction of Homosexuality*; David M. Halperin, *One Hundred Years of Homosexuality* (New York: Routledge, 1990); Celia Kitzinger, *The Social Construction of Lesbianism* (London: Sage, 1987); Ed Cohen, "Are We (Not) What We Are Becoming? 'Gay,' 'Identity,' 'Gay Studies,' and the Disciplining of Knowledge," in *Engendering Men: The Question of Male Feminist Criticism*, ed. Joseph A. Boone and Michael Cadden (New York: Routledge, 1990); Michel Foucault, "Technologies of the Self," in *Technologies of the Self: A Seminar with Michel Foucault*, ed. Luther H. Martin, Huck Gutman, and Patrick H. Hutton (London: Tavistock, 1988); Jonathan Ned Katz, *The Invention of Heterosexuality* (New York: Dutton, 1995); Marjorie Garber, *Vice Versa: Bisexuality and the Eroticism of Everyday Life* (New York: Simon & Schuster, 1995); Judith Butler, *Gender Trouble: Feminism and the Subversion of Identity* (New York: Routledge, 1990); idem, *Bodies That Matter: On the Discursive Limits of "Sex"* (New York: Routledge, 1993), Steven Seidman, "Identity and Politics in a 'Postmodern' Gay Culture: Some Historical and Conceptual Notes," in *Fear of a Queer Planet: Queer Politics and Social Theory*, ed. Michael Warner (Minneapolis: University of Minnesotta Press, 1993).

[20] On the conceptualization of bisexuality, see Michael du Plessis, "Blatantly Bisexual: Or, Unthinking Queer Theory," in *RePresenting Bisexualities: Subjects and Cultures of Fluid Desire*, ed. Donald E. Hall and Maria Pramaggiore (New York: New York University Press, 1996).

[21] Peter Collier and David Horowitz, *Destructive Generation: Second Thoughts About the Sixties* (New York: Summit, 1989), 72–73, 85. Although their book is highly polemical, it does offer a colorful picture of the New Left.

[22] Harold Jacobs, ed., *Weatherman* (Palo Alto, Calif.: Ramparts Press, 1970), 306. Some feminists, among them Robin Morgan, denounced the "smash monogamy" campaign as entirely misguided. Morgan believed Weatherman atti-

tudes toward sexuality — even those of the women in the movement — merely mimicked those of mainstream society. When Weather leaders embraced Charles Manson as a hero and glorified his group marriage commune, many left-wing radicals moved quickly to distance themselves from the "Weather Machine."

[23] "Inside the Weather Machine," *Rat*, 6 February 1970. See also Susan Stern, *With The Weatherman: The Personal Journey of a Revolutionary Woman* (New York: Doubleday, 1975), 180–81. A former member of the Cambridge collective remembers the situation less fondly: "One day we got a directive that monogamy was no longer acceptable. I was dating this woman. When she started sleeping with another guy, I, of course, felt jealous. She told me I was wrong to feel that way." Interview with Michael Kazin by the author, telephone, 6 February 1998.

[24] Quoted in Collier and Horowitz, *Destructive Generation*, 86.

[25] Andrea Dworkin, *Woman Hating* (New York: Dutton, 1974), 84.

[26] Ibid., 79–80. Interview with Andrea Dworkin by the author, New York, 22 February 1995. See also "Fighting Talk," *New Statesman and Society*, 21 April 1995, 16–18; "Andrea Dworkin," *Contemporary Authors Autobiography Series*, vol. 21, 1994, 1–21.

[27] Dworkin, *Woman Hating*, 192.

[28] Germaine Greer, *The Female Eunuch* (New York: McGraw-Hill, 1971), 11. Claudia Dreyfus wrote a very negative review of *The Female Eunuch* for the *Nation*, which was reprinted in Anne Koedt et al., eds., *Radical Feminism* (New York: Quadrangle, 1973), 358–61. Dreyfus writes, "The whole tone of *The Female Eunuch* is shallow, anti-woman, regressive, three steps backward to the world of false sexual liberation from which so many young women have fled," 359.

[29] Germaine Greer, "Suck Now," Wet Dream Festival brochure, Betty Dodson's personal papers.

[30] Anon., Wet Dream Festival brochure, Dodson papers.

[31] Bodil Joensen, "My Men, My Pigs, My Orgasms," Wet Dream Festival brochure, Dodson papers.

[32] "Arguments About Otto," Wet Dream Festival brochure, Dodson papers.

[33] Greer, "Suck Now."

[34] Interview with Iris Brent [pseud.] by the author, Los Angeles, 28 November 1995.

[35] Iris Brent [pseud.], *Swinger's Diary* (New York: Pinnacle, 1973), 215.

[36] Ibid., 163–75. In her description of the event, she avoided the tendency toward exoticism and romanticism that was then common in white writings about black sexuality. "Most people in our society are sexually inhibited, whether they're black or white," she wrote. "Color certainly isn't the determining factor in sexual inhibitions."

[37] Ibid., 213; 214.

[38] Robert Rimmer, Introduction, Tom Hatfield, *The Sandstone Experience* (1975; reprint, New York: New American Library, 1976), 1–15.

[39] Herbert Gold, "Along the Frontiers of Sex," *Oui*, June 1975, 117–18.

[40] Quoted in ibid., 117.

[41] Sandstone flier, vertical file, Institute for Research on Sex, Gender and Reproduction, Indiana University.

[1] *Los Angeles Times,* 4 June 1974. The actual authorship of *The Joy of Sex* is unclear. In the introduction, Comfort says that the text was written by a couple who wished to remain anonymous. The body of the text is written in the first person plural. By convention, however, Comfort is always referred to as the author. No one at Crown Books was able to give me more information, and I was unable to contact Comfort himself because he is very ill. There are no further clues in the Comfort papers at the University of London.

[2] Alex Comfort, ed., *The Joy of Sex: A Cordon Bleu Guide to Lovemaking* (New York: Crown, 1972), 8; 220; 89.

[3] Ibid., 81–82, 150–51; 64.

[4] Interview with Sara Evans by the author, telephone, 1 February 1996.

[5] Comfort, *Joy of Sex,* 158, 248.

[6] Mark Gabor, *The Illustrated History of Girlie Magazines: From National Police Gazette to the Present* (New York: Harmony Books, 1984), 123. Interview with Bob Guccione by the author, New York, 30 May 1996. Early issues can be found at the Institute for Research on Sex, Gender and Reproduction.

[7] Letters to the editor, *Penthouse,* November 1969.

[8] "Mandi's Middle Finger," *Eros* (Sunrise Publishing, ed. Ross Lanning), 1, no. 1: 7–8, Institute for Research in Sex, Gender and Reproduction. For a class-based analysis of pornography, see Laura Kipnis, "(Male) Desire and (Female) Disgust: Reading Hustler," in *Cultural Studies,* ed. Lawrence Grossberg, Cary Nelson, and Paula A. Treichler (New York: Routledge, 1992), 373–91.

[9] Quoted in Norma McLain Stoop, "Burt Reynolds: A Hidden Iceberg that Broke Out like Gangbusters," *After Dark,* August 1972, 49.

[10] Interview with Susan Baerwald by the author, Los Angeles, 20 December 1998.

[11] Maitland Zane, "Skinflicks Perplex," *San Francisco Chronicle,* 9 December 1970.

[12] Joe Hyams, "Birth of the Porno Blues," *Cosmopolitan,* March 1971, 170. Maitland Zane, "The Porn Film Boom in S.F.," *San Francisco Chronicle,* 16 November 1970; Maitland Zane, "The Blue-Movie Battlers," *San Francisco Chronicle,* 18 November 1970. See also Kenneth Turan and Stephen F. Zito, *Sinema: American Pornographic Films and the People Who Make Them* (New York: Praeger, 1974). John Wasserman, "Erotic Films Made with Skill and Wit," *San Francisco Chronicle,* 4 December 1970. In 1971, a jury of eight women and four men found Arlene Elster guilty of showing obscenity. The judge, Agnes O'Brien Smith, refused to allow any testimony from psychiatrists, critics, or other experts. Yet Smith elected to fine Elster $1,000 rather than sentence her to jail. "Woman Guilty of Screening Obscene Films," *San Francisco Chronicle,* 28 January 1971.

[13] Quoted in Bruce Williamson, "Porno Chic," *Playboy,* August 1973.

[14] Foster Hirsch, "He's Happy in His 'Blue' Heaven," *New York Times,* 24 January 1971.

[15] *Screw,* 19 July 1972, 14. In 1980, Linda Lovelace testified in a memoir titled *Ordeal* (Secaucus, N.J.: Citadel, 1980) that she lived as her husband's sex slave (he allegedly coerced her into having sex with other men — and with animals — at gunpoint) and was forced to make *Deep Throat.*

[16] "Pornography on Trial," *New York Times Magazine*, 6 March 1977, 28. *New York Times*, 28 September 1972, 98; *Newsweek*, 15 January 1973, 50–51. "Wonder Woman," *Time*, 15 January 1973, 46. "TV Critic Tackles Pornography," *Variety*, 5 April 1972.

[17] "Wonder Woman."

[18] Quoted in *New York Times*, 2 March 1973. See also Arthur Lenning, "A History of Censorship of the American Film," in *Sexuality in the Movies*, ed. Thomas R. Atkins (Bloomington: Indiana University Press, 1975), 73.

[19] Freedman and D'Emilio, *Intimate Matters*, 328. Leonard J. Leff and Jerold L. Simmons, *The Dame in the Kimono: Hollywood, Censorship, and the Production Code from the 1920s to the 1960s* (New York: Grove and Weidenfeld, 1990), 276.

[20] The poll was part of the General Social Survey conducted by the University of Chicago; the results are summarized in Tom Smith, "The Polls — A Report: The Sexual Revolution?," *Public Opinion Quarterly* 54, no. 3 (Fall 1990): 428.

[21] "Cops Who Smoke Fags," *Screw*, 19 January 1970, 18; "Up Against the Wall Cocksucker!" *Screw*, 26 January 1970, 19.

[22] Tom Burke, "King, Queen," *Rolling Stone*, 6 May 1976, 83.

[23] Interview with Amy Hamilton [pseud.] by the author, telephone, 7 June 1998.

[24] Interview with Howard Bellin by the author, New York, 3 February 1998.

[25] "Is There Life in a Swinger's Club?" *Time*, 16 January 1978, 53.

[26] Don Dorfman, "Upstairs, Downstairs at the Ansonia," *New York*, 28 November 1977, 38–40. See also "Sex Goes Public," *Playboy*, July 1977, which actually consists of two articles: "The Gays Pioneer" by gay activist Arthur Bell and "The Straights Follow" by Dan Rosen.

[27] Quoted in Sanders, *Gay Source*, 243.

[28] Advertisement for Sutro Baths, COYOTE collection, Schlesinger Library.

[29] Sanders, *Gay Source*, 243.

[30] Charles Silverstein and Edmund White, *The Joy of Gay Sex: An Intimate Guide for Gay Men to the Pleasures of a Gay Lifestyle* (New York: Simon & Schuster, 1977), 36.

[31] Interview with Larry Kramer by the author, New York, 29 December 1998.

[32] Ironically, it was the federal government that first mass produced s/m images in twentieth-century America. During World War II, Washington commissioned quasi-pornographic, sadomasochistic propaganda films as part of the effort to mobilize the home front. Such films typically showed Japanese soldiers abusing, raping, murdering, and torturing white women. Often the women were bound and gagged by their prosecutors for added effect. *Behind the Rising Sun, China Sky*, and *Dragon Seed* were three of the most famous examples of this popular genre. The poster for *Behind the Rising Sun* invited spectators to see "Jap Brutes Manhandling Helpless Women — By Official Proclamation" and showed a Japanese soldier about to rape his victim. Thomas Doherty, *Projections of War: Hollywood, American Culture and World War II* (New York: Columbia University Press, 1993), 134; John Dower, *War Without Mercy* (New York: Pantheon, 1986), 189.

[33] Adrienne Rich to Andrea Dworkin, 20 January 1974, box 14, folder 260, Barbara Demming collection, Schlesinger Library.

34 Rita Mae Brown, "Queen for a Day," *Real Paper,* n.d., 1975, clipping, papers of Arthur Bell, International Gay Information Center Collection, New York Public Library.

35 *San Francisco Examiner,* 29 April 1979.

36 *San Francisco Examiner,* 18 October 1976.

37 Margo St. James to Laura, 2 October 1972, COYOTE collection, Schlesinger Library.

38 *Berkeley Barb,* 10–16 May 1974.

39 Allison Pritchard, WGBH, to Mr. Desmond, 26 June 1972, COYOTE collection.

40 COYOTE mailing, January 1975, COYOTE collection. By 1979, with an estimated 1 million prostitutes, professional escorts, and erotic masseuses in the United States, COYOTE had 13 sister organizations. The estimate on the number of prostitutes comes from *The Adult Business Report,* April 1979. Using FBI statistics and police accounts, *TAB* estimated that there were 1,323,600 prostitutes. COYOTE lost steam in the late seventies; see Ronald Weitzer, "Prostitutes' Rights in the United States: The Failure of a Movement," *Sociological Quarterly* 32 (Spring 1991): 23–41. See also Valerie Jenness, "From Sex as Sin to Sex as Work: COYOTE and the Reorganization of Prostitution as a Social Problem," *Social Problems,* 37 (August 1990): 403–20.

41 "Sexually Free?" *Open City,* 9 August 1968, 5.

42 Roszak, *Making of a Counter Culture,* 14–15.

43 Rollo May, *Love and Will* (1969; reprint, New York: Dell, 1970), 57.

44 "Orgynization," *Good Times,* 19 March 1971, 6.

45 "Orgynization," 42.

46 The Red Butterfly, "Comments on Carl Whitman's 'A Gay Manifesto,'" in *We Are Everywhere: A Historical Sourcebook of Gay and Lesbian Politics,* ed. Mark Blasius and Shane Phelan (New York: Routledge, 1997), 389.

47 Xaviera Hollander, *The Happy Hooker* (New York: Dell, 1972), 199; 204.

48 Roszak, *Making of a Counter Culture,* 14, 21.

49 Quoted in Andrea Dworkin, *Woman Hating,* 195.

CHAPTER 19

1 Marcus, *Making History,* 104–21; interview with Barbara Gittings by the author, telephone, 5 October 1997.

2 Elizabeth Lapovsky Kennedy and Madeline D. Davis, *Boots of Leather, Slippers of Gold: The History of a Lesbian Community* (New York: Routledge, 1993), 71.

3 Petronius [pseud.], *New York Unexpurgated: An Amoral Guide for the Jaded, Tired, Evil, Non-Conforming, Corrupt, Condemned, and the Curious — Humans and Otherwise — to Under Underground Manhattan* (New York: Matrix House, 1966), 60–108.

4 Interview with Sarah Holland by the author, New York, 10 December 1998.

5 Quoted in Deborah Goleman Wolf, *The Lesbian Community* (Berkeley: University of California Press, 1980), 36–37.

[6] Carl Whitman, "A Gay Manifesto," in *We Are Everywhere*, 385.

[7] Quoted in Teal, *Gay Militants*, 39–40.

[8] Whitman, "Gay Manifesto," 385.

[9] Robin Morgan, "Lesbianism and Feminism: Synonyms or Contradictions?" in *We Are Everywhere*, 425.

[10] Cleaver, *Soul on Ice*, 184.

[11] Interview with Rita Mae Brown by the author, telephone, 22 December 1997.

[12] Radicalesbians, "The Woman-Identified Woman," in *We Are Everywhere*, 397.

[13] Morgan, *Going Too Far*, 179, 181.

[14] Sue Katz, "The Sensuous Woman" (originally titled "Smash Phallic Imperialism," but retitled by the Liberation News Service), *Rat*, 12–29 January 1971, quoted in Echols, *Daring to Be Bad*, 219–20.

[15] Alice, Gordon, Debbie and Mary, "Separatism," in *For Lesbians Only*, 35.

[16] Barbara to Mickey Zacuto, 2 February 1972. Mickey Zacuto collection, Lesbian History Archives.

[17] Martha Shelley, "Gay is Good," in *We Are Everywhere*, 391–92. Alice Echols, *Daring to Be Bad: Radical Feminism in America, 1967–1975* (Minneapolis: University of Minnesota Press), 1989.

[18] Wilma Scott Heide to Del Martin, 29 May 1973, NOW collection, Schlesinger Library.

CHAPTER 20

[1] Quotations are from "An American Family," *Newsweek*, 15 January 1973, 68.

[2] Steven Mintz and Susan Kellogg, *Domestic Revolutions: A Social History of American Family Life* (New York: Free Press, 1988), 109. Roderick Phillips, *Putting Asunder: A History of Divorce in Western Society* (Cambridge, England: Cambridge University Press, 1988), 569.

[3] Mervyn Cadwallader, "Marriage as a Wretched Institution," *Atlantic Monthly*, November 1966, 62.

[4] See Morgan, *Going Too Far*, 73–74, and Echols, *Daring to Be Bad*, 97–98.

[5] Erhenreich, *Hearts of Men*, 97. Conservative journalist Barbara Dafoe Whitehead expands on this theme in her polemical but at times perceptive essay "Dan Quayle Was Right," *Atlantic*, April 1993.

[6] Groves Conference Report, Small Group on Adult Single Living, 1973, 17, box 6, folder 400, Emily Mudd collection, Schlesinger Library, Harvard University. The Groves Conference was founded in 1934 by Professor Ernest Groves of the University of North Carolina at Chapel Hill.

[7] Statutory law did not always specify that physicians had the right to administer abortions, but this right was consistently upheld in common law court decisions. See Kristen Luker, *Abortion and Politics of Motherhood* (Berkeley: University of California Press, 1984), 68.

[8] See Leslie J. Reagan, *When Abortion Was a Crime: Women, Medicine, and Law in the United States, 1867–1973* (Berkeley: University of California Press, 1997).

[9] Interview with Helen Gurley Brown by the author, New York, 29 January 1996.

[10] *Newsweek,* 17 February 1969, 92. See also Ellen Messer and Katherine E. May, eds., *Back Rooms: Voices from the Illegal Abortion Era* (New York: St. Martin's Press, 1988), 218–24; Reagan, *When Abortion Was a Crime,* 42–47.

[11] Luker, *Abortion,* 62–65; Garrow, *Liberty and Sexuality,* 285–89.

[12] Susan Brownmiller, "Abortion Counseling," *New York,* 4 August 1965. Rocky River, Ohio, *Plain Dealer,* 13 October 1967, 10 October 1967, clippings, Patricia Maginnis Oral History, Family Planning Oral History Project, Schlesinger Library. Garrow, *Liberty and Sexuality,* 308.

[13] Interview with Howard Moody by the author, telephone, 30 March 1997.

[14] On Baird's arrest, see Garrow, *Liberty and Sexuality,* 320–23, 325, 343, 372–74, 376, 410. The Supreme Court eventually overturned Baird's conviction in *Eisenstadt v. Baird* in March 1972.

[15] Interview with Bill Baird by the author, telephone, 12 December 1997; "Baird to Lead Protest March," *Long Island Press,* 7 March 1967, 2; Myra MacPherson, "Abortion: A Whispered Word Takes on a New Voice," *Washington Post,* 9 December 1968; Naomi Rock, "Risking Prison, Fighting Mostly Alone, He Crusades for Abortion Rights," Associated Press, 23 January 1970; *Harvard Graduate Bulletin,* 16 December 1967; "Birth Control Crusader Starts Three Month Jail Term," UPI, 21 February 1970. The *New York Times* reported: "Mention his name on the phone and Betty Friedan's gravelly voice turns to liquid vitriol" (Lindsey Gruson, "The Devil of Abortion," *New York Times,* 14 April 1993).

[16] See Linda Rockey, "Why They Ask for Repeal of Abortion Laws," *Des Moines Register,* 26 February 1969.

[17] "Abortion Rally Speech," Notes from the First Year, June 1968.

[18] Morgan, *Going Too Far,* 88. "Unsafe Abortion Methods," *Everywoman,* 26 March 1971, 14. "How Not to Abort," *Good Times,* 9 April 1971, 15. Baird was eventually forced out of the women's movement because he was perceived as arrogant. After learning that his help was no longer wanted, Baird declared, "Since when did it become their movement?" (*New York Post,* 5 May 1976, quoted in Morgan, *Going Too Far,* 85).

[19] Norma McCorvey, *I Am Roe: My Life, Roe v. Wade, and Freedom of Choice* (New York: HarperCollins, 1994), 114–15.

[20] Garrow, *Liberty and Sexuality,* 402–403.

[21] *Eisenstadt v. Baird,* 405 U.S. 438 (1972).

[22] *Contemporary Authors, New Revision Series,* vol. 52, 227.

[23] Erica Jong, *Fear of Flying* (New York: Signet, 1973), 76.

[24] For reviews of *Fear of Flying,* see Walter Clemons, "Beware of the Man," *Newsweek,* 12 November 1973, 111; *New York Times Book Review,* 11 November 1973; John Updike, "Jong Love," *New Yorker,* 17 December 1973, 149.

[25] *Current Biography,* 1975, 207.

[26] *Contemporary Authors, New Revision Series,* vol. 26, 190.

[27] Caroline Seebohm, *New York Times Book Review,* 7 October 1973, 20.

[28] Nancy Friday, *My Secret Garden: Women's Sexual Fantasies* (New York: Pocket Books, 1973), 217, 270.

[29] Ibid., 1–11.

[30] John Money, "The Birth Control Revolution," *Chronicle of Higher Education,* 12 November 1973, 20.

CHAPTER 21

[1] Bob Greene, "Beyond the Sexual Revolution," *Newsweek,* 29 September 1975, 13.

[2] Andrew Kopkind, *Village Voice,* 25 June 1979.

[3] See Robert M. Collins, "Growth Liberalism in the Sixties," in *The Sixties,* ed. Farber, 37. See also William C. Berman, *America's Right Turn: From Nixon to Bush* (Baltimore: Johns Hopkins University Press, 1994), 14.

[4] "Avant-Garde Retreat?" *Time,* 25 November 1974, 103.

[5] See Talese, *Thy Neighbor's Wife,* 482; 484–95.

[6] Berman, *America's Right Turn,* 10.

[7] Kenneth D. Wald, *Religion and Politics in the United States* (New York: St. Martin's, 1987), 222.

[8] Ibid., 241; 238–39. The modernization of the South also encouraged evangelical political mobilization; see Wald, 325. Meanwhile, the migration of many evangelicals to urban centers precipitated a direct confrontation with the secular world and its commercialization of sex. At the same time, sex books, pornographic movie theaters, and gay bars penetrated the Midwest and South — North and South Carolina in fact had the largest concentration of X-rated theaters in the country — sparking reactionary censorship and police efforts in traditionally isolated and conservative communities. D'Emilio and Freedman, *Intimate Matters,* 328.

[9] United States Bureau of the Census, *Statistical Abstract of the United States* (Washington, D.C.: Government Printing Offfice, 1960), 143; (1970), 147; (1976), 163.

[10] Stephanie Coontz, *The Way We Never Were: American Families and the Nostalgia Trap* (New York: Basic, 1992), 202. See also Maris Vinovskis, *An "Epidemic" of Adolescent Pregnancy?: Some Historical and Policy Considerations* (New York: Oxford University Press, 1988), 25–28. See also Kenneth D. Wald, *Religion and Politics in the United States,* 2nd ed. (Washington, D.C.: Congressional Quarterly Press, 1992).

[11] Tom W. Smith, "The Polls — A Report, The Sexual Revolution?" *Public Opinion Quarterly,* Fall 1990, 415–35.

[12] Wald, *Religion and Politics,* 1st ed., 228–31.

[13] Toni Carabillo et al., *Feminist Chronicles 1953–1993* (Los Angeles: Women's Graphic, 1993), 65; 72.

[14] Jack T. Chick, "The Gay Blade," n.p., 1972. Although evangelical leaders were outspoken in their attacks on feminism, abortion, sex education, and homosexuality, surveys showed that the majority of American evangelicals actually held fairly liberal views. Yet socially conservative evangelicals who aimed their fire at "the sexual revolution" generated enough money and cast enough doubt on the values of the "new morality" to halt the revolution's progress. Wald, *Religion and Politics,* 1st ed., 251–54.

[15] John Neary, "Pornography Goes Public," *Life,* 28 August 1970, 19–25.

16 *Louisville Courier-Journal,* 10 February 1977; 18 November 1977.

17 Richard Neville, "Has the First Amendment Met Its Match?" *New York Times Magazine,* 6 March 1977, 18.

18 Interview with Gay Talese by the author, New York, 19 February 1995.

19 T. Morgan, "United States versus the Princes of Porn," *New York Times Magazine,* 6 March 1977, 15–37. Invitation to benefit sponsored by Harry Reems Defense Fund, vertical file, Institute for Research in Sex, Gender and Reproduction.

20 Morgan, "Princess of Porn," 35–36.

21 Erazim Kohak, "Turning On for Freedom," in *Beyond the New Left,* ed. Irving Howe (New York: McCall, 1970), 239–49.

22 "Excerpts from Interview with Warren on His Court's Decisions," *New York Times,* 27 June 1969.

23 "N.Y. Times Restricts Ads for Porno Films," *Editor and Publisher,* 25 June 1977, 25.

24 Evelyn Reynold, "The Contemporary Movie Rating System in America," in *Sexuality in the Movies,* 82. The M rating was quickly changed to GP (general patronage) in 1970. A second category, GP-Tag, was introduced; GP and GP-Tag evolved into PG (parental guidance) and PG-13 (parental guidance especially suggested for children under age thirteen).

25 "N.Y. Times Restricts Ads," 25.

26 Arthur Sulzberger to Lord Thomson of British Advertising Standards Authority, 18 July 1977, *New York Times* archives.

27 Memo from Katherine P. Darrow to Arthur Sulzberger, 13 June 1977; memo from John D. Pomfret to Sulzberger, 19 May 1977, *Times* archives.

28 "Theater Leaders Applaud Curb on Ads in The Times," 22 June 1977, *Times* archives; *Variety,* 22 July 1977.

29 Michael Azzolina, 42nd St. Theater Row, to Susan Brownmiller, 20 September 1979, Women Against Pornography collection, Schlesinger Library.

30 *Trentonian,* 15 March 1971, Historical Subject files, Mudd Library, Princeton University.

31 On reflection, Stansell describes her actions as an "adolescent act of bravado." "The 'action' was undertaken in the spirit of feminist anarchist high jinks more than morally exemplifying instruction. It was civil disobedience in the sense that we didn't cover our faces like bandits and fully owned up to it when confronted by the proctors, whom [the male student] promptly called." There was a disciplinary hearing and a trial; the two women were represented by Ann Wood, the first woman professor in Princeton's English department. "[We] made stirring speeches. I remember mine was on Virginia Woolf's *Room of One's Own* and the lack of such on the campus — the lack of space for women to call their own." Letter to the author, 9 January 1998.

32 H. Jayne Vogan and Sidney Abbott, Statement of Purpose, Task Force on Sexuality and Lesbianism, November 1973, NOW collection, Schlesinger Library.

33 Interview with Jason Glick [pseud.] by the author, Cambridge, 17 October 1993.

34 Morgan, *Going Too Far,* 167.

35 See Karen Durbin, "Can a Feminist Love the World's Greatest Rock Band?" *Ms.,* October 1974.

36 In her analysis of pornography, Linda Williams states that no actual snuff film has ever been found. While Williams may be correct, her book should be treated with caution. She also claims, for example, that the "cum shot" is a recent invention and thus the defining feature of modern hard-core pornography. The rest of her analysis is premised on this assumption. In fact, the cum shot is as old as the pornographic film itself, but in early stag films the lighting is so bad one can barely see the actors ejaculating. Linda Williams, *Hard Core: Power, Pleasure, and the "Frenzy of the Visible"* (Berkeley: University of California Press, 1989).

37 Morgan, *Going Too Far*, 167.

38 Quoted in Miller, *Bunny*, 193.

39 Quoted in ibid., 194.

40 Interview with Susan Brownmiller by the author, New York, 29 December 1995.

41 Lois Gould, "Hers," *New York Times*, 30 June 1997.

42 Andrea Dworkin to the *New York Times*, 30 June 1997, Barbara Demming collection, Schlesinger Library. Leah Fritz to the *New York Times*, 1 July 1997, Barbara Demming collection, Schlesinger Library.

43 Thompson, *Long Road to Freedom* 147; D'Emilio and Freedman, *Intimate Matters*, 346–47.

44 Kenneth A. Briggs, "Homosexuals Among the Clergy," *New York Times*, 24 January 1977.

45 Grace Lichtenstein, "Homosexuals Are Moving Toward Open Way of Life As Tolerance Rises Among General Population," *New York Times*, 17 July 1977.

46 Norman Podhoretz, "The Culture of Appeasement," *Harper's*, October 1977. See also Gayle Rubin, "Thinking Sex," *Lesbian and Gay Studies Reader*, 273. Neoconservatives were onetime liberals who had grown disillusioned by the drift of the left toward radicalism in the sixties.

47 Dennis Altman, "Fear and Loathing and Hepatitis on the Path of Gay Liberation," *Christopher Street*, January 1977, reprinted in *New Gay Liberation Book*, 200–201.

48 *U.S. v. Womack*, U.S. District Court for District of Columbia, 3 November 1969, box 1, folder 1.1, Lynn Womack papers, Carl A. Kroh Library, Cornell University.

49 Aquarius Press newsletter and catalog, box 2, folder 2.68, Womack papers.

50 Titles included *Better Life, Broadstreet Journal,* and *Hermes.* See *Drummer*, vol. 1, no. 2, 7.

51 John Mitzel, *The Boston Sex Scandal* (Boston: Glad Day Books, 1980), 12.

52 "Chicago Is Center of National Child Porno Ring," *Chicago Tribune*, 16 May 1977, front page.

53 Typescript, WAP collection, Schlesinger Library.

54 Take Back the Night steering committee meeting minutes, 13 August 1979, WAP collection.

55 Joe Conforti to Women Against Pornography, n.d.; David Horch to WAP, WAP collection.

56 Smith, "The Polls," 415–35.

[57] "Public Opinion Polls on Lesbian and Gay Rights," National Organization for Women, Lesbian Rights Resource Kit, 1980, NOW collection, Schlesinger Library. Relevant surveys were conducted by Gallup, Harris, Time Magazine–Daniel Yankelovich, and the American Institute of Public Opinion.

[58] Eunice Lake diary, 3 February 1975.

[59] *Lovisi vs. Slayton*, 363 F. Supp. 620 (1973); "Three's a Crowd in Sex, Court Says," *San Francisco Chronicle*, 15 May 1976. The two girls testified in court that they took the photographs; the Lovisis insisted that the girls were not present during the sexual encounters.

[60] See Vito Russo, *The Celluloid Closet: Homosexuality in the Movies* (New York: Harper & Row, 1981), 238.

[61] *Congressional Record*, 30 April 1981.

[62] Gloria Steinem, *Outrageous Acts and Everyday Rebellions* (New York: Holt, Rinehart and Winston, 1983), 27. Interview with Steinem by the author.

[63] All quotations appear in Allan M. Brandt, *No Magic Bullet: A Social History of Venereal Disease in the United States Since 1880* (New York: Oxford University Press, 1985), 179–82. See "Herpes: The New Sexual Leprosy," *Time*, 28 July 1980, 76; "The New Scarlet Letter," *Time*, 2 August 1982, 62–66; "The Misery of Herpes II," *Newsweek*, 10 November 1980, 105; Lois Draegin, "Sex Makes You Sick," *Soho Weekly News*, 24 November 1981, 12–14.

[64] William H. Masters and Virginia E. Johnson, and Robert C. Kolodny, *Crisis: Heterosexual Behavior in the Age of AIDS* (New York: Grove, 1988), 94.

EPILOGUE

[1] It is possible that the sexual revolution has meant a certain loss of freedom — a freedom, for instance, to experiment with members of the same sex without questioning one's own whole identity. Some claim that in the days before sexual liberation, men felt entitled to accept sexual favors from other men, so long as strict rules about who did what to whom were followed. "No one talks about this fleeting flexibility anymore," writes Richard Goldstein, executive editor of the *Village Voice*, "but back then, lots of guys bragged about getting a blow job from a 'fag.' The common belief was that real men were so horny they would fuck anything. As long as they put it out and didn't take it in, they considered themselves straight." But, laments Goldstein, today the sharp lines between "straight" and "gay" make such bisexual boundary crossings virtually impossible. Perhaps, in the end, shining the light of liberation into every dark corner of daily life has made it more difficult to indulge in some sexual pleasures spontaneously and unself-consciously. See Richard Goldstein, *Nerve*, www.nerve.com, 3 August 1999. When he was in college in the 1950s, my own father received oral sex from another male student; my father says he never thought twice about the experience. In *Gay New York*, George Chauncey suggests that, prior to the construction of modern sexual identities in the 1920s and '30s, men easily slid between the worlds of same-sex and different-sex activities; again, the emphasis was on the role one played in sexual activities ("top" vs. "bottom") rather than the gender of one's partner. On the other hand, it is possible that all the "straight" men who indulged in sex with other men before the sexual revolution would now happily consider themselves gay or bisexual. The basic argument that openness brings

its own oppression is most often associated with Foucault and his metaphor (borrowed from Jeremy Bentham) of the panopticon: the circular prison where no physical restraints are needed because every prisoner is visible at all times to every other.

Even the idea of sexual freedom can have its limitations. Some people, for instance, like their sex dangerous. They find it more thrilling when it is illicit. For them, "sexual freedom," by eliminating the taboos surrounding sex, also eliminates some of the thrill. The more "freedom" they gain, the more they seek out new rules to break, new boundaries to push — not because they believe the rules ought to be eliminated, but because they enjoy the excitement of transgressing social norms. One would have to say that for them, the sexual revolution was ultimately counterproductive. But I don't think that even they would want to turn back the cultural clock. There are people who would find life under an oppressive political regime far more exciting than life in a democracy. But who would suggest that democracy be abolished simply to make everyday existence more interesting?

[2] Eunice Lake diary, 11 December 1974.

[3] Interview with Glen Murphy [pseud.] by the author, telephone, 20 April 1998.

[4] Interview with Tom Murphy [pseud.] by the author, telephone, 21 April 1998.

[5] See, for instance, *Taxi Driver* or *Little Darlings*.

[6] "Childhood Sensuality Circle Newsletter," vol. 3, no. 2 (June 1977), COYOTE collection, Schlesinger Library.

[7] Interview with Valerie Goldberg [pseud.] by the author, telephone, 30 August 1997.

[8] Interview with Jody West [pseud.] by the author, Washington, D.C., 21 December 1996.

[9] This example illustrates why, though I have referred to "sexual liberals" and "sexual liberalism" throughout the book, I have done so reluctantly. Was it liberal of my stepmother to encourage me to have sex with a prostitute when I was twelve? Obviously, our sexual attitudes are too complex to be reduced to simplistic political categories.

SELECTED BIBLIOGRAPHY

BOOKS AND ARTICLES

ABBOT, SIDNEY, AND BARBARA LOVE. *Sappho Was a Right-On Woman: A Liberated View of Lesbianism.* New York: Stein and Day, 1973.

ABELOVE, HENRY, MICHELE AINA BARALE, AND DAVID HALPERIN, eds. *The Lesbian and Gay Studies Reader.* New York: Routledge, 1993.

ABERLE, SOPHIE, AND G. W. CORNER. *Twenty-Five Years of Sex Research.* Philadelphia: Saunders, 1953.

ABRAMSON, P., AND B. MECHANIC. "Sex and the Media: Three Decades of Best-Selling Books and Major Motion Pictures," in *Archives of Sexual Behavior,* vol. 12, no. 3 (1983): 185–205.

ALTMAN, MERYL. "Everything They Always Wanted You to Know: The Ideology of Popular Sex Literature," in *Pleasure and Danger,* 115–130.

ARCHER, JULES. *The Incredible Sixties: The Stormy Years that Changed America.* San Diego: Harcourt Brace Jovanovich, 1986.

ASBELL, BERNARD. *The Pill: A Biography of the Drug that Changed the World.* New York: Random House, 1995.

ATKINS, THOMAS, ed. *Sexuality in the Movies.* Bloomington: Indiana University Press, 1975.

BAILEY, BETH. *From Front Porch to Back Seat.* Baltimore: Johns Hopkins, 1989.

BARITZ, LOREN. *The Good Life: The Meaning of Success for the American Middle Class.* New York: Perennial, 1982.

BANES, SALLY. *Greenwich Village 1963: Avant-Garde Performance and the Effervescent Body.* Durham, NC: Duke University Press, 1993.

BARNHART, JACQUELINE BAKER. *The Fair But Frail: Prostitution in San Francisco, 1849–1900*. Reno: University of Nevada Press, 1986.

BARRY, KATHLEEN. *Female Sexual Slavery*. Englewood Cliffs, NJ: Prentice-Hall, 1979.

BARTELL, GILBERT. "Group Sex among the Mid-Americans," in *Journal of Sex Research*, vol. 6, no. 2 (May 1970): 113–130.

BAYER, RONALD. *Homosexuality and American Psychiatry: The Politics of Diagnosis*. New York: Basic Books, 1981; 2nd ed. Princeton University Press, 1987.

BELL, ROBERT, AND JAY CHASKES. "Premarital Sexual Experiences among Coeds, 1958–1968," in *Journal of Marriage and the Family*, vol. 32 (1970): 81–84.

BENNETT, PAULA, AND VERNON A. ROSARIO. *Solitary Pleasures: The Historical, Literary and Artistic Discourses of Autoeroticism*. New York: Routledge, 1995.

BERGLER, EDMUND. "A Psychoanalyst's Case for Monogamy," in *Harper's Bazaar*, May 1957, 120–21, 172–80.

———. *Counterfeit-Sex: Homosexuality, Impotence, Frigidity*. New York: Grune and Stratton, 1958.

BERMAN, WILLIAM. *America's Right Turn: From Nixon to Bush*. Baltimore: Johns Hopkins University Press, 1994.

BERUBÉ, ALLAN. *Coming Out under Fire: The History of Gay Men and Women in World War Two*. New York: Free Press, 1990.

BIRKIN, LAWRENCE. *Consuming Desire: Sexual Science and the Emergence of a Culture of Abundance, 1871–1914*. Ithaca, NY: Cornell University Press, 1988.

BOADELLA, DAVID. *Wilhelm Reich: The Evolution of His Work*. London: Vision Press, 1973.

BRADLEY, DONALD, JACQUELINE BOLES, AND CHRISTOPHER JONES. "From Mistress to Hooker: 40 Years of Cartoon Humor in Men's Magazines," in *Qualitative Sociology*, vol. 2, no. 2 (September 1979): 42–62.

BRADY, FRANK. *Hefner*. New York: Macmillan, 1974.

BRANDT, ALLAN. *No Magic Bullet: A Social History of Venereal Disease in the U.S. since 1880*. New York: Oxford University Press, 1987.

BRECHER, EDWARD, AND RUTH BRECHER. *The Sex Researchers*. Boston: Little, Brown, 1969.

BRECHER, EDWARD. "Kraft-Ebbing vs. Havelock Ellis: Contrasting Attitudes in Two Pioneering Students of Sexual Behavior," in *Medical Aspects of Human Sexuality*, vol. 7, no. 7 (July 1973): 147–154.

BRENT, IRIS [pseud.]. *My Love Is Free*. New York: Pinnacle, 1975.

———. *Swinger's Diary*. New York: Pinaccle, 1973.

BROWN, HELEN GURLEY. *Sex and the Single Girl*. New York: Bernard Geis Associates, 1962.

BROWN, NORMAN O. *Life Against Death*. Middletown, CT: Wesleyan University Press, 1959.

———. *Love's Body*. New York: Random House, 1966.

BROWNMILLER, SUSAN. *Against Our Will: Men, Women and Rape.* New York: Simon & Schuster, 1975.

BRUCE, LENNY. *How to Talk Dirty and Influence People.* Chicago: Playboy Press, 1972.

BRUNS, ROGER. *The Damnedest Radical: The Life and World of Ben Reitman, Chicago's Celebrated Social Reformer, Hobo King and Whorehouse Physician.* Chicago: University of Illinois Press, 1987.

BUCKLEY, JIM, AND AL GOLDSTEIN, eds., *The Screw Reader.* New York: Lyle Stuart, 1971.

BUGLIOSI, VINCENT, WITH CURT GENTRY. *Helter Skelter: The True Story of the Manson Murders.* New York, Bantam, 1976.

BULLOUGH, VERN L. "Katherine Bement Davis, Sex Research, and the Rockefeller Foundation," in *Bulletin of the History of Medicine,* vol. 62, no. 1 (1988).

———. "The Rockefellers and Sex Research," in *Journal of Sex Research,* vol. 21, no. 2 (May 1985).

———. *Science in the Bedroom: A History of Sex Research.* New York: Harpers, 1994.

———. "The Society for the Scientific Study of Sex: A Brief History." Foundation for the Scientific Study of Sexuality, 1989.

BURNHAM, JOHN. *Bad Habits: Drinking, Smoking, Taking Drugs, Gambling, Sexual Misbehavior and Swearing in American History.* New York: New York University Press, 1993.

———. "The Progressive Era Revolution in American Attitudes Toward Sex," in *Journal of American History,* vol. 59 (1972): 885–908.

BUTLER, JUDITH. *Bodies that Matter: On the Discursive Limits of "Sex."* New York: Routledge, 1993.

———. *Gender Trouble: Feminism and the Subversion of Identity.* New York: Routledge, 1990.

CALIFIA, PAT. "The Great Kiddy Porn Scare of '77 and Its Aftermath," in *Advocate,* 6 October 1980.

———. "A Personal View of the History of the Lesbian S/M Community and Movement in San Francisco," in *Coming to Power: Writings and Graphics on Lesbian S/M,* ed. Samois. Boston: Alyson Books, 1982, 243–281.

———. "A Thorny Issue Splits a Movement," in *Advocate,* 30 October 1980.

CAMPBELL, PATRICIA. *Sex Education Books for Young Adults: 1892–1979.* New York: R. R. Boucher, 1979.

CANAVAN, FRANCIS. "Reflections on the Revolution in Sex," in *America,* 6 March 1965, 312–15.

CAPLAN, PAULA J. *The Myth of Women's Masochism.* New York: Dutton, 1985.

CASTRO, GINETTE. *American Feminism: A Contemporary History.* New York: New York University Press, 1990.

CAUTE, DAVID. *The Year of the Barricades: A Journey Through 1968.* New York: Harper & Row, 1988.

CAVANAGH, JOHN R. *The Popes, the Pill and the People.* Milwaukee: Bruce, 1965.

CHARTERS, ANN, ed. *The Portable Beat Reader.* New York: Penguin, 1992.

CHAUNCEY, GEORGE. *Gay New York: Gender, Urban Culture, and the Making of the Gay Male World, 1890–1940.* New York: Basic, 1994.

CHESLER, ELLEN. *Woman of Valor: Margaret Sanger and the Birth Control Movement in America.* New York: Simon & Schuster, 1992.

CLAPHAM, ADAM, AND ROBIN CONSTABLE. *As Nature Intended.* London: Heinemann, 1982.

CLEAVER, ELDRIDGE. *Soul on Ice.* New York: McGraw-Hill, 1967.

COCHRAN, WILLIAM, FREDERICK MOSTELLER, AND JOHN TUKEY. *Statistical Problems of the Kinsey Report.* Washington, D.C.: The American Statistical Association, 1954.

COLEMAN, ROSALIND, AND JAMES ROLLESTON. "Anatomy Lessons: The Destiny of a Textbook," in *South Atlantic Quarterly,* vol. 90, no. 1 (Winter 1991): 153–174.

COMFORT, ALEX. *Barbarism and Sexual Freedom: Lectures on the Sociology of Sex from the Standpoint of Anarchism.* London: Freedom Press, 1948.

———. *The Joy of Sex: A Gourmet Guide to Lovemaking.* New York: Simon & Schuster, 1972.

———. *More Joy of Sex.* New York: Simon & Schuster, 1972.

COMMITTEE ON THE COLLEGE STUDENT, GROUP FOR THE ADVANCEMENT OF PSYCHIATRY. *Sex and the College Student.* New York: Atheneum, 1966.

COOK, BRUCE. *The Beat Generation.* New York: Scribners, 1971.

COONTZ, STEPHANIE. *The Way We Never Were: American Families and the Nostalgia Trap.* New York: Basic, 1992.

COSTELLO, JOHN. *Virtue under Fire: How World War II Changed Our Social and Sexual Attitudes.* Boston: Little, Brown, 1985.

COTT, NANCY, AND ELIZABETH PECK. *A Heritage of Her Own: A New Social History of American Women.* New York: Simon & Schuster, 1979.

CRITCHLOW, DONALD. "Birth Control, Population Control, and Family Planning: An Overview," in *Journal of Policy History* 7 (1995): 1–21.

CUBER, JOHN F., AND PEGGY HARROFF. *The Significant Americans: A Study of Sexual Behavior among the Affluent.* New York: Appleton Century, 1965.

DEGLER, CARL. "What Ought to Be and What Was: Women's Sexuality in the 19th Century," in *American Historical Review,* vol. 79 (December 1974): 1467–1490.

———. *At Odds: Women and the Family in America from the Revolution to the Present.* New York: Oxford University Press, 1980.

DE GRAZIA, EDWARD. *Girls Lean Back Everywhere: The Law of Obscenity and the Assault on Genius.* New York: Random House, 1992.

D'EMILIO, JOHN. *Sexual Politics, Sexual Communities: The Making of a Homosexual Minority in the United States, 1940–70.* Chicago: University of Chicago Press, 1983.

————, AND ESTELLE FREEDMAN. *Intimate Matters: A History of Sexuality in America*. New York: Harper & Row, 1988.

DENFELD, DUANE, AND MICHAEL GORDON. "The Sociology of Mate Swapping: Or, the Family that Swings Together Clings Together," in *Journal of Sex Research*, vol. 6, no. 2 (May 1970): 85–100.

DICKSTEIN, MORRIS. *Gates of Eden: American Culture in the Sixties*. New York: Basic, 1977.

DIDION, JOAN. *Slouching Towards Bethlehem*. New York: Farrar, Straus & Giroux, 1968.

DI LAURO, AL, AND GERALD RABKIN. *Dirty Movies: An Illustrated History of the Stag Film, 1915–1970*. New York: Chelsea House, 1976.

DODSON, BETTY. *Liberating Masturbation*. New York: Betty Dodson, 1974.

DRAKE, GORDON. *SEICUS: Corrupter of Youth*. Tulsa: Oklahoma Christian Crusade Publications, 1969.

DWORKIN, ANDREA. *WomanHating*. New York: E. P. Dutton, 1974.

DUBERMAN, MARTIN. *Stonewall*. New York: Dutton, 1993.

ECHOLS, ALICE. *Daring to Be Bad: Radical Feminism in America, 1967–1975*. Minneapolis: University of Minnesota Press, 1989.

EDGREN, GRETCHEN. *The Playboy Book: Forty Years*. Santa Monica, CA: General Publishing Group, 1994.

EHRENREICH, BARBARA. *The Hearts of Men: American Dreams and the Flight from Commitment*. New York: Doubleday, 1983.

————, AND DIEDRE ENGLISH. *For Her Own Good: 150 Years of the Experts' Advice to Women*. Garden City, NY: Anchor, 1978.

————, ELIZABETH HESS, AND GLORIA JACOBS. *Remaking Love: The Feminization of Sex*. Garden City, NY: Anchor, 1987.

ELLIOT, M. L. "The Use of 'Impotence' and 'Frigidity': Why Has 'Impotence' Survived?" in *Journal of Sex and Marital Therapy*, vol. 11: 51–56.

ELLIS, ALBERT. *The American Sexual Tragedy*. New York: Lyle Stuart, 1962.

————. *The Folklore of Sex*. New York: Grove Press, 1961.

————. "On the Cure of Homosexuality," in *International Journal of Sexology*, vol. 5, no. 3 (February 1952): 135–142.

————. *Sex and the Single Man*. New York: Dell, 1965.

————. "The Sexual Psychology of Human Hermaphrodites," in *Psychosomatic Medicine*, vol. 7: 108–125.

————. *Sex Without Guilt*. New York: Lyle Stuart, 1958.

ELLIS, KATE, ET AL. *Caught Looking: Feminism, Pornography and Censorship*. East Haven, CT: Long River Books, 1992.

EVANS, DAVID. *Sexual Citizenship: The Material Construction of Sexualities*. New York: Routledge, 1993.

EVANS, SARAH. *Personal Politics: The Roots of Women's Liberation in the Civil Rights Movement and the New Left*. New York: Vintage, 1980.

FADERMAN, LILLIAN. *Odd Girls and Twilight Lovers: A History of Lesbian Life in Twentieth Century America.* New York: Penguin, 1991.

FALK, CANDICE. *Love, Anarchy and Emma Goldman: A Biography,* rev. ed. New Brunswick, NJ: Rutgers University Press, 1990.

FARBER, DAVID, ed. *The Sixties: From Memory to History.* Chapel Hill: University of North Carolina Press, 1994.

FASS, PAULA. *The Damned and the Beautiful: American Youth in the 1920s.* New York: Oxford University Press, 1977.

FEINBERG, BARRY, AND RONALD KASRILS, eds. *Bertrand Russell's America,* vol. 1. 1973; reprint, New York: Viking, 1974.

FILENE, PETER. *Him/Her/Self: Sex Roles in Modern America,* 2nd ed. Baltimore: Johns Hopkins University Press, 1986.

FIRESTONE, SHULAMITH. *The Dialectic of Sex: The Case for Feminist Revolution.* New York: Morrow, 1970.

FISKE, MARJORIE. *Book Selection and Censorship.* Berkeley: University of California Press, 1959.

FITZPATRICK, ELLEN, ed. *Katherine Bement Davis, Early Twentieth-Century American Women and the Study of Sex Behavior.* New York: Garland, 1987.

FLEMING, KARL, AND ANNE TAYLOR FLEMING. *The First Time.* New York: Simon & Schuster, 1975.

FORD, CLELLAND, AND FRANK BEACH. *Patterns of Sexual Behavior.* New York: Harper and Brothers, 1951.

FOUCAULT, MICHEL. *The History of Sexuality,* vol. 1, trans. Robert Hurley. New York: Pantheon, 1978.

FRASER, RONALD, ed. *1968: A Student Generation in Revolt.* New York: Pantheon, 1988.

FREUD, SIGMUND. *General Introduction to Psychoanalysis.* 1917; reprint, New York: Collier, 1963.

FRIEDAN, BETTY. *The Feminine Mystique.* New York: W. W. Norton, 1963.

FRIEDMAN, LEON. *Obscenity: The Complete Oral Arguments Before the Supreme Court in the Major Obscenity Cases.* New York: Chelsea House, 1970.

FROMM, ERICH. *Man for Himself.* New York: Rinehart, 1947.

GABOR, MARK. *An Illustrated History of Girlie Magazines: From National Police Gazette to the Present.* New York: Harmony Books, 1984.

GAILLARD, FRYE. *Watermelon Wine: The Spirit of Country Music.* New York: St. Martin's, 1978.

GALLUP REPORT. *Religion in America: 50 Years, 1935–1985,* report no. 236, May 1985.

GARBER, MARJORIE. *Vice Versa: Bisexuality and the Eroticism of Everyday Life.* New York: Simon & Schuster, 1995.

GARDELLA, PETER. *Innocent Ecstasy: How Christianity Gave America an Ethic of Sexual Pleasure.* New York: Oxford University Press, 1986.

GARROW, DAVID. *Liberty and Sexuality: The Making of Roe v. Wade.* New York: Macmillan, 1994.

GEBHARD, PAUL. "The Institute," in *Sex Research: Studies from the Kinsey Institute,* ed. Martin Weinberg. New York: Oxford University Press, 1976.

GEDDES, DONALD PORTER, ed. *An Analysis of the Kinsey Reports on Sexual Behavior in the Human Male and Female.* New York: New American Library 1954.

GENTRY, CURT. *The Madames of San Francisco.* New York: Ballantine, 1971.

GERASSI, JOHN. *The Boys of Boise.* New York: Collier, 1968.

GILBERT, JAMES. *Cycle of Outrage: America's Reaction to the Juvenile Delinquent in the 1950s.* New York: Oxford University Press, 1986.

GILMARTIN, BRIAN. *The Gilmartin Report.* Secaucus, NJ: Citadel, 1978.

GINZBURG, RALPH. *Castrated: My Eight Months in Prison.* New York: Avant-garde Books, 1973.

GILFOYLE, TIMOTHY J. *City of Eros: New York City, Prostitution, and the Commercialization of Sex, 1790–1920.* New York: W. W. Norton, 1994.

GITLIN, TODD. *The Sixties: Years of Hope, Days of Rage.* New York: Bantam Books, 1987.

GLENN, NORVAL, AND CHARLES WEAVER. "Attitudes Toward Premarital, Extramarital and Homosexual Relations in the U.S. in the 1970s," in *Journal of Sex Research,* vol. 15 (1979): 108–118.

GLESSING, ROBERT. *The Underground Press in America.* Bloomington: Indiana University Press, 1970.

GOLDMAN, WILLIAM. *Boys and Girls Together.* New York: Bantam, 1965.

GOLDSTEIN, MARTIN, ERWIN HAEBERLE, AND WILL McBRIDE. *The Sex Book.* New York: Herder and Herder, 1971.

GOODMAN, MICHAEL. *Contemporary Literary Censorship: The Case History of Burroughs' The Naked Lunch.* Lanham, MD: Scarecrow Press, 1981.

GORDON, LINDA. *Woman's Body, Woman's Right: Birth Control in America.* New York: Penguin, 1990.

GORDON, MICHAEL. *The American Family in Social-Historical Perspective.* New York: St. Martin's, 1973.

GONTARSKI, S. E. "Dionysus in Publishing: Barney Rosset, Grove Press, and the Making of a Countercanon," in *Review of Contemporary Fiction,* vol. 10, no. 3 (Fall 1990): 7–19.

———. "Don Allen: Grove's First Editor," in *Review of Contemporary Fiction,* vol. 10, no. 3 (Fall 1990): 132–136.

GRANT, LINDA. *Sexing the Millenium.* New York: Grove, 1994.

GREENBERG, DAVID F. *The Construction of Homosexuality.* Chicago: University of Chicago Press, 1988.

GREER, GERMAINE. *The Female Eunuch.* New York: McGraw-Hill, 1970.

GRIFFON, JULES. *The Golden Years: Masterpieces of the Erotic Postcard.* Los Angeles: Profile Publications, 1978.

GROSS, LEONARD, ed. *Sexual Issues in Marriage: A Contemporary Perspective.* New York: Spectrum, 1975.

GROSSBERG, LAWRENCE, CARY NELSON, AND PAULA TREICHLER. *Cultural Studies.* New York: Routledge, 1992.

GROSSKURTH, PHYLLIS. *Margaret Mead.* New York: Penguin, 1988.

GROUP FOR THE ADVANCEMENT OF PSYCHIATRY, COMMITTEE ON THE COLLEGE STUDENT. *Sex and the College Student.* New York: Atheneum, 1966.

GURSTEIN, ROCHELLE. *The Repeal of Reticence.* New York: Hill and Wang, 1996.

HAAG, PAMELA. "In Search of 'The Real Thing': Ideologies of Love, Modern Romance, and Women's Sexual Subjectivity in the United States, 1920–1940," in *Journal of the History of Sexuality,* vol. 2 (April 1992): 547–577.

HAEBERLE, ERWIN. "The Birth of Sexology: A Brief History in Documents." World Association for Sexology Conference, Sixth World Congress of Sexology. Washington, DC, May 22–27, 1983.

HAIKEN, ELIZABETH. *Venus Envy: A History of Cosmetic Surgery.* Baltimore: Johns Hopkins University Press, 1997.

HAMILTON, MARYBETH. *"When I'm Bad, I'm Better": Mae West, Sex, and American Entertainment.* New York: HarperCollins, 1995.

HANEY, ROBERT. *Comstockery in America: Patterns of Censorship and Control.* Boston: Beacon, 1960.

HANSEN, BERT. "The Historical Construction of Homosexuality," in *Radical History Review,* vol. 20 (1979): 66–73.

HANSEN, GLADYS C. *San Francisco Almanac: Everything You Want to Know About the City.* San Francisco: Chronicle Books, 1975.

HARTMAN, WILLIAM, MARILYN FITHIAN, AND DONALD JOHNSON. *Nudist Society: The Controversial Study of the Clothes-Free Naturist Movement in America.* 1970; reprint, Los Angeles: Elysium Growth Press, 1991.

HARVEY, BRETT. *The Fifties: A Woman's Oral History.* New York: HarperCollins, 1993.

HATFELD, TOM. *The Sandstone Experience.* 1975; reprint, New York: New American Library, 1976.

HEIDENARY, JOHN. *What Wild Ecstasy. The Rise and Fall of the Sexual Revolution.* New York: Simon & Schuster, 1997.

HEILBRUN, CAROLYN G. *The Education of a Woman: The Life of Gloria Steinem.* New York: Dial, 1995.

HEINLEIN, ROBERT A. *Grumbles from the Grave,* ed. Virginia Heinlein. New York: Del Rey, 1989.

HENSLIN, JAMES, ed. *Studies in the Sociology of Sex.* New York: Meredith, 1971.

HERLIHY, JAMES LEO. *Midnight Cowboy*. New York: Dell, 1969.

HERON, ALASTAIR, ed. *Toward a Quaker View of Sex*. London: Friends House Service Committee, 1963.

HITE, SHERE. *The Hite Report: A Nationwide Study of Female Sexuality*. New York: Macmillan, 1976.

HODES, MARTHA, ed. *Sex, Love, Race: Crossing Boundaries in North American History*. New York: New York University Press, 1999.

HOGELAND, LISA MARIA. "Sexuality in the Consciousness-Raising Novel of the 1970s," in *Journal of the History of Sexuality*, vol. 5 (April 1995): 601–632.

HOLLANDER, XAVIERA. *The Happy Hooker*. New York: Dell, 1972.

HOOVEN, F. VALENTINE, III. *Beefcake: The Muscle Magazines of America, 1950–1970*. Cologne: Taschen, 1995.

HOWARD, JANE. *Please Touch*. New York: Dell, 1970.

HUBNER, JOHN. *Bottom Feeders: From Free Love to Hard Core — The Rise and Fall of Counter-culture Heroes Jim and Artie Mitchell*. New York: Doubleday, 1993.

HUMPHREYS, LAUD. *Tearoom Trade: Impersonal Sex in Public Places*. 1970; reprint, Chicago: Aldine, 1975.

HUNT, MORTAN. *Sexual Behavior in the 1970s*. New York: Dell, 1974.

HUREWITZ, DANIEL. *Stepping Out: Nine Tours Through New York City's Gay and Lesbian Past*. New York: Holt, 1997.

IRVINE, JANICE. *Disorders of Desire: Sex and Gender in Modern American Sexology*. Philadelphia: Temple University Press, 1990.

JACOBS, HAROLD, ed. *Weatherman*. Palo Alto: Ramparts Press, 1970.

JACOBY, RUSSELL. *Social Amnesia: A Critique of Conformist Psychology from Adler to Laing*. Boston: Beacon, 1975.

JAMISON, ANDREW, AND RON EYERMAN. *Seeds of the Sixties*. Berkeley: University of California Press, 1994.

JAY, KARLA, AND ALLEN YOUNG, eds. *Out of the Closets: Voices of Gay Liberation*. New York: Douglas, 1972.

JEFFREYS, SHEILA. *Anticlimax: A Feminist Perspective on the Sexual Revolution*. London: The Woman's Press, 1990.

JEZER, MARTY. *The Dark Ages: Life in the United States, 1945–60*. Boston: South End Press, 1970.

JONES, LANDON. *Great Expectations: America and the Baby Boom Generation*. New York: Baltimore Books, 1981.

JONG, ERICA. *Fear of Flying*. New York: Holt, Rinehart and Winston, 1974.

KATZ, JONATHAN NED. *The Invention of Heterosexuality*. New York: Dutton, 1995.

KENDRICK, WALTER. *The Secret Museum: Pornography in Modern Culture*. New York: Viking, 1987.

KENNEDY, ELIZABETH LAPOVSKY, AND MADELINE D. DAVIS. *Boots of Leather, Slippers of Gold: The History of a Lesbian Community.* New York: Routledge, 1993.

KINSEY, ALFRED, et al. *Sexual Behavior in the Human Female.* Philadelphia: Saunders, 1953.

———. *Sexual Behavior in the Human Male.* Philadelphia: Saunders, 1948.

KIRKENDALL, LESTER. *A New Bill of Sexual Rights and Responsibilities.* Buffalo: Prometheus Books, 1976.

———. *The New Sexual Revolution.* New York: D. W. Brown, 1972.

———. *Pre-Marital Intercourse and Interpersonal Relationships.* New York: Julian Press, 1961.

KOPKIND, ANDREW, AND JAMES RIDGEWAY, eds. *Decade of Crisis: America in the '60s.* New York: World, 1972.

KRASSNER, PAUL. *Confessions of a Raving, Unconfirmed Nut.* New York: Simon & Schuster, 1993.

KRONHAUSEN, PHYLLIS, AND EBERHARD KRONHAUSEN. *Erotic Art.* New York: Bell, 1968.

———. *Pornography and the Law.* New York: Ballantine, 1959.

KUH, RICHARD. *Foolish Figleaves: Pornography in — and out of — Court.* New York: Macmillan, 1967.

LAQUER, THOMAS. *Making Sex: Body and Gender from the Greeks to Freud.* Cambridge: Harvard University Press, 1990.

LEFF, LEONARD, AND JEROLD SIMMONS. *The Dame in the Kimono: Hollywood, Censorship and the Production Code from the 1920s to the 1960s.* New York: Grove, Weidenfeld, 1990.

LIPTON, LAWRENCE. *The Erotic Revolution: An Affirmative View of the New Morality.* Los Angeles: Sherbourne Press, 1965.

LOCKWOOD, CHARLES. *Suddenly San Francisco: The Early Years of an Instant City.* San Francisco: San Francisco Examiner Special Projects, 1978.

LOWNES, VICTOR. *The Day the Bunny Died.* Secaucus, NJ: Lyle Stuart, 1983.

LOWRY, RICHARD, ed. *The Journals of A. H. Maslow.* Belmont, CA: Wadsworth, 1979.

LUKER, KRISTIN. *Abortion and the Politics of Motherhood.* Berkeley: University of California Press, 1984.

———. *Dubious Conceptions: The Politics of Teenage Pregnancy.* Cambridge, MA: Harvard University Press, 1996.

MAILER, NORMAN. "The Homosexual Villain," in *One.* January 1955, 8–12.

———. "The White Negro: Superficial Reflections on the Hipster," in *Dissent,* Summer 1957, 276–293; reprinted in *The Portable Beat Reader,* ed. Ann Charters. New York: Viking, 1992.

MANFULL, HELEN, ed. *Additional Dialogue: Letters of Dalton Trumbo, 1942–1962.* New York: Evans & Co., 1970.

MANNING, CAITLIN. "Whatever Happened to the Sexual Revolution?" in *Socialist Review,* no. 91 (Jan–Feb, 1987).

MANSO, PETER. *Mailer: His Life and Times.* New York: Penguin, 1985.

MARCUS, ERIC, ed. *Making History: The Struggle for Gay and Lesbian Equal Rights, 1945–1990: An Oral History.* New York: HarperCollins, 1993.

MARCUS, STEVEN. *The Other Victorians.* New York: Basic Books, 1966.

MARCUSE, HERBERT. *Eros and Civilization.* Boston: Beacon, 1955.

———. *One Dimensional Man.* Boston: Beacon, 1966.

MAROTTA, TOBY. *The Politics of Homosexuality.* Boston: Houghton Mifflin, 1981.

MASLOW, ABRAHAM. *Toward a Psychology of Being.* New York: D. Van Nostrand, 1962.

MASS, LAWRENCE. *Dialogues of the Sexual Revolution.* New York: Haworth Press 1990.

MASTERS, WILLIAM, AND VIRGINIA JOHNSON. *Human Sexual Inadequacy.* Boston: Bantam Books, 1981.

———. *Human Sexual Response.* Boston: Little, Brown, 1966.

———. *The Pleasure Bond: A New Look at Sexuality and Commitment.* Boston: Little, Brown, 1970.

MAY, ELAINE TYLER. *Homeward Bound: American Families in the Cold War Era.* New York: Basic, 1988.

McCUMBER, DAVID. *X-Rated: The Mitchell Brothers, a True Story of Sex, Money and Death.* New York: Simon & Schuster, 1992.

McGOVERN, JAMES. "The American Woman's Pre-World War I Freedom in Manners and Morals," in *Journal of American History,* vol. 55 (1968): 315–33.

McLAUGHLIN, LORETTA. *The Pill, John Rock and the Church: The Biography of a Revolution.* Boston: Little, Brown, 1982.

MESSER, ELLEN, AND KATHERINE E. MAY, eds. *Back Rooms: Voices from the Illegal Abortion Era.* New York: St. Martin's Press, 1988.

METALIOUS, GRACE. *Peyton Place.* New York: Julien Messner, 1956.

MEYEROWITZ, JOANNE, ed. *Not June Cleaver: Women and Gender in Postwar America, 1945–60.* Philadelphia: Temple University Press, 1994, 29–262.

MILES, BARRY. *Ginsberg: A Biography.* New York: Viking, 1989.

MILLER, HENRY. *Tropic of Cancer.* 1934; reprint, New York: Evergreen, 1980.

MILLER, JAMES. *Democracy Is in the Streets: From Port Huron to the Siege of Chicago.* New York: Simon & Schuster, 1987.

MILLER, TIMOTHY. *The Hippies and American Values.* Knoxville: University of Tennessee Press, 1991.

MILLET, KATE. *Sexual Politics.* New York: Simon & Shuster, 1970.

MILLS, HILLAR. *Mailer: A Biography.* New York: Empire, 1982.

MINTZ, STEVEN, AND SUSAN KELLOGG. *Domestic Revolutions: A Social History of Family Life.* New York: Macmillan, 1988.

MITZEL, JOHN. *The Boston Sex Scandal.* Boston: Glad Day Books, 1980.

MOORHEAD, CAROLINE. *Bertrand Russell: A Life.* New York: Viking, 1992.

MORANTZ, REGINA MARKELL. "The Scientist as Sex Crusader: Alfred C. Kinsey and American Culture," in *American Quarterly* 29 (Winter 1979), 563–89.

MORDEN, ETHAN. *Medium Cool: The Movies of the 1960s.* New York: Knopf, 1990.

MORGAN, EDWARD. *The 60s Experience: Hard Lessons about Modern America.* Philadelphia: Temple University Press, 1991.

MORGAN, ROBIN, ed. *Sisterhood Is Powerful: An Anthology of Writings from the Women's Liberation Movement.* New York: Vintage, 1970.

MOSHER, WILLIAM, AND WILLIAM PRATT. *Contraceptive Use in the United States, 1973–1988.* Atlanta: U.S. Department of Health and Human Services, Public Health Service, Centers for Disease Control, National Center for Health Statistics, 1990.

MUSCATINE, DORIS. *Old San Francisco: The Biography of a City, from Early Days to Earthquake.* New York: Putnam, 1975.

NEILL, A. S. *Summerhill.* New York: Hart, 1960.

NESTLE, JOAN. "Butch-Fem Relationships: Sexual Courage in the Fifties," in *Heresies Sex Issue* #12, vol. 3, no. 4 (1981): 21–24.

NOONAN, JOHN. *Contraception. A History of Its Treatment by Catholic Theologians and Canonists.* Cambridge: Harvard University Press, 1966.

O'NEILL, GEORGE, AND NENA O'NEILL. *Open Marriage: A New Lifestyle for Couples.* New York: Avon, 1972.

O'NEILL, WILLIAM L. *American High: The Years of Confidence, 1945–1960.* Garden City, NY: Free Press, 1986.

OSTERMAN, ROBERT, AND MARK ARNOLD. *The Pill and Its Impact.* Silver Spring, MD: Dow Jones & Co., 1967.

PACKARD, VANCE. *The Sexual Wilderness.* New York: David McCay, 1968.

PAGLIA, CAMILLE. *Vamps and Tramps: New Essays.* New York: Vintage Books, 1994.

PALLADINO, GRACE. *Teenagers.* New York: Basic, 1966.

PECK, ABE. *Uncovering the Sixties: The Life and Times of the Underground Press.* New York: Citadel, 1991.

PEISS, KATHY. *Cheap Amusements: Working Women and Leisure in Turn-of-the-Century New York.* Philadelphia: Temple University Press, 1986.

PERRY, CHARLES. *The Haight-Ashbury: A History.* New York: Random House, 1984.

PHILLIPS, RODERICK. *Putting Asunder: A History of Divorce in Western Society.* Cambridge, England: Cambridge University Press, 1998.

PIVAR, DAVID. *Purity Crusade: Sexual Morality and Social Control, 1868–1900.* Westport, CT: Greenwood, 1973.

PILKINGTON, JAMES, ed. "Television News Index and Abstracts: A Guide to the Videotape Collection of the Network Evening News Programs in the Vanderbilt Television News Archive." Vanderbilt University Library.

POLAND, JEFFERSON, AND SAM SLOAN. *The Sex Marchers.* Los Angeles: Elysium Press, 1968.

POMEROY, WARDELL. *Dr. Kinsey and the Institute for Sex Research.* 1972; reprint, New Haven, CT: Yale University Press, 1982.

RAINWATER, LEE. *Family Design: Marital Sexuality, Family Size and Contraception.* Chicago: Aldine Publishing Co., 1965.

RAYMOND, OTIS. *An Illustrated History of Sex Comic Classics.* New York: Comic Classics, 1972.

RICHMOND, LEN, WITH GARY NOGUERA. *The New Gay Liberation Book: Writings and Photographs about Gay (Men's) Liberation.* Palo Alto: Ramparts, 1979.

REAGAN, LESLIE. *When Abortion Was a Crime: Women, Medicine and Law in the United States, 1867–1973.* Berkeley: University of California Press, 1997.

RECHY, JOHN. *City of Night.* Grove Press, 1963.

REED, JAMES. *The Birth Control Movement and American Society: From Private Vice to Public Virtue.* Princeton, NJ: Princeton University Press, 1983.

REMBAR, CHARLES. *The End of Obscenity.* New York: Random House, 1968.

REUBEN, DAVID. *Everything You Always Wanted to Know About Sex But Were Afraid to Ask.* New York: Bantam, 1969.

REICH, WILHELM. *The Function of the Orgasm.* New York: Farrar, Straus and Giroux, 1961.

———. *The Sexual Revolution: Toward a Self-Governing Character Structure.* 1945; reprint, New York: Farrar, Straus and Giroux, 1969.

REIK, THEODORE. *Of Love and Lust.* New York: Grove, 1959.

RIMMER, ROBERT. *The Harrad Experiment.* New York: Bantam, 1967.

———. *The X-Rated Videotape Guide.* Bayside, NY: Arlington House, 1984.

ROBINSON, IRA. "Twenty Years of the Sexual Revolution, 1965–1985: An Update," in *Journal of Marriage and the Family,* vol. 53, no. 1 (February 1991): 216–220.

ROBINSON, PAUL. *The Freudian Left.* New York: Harper, 1969.

———. *The Modernization of Sex: Havelock Ellis, Alfred Kinsey, William Masters and Virginia Johnson.* New York: Harper Colophon, 1976.

ROSE, JUNE. *Sex and the Singular Woman: Marie Stopes and the Sexual Revolution.* London: Faber, 1992.

ROSEN, RUTH. *The Lost Sisterhood: Prostitution in America, 1900–1918.* Baltimore: Johns Hopkins University Press, 1982.

ROSENBERG, CAROL SMITH. "The Female World of Love and Ritual: Relations Between Women in Nineteenth Century America," in *Signs*, vol. 1, no. 1, (Autumn 1975): 1–35.

ROTHMAN, STANLEY, AND ROBERT LICHTER. *Roots of Radicalism: Jews, Christians and the New Left*. New York: Oxford University Press, 1982.

ROTUNDO, E. ANTHONY. *American Manhood: Transformations in Masculinity from the Revolution to the Modern Era*. New York: Basic Books, 1994.

ROSZAK, THEODORE. *The Making of a Counter Culture*. New York: Doubleday, 1968.

RUBENSTEIN, PAUL, AND HERBERT MARGOLIS. *The Group Sex Tapes*. New York: David McKay, 1971.

RULE, JANE. *Lesbian Images*. New York: Doubleday, 1975.

RUSSELL, BERTRAND. *Marriage and Morals*. New York: Liveright, 1929.

SANDERS, DENNIS. *Gay Source: A Catalog for Men*. New York: Berkley, 1977.

SANDERS, JOEL. *Stud: Architectures of Masculinity*. New York: Princeton Architectural Press, 1980.

SCHLOSSMAN, STEVEN, AND STEPHANIE WALLACH. "The Crime of Precocious Sexuality: Female Juvenile Delinquency in the Progressive Era," in *Harvard Educational Review*, vol. 48, no. 1 (February 1978): 65–94.

SCHUR, EDWIN. *The Americanization of Sex*. Philadelphia: Temple University Press, 1988.

———. *The Family and the Sexual Revolution*. Bloomington: Indiana University Press, 1964.

SCHMACH, MURRAY. *The Face on the Cutting Room Floor: The Story of Movie and Television Censorship*. New York: De Capo Press, 1974.

SCHUSTER, READ. "Nudist Beginnings," in *Clothed with the Sun*, Spring 1986: 21–29.

SCHWARTZ, JUDITH. *Radical Feminists of Heterodoxy: Greenwich Village 1920–1940*. Norwich, VT: New Victoria, 1982.

SCOTT, JOSEPH E., AND JACK L. FRANKLIN. "Sex References in the Mass Media," in *Journal of Sex Research*, vol. 9, no. 3 (August 1973): 196–209.

SEARS, HAL. *The Sex Radicals: Free Love in High Victorian America*. Lawrence: Regents Press of Kansas, 1977.

SELTH, JEFFERSON. *Alternative Lifestyles: A Guide to Research Collections on International Communities, Nudism and Sexual Freedom*. Bibliographies and Indexes in Sociology, no. 6. Westport, CT: Greenwood Press, 1985.

SHARAF, MYRON. *Fury on Earth: A Biography of Wilhelm Reich*. New York: St. Martin's Press, 1983.

SHEPARD, MARTIN. *Fritz: An Intimate Portrait of Fritz Perls and Gestalt Therapy*. New York: E. P. Dutton, 1975.

SHARPLESS, JOHN. "World Population Growth, Family Planning and American Foreign Policy," in *Journal of Policy History*, vol. 7 (1995): 72–102.

SHILTS, RANDY. *And the Band Played On: Politics, People and the AIDS Epidemic*. New York: St. Martin's Press, 1987.

SHOWALTER, ELAINE. *Sexual Anarchy: Gender and Culture at the Fin de Siecle*. New York: Penguin, 1990.

SKINNER, JAMES. *The Cross and the Cinema: The Legion of Decency and the National Catholic Office for Motion Pictures, 1933–1970*. Westport, CT: Praeger, 1993.

SMITH, JAMES, AND LYNN SMITH, eds. "Comarital Sex and the Sexual Freedom Movement," in *Journal of Sex Research*, vol. 6, no. 2 (May 1970): 131–142.

———. *Beyond Monogamy*. Baltimore: Johns Hopkins University Press, 1974.

SMITH, TOM. "The Polls — A Report: The Sexual Revolution?" in *Public Opinion Quarterly*, vol. 54, no. 3 (Fall 1990): 415–435.

SNITOW, ANN. "The Front Lines: Notes on Sex in Novels by Women, 1969–1979," in *Women, Sex and Sexuality*, ed. Catherine Stimpson and Ethel Spector Person. Chicago: University of Chicago Press, 1980.

———, CHRISTINE STANSELL, AND SHARON THOMPSON, eds. *Powers of Desire: The Politics of Sexuality*. New York: Monthly Review Press, 1983.

SOLLINGER, RICKIE. *Wake Up Little Susie: Single Pregnancy and Race before Roe v. Wade*. New York: Routledge, 1992.

SOMMERVILLE, ROSE. "Family Life and Sex Education in the Turbulent Sixties," in *Journal of Marriage and the Family*, vol. 33 (1971): 11–35.

SONTAG, SUSAN. *Against Interpretation*. 1966; reprint, New York: Anchor, 1990.

SOROKIN, PITIRIM. *The American Sex Revolution*. Boston: P. Sargent, 1956.

SPURLOCK, JOHN. *Free-Love: Marriage and Middle-Class Radicalism in America, 1825–1860*. New York: New York University Press, 1988.

STANSELL, CHRISTINE. *City of Women: Sex and Class in New York, 1789–1860*. New York: Knopf, 1986.

STOEHR, TAYLOR. *Free Love in America: A Documentary History*. New York: AMS Press, 1979.

STREITMATTER, RODGER. "The *Advocate*: Setting the Standard for the Gay Liberation Press," in *Journalism History*, vol. 19, no. 3 (Autumn 1993): 93–102.

———. *Unspeakable: The Rise of the Gay and Lesbian Press in America*. Boston: Faber and Faber, 1995.

SYMONDS, CAROLYN. "Sexual Mate Swapping and the Swingers," in *Marriage Counseling Quarterly* 6 (Spring 1971): 1–12.

TALESE, GAY. *Thy Neighbor's Wife*. New York: Doubleday, 1980.

TANNAHILL, REAY. *Sex in History*. New York: Scarborough Press, 1982.

TANNER, LESLIE, ed. *Voices from Women's Liberation*. New York: New American Library, 1970.

TEAL, DONN. *The Gay Militants*. 1971; reprint, New York: St. Martin's Press, 1995.

THOMPSON, MARK, ed. *Leatherfolk: Radical Sex, People, Politics and Practice*. Boston: Alyson, 1991.

TOEPFER, KARL ERIC. *Empire of Ecstasy: Nudity and Movement in German Body Culture, 1910–1935*. Berkeley: University of California Press, 1997.

TOTH, EMILY. *Inside Peyton Place: The Life of Grace Metalious.* Garden City, NY: Doubleday, 1981.

TYNAN, KATHLEEN. *The Life of Kenneth Tynan.* New York: Morrow, 1987.

United States Technical Report of the Commission on Obscenity and Pornography. United States Govt. Printing Office, Washington, DC, 1971. Also published as *Report of the Commission on Obscenity and Pornography.* New York: Bantam, 1970.

VANCE, CAROLE, ed. *Pleasure and Danger: Exploring Female Sexuality.* London: Pandora, 1992.

VIDAL, GORE. *The City and the Pillar.* New York: Random House, 1995, rev. ed.

VILGOT, SJÖRMAN. *I Am Curious (Yellow): The Complete Scenario of the Film.* New York: Grove Press, 1968.

VIORST, MILTON. *Fire in the Streets: America in the 1960s.* New York: Simon & Schuster, 1979.

WALD, KENNETH D. *Religion and Politics in the United States.* Washington, DC: Congressional Quarterly, 1992.

WALKER, SAMUEL. *In Defense of American Liberties: A History of the ACLU.* New York: Oxford, 1990.

WALKOWITZ, JUDITH. *Prostitution and Victorian Society: Women, Class and the State.* Cambridge: Cambridge University Press, 1980.

WALTER, AUBREY, ed. *Come Together: The Years of Gay Liberation, 1970–73.* London: Gay Men's Press, 1980.

WARNER, MICHAEL. *Fear of a Queer Planet: Queer Politics and Social Theory.* Minneapolis: University of Minnesota Press, 1993.

WATSON, STEVEN. *The Birth of the Beat Generation.* New York: Pantheon, 1995.

WEEKS, JEFFREY. *Coming Out: Homosexual Politics in Britain from the Nineteenth Century to the Present.* New York: Quartet, 1977.

———. *Sex, Politics and Society: The Regulation of Sexuality since 1800.* New York: Longman, 1981.

WEINBERG, MARTIN AND COLIN WILLIAMS. "Sexual Embourgeoisment? Social Class and Sexual Activity: 1938–1970." *American Sociological Review,* vol. 45 (1980): 33–48.

———. "Gay Baths and the Social Organization of Impersonal Sex," *Social Problems* 23, (1975): 124–136.

WEINBERG, M. S., R. G. SWENSSON & S. K. HAMMERSMITH, "Sexual Autonomy and the Status of Women: Models of Female Sexuality in U.S. Sex Manuals from 1950 to 1980." *Social Problems,* vol. 30: 312–324.

WEINER, DONALD. *Passionate Skeptic: Albert Ellis and Rational-Emotive Therapy.* New York: Praeger, 1988.

WESTOFF, CHARLES, AND NORMAN RYDER. *The Contraceptive Revolution.* Princeton: Princeton University Press, 1977.

WHITE, KEVIN. *The First Sexual Revolution: The Emergence of Male Heterosexuality in Modern America.* New York: New York University Press, 1992.

WHYTE, WILLIAM FOOTE. *Street Corner Society: The Social Structure of an Italian Slum.* Chicago: University of Chicago Press, 1943.

WIESEN-COOK, BLANCHE. "The Historical Denial of Lesbianism," in *Radical History Review* 20 (Spring/Summer 1979).

WILLIAMS, LINDA. *Hard Core: Power, Pleasure and the Frenzy of the Visible.* Berkeley: University of California Press, 1989.

WUTHNOW, ROBERT. *The Restructuring of American Religion: Society and Faith since World War II.* Princeton: Princeton University Press, 1988.

YANKELOVICH, DANIEL. *The New Morality: A Profile of American Youth in the 1970s.* New York: McGraw Hill, 1974.

YOUNG, ALLEN, AND KARLA JAY, eds. *Out of the Closets.* New York: Harcourt Brace Jovanovich, 1972.

YOUNG, WAYLAND. *Eros Denied: Sex in Western Society.* New York: Grove, 1964.

INTERVIEWS

TI-GRACE ATKINSON, 20 May 1997, New York.

SUSAN BAERWALD, 20 December 1998, Los Angeles.

BILL BAIRD, 12 December 1997, telephone.

LEE BAXANDALL, 21 April 1996, Oshkosh, WI, telephone.

HOWARD BELLIN, 3 February 1998, New York.

STEPHANIE BLACK (pseud.), 20 June 1998, telephone.

SCOTT BLOOM (pseud.), 3 July 1998, telephone.

IRIS BRENT (pseud.), 28 November 1995, Los Angeles.

MICHAEL BRONSKI, 29 April 1994, Cambridge, MA.

HELEN GURLEY BROWN, 29 January 1996, New York.

RITA MAE BROWN, 22 December 1997, telephone.

SUSAN BROWNMILLER, 29 December 1995, New York.

HAL CALL, 8 July 1996, San Francisco, telephone.

CHARLIE DELLIN (pseud.), 22 May 1998, telephone.

SYDNEY DICKSTEIN, 25 November 1997, telephone.

BETTY DODSON, 12 September 1995, New York.

CUTLER DURKEE, 10 February 1998, telephone.

ANDREA DWORKIN, 22 February 1995, New York.

EDWARD EICHEL, 22 April 1996, New York.

ALBERT ELLIS, 8 January 1995, New York.

SARA EVANS, 1 February 1996, telephone.

ROGER FISHER, 5 September 1994, Cambridge, MA.

STANLEY FLEISHMAN, 27 November 1995, Los Angeles.

Larry Flynt, 29 November 1995, Los Angeles.

Jack Gelfand, 10 August 1997, Princeton.

Marsha Gillespie, 12 December 1997, telephone.

Elizabeth Gipps, 20 June 1998, telephone.

Barbara Gittings, 5 October 1997, telephone.

Jason Glick (pseud.), 17 October 1993, Cambridge, MA.

Valerie Goldberg (pseud.), 30 August 1997, telephone.

Art Green (pseud.), 17 May 1998, telephone.

Bob Guccione, 30 May 1996, New York.

Amy Hamilton (pseud.), 7 June 1998, telephone.

Hugh Hefner, 29 March 1995, Los Angeles.

Sarah Holland, 10 December 1998, New York.

Ronald Jones (pseud.), 27 August 1997, telephone.

Michael Kazin, 6 February 1998, telephone.

Jim Kepner, 27 November 1995, Los Angeles.

Anne Koedt, 28 January 1996, New York.

Howard Kolding (pseud.), 6 June 1998, telephone.

Larry Kramer, 29 December 1998, New York.

Tuli Kupferberg, 30 December 1995, New York.

Eunice Lake (pseud.), 9 December 1994, Peru, IN.

Jacques Levy, 7 June 1998, telephone.

John Lobel, 2 May 1998, telephone.

Mimi Lobel, 3 May 1998, telephone.

Marvin and Betty Mandel, 2 October 1994, Boston.

George Mansour, 15 October 1994, Cambridge, MA.

Peter Marcuse, 2 February 1997, telephone.

Ted McIllvenna, 20 March 1995, San Francisco.

Bob McGinley, 23 January 1997, telephone.

Howard Moody, 30 March 1997, telephone.

Glen Murphy (pseud.), 20 April 1998, telephone.

Tom Murphy (pseud.), 21 April 1998, telephone.

Osha Neumann, 12 February 1997, telephone.

Camille Paglia, 17 February 1997, telephone.

Nell Painter, 13 November 1997, Princeton.

Kenneth Pitchford, 22 February 1995, New York.

Linda Price (pseud.), 3 July 1998, telephone.

JOHN RECHY, 27 November 1995, Los Angeles.

CHARLES RENSLOW, 1 December 1994, Chicago.

MARGO RILA, 21 March 1995, San Francisco.

ROBERT RIMMER, 15 April 1994, Boston.

BARNEY ROSSET, 20 February 1994, New York.

MAGGIE RUBENSTEIN, 21 March 1995, San Francisco.

BARBARA SEAMAN, 22 April 1996, New York.

MYRON SHARAF, 3 October 1994, Boston.

JIM SHENTON, 14 October 1998, telephone.

CHARLIE SHIVELY, 28 April 1994, Cambridge, MA.

DONNA STANTON (pseud.), 10 November 1997, telephone.

GLORIA STEINEM, 5 December 1997, Princeton.

GAY TALESE, 19 February 1995, New York.

LYNN TYLMAN, 22 February 1995, New York.

ANDREW WALLACE (pseud.), 30 April 1997, New York.

SYLVIA WEIL, 7 August 1998, telephone.

JONATHAN WEST (pseud.), 10 June 1998, telephone.

RANDY WICKER, 29 December 1995, New York.

SEAN WILENTZ, 17 November 1997, Princeton.

J. X. WILLIAMS (pseud.), 14 December 1993, Cambridge.

ELLEN WILLIS, 20 May 1997, New York.

REV. ROBERT WOOD, 11 July 1994, New Hampshire.

BRIAN ZELL, 11 June 1998, telephone.

OBERON ZELL, 9 June 1998, telephone.

VIDEO INTERVIEWS

"Lyle Stuart — Breaking Through in Sex Publishing," 22 June 1982, Institute for the Advanced Study of Human Sexuality Video Library, San Francisco.

"Paul Krassner — An Evening of Sex and Politics," Society for the Scientific Study of Sex, Western Regional Meeting, San Francisco, April 1994, Institute for the Advanced Study of Human Sexuality Video Library, San Francisco.

"Al Goldstein," 21 June 1987, Institute for the Advanced Study of Human Sexuality Video Library, San Francisco.

"Phil Donahue Show," 1978, Mary Steichen Calderone Collection, Schlesinger Library.

Bill of Rights Fund Collection, Columbia University.

American Civil Liberties Union Papers, Mudd Library, Princeton University.

Arthur Bell and the International Gay Information Center Papers, New York Public Library.

Betina Berch Collection, Columbia University.

Ilsley Boone Papers, Institute for Research on Sex, Gender and Reproduction.

William Burroughs Papers, Columbia University.

Mary Steichen Calderone Collection, Schlesinger Library.

Zachariah Chafee Papers, Harvard University Law School.

Alex Comfort Papers, London Library, University College, London.

Committee on Research of Problems of Sex Records, Rockefeller Archives Center.

COYOTE Collection, Schlesinger Library.

Barbara Demming Papers, Schlesinger Library.

Robert Latou Dickinson Papers, Countway Medical Library, Harvard University.

Betty Dodson Papers, personal collection, New York.

Frank Donahue Papers, Langdell Library, Harvard University Law School.

Family Planning Oral History Project, Schlesinger Library.

Albert Ellis Papers, Institute for Rational Emotive Therapy, New York.

Frances Fitzgerald Papers, Mugar Memorial Library, Boston University.

Gay Media Task Force Records, Cornell University Library.

Gay Publishing Co. Records, Cornell University Library.

Allen Ginsberg Papers, Columbia University Library.

Sheldon Glueck Papers, Langdell Library, Harvard Law School.

Grove Press Papers, Syracuse University Library.

James Leo Herlihy Papers, Mugar Memorial Library, Boston University.

Joseph Ishill Papers, Houghton Library, Harvard University.

International Gay Information Center Collection, New York Public Library.

Institute for Sex Education Collection, University of Illinois at Chicago Center.

Alfred Kinsey Papers, Institute for Research in Sex, Gender and Reproduction.

Linda LeClair Collection, Barnard College Archives.

Massachusetts Society for Social Hygiene Records, Schlesinger Library.

Harold Matson Company Collection, Columbia University.

Hygiene Course Reports, Barnard College Archives.

Emily Mudd Papers, Schlesinger Library.

Leather History Archives, Chicago, IL.

Ms. Magazine Collection, Schlesinger Library, Harvard University.

Pauli Murray Papers, Schlesinger Library, Harvard University.

Lonny Myers Papers, University of Illinois at Chicago Center.

National Catholic Welfare Conference Records, Catholic University.

National Organization for Women Records, Schlesinger Library, Harvard University.

Rochelle Owens Papers, Mugar Memorial Library, Boston University.

Pill Project Collection, Biological Sciences Division, Smithsonian Institution.

Playboy Enterprises Records, Playboy Enterprises, Chicago, IL.

John Preston Papers, Mugar Memorial Library, Boston University.

John Preston Collection, John Hay Library, Brown University.

Robert Rimmer Papers, Mugar Memorial Library, Boston University.

John Rock Papers, Countway Medical Library, Harvard University

Froma Sand Papers, Mugar Memorial Library, Boston University.

Sexual Freedom League Collection, Bancroft Library, UC Berkeley.

Social Protest Collection, Bancroft Library, UC Berkeley.

Peter Stafford Collection, Columbia University.

Vertical Files, American Academy of Motion Picture Arts and Sciences Library.

Vertical Files, Institute for Research in Sex, Gender and Reproduction.

Vertical Files, Schlesinger Library.

Lynn Womack Papers, Human Sexuality Collection, Carl A. Kroch Library, Cornell University.

Women Against Pornography Collection, Schlesinger Library.

INDEX

Buckley, Jim, 163
Burger, Warren, 276, 276n
burlesque, 27
Burroughs, William, 44, 68–70
butch/femme roles, 248
Byrd, Robert, 193

Calderone, Mary Steichen, 154, 179
Callahan, Sidney, 115
Camelot, 12
Canavan, Francis, 112
Canby, Vincent, 129–30
Candy (Southern), 66
Cannon, Dyan, 14
Capp, Al, 138
Carmichael, Stokely, 90
Carnal Knowledge (film), 276n
Cartoon and Model Parade, 187
castration, of African-Americans, 86
casual sex, opposition to, 179
Catholic church, on contraception, 31
Catholic Legion of Decency, 128
censorship
    of books, 48–70
    of nudist magazines, 25, 62
    as social control, 48
    See also pornography
Censorship in Denmark (film), 233
Chambers, Marilyn, 235
Chapman Report, The (Wallace), 20
Chattleman, Lord, 211
Che (play), 126–27, 161
Chester, Alfred, 154
children, sexual revolution and, 296–99
child pornography, 285–87. *See also*
    pedophilia
child-rearing, sex and, 20
Christianity, during Middle Ages, 31
Christians, early, 12
Church of All Worlds, 80

Ciardi, John, 64
City Lights bookstore, 26, 69
City of Night (Rechy), 65, 154
Citizens for Decent Literature, 61, 122
civil rights movement
    influence of, 29, 44, 152
    sexual politics in, 89–90
Civilization and Its Discontents (Freud),
    197–202
Civil War, draft riots during, 86
Clark, Dick, 231
Clark, Lige, 163
class conflict, 231
Cleaver, Eldridge, 90–91, 250
Cleland, John, 56
Clinton, Bill, 295
Clockwork Orange, A (film), 130
Club Baths, 238–39
Club Wide World, 208
Coffee, Linda, 265–66
coitus interruptus, Church view of, 31
Cold War, 148. *See also*
    anticommunism
Columbia University, 152–53
Come Out Cell, 249–50
Comfort, Alex, 229–30
comic books, censorship of, 61
commercialism, critique of, 242–45
Committee for Fair Divorce and
    Alimony Laws, 258
communes, 80–81
Comstock, Anthony, 32, 56
Comstock Law, 13, 31, 56
Condor Club, 25–26, 28–29
condoms, 31
Continental Baths, 236–37
contraception, history of, 30–32.
    See also birth control
Cornell University, 51, 95, 153
Corner, George Washington, 167
Cosmopolitan, 232

Marcuse, Herbert, 196–200, 202–205, 242, 294

Marmor, Judd, 178

marriage, in ancient times, 12

Marshall, Thurgood, 130

Martin, Bob. *See* Donaldson, Stephen

Martin, Dell, 247

Marx, Karl, 197–202

masculinity, evolution of, 147–48
  alleged fragility of, 159

Maslow, Abraham, 73

Masters, William (and Johnson), 166–75, 229

masturbation, 135–46, 177, 295
  and child-rearing practices, 135–36
  among female mammals, 139
  among male mammals, 137
  AMA opposition to, 181

materialism, 28

Mattachine Society, creation of, 24, 151
  and Barney Rosset, 63
  and Randy Wicker, 45

May, Rollo, 242

McCarthy, Eugene, 110

McCarthyism. *See* anticommunism

McCluhan, Marshall, 202

McClure, Michael, 26

McCormick, Katherine Dexter, 33

McCorvey, Norma, 265–66

McGinley, Bob, 208

McIlvenna, Rev. Ted, 115–16, 142, 163

McNight, Bob, 233

Mead, Margaret, 17

Medical Aspects of Human Sexuality, 154, 173, 180

Mekas, Jonas, 47

Metalious, Grace, 17–18

Metzger, Randy, 235

Meyer, Russ, 128

Michaels, Dick, 153

Midler, Bette, 236

Midnight Cowboy (film), 130

Milk, Harvey, 285

Mill, James, 30

Miller, Henry, 57, 64–65, 104

Miller v. California, 276

Miller, Virginia, 241–42

Millett, Kate, 104, 241, 252

mind/body dualism, 59, 204

miscegenation laws, 86
  opposition to, 46, 51
  unconstitutionality of, 92

Miss America pageant, 105

Mitch, Richard. *See* Dick Michaels

Mitchell, Jim and Artie, 233, 235

Mitchell, John, 194

Mizer, Bob, 150

Money, John, 233, 269

monogamy
  in ancient times, 12
  critique of, 43, 72, 75–76
  Masters and Johnson on, 173
  persistence of, 99–100

monokini. *See* swimsuit, topless

Montague, Ashley, 33

Moody, Rev. Howard, 262–63

Moon Is a Harsh Mistress, The (Heinlein), 78

More Joy (Comfort), 230

Morgan, Robin, 105, 250, 252

Morrison, Jim, 130–31, 204

Morrissey, Paul, 128

Motion Picture Association of America, 279

motion pictures, regulation of, 127–130
  ratings system, 278–79

Moynihan, Daniel Patrick, 88

Moynihan Report, 88

Mudd, Emily, 171

Muehl, Otto, 223

Murphy, John, 292

Myers, Lonny, 264

Redstockings, 105

Reece, B. Carroll, 17

Rechy, John, 65

Reems, Harry, 234, 277

Reich, Wilhelm, 4, 45, 200, 204
  influence on Norman Mailer, 87

Reik, Theodore, 58, 169
  on gender roles, 21–22

Reiss, Ira, 99

Reitman, Ben, 43

Reproductive Biology Research
  Foundation, 167, 170–72

Republic, The (Plato), 77

"revolution," definitions of, 7

Reuben, David, 175–77

Rexroth, Kenneth, 26, 233

Rexroth, Mary, 233

Reynolds, Burt, 232

Rhodes, Richard, 166–67

Rich, Adrienne, 239

Riggs, Bobby, 246

"right-to-life" movement, 275. *See
  also* anti-abortion

Rila, Margo, 216

Rimmer, Robert, 71–77, 83–84, 158
  group marriage of, 74–75

Ritz, The (play), 237

Robinson, John T., 113

Robinson, Paul, 168

rock concerts, 131

Rock, John, 33, 109

Roe v. Wade, 260, 265–66

Rolling Stones, the, 37, 280

romantic love, critique of, 72

Rome, ancient, 12

Roosevelt, Eleanor, 37

Ross, Mike, 237–38

Rosset, Barney, 63, 129, 163

Roszack, Theodore, 197, 242, 244

Roth, Philip, 136–37

Roth, Samuel, 61

Roth v. United States, 61–62, 65

Rousseau, J. J., 13
  on masturbation, 137

Rosenberg, Davey, 25, 28

Rudd, Mark, 220

Rugart, Karl, 178

Run, Little Leather Boy (Townsend),
  239

Rusk, Dean, 91

Rusk, Margaret, 91–92

Russell, Bertrand, 16

Russell, Ken, 129

Sadomasochism, 239, 239n, 281
  in 1950s, 187

Sahl, Mort, 21

Sanders, Ed, 44–45

Sandstone, 225–27

Sanger, Margaret, 32, 34

Sappington, Margo, 122

Sartre, Jean-Paul, 111, 124

Save Our Children campaign, 284

Savio, Mario, 49

Scandanavian attitudes toward sex,
  125

Scarlet Letter, The (Hawthorne), 48

Schlafly, Phyllis, 274

Schoomaker, Craig, 155, 160

Schroeder, Theodore, 56–57

science, Americans' love of, 41

Score (film), 235

Screw, 130, 163, 176, 232, 234

Screwtape Letters, The (Lewis), 138

Seale, Bobby, 90

Seaman, Barbara, 182–83

SIECUS, 178–79

self-acceptance, importance of, 20

Sensuous Woman, The (Garrity), 268n

Sex and the College Student (GAP), 51

Sex and the Single Girl (Gurley
  Brown), 10–12, 19–21, 228